The World of Scripting Languages

WORLDWIDE SERIES IN COMPUTER SCIENCE

Series Editors **Professor David Barron, Southampton University, UK**
Professor Peter Wegner, Brown University, USA

The Worldwide series in Computer Science has been created to publish textbooks which both address and anticipate the needs of an ever evolving curriculum thereby shaping its future. It is designed for undergraduates majoring in Computer Science and practitioners who need to reskill. Its philosophy derives from the conviction that the discipline of computing needs to produce technically skilled engineers who will inevitably face, and possibly invent, radically new technologies throughout their future careers. New media will be used innovatively to support high quality texts written by leaders in the field.

The World of Scripting Languages

David W. Barron
University of Southampton, UK

John Wiley & Sons, Ltd

Chichester • New York • Weinheim • Brisbane • Singapore • Toronto

Other Wiley Editorial Offices
John Wiley & Sons, Inc., 605 Third Avenue,
New York, NY 10158-0012, USA

Weinheim • Brisbane • Singapore • Toronto

Library of Congress Cataloging-in-Publication Data

Barron, D. W. (David William), 1935–
        The world of scripting languages / David W. Barron.
            p.   cm. – (Worldwide series in computer science)
        Includes bibliographical references and index.
        ISBN 0-471-99886-9 (alk. paper)
        1. Programming languages (Electronic computers)   2. CGI (Computer network
    protocol)   3. World Wide Web.   I. Title.   II. Series.
        QA76.6-B3715 2000

                                                                    99–089450

British Library Cataloguing in Publication Data

ISBN 0-471-99886-9

Typeset in 9/12 Garamond by Mayhew Typesetting, Rhayader, Powys
Printed and bound in Great Britain by Biddles Ltd, Guildford, Surrey
This book is printed on acid-free paper responsibly manufactured from sustainable forestry, in which
at least two trees are planted for each one used for paper production.

Contents

Preface

Recent developments in the world of computing have made us think about computer systems in entirely new ways and have given a very high profile to a disparate group of languages – the so-called 'scripting languages' – to the extent that some commentators are expressing the view that traditional compiled languages have had their day. While this is certainly an over-statement, it is nevertheless true that an increasing amount of programming nowadays takes the form of scripting, and much of it is done by people who are not employed as programmers in the traditional sense, and who certainly would not regard themselves as programmers, and are taking advantage of the way in which scripting languages combine power with ease of use.

Readers of the popular computer press may associate scripting and scripting languages exclusively with the World Wide Web – CGI scripts to process form input and access remote databases, client-side scripting and Dynamic HTML to create 'cool' Web pages with animations and other special effects, and server-side scripting to implement 'Active Server Pages'. However, scripting is also at the heart of tools like Visual Basic, and forms an important component of suites like Microsoft Office and systems such as Lotus Notes. (And like M. Jourdain in Molière's *Le Bourgeois Gentilhomme*, who discovered that he had been speaking prose for the past forty years, many users will have made unknowing use of a form of scripting language when creating macros for word processor and spreadsheet applications.)

Scripting languages have been around almost since the invention of computers, certainly since the invention of operating systems. Scripting originated in the UNIX world, and independently in the IBM mainframe world, in the early 1980s as a way of automating interactive applications that were designed to be controlled from a keyboard. (The concept of scripting as a form of automation reappears in a modern context in various guises, in particular in the so-called macro languages associated with desktop applications – word processor, spreadsheet etc.) Similar techniques of shell scripting were used in the UNIX world to develop system administration tools, and this led to the development of specialized languages for system administration and for development of command-line applications, in particular Perl and Tcl. These languages introduced the concept now known as *Open Source*: they attracted a large number of enthusiasts, who have contributed large amounts of software in the form of add-on libraries. The languages have spread from their UNIX roots into the worlds of Windows and the Apple Macintosh, and have achieved great popularity since they turned out to be exactly what was required for developing CGI scripts on the Web and for administrating NT server systems. Beyond that, they are increasingly being chosen as the tools of choice to develop substantial applications, in preference to languages like C++.

Alongside this world of what (with a nod on the side to the manufacturers of Coca-Cola) we might call 'classic' scripting there has grown a new world of scripting tied to Web browsers and servers, and to Microsoft Windows, where scripting languages are used to control the interaction between objects in an object model that reflects the structure of some entity of interest to a user, e.g. a Web page or a graphical user interface. Used in this context, a scripting language is often described as a 'glue language', since it provides the glue to link a collection of disparate components into an application. Scripting languages, being (with a few exceptions) platform independent, can thus be used to link platforms, processes, components and users: many major Web sites and many major applications are constructed in this way.

The ease of use of scripting languages, and the consequent accessibility to those for whom programming is not their main occupation, is shared by a number of recently developed *alternative programming languages*, e.g. Python and Dylan. However, although these languages are often described as scripting languages, they are really more akin to programming languages like C++, and as such they fall outside the scope of this book.

Like all programming languages, scripting languages exhibit many of the characteristics usually associated with religions – sacred books, high priests, and most notably, bands of enthusiastic followers who proclaim 'their' language as the only true path to salvation. I take no sides: as the title implies, the book aims to give an overview of the use of scripting languages and their many applications. To this end, I have not attempted to give a comprehensive coverage of all scripting languages, preferring instead to concentrate on the half-dozen or so languages currently in widespread use. (Languages such as AWK and REXX, which although of great intrinsic interest are no longer part of the mainstream, are covered in a chapter at the end of the book, along with other loose ends.) I have tried to keep the material as up to date as possible, but the world of scripting languages is one of rapid change, not only in the languages themselves, but also in the way they are used. My text will inevitably have been overtaken by events by the time it appears in print: to help the reader I have indicated clearly in every chapter the precise version of the language that I am describing.

This is not one of the blockbuster 'how to' books – '[Learn | Teach Yourself][Perl | JavaScript | VBScript] in [a Week | 21 Days]' – that can be found in any bookstore, nor does it provide exhaustive accounts of the syntax and semantics of every language discussed – it would require a book of several thousand pages to do that. My objective is rather to convey the distinctive flavour of each language, and to explain why particular languages are the way they are, and how that makes them suited to particular tasks. By the end of the book the reader will have an understanding of what scripting languages can be used for, and will be able to read a script in any of the languages covered and make reasonable sense of it, choose the right language for a job, and know enough about it to make sense of more detailed documentation. An annotated guide to sources of further information, both paper and electronic, appears at the end of the book.

While readers are expected to have some familiarity with programming in a procedural language – a passing acquaintance with C, C++ or Java will be particularly useful – I have tried to make the material accessible to a readership with a very varied amount of background knowledge and coming from dissimilar environments. The book is structured so that readers can pick out those parts which match their particular interests: as the Spanish proverb says, 'Traveller, there are no paths: paths are made by walking'.

David Barron
Southampton, 1999

Acknowledgements

I owe a debt of gratitude to O'Reilly & Associates Inc., whose books have been an invaluable source of information. (I wish I could say the same about some of the Microsoft on-line documentation.) Special thanks are due to Nigel Chapman, who went through a draft version of the book with a fine-tooth comb and provided lots of helpful comments, and to Nick Barron for his eagle-eyed proof-reading. But the greatest thanks must go to the successive generations of students who have attended my course 'PLD2': it is only by teaching a subject that you discover the true depths of your own ignorance, and my understanding of scripting languages improved by leaps and bounds as I endeavoured to convey the subject to my students.

Trademark notices

ActiveX, Microsoft, MS-DOS, JScript, Visual Basic, Win32, Windows and Windows NT are trademarks of Microsoft Corporation.

Java and JavaScript are trademarks of Sun Microsystems Inc.

Netscape and Netscape Navigator are trademarks of Netscape Communications Corporation.

HyperCard, HyperTalk and Macintosh are trademarks of Apple Computer Inc.

UNIX is a registered trademark licensed exclusively by X/Open Company Ltd.

Other product and company names mentioned herein may be the trademarks of their respective owners.

The term 'hacker" has fallen into sad disrepute, nowadays being used as a pejorative term for someone who maliciously interferes with computer systems. The original meaning is captured accurately in the *Jargon File* (the on-line Jargon File, 4.0.0 version, released 25 July 1996. Available at http://sagan.earthspace.net/jargon/)

---

hacker [originally, someone who makes furniture with an axe] n.

1. A person who enjoys exploring the details of programmable systems and how to stretch their capabilities, as opposed to most users, who prefer to learn only the minimum necessary.

2. One who programs enthusiastically (even obsessively) or who enjoys programming rather than just theorizing about programming.

This book is dedicated to everyone who fits one or other of the above descriptions, and to the hackers like Larry Wall and John Ousterhout who have made programming fun again.

Part one

The big picture

## Chapter 1

Introduction to scripts and scripting

Like many things in the computing world, scripting languages are hard to define, though practitioners in the field will have no difficulty in recognizing a scripting language when they see one. In everyday life it is common to classify things by a combination of visual and behavioural characteristics – if it has feathers and a bill, swims and quacks, then it is probably a duck – so in this chapter we explore what it is that characterizes scripting languages, what distinguishes them from conventional programming languages and why they are so useful.

1.1 Scripts and programs

If you look up 'scripting' in a dictionary, you will not find it defined as an adjective, though you may find it defined as a verbal noun derived from 'script', in the sense of the typescript for a film or television broadcast. (The OED gives as an example a television critic praising 'cunning scripting and polished production'.) However, we are familiar with the idea of a programming language, which is a language in which we can write programs, so by association a scripting language must be one in which we can write scripts. This apparently circular definition is not so silly as it sounds: programming is well understood to be the action of writing programs using a programming language, and our definition suggests that scripting is the action of writing scripts using a scripting language, distinguishing neatly between *programs*, which are written in conventional programming languages such as C, C++ and Java, and *scripts*, which are written using a different kind of language.

Why make the distinction? After all, we could reasonably argue that the use of scripting languages is just another kind of programming. While this is true, the distinction is useful, because the kind of programming that scripting languages are used for is qualitatively different from conventional programming. Languages like C++ and Ada address the problem of developing large applications from the ground up, employing a team of professional programmers, starting from well-defined specifications, and meeting specified performance constraints. (At least, that's the theory. In practice, if you look at real-world programming projects you soon realize that this paradigm for software production is naïvely optimistic. Most major projects are late, bug-ridden and grossly over budget.) Scripting languages, on the other hand, address different problems:

It is common to speak of programming the video recorder to record a programme at a later time – an association of programming with control of a device. Perhaps we should say 'scripting the video recorder'?

- Building applications from 'off the shelf' components
- Controlling applications that have a programmable interface
- Writing programs where speed of development is more important than run-time efficiency.

The resulting languages have very distinctive characteristics that set them apart from 'real' programming languages. Perhaps the most important difference is that scripting languages incorporate features that enhance the productivity of the user in one way or another, making them accessible to people who would not normally describe themselves as programmers, their primary employment being in some other capacity. Scripting languages make programmers of us all, to some extent. (There is an analogy here with the written word. Before the days of universal literacy, the ability to write was strictly the preserve of the educated classes, and a working man who needed a letter written would seek the assistance of the village parson or doctor; similarly, until recently if an end-user needed a program, he or she would have to find a programmer to write it. It is interesting to observe in this context that Visual Basic, originally targeted at the non-professional market as a way of developing Windows applications without the horrors of the SDK or the Microsoft Foundation Classes and C++, has become instead a tool for professional developers to prototype and develop applications, and now appears in 'Professional' and 'Enterprise' editions.)

1.2 Origins of scripting

The use of the word 'script' in a computing context dates back to the early 1970s, when the originators of the UNIX operating system coined the term 'shell script' for a sequence of commands that were to be read from a file and obeyed in sequence as if they had been typed in at the keyboard. This usage has persisted in the UNIX world, being extended to sequences of instructions for other language processors, e.g. an 'AWK script', a 'Perl script' etc., the name *script* being used for a text file that was intended to be executed directly rather than being compiled to a different form of file prior to execution.

Other early occurrences of the term 'script' can be found. For example, in a DOS-based system, use of a dial-up connection to a remote system required a communication package that used a proprietary language to write *scripts* to automate the sequence of operations required to establish a connection to a remote system. This usage probably arose by analogy with film and television scripts, which contain detailed instructions for the actors and the camera operators. Another early occurrence was in the Apple Macintosh Hyper-Card application, one of the early hypertext systems. The associated HyperTalk language allowed the user to define sequences of actions to be associated with mouse clicks or movements, and these were called scripts (another analogy with the world of films and television) rather than programs so as not to frighten the user, who was assumed to be a non-programmer. In both these cases the function of the script is one of control: causing the modem to perform certain actions in the first case, and changing some aspects of the display in the second. (This association of scripts and control is common, but it is not the only way in which scripts are used.)

Note that if we regard a script as a sequence of commands to control an application or a device, a configuration file such as a UNIX 'makefile' could be regarded as a script.

However, scripts only become interesting when they have the added value that comes from using programming concepts such as loops and branches.

1.3   Scripting today

The term 'scripting' is nowadays used with three different meanings.

1. A new style of programming which allows applications to be developed much faster than traditional methods allow, and makes it possible for applications to evolve rapidly to meet changing user requirements. This style of programming frequently uses a scripting language to interconnect 'off the shelf' components that are themselves written in a conventional language. Applications built in this way are sometimes called 'glue applications', and the scripting language is called a 'glue language'. The use of Visual Basic to develop graphical user interfaces using pre-built visual 'controls' is a prime example.

2. Using a scripting language to 'manipulate, customize and automate the facilities of an existing system', as the ECMAScript definition puts it. Here the script is used to control an application that provides a programmable interface: this interface may be an API, though more commonly the application is constructed from a collection of objects whose properties and methods are exposed to the scripting language: we speak of 'scripting the objects'. Examples are the use of client-side scripting and Dynamic HTML to create interactive and feature-rich enhanced Web pages, and the use of Visual Basic for Applications to control the applications in the Microsoft Office suite. These are really more applications of 'glue'.

3. Using a scripting language with its rich functionality and ease of use as an alternative to a conventional language for general programming tasks, particularly system programming and system administration. UNIX system administrators have for a long time used scripting languages for system maintenance tasks, and administrators of Windows NT systems are adopting a scripting language, Perl, for their work. Perl is also the language of choice for CGI scripting in Web servers. (The most widely used Web server, Apache, has an embedded Perl interpreter for CGI scripts, and although Microsoft promotes its ISAPI technology as an alternative to CGI scripts, it has recently agreed to support development of the Win32 version of Perl.)

Much trouble will be avoided if we keep this multiple meaning of the term 'scripting' firmly in mind.

1.4   Characteristics of scripting languages

The languages used for these different kinds of scripting have many features in common, which serve to define an overall concept of a scripting language, and to differentiate it from the concept of programming language. We list here some of the features that characterize scripting languages.

■   *Integrated compile and run.* This is perhaps the most important feature. Scripting languages are usually characterized as interpreted languages, but this is an oversimplification. What matters is that they behave as if they were interpreted, i.e. they operate on an immediate execution basis, without the need to issue separate commands to compile the program and then to run the resulting object file, and without the need to link extensive libraries into the object code. This notion of immediate execution (sometimes described as 'hack-it-and-run') is vital, because scripting is often an inter-active, experimental activity that does not fit well with the edit–compile–link–run cycle of conventional programming.

A few scripting languages are indeed implemented as strict interpreters, reading the source file in a single forward pass without lookahead or backtracking, and performing appropriate operations as soon as a valid keyword or construct is recognized: the UNIX shell and versions of Tcl up to version 7.6 are good examples. However, most of the languages in current use (including Tcl 8.0x) employ a hybrid technique, com-piling to an intermediate form which is then interpreted. This intermediate form is usually a representation of the parse tree: the attraction of this approach is that the source is still available (in the form of the parse tree) at run-time, making it possible to provide informative diagnostics in case of error. Indeed, Visual Basic actually builds the parse tree as you type the code, thus providing immediate feedback on many syntax errors. When discussing this class of languages, it is very common to refer to 'compile time' even though they are only partially compiled.

- *Low overheads and ease of use.* Scripting languages endeavour not to come between the user and the problem, which means that they have a minimum of 'clutter'. Variable declarations are often optional: variables can be declared by use, and initialized to something sensible when first used. (However, as the languages have matured and have been used for ever larger applications, the benefits of explicit variable declarations have been recognized, and languages that allow declaration-by-use usually provide an option to require explicit declaration.) The number of different data types is usually limited: frequently, everything is a string, with automatic string to number conversion (or vice versa) when the context requires it. The number of different data structures is likewise limited: quite often the only data structures are arrays, frequently associative arrays rather than conventional indexed arrays. It is generally the case that there is no architecture-determined limit on the size of numbers, nor are there size or shape limits on arrays.

- *Enhanced functionality.* Scripting languages usually have enhanced functionality in some areas. For example, most languages provide powerful string manipulation based on the use of regular expressions, while other languages provide easy access to low-level operating system facilities, or to the API or object model exported by an application.

- *Efficiency is not an issue.* Ease of use is achieved at the expense of efficiency (e.g. interpretation rather than compiling), because efficiency is not an issue in the appli-cations for which scripting languages are designed. Many scripts (e.g. shell scripts written by a system administrator) will be used only once. Other scripts (e.g. CGI scripts) will be used on a regular basis but do not call for high performance: rapid development is more important, together with the ability to make speedy changes to meet new or unanticipated requirements. (This argument appears to fall down in the case of Visual Basic, which has become a tool of choice for many Windows developers, who use it to generate the final delivered application. For this reason, the latest version of Visual Basic still employs the semi-interpretive approach at design time, but has the capability to compile native code executable files for delivery of the shipping version of the application.)

The characteristics of ease of use, particularly the lack of an explicit compile–link–load sequence, are sometimes taken as the sole definition of a scripting language. On this basis, languages such as Python and Dylan are often described as scripting languages: however, we define them as *alternative programming languages*, keeping the designation of 'scripting language' for the languages characterized in Section 1.3.

1.5 Uses for scripting languages

The previous section describes some of the attributes of scripting languages, what they *are*. Equally important is what they *do*, and we explore this issue further in this section.

1.5.1 Traditional scripting

The activities that comprise traditional scripting include

- System administration: automating everyday tasks, building data reduction tools
- Controlling applications remotely
- System and application extensions
- 'Experimental' programming
- Building command-line interfaces to applications based on C libraries
- Server-side form processing on the Web using CGI.

Traditional scripting is the province of what are nowadays called 'Open Source' languages, particularly Perl and Tcl. (These languages are among the earliest exemplars of Open Source software, along with the GNU software produced by the Free Software Foundation.)

System administration

The concept of scripting first arose out of the requirements of system administration in the UNIX world. The administrators used shell scripts – sequences of shell commands executed from a file - to automate everyday tasks such as adding a new user to the system or backing up the file system With the advent of the programmable Bourne shell and its successors, sophisticated effects could be obtained with shell scripts, which became viable alternatives to C programming for most activities of this kind. Indeed, the Bourne shell can claim to be one of the first scripting languages: the other was REXX, developed at about the same time, which provided a similar kind of programmable control over the IBM mainframe VM/CMS system.

The Bourne shell was well suited to system administration since (i) it was fully programmable (within limits; see Chapter 16) and (ii) it provided full access to the underlying system calls. This is vital since system administration is more about manipulating files and processes than performing numerical computations. The other requirement for system administration is the ability to process the contents of the files, e.g. for digesting log files and presenting the results in a readable format, tabulating disk usage etc. as well as manipulating the files themselves. This typically involves extensive processing of textual data, which is not something for which shell scripts are well suited (nor is it something that is easily done in C). In addition, many of the programs of this nature that are required may only be used once, so the overhead of development must be low. There is thus a requirement for a low-overhead language that provides easy access to the underlying functions of the operating system, and specialized towards the handling of textual data.

The requirement for powerful but easy-to-use facilities for processing of textual data was first met by the development of scripting languages specialized to that purpose: AWK is the prime example in this category. Although AWK was extremely effective as a text manipulation tool, to meet the needs of the 'sysadmins' (as system administrators are colloquially known) it was necessary to embed AWK scripts (to manipulate the file contents) in shell scripts which manipulated the files themselves. This was a messy business, mainly due to incompatible syntaxes (AWK and the shell both make extensive use of the $ character, but for quite different purposes), and the problem was solved by the development of Perl, which combines the capabilities of shell scripts and AWK, together with many other powerful facilities, in a uniform framework. It is worth remarking that although Perl is now the language of choice for this kind of activity, AWK played an important role in the evolution of scripting languages, and remains an interesting language in its own right: see Chapter 16 for more details of the language.

Driving applications remotely

As we have seen, an early application of scripting was to control a dial-up link to a remote computer. The use of a scripting *language*, rather than a utility that just plays back a previously recorded sequence of keystrokes, is necessary because there is often an element of conditional logic involved. For example, having dialled the number it is necessary to wait until the distant computer responds: it may then be necessary to acknowledge the response and wait for the 'login' prompt, and, having sent the user identifier, wait again for the 'password:' prompt. Any of these stages may fail, and so the script must also include conditional logic to deal with failures, and retry the operation if appropriate.

This was a precursor of the use of scripting languages to allow remote control of an application (often, but not necessarily, an application with an interactive interface). This *application automation* is increasingly important, and can be applied to any *scriptable application*, i.e. one that has some sort of control interface that allows it to be controlled or used by another program. The control interface exposed by the application may be as simple as the ability to accept text strings as commands (e.g. DOS or the UNIX shell), or as complicated as the Windows API, or anything in between. In the operating system world these remote control languages are often described as *batch languages*.

System and application extensions

In terms of the definition given in the preceding section, the UNIX system is a scriptable application, since it exposes a programmable API in the form of the system calls. Thus, a shell script could be regarded as an example of automation, in which the command interpreter is driven by a script held in a file rather than by a real user. However, we tend to regard this kind of behaviour as *application extension* rather than as application automation. The distinction can perhaps be made clear by considering the changing nature of macros in desktop applications such as word processors and spreadsheet programs. From the very early days these applications provided automation of common sequences of operations in the form of keystroke recording and subsequent replay. With more sophisticated applications and graphical user interfaces, keystroke recording becomes less effective, and many modern applications expose a programmable API together with a scripting language, still called a macro language but strictly an extension language, to extend the user interface. (For ordinary users a macro appears to be just a way of recording menu selections and keystrokes to automate common operations, but what is really happening is that a 'keystroke compiler' is generating a program in the underlying macro language.) A prime example of this technique was the use of WordBasic as the extension language (macro language) for Microsoft Word prior to the release of Microsoft Office 97, providing an easy way to control the editing and formatting engine of Microsoft Word. In addition, 'power users' of spreadsheet and word processing packages were unknowing users of scripting languages when they used so-called macro languages to extend the functionality of the package.

A modern form of extension is found in the use of scripting to provide an 'escape' from a declarative system for tasks that require an element of programmability. Thus HTML is a declarative system, using tags to define a static structure with only the simplest interactive component in the guise of forms: more elaborate interaction requires the use of a scripting language such as JavaScript or VBScript.

Experimental programming

Traditional languages like C were developed as tools for writing large and complex programs, many of which require teams of programmers. Not all programming is like that: as the early system administrators discovered, there is another class of programs, the writing of which involves experimentation, since the precise requirements are not clear at the outset, and it is often necessary to produce several versions before the tool is satisfactory. Low-overhead scripting languages are well suited to this kind of 'experimental programming' since ideas can be tried out without incurring a time-consuming penalty from the overhead of the edit–compile–link–load cycle. (Experimental programming is just one instance of 'throw-away' programming – writing programs that will only be used once.) The convenience of Perl for this kind of programming caused its use to spread beyond the confines of system programming as a tool for rapid application development and for building prototypes – an inherent part of the software development process, which leads to a better quality product in the end. Sometimes a prototype in Perl is a prelude to a final application coded in C or C++: however, unless there are strong requirements for run-time efficiency, the application may never be re-coded – the last prototype becomes the production version.

Command-line interfaces

A major use of scripting languages in traditional scripting is as a form of 'glue' to connect together sections of code written in some other language or languages through a command-line interface, making it possible to build new applications by combining other applications, or parts of other applications. In the UNIX world, a glue language is one that is able to start up another program, collect its output, process it and perhaps pass it as input to a third program, and so on. The shell offers a simple form of glue in the form of pipes, and languages like Perl provide much more comprehensive glue capabilities. An extension to this line of thought is the idea that large software systems should be developed using a combination of *two* languages: one, such as C, C++ or Java, for manipulating the complex internal data structures and other operations for which performance is important, and a scripting language for writing scripts that 'glue' the C pieces together. In this way we can speed the development of powerful and media-rich applications that can call upon compiled routines written in an efficient low-level language when they want to. Tcl is a very good example of this approach to application development.

1.5.2 Modern scripting

To complement our discussion of traditional scripting, we now survey the world of modern scripting based on scriptable objects. The applications that comprise modern scripting include:

- Visual scripting
- Using scriptable components – macros for desktop applications and compound documents
- Client-side and server-side Web scripting.

Visual scripting

Visual scripting is the process of constructing a graphical interface from a collection of visual objects ('controls' in Microsoft terminology, 'widgets' in Tcl/Tk and Perl-Tk), which have properties (attributes), e.g. foreground and background colours, text on a button etc. that can be set by a program written in an appropriate language. Some objects (e.g. buttons) respond to external *events* such as mouse clicks, and the response to each action is defined by a script. Programming such an interface is described as 'scripting the objects'.

Visual Basic is the pre-eminent visual scripting system, used to develop new applications and to provide visual interfaces for 'legacy' applications, either as prototypes to be replaced later by production versions written in C++, or as final products in their own right, the objects being scripted using a dialect of the BASIC language, confusingly also called Visual Basic. Alternatives to Visual Basic for visual scripting in the Windows environment include Tcl/Tk and Perl-Tk. In the UNIX environment Tcl/Tk, Perl-Tk and the Desktop Kornshell facilitate the construction of visual interfaces under the X Window System: these are much more accessible than the alternative of using one of the C-based X Window System development libraries. In all these cases we see the power of scripting: controls (widgets), created by professional programmers using C++, can easily be assembled ('glued') into applications using a scripting language, without necessarily requiring expert programming skills.

Another use of visual scripting is creating enhanced Web pages: we return to this later.

Scriptable components

In this modern world the idea of glue reappears in the use of scripting languages to manipulate a collection of objects or components which expose an interface that conforms to a particular scripting architecture: in brief, scriptable objects. The first applications to be built round the concept of scriptable objects were Microsoft's Visual Basic and Excel: the concept has since developed to underpin all of Microsoft's application development.

Scriptable objects include:

- Visual components ('controls') whose properties can be manipulated by a scripting language. These may form part of an application like Visual Basic, or they may be embedded in an application such as a Web browser to provide dynamic interaction.
- Parts of a compound document, e.g. a spreadsheet embedded in a word-processor document.
- More substantial 'component objects' encapsulating the data and functionality of all or part of an application, e.g. the spellchecker in a word processor, an interface to an external database or a low-level interface to the Internet.
- Elements in an object model that reflects the structure of some entity of interest to a user, e.g. a Web page.

This idea of scripting objects extends to 'component-ware', the construction of an application from several off-the-shelf component objects, and to the manipulation of *compound documents* made up of a number of components (paragraphs, graphics, spreadsheets etc.) that are seen as objects 'belonging' to a number of different applications. As well as having properties that can be set, the objects used in these contexts encapsulate data and functionality, providing *methods* that can be invoked externally (e.g. 'compute the sum of the selected cells'). In much modern writing the term 'scripting' is used exclusively to describe this activity of controlling the interworking of components and objects.

Components can be controlled by any program that can invoke their methods. Such a program might be written in a conventional language like C++, but component architectures come into their own when they are based on *scriptable* components, i.e. components whose external interface is accessible from one or more scripting languages. In the Microsoft implementation of components the external interface to an object is defined by the Component Object Model (COM), and the scripting language is a version of Visual Basic called Visual Basic for Applications (VBA) or Visual Basic Applications Edition. All the applications in the Office suite follow the COM architecture; thus, *compound documents* may be created, typically combining text, spreadsheet data and graphics. Each component is manipulated by a different application, and the interactions are mediated by VBA, which becomes a common macro language for all the applications: another form of 'glue'. (This was Microsoft's first component architecture. We shall see shortly that Internet Explorer implements a powerful component architecture with support for multiple scripting languages.)

As we have observed above, the idea of building applications from components – 'component-ware' – is not tied to scripting: indeed, one of the most elaborate component architectures, OpenDoc, was implemented as a collection of C++ classes. However, it is likely that the run-away success of Microsoft's component architecture – exemplified by

Microsoft's Office 97 suite and the related OLE and ActiveX technologies – and the simultaneous demise of OpenDoc owe much to the fact that the components in the Microsoft
architecture are scriptable, and powerful scripting languages are available. (The slow take-
up of the CORBA architecture can be attributed in part to the same reason.)

1.6 Web scripting

The Web is one of the most fertile areas for the application of scripting languages at the
present time, and readers of the popular technical press probably believe that scripting is
solely concerned with generating interactive Web pages. Web scripting divides into three
areas: (i) processing forms, (ii) creating pages with enhanced visual effects and user
interaction and (iii) generating pages 'on the fly' from material held in a database.

Processing Web forms

*'Vanilla' HTML can in
fact be considered to be a
scripting language, since
it controls the Web
browser and
consequently the screen
display. If we take this
view, it is the first
declarative scripting
language. Alternatively,
it can be regarded as a
notation: the distinction
between notations and
programs is too subtle to
pursue here.*

From the early days, HTML has allowed a limited kind of user interaction through the use
of *forms* – a rather primitive visual interface, defined by tags in an HTML document. In
the original implementation of the Web, when the form is submitted for processing, the
information entered by the user is encoded and sent to the server for processing by a CGI
script that eventually generates an HTML page to be sent back to the Web browser. This
processing requires string manipulation to decode the form data and text manipulation to
construct the HTML page that constitutes the reply, and may also require system access,
to run other processes and/or establish network connections. These are exactly the
requirements that we have already identified as those of the UNIX system administrator,
and it is not surprising that the system administrator's favourite language, Perl, is also the
language of choice for CGI scripting. (Perl's handling of untrusted data is also a major
reason why it is used for CGI scripts; see Chapter 3.)

  As an alternative to doing all the processing of a form with a script running on the
server, it is possible to do some client-side processing within the browser to validate form
data before sending it to the server, using a scripting language designed for the purpose,
e.g. JavaScript/JScript or VBScript. (JavaScript/JScript can be used in both Netscape
Navigator and Internet Explorer. VBScript – Visual Basic Scripting Edition – is available
only in Internet Explorer.)

Dynamic Web pages

*Note that Netscape uses
the term 'Dynamic
HTML' to encompass an
object model in which
only a few components of
the HTML page are
scriptable objects,
together with their
proprietary technology
for positioning of
content. See Chapter 12
for more details.*

'Dynamic HTML', as implemented in Internet Explorer, makes every component of a Web
page – headings, anchors, emphasized text, tables, form components etc. – a scriptable
object. This makes it possible to provide very elaborate dynamic control over the appearance of a Web page and to provide simple interaction with the user using scripts written in
JavaScript/JScript or VBScript, which are interpreted by the browser. Scripts can also be
used to obtain information about the browser, and thus optimize pages to match the
browser's capabilities.

  Microsoft's ActiveX technology (so far available only in Internet Explorer) allows the
creation of pages with more elaborate user interaction by using embedded visual objects

called ActiveX controls (analogous to the controls in Visual Basic). These controls are scriptable objects, and can in fact be scripted in a variety of languages, since Explorer implements a scripting architecture called ActiveX Scripting. An ActiveX *scripting host* does not interface directly to an embedded scripting language; instead it can access any of a number of *scripting engines* to run a script written in the language associated with the particular engine. Thus, while Internet Explorer comes with scripting engines for VBScript and JavaScript (JScript), it can also be scripted in Perl using a Perl scripting engine supplied by a third party. The ActiveX and OLE specifications are non-proprietary, and so in principle ActiveX scripting need not be limited to Microsoft languages and applications.

Dynamically generated HTML

Another form of dynamic Web page is one in which some or all of the HTML is generated by scripts executed on the server. A common application of the technique is to construct pages whose content is retrieved from a database. For example, Microsoft's IIS Web server (incorporated in the Windows NT Server product) implements so-called Active Server Pages (ASP), which incorporate scripts in JScript or VBScript. Netscape provides a functionally equivalent facility in its server, based on JavaScript, and Sun has recently introduced Java Server Pages, which emulate ASP. We explore the Microsoft version further in Chapter 11.

1.7 Java

Java is not a scripting language by any of the definitions given previously: it is an object-oriented procedural programming language having much in common with C++. However, it merits a mention here because of its tight integration with the Web – in the world of the Web, programmers do it in a scripting language or they do it in Java. In particular, JavaScript can be used as an interface to objects written in Java, and Java can be used as an implementation language for ActiveX controls, so from the scripting language point of view, Java is a rich source of scriptable objects. 'JavaBeans' are the basis of the Java component architecture; although the original concept was that their interaction would be entirely a matter of programming in Java, they can be regarded as scriptable components, and a Java-based version of Tcl, Jacl, makes it possible to script JavaBeans from Tcl. (See Chapter 5 for more details.)

1.8 The universe of scripting languages

In describing the world of scripting languages we have identified traditional and modern scripting, and we have seen that Web scripting forms an important part of modern scripting. An alternative view is that there is a scripting universe, containing multiple overlapping worlds:

- the original UNIX world of traditional scripting using Perl and Tcl, which are now available on most platforms

- the Microsoft world of Visual Basic and ActiveX controls
- the world of VBA for scripting compound documents
- the world of client-side and server-side Web scripting.

(If you find the concept of overlapping worlds difficult, think of them as resembling the Discworld that features in the novels of Terry Pratchett – but without the giant turtle and the elephants!) The overlap is complex: for example, Web scripting can be done in VBScript, JavaScript/JScript, Perl or Tcl.

This universe has recently been enlarged by the appearance of another world, in which Perl and Tcl are used to implement complex applications for large organizations – for example, Tcl has been used to develop a major banking system, and Perl has been used to implement an enterprise-wide document management system for a leading aerospace company. The enormous increase in processor power in recent years means that the performance hit of interpretation rather than compiling is no longer a serious considera-tion, and the order-of-magnitude increase in productivity gained by using a scripting language pays off handsomely. We live in interesting times.

## Part two

Languages

## Chapter 2

Getting the job done in Perl

The arrival of Perl (Practical Extraction and Report Language) in the late 1980s was a defining event in the development of scripting languages. Perl rapidly developed from being a fairly simple text-processing language to a fully featured language with extensive capabilities for interacting with the system to manipulate files and processes, establish network connections and other similar system-programming tasks. The current version, Version 5, also provides a full range of object-oriented capabilities. This chapter explores the capabilities of Perl, and shows how it has gained the sobriquet 'the Swiss Army chain saw of languages', partly because its versatility resembles that of the Swiss Army knife, and partly because it is able to cut through difficulties with ease.

2.1 The Perl phenomenon

In less than ten years, Perl has become one of the world's most popular programming languages, spreading from its UNIX roots to every major operating system. A Perl script will run unchanged on a bewildering number of platforms – virtually all known and current UNIX derivatives are supported, as are the Amiga, BeOS, DOS, the Macintosh, OS/2, QNX, Windows and VMS – provided you do not use anything that is special to a particular operating system. (Initially, the UNIX version was ported to each of the other platforms but as from Perl 5.005 all implementations are derived from a common source file.)

Perl is an example of a phenomenon that we see increasingly often – someone develops a piece of software primarily for their own use, or just out of interest, and makes it freely available to the community over the Internet: people find the software useful, and an enthusiastic band of users begin to develop enhancements, which they again circulate freely via the net. Before we know it, there is a high-quality free product available, with better support than many commercial products, thanks to the networked user community. It is a prime example of what has come to be called Open Source Software. Other examples are the GNU software suite, Tcl/Tk (discussed in Chapters 4, 5 and 6) and, most recently, the rise and rise of Linux and the Apache Web server – the free software/Open source movement comes from the UNIX world, which has a long tradition of cooperation and self-help.

The original author of Perl, Larry Wall, has observed that the explosive growth of Perl outside the UNIX environment has been driven by former UNIX programmers whose jobs have taken them into other less congenial environments: as a result of its origins in the UNIX world, Perl is a 'portable distillation of UNIX culture' that such refugees can take with them. Another reason for the explosive growth can be found in the all-enveloping World Wide Web. The Web originated in the UNIX world: the original Web servers were UNIX machines, and it is not surprising that Perl was rapidly adopted as the language of choice for server-side scripting: the development of CGI scripts is similar in many ways to the development of system-administration tools, and the original webmasters were in many cases also the system administrators for the server machines. More recently it has become possible to use Perl scripts as alternatives to JavaScript and VBScript for client-side Web scripting (see Chapter 11). Although we have classified Perl as a programming language rather than a 'glue' language, it has an element of glue: as Larry Wall has remarked, 'Perl tries to hook up to everything on your system that it can: that's the glue part of it'.

2.2 Introducing Perl

Perl originated in the late 1980s when Larry Wall was the system guru for a project developing secure wide-area networks. The installation comprised three VAXen [1] and three Sun workstations on the east coast of the USA and the same on the west coast. At first he used the shell and AWK to produce management reports, but finding this combination insufficiently powerful for his needs, he decided to develop a new language rather than code a variety of special-purpose tools. Originally called Pearl, the name was abbreviated to Perl, partly because there was a graphics language at the time called Pearl, and partly because it's quicker to type four characters than five. The name expands to 'Practical Extraction and Report Language', though it is possible that, as with many acronyms, the name predates its alleged expansion.

The description of the language provided in the UNIX 'man' (manual) page for Version 1 is of interest:

> Perl is an interpreted language optimized for scanning arbitrary text files, extracting information from those text files, and printing reports based on that information. It's also a good language for many system management tasks. The language is intended to be practical (easy to use, efficient, complete) rather than beautiful (tiny, elegant, minimal). It combines (in the author's opinion, anyway) some of the best features of C, sed, awk, and sh, so people familiar with those languages should have little difficulty with it. (Language historians will also note some vestiges of csh, Pascal, and even BASIC.)

Perl started as a data reduction language which could navigate the file system, scan large amounts of text, and produce easily formatted reports using powerful pattern matching and text manipulation capabilities. As it developed it gained the facility to manipulate the files themselves, as well as their contents, and to create and control processes. As networking became more common, Perl also became a networking language, providing system-independent abstractions of files, processes, sockets etc. in so far as this is possible in specific systems. The current version (Version 5, on which this chapter is based) also provides a full range of object-oriented capabilities. Perl provides 'one-stop shopping' for system administrators, but its capabilities, especially its powerful dynamic data structures and string handling, make it applicable way beyond the area of system administration: it is, for example, the language of choice for CGI scripting. It is often called 'the Swiss Army chain saw of languages', partly because its versatility resembles that of the Swiss Army knife, and partly because it is able to cut through difficulties with ease. It has also been described as 'a shell for C programmers' and, more controversially, 'BASIC for UNIX'.

The Perl philosophy is embodied in the observation that Perl 'makes easy things easy while making difficult things possible'. (This is stated explicitly. An implicit, but significant, part of the Perl philosophy is that programming should be fun.) An important design objective embodied in the quotation given above was that the language should be 'practical (easy to use, efficient, complete) rather than beautiful (tiny, elegant, minimal)'. As a result, although most of the underlying ideas are simple, Perl is an immensely rich language. It is also at times a messy language, but that is no accident: as Larry Wall has explained [2]:

> English is useful because it's a mess. Since English is a mess, it maps well onto the problem space which is also a mess, which we call reality. Similarly, Perl was designed to be a mess (though in the nicest of possible ways).

Perl has unashamedly borrowed the best ideas from many sources, particularly the C language, the UNIX utilities *sed* and *awk*, and the UNIX shell, and as a result of its borrowing you can use Perl for anything you would program in *sh*, *sed* or *awk* – sed2perl and awk2perl converters are available – and you can use it instead of C for all system-level UNIX programming.

Unlike most languages, which make a virtue out of forcing the programmer to do things in a particular way, Perl espouses the principle that 'there's more than one way to do it'. Consciously modelled on English usage, it allows different ways of expressing the same concept, e.g. the ability to put an if condition after a statement rather than before, or the ability to replace if by unless if this makes the condition more perspicuous. Perl makes sensible assumptions in the face of apparently incomplete information, and it takes a relaxed view of syntactic conformity, e.g. brackets are required round function arguments only if they are needed to resolve ambiguity: if the meaning is unambiguously clear without the brackets, they can be omitted. Throughout the language there is a policy of 'no surprises': Perl always tries to do what is obviously sensible in the circumstances. Finally, Perl is not prescriptive: the programmer is free to adopt whatever style he or she feels most comfortable with. If you prefer to put brackets round function arguments, you can. If you disagree with the Perl default of no declarations, you can tell the system to behave as what is sometimes called a 'bondage language' by insisting on their presence. Just add the line

```
use strict;
```

at the start of your script. (Experienced Perl programmers invariably do this, being aware of their own limitations and of the havoc that can be caused by a misspelled variable name.)

Perl is affectionately known in some circles as the 'Pathologically Eclectic Rubbish Lister'. When you have learned more about the language, come back to the dictionary definitions, and see if you agree.

pathologically: in a morbid manner. **morbid**: 1. Of persons or animals, their parts etc.: affected by disease, diseased, unhealthy. 2. Of mental conditions, ideas, etc.: unwholesome, sickly: chiefly applied to unreasonable feelings of gloom, apprehension or suspicion. **eclectic**: 1. In ancient use, the distinguishing epithet of a class of philosophers who neither attached themselves to any recognised school, nor constructed independent systems, but 'selected such doctrines as pleased them in every school'. 2. More vaguely: That borrows or is borrowed from diverse sources. Also, of persons or personal attributes: Unfettered by narrow system in matters of opinion or practice: broad not exclusive in matters of taste.

2.2.1 Hello world!

It is traditional for any description of a new programming language to start with a program that displays the message 'Hello World!' to the user: one purpose of this is to illustrate the overhead that a particular language attaches to the simplest of programs. For example, here is the 'Hello World!' program in C:

```
#include <stdio.h>
main()
{
     printf("Hello World!\n");
}
```

and here it is in Java:

```
public class Hello {
   public static void main(String[ ] args)
   {
      System.out.println("Hello World!");
   }
}
```

By contrast, the Perl version is a single line, with no additional clutter:

```
print "Hello World!\n";
```

Note that while C functions and Java methods require their arguments to be enclosed in round brackets, in the Perl version the brackets are not required. What makes Perl *really* special is that we could have put the brackets in if we wanted to – if you're used to another language, putting brackets round function arguments comes automatically. Thus Perl is equally happy to accept any of the following variations:

There's usually more than one way to do it. If the meaning is obvious, the syntax is probably OK.

```
print("Hello World!\n");
print ("Hello World!\n");
print "Hello World!", "\n";
print "Hello", " ", "World!", "\n";
```

To complete the comparison, we need also to look at what is involved in running the program. In C, we would put the code into a file called `test.c`, then (in UNIX) type

```
$  cc test.c
$  a.out
```

(Here, $ is the UNIX shell prompt.) The command `cc test.c` compiles the C code and generates an executable file called `a.out`, which is run by the following command. In Java we would put the code into a file called `Hello.java` (the file name must be identical to the class name), and compile and run it with the commands

```
$  javac Hello.java
$  java Hello
```

The `javac` command compiles the Java code and generates a class file called `Hello.class` which is run by the `java` command.

A similar approach can be used in Perl: if we put the `print` command in a file called `hello.pl`, we can run it with the command

```
$  perl hello.pl
```

Since Perl is an immediate execution ('hack it and go') language, we do not need separate commands to compile and run. In the UNIX environment we normally make a Perl script into an executable command by placing it in an executable file with a 'magic' first line that causes the system to invoke the Perl interpreter on the rest of the text. This magic line is typically

```
#!/usr/bin/perl
```

though the path name for the Perl interpreter may be different on your system – consult the system administrator for details of local conventions. Thus if we have an executable file called *greet* containing the text

```
#!/usr/bin/perl
print "Hello World!\n"
```

we can run our script by just typing `greet` at the UNIX shell prompt. The same script can be run in Windows (in a DOS box) by the command

```
c:\> perl greet
```

since the first line will be discarded as a comment. Making the script into an executable file is overkill for a single liner, but it illustrates an important facility. In practice, for anything more than a one-liner we would make the first line

```
#!/usr/bin/perl -w
```

in order to switch on 'warning mode': this provides a variety of helpful messages in the event of errors in the script. To obtain the same effect in DOS we invoke the script with

```
perl -w greet
```

2.2.2 Beyond 'Hello world!'

Before we go on to look at Perl in detail, here are six small examples to give you the flavour of Perl and some indication of its power.

Example 1: Print lines containing the string 'Shazzam!'

```
#!/usr/bin/Perl
while (<STDIN>) {
  print if /Shazzam!/
};
```

This one-liner reads from standard input and prints out all the lines that contain the string '*Shazzam!*'. `<STDIN>` is a bit of Perl magic that delivers the next line of input each time round the loop. At end-of-file it delivers a special value called undef, which terminates the while loop. Note the English-like simplicity of putting the if condition after the operation. Note also the use of an implied anonymous variable analogous to the pronoun 'it', and the implied pattern match – 'print *it* if *it* matches /Shazzam!/'. If we wanted to spell everything out, we would have changed the code to the version shown in Example 2: needless to say, the earlier form is the preferred idiom in Perl.

Example 2: The same thing the hard way

Here we use a variable instead of the anonymous 'it'. $line indicates that it is a scalar variable (as opposed to an array).

```
while ($line = <STDIN>) {
  print $line if $line =~
   /Shazzam!/
};
```

Example 3: Print lines not containing the string 'Shazzam!'

If we want to print all lines except those containing the pattern, we just change if to unless.

```
/!/usr/bin/Perl
while (<STDIN>) {
print unless /Shazzam!/
};
```

Example 4: A script with arguments

When we invoke a Perl script we can add command-line arguments, e.g.

```
$  match  abracadabra
$  match  Shazzam!  file1  file2
```

in UNIX, or

```
c:\> perl match.pl abracadabra
c:\> perl match.pl shazzam! file1 file2
```

in Windows. Called with one argument, `match` is a generalization of Example 1: it reads standard input and prints those lines which contain the word given as the argument. Called with two or more arguments, the first argument is the word to be searched for, and the second and subsequent arguments are names of files that will be searched in sequence for the target word. The script is remarkably short:

```
#!/usr/bin/perl
$word = shift;
while (<>) {print if /$word/};
```

The `shift` operator returns the first argument from the command line, and moves the others up one place. Note the extreme magic of <>, which delivers the lines of input from each of the files given as arguments in sequence, and is clever enough to deliver lines from STDIN (standard input) if no file-name arguments are provided. (Execution of the script is terminated if any of the files named on the command line cannot be opened.)

Example 5: Error messages

```
#!/usr/bin/perl
die "Need word to search for\n"
  if @ARGV == 0;
$word = shift;
while (<>) {print if /$word/};
```

The command-line arguments can be accessed in the array @ARGV. This script is a variant of Example 4 that calls the built-in function `die` if no arguments are provided. This terminates execution of the script, after writing its argument string to STDERR, the standard error channel (usually the screen).

Example 6: Reverse order of lines in a file

```
#!/usr/bin/perl
open IN, $ARGV[0] or die
  "Can't open $ARGV[0]\n";
@file = <IN>;
for ($i = @file - 1; $i >= 0; $i--) {
  print $file[$i]
};
```

This script reads the file whose name is given as an argument (with an error message if the file cannot be opened), and prints the lines of the file in reverse order. Think about the complexity of a program to achieve this in a language like C, and marvel that Perl requires just three lines of code for the actual reversal! (The job can in fact be done in one line using the built-in function `reverse`, but for educational reasons we are pretending that this function does not exist. The magic embodied in the second line will be explained later.) Line 4 in the script reads the entire file into the array @file – which may cause memory problems if the file is truly gigantic.

2.3 Names and values in Perl

2.3.1 Names

This chapter, and the next, are based on Perl 5.005. Perl 5 was a major rewrite of the system, and some of the features we describe are present in different forms, or not present at all, in earlier versions.

Like any other procedural language, Perl manipulates *variables* which have a *name* (or *identifier*) and a *value*: a value is assigned to (or *stored in*) a variable by an *assignment statement* of the form

```
name = value;
```

Variable names resemble nouns in English (command names are verbs), and, like English, Perl distinguishes between singular and plural nouns (names). A singular name is associated with a variable that holds a single item of data (a *scalar value*): a plural name is associated with a variable that holds a collection of data items (an *array* or *hash*).

A notable characteristic of Perl is that variable names start with a special character that denotes the kind of thing that the name stands for – scalar data ($), array (@), hash (%), subroutine (&) etc. (In practice we rarely need to attach a prefix character to a subroutine name: the reason why will be explained later.) The remainder of the name follows the more-or-less standard convention: valid characters are letters, digits and underscores, and the first character after the special character must be a letter or an underscore. (A single quote is also a valid character in a name, but use of this feature is deprecated.) The syntax also allows a name that consists of a single non-alphanumeric character after the initial special character, e.g. $$, $?; such names are usually reserved for the Perl system and we shall see a number of examples as we delve deeper into the language.

The use of a special character at the start of a name means that each kind of data has a separate namespace, but this is not the whole story. The special character also determines the context in which the name is being used and thus the kind of thing it stands for. This somewhat subtle point will become clearer when we come to discuss collections of data, where a name may refer to the entire collection, part of the collection, or to a single element of the collection, depending on the context. This way of handling names is more than just a convenience: a naming convention that establishes the evaluation context unequivocally makes life easier for the user, by removing the possibility of errors due to ambiguity, and makes life simpler for the Perl compiler. (This idea of context is present in a different form in conventional programming languages. If we write an assignment, e.g. j = j + 1, the occurrence of j on the left denotes a storage location, while the right-hand occurrence denotes the contents of the storage location. We sometimes refer to these as the *lvalue* and *rvalue* of the variable: more precisely we are determining the meaning of the identifier in a *left-context* or a *right-context*. In the assignment a[j] = a[j] + 1, both occurrences of j are determined in a right-context, even though one of them appears on the left of the assignment.)

In conventional programming languages, new variables are introduced by a *declaration*, which specifies the name of the new variable and also its *type*, which determines the kind of value that can be stored in the variable and, by implication, the operations that can be carried out on that variable. Thus in C we might write

```
int i = 1;
float data[9];
```

to introduce an integer variable i, initialized to the value 1, and an array of 10 floating-point values called data. In many languages the declaration performs a further function: its placing in the program text determines the *scope* of the variable, i.e. the part of the program in which the variable is visible and available for use. For example, in C and similar languages, variables declared at the head of a function are by default *local* to the function, and only visible (accessible) during execution of the function body.

Scripting languages often allow the user to dispense with declarations: a new variable springs into being on its first use, initialized to some sensible value, and the type is determined implicitly when a value is assigned. This is useful in short 'throw-away' scripts, but for more substantial projects it is good discipline to use declarations. In the absence of declarations, Perl variables appear to spring into life as described above, though the actual behaviour is more subtle. A variable comes into existence when declared or first used with a special 'value' denoted by undef. If this first occurrence of a variable is in a right-context, where a value is required, undef evaluates to zero in a numeric context and to an empty string in a string context. However, it is possible to test for this value, thus a program can find out whether a variable has ever been given a value.

Declarations are used as a way of delimiting scope, as we shall see when we come to subroutines. As we have noted earlier, you can choose to declare all variables if you so wish – Perl won't mind – and experienced programmers usually tell Perl to insist on declarations by placing the line

```
use strict 'vars';
```

or just

```
use strict;
```

at the start of a script. Variables are declared explicitly using my, e.g.

```
my x, y, z;
```

The reason for the choice of my to introduce declarations will become apparent later.

2.3.2   Scalar data

Strings and numbers

In common with many scripting languages, Perl recognizes just two kinds of scalar data: strings and numbers. There is no distinction between integer and real numbers as different types – a number is a number. Internally, numbers are stored as signed integers if possible, and otherwise as double length floating point numbers in the system's native format. Strings are stored as sequences of bytes of unlimited length (subject, of course, to the amount of available memory: you can have a string that fills all the memory, but it is unlikely that you can do anything useful with it). Although we tend to think of strings as sequences of printable characters, Perl attaches no significance to any of the 256 possible values of a byte. You could in principle use Perl's string operations to patch a chunk of executable binary code.

Perl is a *dynamically typed language* [3]: the system keeps track of whether a variable contains a numeric value or a string value, and the user doesn't have to worry about the difference between strings and numbers since conversions between the two kinds of data are done automatically as required by the context in which they are used. (That is how it appears to the user: in fact, once a string has been converted to a number, or vice versa, both versions are retained to avoid the inefficiency of repeatedly doing the same conversion.) Thus if a string value occurs in an *arithmetic context*, e.g. as an operand for an arithmetic operator, Perl will convert it to a number by fair means or foul; if a numerical value occurs in a *string context*, e.g. as an operand for a string operator, Perl will convert it to a string (strictly, the string that would be printed by a C *sprintf* function with the format string "%.14g"). A trap that is likely to ensnare the user arises when a string to be converted to a number contains characters that cannot be part of a number. If the first non-blank character in the string is not a digit, a plus sign or a minus sign the value zero is used: if the string is *a priori* a valid number it will be converted, but any trailing non-digit characters are discarded. In both cases this happens quietly and unobtrusively. (The treatment of trailing non-digit characters is in fact the behaviour of the C *atof()* function: however, *atof* gives the programmer the option of finding out whether the conversion was terminated by an invalid character.)

Boolean values

All programming languages need some way of representing truth values (Boolean values), e.g. in control constructs for conditional execution and repetition of blocks of code, and Perl is no exception. Since scalar values are either numbers or strings, some convention is needed for representing Boolean values, and Perl adopts the simple rule that numeric zero, "0" and the empty string ("") mean false, and anything else means true. (This is a slight oversimplification, but will suffice for the present.)

2.3.3 Numeric constants

Numeric constants (*number literals*) can be written in a variety of ways, including scientific notation, octal and hexadecimal. Although Perl tries to emulate natural human communication, the common practice of using commas or spaces to break up a large integer constant into meaningful digit groups cannot be used, since the comma has a syntactic significance in Perl. Instead, underscores can be included in a number literal to improve legibility. Some possible number formats are illustrated below.

```
123                 4929712198024
122.45              4929_712_198_024
122.45e-5           0377 (octal)
122.45E-5           0x3fff (hex)
```

2.3.4 String constants

String constants (*string literals*) can be enclosed in single or double quotes. The string is terminated by the first next occurrence of the quote (single or double) which started it, so a single-quoted string can include double quotes and vice versa. Following the widely used convention first introduced in the UNIX shell, single quoted strings are treated 'as is' with no interpretation of their contents except the usual use of backslash to remove special meanings, so to include a single quote in such a string it must be preceded with a backslash, and to include a backslash you use two of them. In a double quoted string, backslash is used to introduce special characters (e.g. newline), and other substitutions can occur, as will be explained later. Thus, `'Friday'` is a string containing six characters, `'Friday\n'` is a string containing eight characters (ending with \ and n), but `"Friday\n"` is a string containing seven characters of which the last is newline. The usual backslash substitutions (\n for newline, \t for tab, etc.) are provided: in addition, backslash substitutions can also be used to effect case modification, e.g. \U forces all following characters (or all characters up to the next \E) to upper case. For details of all the backslash substitutions available, see the Perl documentation.

Choose your own quotes

There's more than one way to do it. The q (quote) and qq (double quote) operators allow you to use any character as a quoting character. Thus

        q/any string/

or

        q(any string)

are the same as

        'any string'

and

        qq/any string/

or

        qq(any string)

are the same as

        "any string"

The character following the q or qq operator is the opening quote character, and the next occurrence of that character is treated as the closing quote character. In fact, Perl adds a little more magic. If the opening quote is specified as an opening bracket – round, square, curly or angle – the closing quote is the next *matching* closing bracket, so

        qq(This is a (very) neat trick)

is the same as

        "This is a (very) neat trick"

2.4 Variables and assignment

2.4.1 Assignment

Borrowing from C, Perl uses '=' as the assignment operator. It is important to note that an assignment statement returns a value, the value assigned. This permits statements like

```
$b = 4 + ($a = 3);
```

which assigns the value 3 to $a and the value 7 to $b. A useful device often used in assignments is to interpolate the value of a scalar variable into a double quoted string: after the assignments

```
$a = "Burger";
$b = "Beef  $a ";
$c = "Turkey  $a";
```

the value of $b is "Beef Burger" and the value of $c is "Turkey Burger", in both cases with a space in the middle. Because scalar variable names start with $, no special syntax is needed for variable interpolation. If it is required to interpolate a variable value without an intervening space the following syntax, borrowed from UNIX shell scripts, is used:

```
$a =   "Java";
$b = "${a}Script";
```

This gives $b the value "JavaScript": the braces (curly brackets) delimit the characters that are part of the variable name.

2.4.2 <STDIN> – a special value

We have already met the magic 'variable' <STDIN>: when it appears in a context where a scalar value is required, it evaluates to a string containing the next line from standard input, *including the terminating newline*. (The standard input is the keyboard, unless you've done something to change it.) If there is no input queued, Perl will wait until a line is typed and the return key pressed. End-of-file (Ctrl-D in UNIX, Ctrl-Z in DOS) causes <STDIN> to return undef, which evaluates to "", since <STDIN> always occurs in a context where a string is expected. The empty string is treated as false in a Boolean context, hence the common idiom

```
while (<STDIN>) {
...
}
```

to process all lines until end-of-file is reached. (A cautious programmer would write

```
while (defined <STDIN>) {
...
}
```

to make sure the loop is not entered if some unusual condition means that STDIN is not available.)

If <STDIN> appears on the right-hand side of an assignment to a scalar variable, the string containing the input line is assigned to the variable named on the left. If it appears in any other scalar context the string is assigned to the *anonymous variable*: this can be accessed by the name $_: many operations use it as a default, as we shall see later. (Wimpish programmers add 'use English;' at the start of a script: they can then use $ARG in place of $_. This is sometimes claimed to be more readable, but since the anonymous variable is not necessarily an argument, this is a moot point.)

2.5 Scalar expressions

Scalar data items (whether literals or values of variables) are combined into *expressions* using *operators*. Perl has a lot of operators, which are ranked in 22 precedence levels: these are carefully chosen so that the 'obvious' meaning is what you get, but the old advice still applies: if in doubt, use brackets to force the order of evaluation. In the following sections we describe the available operators in their natural groupings – arithmetic, string, logical etc. A full list of operators and precedence is given in Section 2.16 at the end of the chapter.

2.5.1 Arithmetic operators

Following the principle of 'no surprises' Perl provides the usual arithmetic operators, including auto-increment and auto-decrement operators after the manner of C: note that in

```
$c = 17; $d = ++$c;
```

the sequence is increment then assign, whereas in

```
$c = 17; $d = $c++;
```

the sequence is assign then increment. As in C, binary arithmetic operations can be combined with assignment, e.g.

```
$a += 3;
```

This adds 3 to $a, being equivalent to

```
$a = $a + 3;
```

As in most other languages, unary minus is used to negate a numeric value; an almost never-used unary plus operator is provided for completeness [4].

2.5.2 String operators

Perl provides very basic operators on strings: most string processing is done using built-in functions and regular expressions, as described later. Unlike many languages which use +

as a concatenation operator for strings, Perl uses a period for this purpose: this lack of overloading means that an operator uniquely determines the context (string or number) for its operands. The other string operator is x, which is used to replicate strings, e.g.

```
$a ="Hello" x 3;
```

sets $a to "HelloHelloHello".

The capability of combining an operator with assignment is extended to string operations, e.g.

```
$foo .= " ";
```

appends a space to $foo.

So far, things have been boringly conventional for the most part. However, we begin to get a taste of the real flavour of Perl when we see how it adds a little magic when some operators, normally used in an arithmetic context, are used in a string context. Two examples illustrate this.

1. **Auto-increment**. If a variable has only ever been used in a string context, the auto-increment operator (but *not* auto-decrement) can be applied to it. If the value consists of a sequence of letters, or a sequence of letters followed by a sequence of digits, the auto-increment takes place in string mode starting with the rightmost character, with 'carry' along the string. For example, the sequence

    ```
    $a = 'a0'; $b = 'Az9';
    print ++$a, ' ', ++$b; "\n";
    ```

    prints a1 Ba0.
2. **Unary minus**. This has an unusual effect on non-numeric values. Unary minus applied to a string which starts with a plus or minus character returns the same string, but starting with the opposite sign. Unary minus applied to an identifier returns a string consisting of a minus prefixed to the characters of the identifier. Thus if we have a variable named $config with value "foo", then -$config evaluates to the string "-foo". This is useful, for example, in constructing command strings to be sent to a UNIX shell, where by convention arguments are introduced by -.

2.5.3 Comparison operators

The value of a comparison is returned as numeric 1 if true, and an empty string ("") if false, in accordance with the convention described earlier. Two families of comparison operators are provided, one for numbers (= < > etc.) and one for strings (eq lt gt etc.): the operator used determines the context, and Perl converts the operands as required to match the operator. This duality is necessary because a comparison between strings made up entirely of numerical digits should apply the usual rules for sorting strings using ASCII as a collating sequence, and this may not give the same result as a numerical comparison. For example, the expression ('5' < '10') returns the value true as a numerical comparison, having been converted into (5 < 10), whereas the string comparison ('5' lt '10') returns false, since 10 comes before 5 in the canonical sort order for ASCII strings.

The comparison operator (<=> for numbers, cmp for strings), performs a three-way test, returning −1 for less-than, 0 for equal and +1 for greater-than. Note that the comparison operators are non-associative, so an expression like

```
$a > $b > $c
```

is erroneous.

2.5.4   Logical operators

The logical operators allow us to combine conditions using the usual logical operations 'not' (!, not), 'and' (&&, and) and 'or' (||, or). Perl implements the 'and' and 'or' operators in 'shortcut' mode, i.e. evaluation stops as soon as the final result is certain, using the rules *false && b = false*, and *true || b = true*.

Before Perl 5, only the !, && and || operators were provided. The new set, not, and, or, are provided partly to increase readability, and partly because their extra-low precedence makes it possible to omit brackets in most circumstances – the precedence ordering is chosen so that numerical expressions can be compared without having to enclose them in brackets, e.g.

```
print "OK\n" if $a < 10 and $b < 12;
```

2.5.5   Bitwise operators

The unary tilde (~) applied to a numerical argument performs bitwise negation on its operand, generating the one's complement. If applied to a string operand it complements all the bits in the string – an effective way of inverting a lot of bits. The remaining bitwise operators – & (and), | (or) and ^ (exclusive or) – have a rather complicated definition. If either operand is a number *or a variable that has previously been used as a number*, both operands are converted to integers if need be, and the bitwise operation takes place between the integers. If both operands are strings, and if variables have never been used as numbers, Perl performs the bitwise operation between corresponding bits in the two strings, padding the shorter string with zeros as required.

2.5.6   Conditional expressions

A *conditional expression* is one whose value is chosen from two alternatives at run-time depending on the outcome of a test. The syntax is borrowed from C:

```
test ? true_exp : false_exp
```

The first expression is evaluated as a Boolean value: if it returns true the whole expression is replaced by *true_exp*, otherwise it is replaced by *false_exp*, e.g.

```
$a = ($a < 0) ? 0 : $a;
```

2.6 Control structures

Although the power of Perl derives largely from its flexible data structures and its powerful string handling, based on the use of regular expressions, we defer discussion of these features until we have covered the basic control structures. As is characteristic of Perl, there are initially no surprises in the control structures for conditional execution and repetition – all the usual control mechanisms are there, and everything is very C-like at first sight. However, the standard mix comes with some ingenious variations, and there are traps for the unwary C expert. Following some introductory generalizations, we illustrate the control constructs by examples.

2.6.1 Blocks

The concept of a block is very important in Perl. A *block* is just a sequence of one or more statements enclosed in braces (curly brackets), e.g.

```
{$positive = 1;
 $negative = -1}
```

The last statement in the block is terminated by the closing brace. (But Perl is happy to let you put a semicolon there, and it's a sensible thing to do, in case you add another statement later.)

The control structures in Perl use *conditions* to control the evaluation of one or more blocks, and we shall see later (Section 2.11) that the body of a subroutine is a block. Blocks can in fact appear almost anywhere that a statement can appear: such a block is sometimes called a *bare block*, and its appearance is often in the context of a clever (or dirty) trick.

2.6.2 Conditions

A condition is just a Perl expression which is evaluated in a Boolean context: if it evaluates to zero or the empty string the condition is treated as false, otherwise it is treated as true in accord with the rules already given. Conditions usually make use of the relational operators, and several simple conditions can be combined into a complex condition using the logical operators described above, e.g.

```
$total > 50
$total > 50 and $total < 100
```

A condition can be negated using the ! operator, e.g.

```
!($total > 50 and $total < 100)
```

2.6.3 Conditional execution

If–then–else statements

```
if ($total > 0) {
  print "$total\n"}

if ($total >0) {
  print "$total\n"
} else {
  print "bad total!\n"}
```

Note particularly that a single statement is a block and requires braces round it: omitting the braces in this case is a common pitfall for programmers versed in other languages. Note also that the syntax of the if statement requires that the expression forming the condition is enclosed in brackets. The construct extends to multiple selections e.g.:

```
if ($total > 70){
  $grade = "A";
} elsif ($total > 50){
  $grade = "B";
} elsif ($total > 40){
  $grade = "C";
} else {
  $grade = "F";
  $total = 0
}
```

Note the error-prone
elsif: C uses 'else if',
some languages use
'elseif', others use 'elif':
disp seems designed to
trip the unwary

Following the Perl principle that there's more than one way to do it, and modelling customary usage in written and spoken English, if can be replaced by unless with the expected effect. This can contribute greatly to readable programs.

Alternatives to if–then–else

A common idiom is to use a conditional expression in place of an if–then–else construct. Thus

```
if ($a < 0)
{$b = 0}
else {$b = 1};
```

can be written

```
$b = ($a < 0) ? 0 : 1;
```

Another common idiom is, as we have seen, to use the 'or' operator between statements, e.g.

```
open(IN, $ARGV[0]) or die
  "Can't open $ARGV[0]\n";
```

Statement qualifiers

Finally, Perl adds a bit more magic: as we have seen in the examples earlier, a single statement (but *not* a block) can be followed by a conditional modifier, as in the English 'I'll come if it's fine'. For example

```
print "OK\n"      if $volts >= 1.5;
print "Weak\n"    if $volts >= 1.2 and
                     $volts < 1.5;
print "Replace\n" if $volts < 1.2;
```

This is readable and self-documenting: compare the following code using conditional expressions, which has the same effect:

```
print (($volts >= 1.5) ? "OK\n" :
(($volts >= 1.2) ? "Weak\n" :
"Replace\n"));
```

2.6.4 Repetition

Perl provides a variety of repetition mechanisms to suit all tastes, including both 'testing' loops and 'counting' loops.

'Testing' loops

You don't have to lay the code out like this: choose a style that suits you, and stick to it.

```
while ($a != $b) {
  if ($a > $b){
     $a = $a - $b
  } else {
     $b = $b - $a
  }
}
```

Note that, as with the `if` statement, the expression that forms the condition must be enclosed in brackets. As you might expect by now, `while` can be replaced by `until` to give the same effect as explicit negation of the condition. Likewise, single statements (but not blocks) can use `while` and `until` as statement modifiers to improve readability, e.g.

```
$a += 2 while $a < $b;
$a += 2 until $a > $b;
```

Note particularly, though, that this is purely *syntactic sugar* – a notational convenience. Although the condition is written after the statement, it is evaluated *before* the statement is executed, just like any other while/until loop: if the condition is initially false the statement will never be executed – a zero-trip loop. Sometimes it is convenient to have the semantics of a FORTRAN-like loop that is always executed at least once: Perl is happy to oblige, and provides the do loop for the purpose – strictly speaking, do is a built-in function rather than a syntactic construct, but don't worry about the difference. The condition attached to a do loop looks superficially the same as a statement modifier, but the semantics are that the condition is tested after execution of the block, so the block is executed at least once.

```
do {
    ...
} while $a != $b;
```

The while can be replaced by until with the obvious meaning, and the modifier can be omitted entirely. A do statement without a modifier executes the statements of the block and returns the value of the last expression evaluated in the block: this construction is typically used if the earlier statements in the block are being executed solely for their side effects – a dirty trick, but none the less useful at times.

'Counting' loops

Counting loops use the same syntax as C:

```
for ($i = 1; $i <= 10; $i++) {
    $i_square = $i*$i; $i_cube = $i**3;
    print "$i\t$i_square\t$i_cube\n";
}
```

There is also a foreach construct, which takes an explicit list of values for the controlled variable. This will be described later, when we come to deal with collections of data, but here we note that real Perl programmers would write the above for loop as

```
foreach $i (1..10) {
    $i_square = $i*$i; $i_cube = $i**3;
    print "$i\t$i_square\t$i_cube\n";
}
```

And if they wanted to count backwards they would write

```
foreach $i reverse (1..10) {
    $i_square = $i*$i; $i_cube = $i**3;
    print "$i\t$i_square\t$i_cube\n";
}
```

Loop refinements

Many 'testing' loops in programs turn out to be what are sometimes called 'n-and-a-half' loops, in which it is required to terminate the loop part-way through an iteration. Strictly speaking an 'n-and-a-half' loop is one from which we *exit* part-way through: equally common is the requirement to abandon the current iteration part-way through and start the next iteration. Perl provides three loop control commands for this purpose: last, next and redo. The last and next commands are analogous to the 'break' and 'continue' statements in C: last breaks out of a loop, and next forces the next iteration of a loop. For example, to terminate input processing if a line containing 'quit' is read, we write

```
while <STDIN> {
   last if /quit/;
   ...
}
```

The `redo` command repeats the current iteration from the beginning. It has been said that it is used 'mainly by programs that want to lie to themselves about what was just input'.

If an undecorated `last`, `next` or `redo` appears in a nested loop structure it operates on the innermost enclosing loop. More elaborate loop control can be achieved by applying the loop control commands to named loops, e.g.

```
OUTER: while (...){
        ...
        INNER: while (...){
                ...
                if (...) then {last OUTER;}
                if (...) then {next INNER;}
                ...
        }}
```

The `last` and `redo` commands can be used in a bare block, as well as in a looping context. For example, the following fragment will read lines from standard input, throwing away blank lines until the first non-blank line is reached:

```
{$line = <STDIN>;
 redo until $line =~ /\S/
}
```

(The expression $line =~ /\S/ evaluates to true if the line contains any characters that are not whitespace characters: see Section 2.12.)

2.7 Built-in functions

We have already met some of Perl's built-in functions, e.g. `print`. Perl provides a large number of built-in functions, which can be grouped in a number of categories including, but not exclusively:

- Numeric functions – trigonometric functions, random numbers, etc.
- Scalar conversion functions – including decimal value to character and vice versa, octal and hex to decimal, etc.
- Structure conversion functions – convert a list of values into a binary structure according to a template, and vice versa
- String functions – mainly for inserting and removing sub-strings
- Input/output and file manipulation functions.

In languages like C, the syntax for calling built-in functions is the same as that for user-defined functions. Perl takes a very different view: a built-in function is regarded as a unary operator identified by a name rather than an ideograph. This means that its arguments need only be enclosed in brackets if precedence demands it. Functions like `print` which take a list of arguments are called *list operators*: functions that take a single argument are called *named unary operators*. Both have rather unusual precedence rules that nevertheless lead to natural and 'obvious' behaviour, as follows.

1. If the token following the function name (operator) on the same line is an opening bracket, the operator and its arguments have highest precedence – if it looks like a function call, it behaves like a function call. For example:

    ```
    $n = rand($m*2) + 1;
    print("Total is $total\n");
    ```

2. A named unary operator has lower precedence than arithmetic operations (but higher precedence than logical operators), thus

    ```
    $n = rand $m*2 + 1;
    ```

    has the same effect as

    ```
    $n = rand($m*2 + 1);
    ```

    We observe that the characteristic Perl style is to omit the parentheses, but programmers experienced in more conventional languages will probably find that the parentheses come naturally (and automatically). Perl is happy in either case.

3. In the absence of the opening bracket, a list operator has very high precedence to the left, and very low precedence to the right. Thus in

    ```
    print "Hello", "World!", "\n";
    ```

    the commas bind tighter than the `print`, giving the desired effect, but if a list operator appears as a component of a list, e.g.

    ```
    ("foo", "bar", substr $line, 10, 5)
    ```

    the commas on the left of `substr` are evaluated after it, but the commas on the right are evaluated before, giving the expected interpretation as

    ```
    ("foo", "bar", substr($line, 10, 5))
    ```

2.8 Collections of data

Collections of data occur in Perl in two forms.

- *Lists.* A list is a collection of scalar data items which can be treated as a whole, and has a temporary existence on the run-time stack.
- *Arrays* and *hashes.* These are collections of scalar data items which have an assigned storage space in memory, and can therefore be accessed using a variable name (or a *reference* – see Chapter 3). The name of such a variable is analogous to a plural noun. The difference between arrays and hashes is that the constituent elements of an array are identified by a numerical *index*, which starts at zero for the first element, while a

hash is an associative array (or table) in which each element is identified by an associated string called the *key*.

Experienced Perl users tend to use hashes in preference to arrays for a variety of reasons. Identifying elements by meaningful strings makes scripts more readable, hashes are 'elastic', and access to an element of a hash is almost as efficient as access to an indexed element in an array, since the hash is stored in an efficient hash table (hence the name).

Lists and arrays are largely interchangeable: if Perl encounters the one in a context where it is expecting the other it will perform a silent transformation. Along the same lines, we can select an element from a list using its index, just as we can select an element from an array.

2.8.1 Lists

A list is a collection of variables, constants (numbers or strings) or expressions, which is to be treated as a whole. It is written as a comma-separated sequence of values, e.g.

```
"red", "green", "blue"
255, 128, 66
$a, $b, $c
$a + $b, $a - $b, $a*$b, $a/$b
```

A list often appears in a script enclosed in round brackets, e.g.

```
("red", "green", "blue")
```

It is important to appreciate that the brackets are not a required part of the list syntax, as they are in, for example, Lisp, but are there for grouping purposes, to satisfy precedence rules. However, it is good practice to use the brackets all the time (except in the case of function arguments, as described above), since it makes scripts more readable and avoids nasty surprises. We shall use brackets for all lists in the remainder of this discussion.

Applying the principle that the language should always do what is natural, 'obvious' shorthand is acceptable in lists, e.g.

```
(1..8)
("A".."H", "O".."Z")
```

and to save tedious typing,

```
qw(the quick brown fox)
```

is a shorthand for

```
("the", "quick", "brown", "fox")
```

qw, the 'quote words' operator, is an obvious extension of the q and qq operators introduced in Section 2.4. It follows that the above list could be written as

```
qw/the quick brown fox/
```

or

```
qw|the quick brown fox|
```

The 'matching brackets' rule also applies to the qw operator.

List magic

Lists are often used in connection with arrays and hashes, and we shall see many examples of this in the sections that follow. However, there is a particularly novel feature of lists that makes them useful in their own right. This is that a list containing only variables can appear as the target of an assignment and/or as the value to be assigned. This makes it possible to write simultaneous assignments, e.g.

```
($a, $b, $c)  =  (1, 2, 3);
```

and to perform swapping or permutation without using a temporary variable, e.g.

```
($a, $b)  =  ($b, $a);
($b, $c, $a) = ($a, $b, $c)
```

Both of these are natural forms of expression that can be a great aid to readability in Perl scripts.

2.8.2 Arrays

An array is an ordered collection of data whose components are identified by an ordinal index: it is usually the value of an array variable. The name of such a variable always starts with an @, e.g. @days_of_week, denoting a separate namespace and establishing a *list context*.

The association between arrays and lists is a close one: an array stores a collection, and a list is a collection, so it is natural to assign a list to an array, e.g.

```
@rainfall = (1.2, 0.4, 0.3, 0.1, 0, 0, 0);
```

This creates an array of seven elements, which can be accessed individually as $rainfall[0], $rainfall[1], ... $rainfall[6]. Note the use of $rainfall[ ] here: each element of the array (or list) is a scalar. We pursue this distinction in the next section.

A list can occur as an element of another list. However, this does not produce a LISP-like list with sub-lists: the inner list is inserted in a linear one-level structure, so that

```
@foo = (1, 2, 3, "string");
@foobar = (4, 5, @foo, 6);
```

gives foobar the value (4, 5, 1, 2, 3, "string", 6). (We shall see in the next chapter how it is possible to create multi-dimensional arrays, i.e. lists of lists.)

List and scalar context

Whenever Perl performs an operation, it does so in a *context*: this can be a *list context* or a *scalar context*. List context implies that the 'target' of an operation is a collection, while scalar context implies that it is a single data item. It follows that in an assignment to an array, the @ of the array name on the left-hand side establishes a list context, but when an element of an array is being accessed the occurrence of the same name but with a leading $ establishes a scalar context.

Some items that can occur in either context modify their behaviour depending on the current context. For example, a list evaluated in a scalar context delivers its *last* item, so

```
@foo = (101, 102, 103);
```

sets all three values of the array foo, but

```
$foo = (101, 102, 103);
```

sets $foo to 103. (This example is somewhat pointless. It is only sensible to use this feature if evaluation of the earlier elements in the list has useful side-effects.) If you assign a scalar value to an array, Perl does the sensible thing and (effectively) puts brackets round it to make it a list of one element, so

```
@a = "candy";
```

has the same effect as

```
@a = ("candy");
```

If you assign an array to a scalar value, the value assigned is the length of the array, thus with the array @foo defined above,

```
$n = @foo;
```

assigns the value 3 to $n.

List context can be established in other ways. For example the print function establishes a list context, since it expects a list of things to print. This can lead to unexpected results: for example, knowing that an array name evaluated in a scalar context delivers the number of elements in the array, we can write

```
$n = @foo
print "array foo has $n elements\n"
```

We might be tempted to abbreviate this to

```
print "array foo has @foo elements"
```

but this would print the entire contents of the array. We can get the desired effect by using what computer scientists call a 'cast', and writing

```
print "array foo has scalar @foo elements"
```

2.8.3 Hashes

In the world of scripting languages it is common to find associative arrays (sometimes called *content-addressable arrays*). An associative array is one in which each element has two components, a key and a value, the element being 'indexed' by its key (just like a table). Such arrays are usually stored in a hash table to facilitate efficient retrieval, and for this reason Perl uses the term *hash* for an associative array. Hashes are a very natural way of storing data, and are widely used in Perl – probably more than conventional arrays. A particular attraction of hashes is that they are elastic – they expand to accommodate new elements as they are introduced.

Names of hashes in Perl start with a % character: such a name establishes a list context. As with arrays, since each element in a hash is itself a scalar, a reference to an element uses $ as the first character, establishing a scalar context. The index (or key) is a string enclosed in braces (curly brackets): if the key is a single 'word', i.e. does not contain space characters, explicit quotes are not required. Consider the following assignment statements:

`$somehash{aaa}   = 123;`	*The braces establish that the scalar item is being assigned to an element of a hash.*
`$somehash{234}   = "bbb";`	*The key is a three-character string, not a number.*
`$somehash{"$a"} = 0;`	*The key is the current value of $a.*
`%anotherhash = %somehash;`	*The leading % establishes a list context: the target of the assignment is the hash itself, not one of its values.*

2.9 Working with arrays and lists

2.9.1 Accessing array elements

Elements of an array are selected using a C-like square-bracket syntax, e.g.

```
$bar = $foo[2];
$foo[2] = 7;
$foo = $foo[2];
```

The leading $ in `$foo[2]` establishes a scalar context, and the square brackets make it clear that this instance of `foo` is an element of the array `foo`, not the scalar variable `foo`, nor the entire array `foo`.

Perl provides a number of powerful facilities for accessing collections of array elements. A group of contiguous elements is called a *slice*, and is accessed using a simple syntax:

```
@foo[1..3]
```

is the same as the list

```
($foo[1], $foo[2], $foo[3])
```

A slice can be used as the destination of an assignment, e.g.

```
@foo[1..3] = ("hop", "skip", "jump");
```

The idea of a slice extends to a non-contiguous *selection* of array elements, thus `@foo[1,3,5]` and the list `($foo[1],$foo[3],$foo[5])` are one and the same thing. Like a slice, a selection can appear on the left of an assignment: this leads to a useful idiom for rearranging the elements in a list, e.g. to swap the first two elements of an array we write

```
@foo[0, 1] = @foo[1, 0];
```

Array variables and lists (either literal lists or those generated as slices or selections) can be used interchangeably in almost any sensible situation: in particular you can subscript a list expression to obtain an element or a slice, e.g.

```
$front = ("Bob", "Carol", "Ted", "Alice")[0];
@rest = ("Bob", "Carol", "Ted", "Alice")[1..3];
```

or even

```
@rest = qw/Bob Carol Ted Alice/[1..3];
```

Using this technique we can select the smaller of two values without using an if statement or a conditional expression:

```
$smaller = ($foo, $bar)[$foo > $bar];
```

(Before reading further, be sure you understand why this trick works.)

In the same spirit, elements of an array can be selected by using another array as the selector, e.g. if we write

```
@foo = (7, "fred", 9);
@bar = (2, 1, 0);
```

then

```
@foo = @foo[@bar];
```

reverses the order of foo.

As we have noted earlier, an array name evaluated in a scalar context delivers the number of elements in the array: $#foo evaluates to the index of the last element of @foo.

2.9.2 Manipulating lists

Perl provides several built-in functions for list manipulation. Three useful ones are

- shift LIST. Returns the first item of LIST, and moves the remaining items down, reducing the size of LIST by 1.
- unshift ARRAY, LIST. The opposite of shift: puts the items in LIST at the beginning of ARRAY, moving the original contents up by the required amount.
- push ARRAY, LIST. Similar to unshift, but adds the values in LIST to the end of ARRAY.

(The name 'shift' originates in UNIX shell scripting, where *shift* discards the first argument and moves all the others up. Purists would argue that unshift should be called push, and push should be called append.)

2.9.3 Iterating over lists

It is common to want to perform the same operation on all the items in a list, or a selection of the items. Perl provides a number of mechanisms to achieve this.

foreach

The `foreach` loop performs a simple iteration over all the elements of a list:

```
foreach $item (list) {
  ...
}
```

The block is executed repeatedly with the variable `$item` taking each value from the list in turn. The variable can be omitted, in which case `$_` will be used. Since Perl will automatically convert an array into a list if required, the natural Perl idiom for manipulating all items in an array is

```
foreach (@array) {
  ... # process $_
}
```

For example, we can reverse the sign of every element in an array of numbers `@a` with the simple code

```
foreach (@a) {
  $_ = -$_
}
```

A seasoned Perl hacker might write

```
for (@a) {
  $_ = -$_
}
```

since Perl is happy to accept `for` in place of `foreach` – the fact that it is followed by a list makes the construction unambiguous. However, this usage is deprecated.

Compare the elegant simplicity of the `foreach` loop with the (equally valid) Perl code that might be written by a beginner who was familiar with C:

```
$n = @a-1;
for ($i=0; $i < $n; $i++){
  $a[$i] = -$a[$i]
}
```

map

It is not uncommon to want to generate a list by applying the same operation to an original list. For example, suppose we have a list of words, e.g.

```
('cat', 'dog', 'rabbit', 'hamster', 'rat')
```

and we want to create a list of the same words with a terminal 's' added to form the plural:

```
('cats', 'dogs', 'rabbits', 'hamsters', 'rats')
```

This could be done with a `foreach` loop:

```
@s = qw/cat, dog, rabbit, hamster, rat/;
@pl = ();
foreach (@s) {
  push @pl, $_.'s'
}
```

However, this is such a common idiom that Perl provides an in-built function `map` to do the job:

```
@pl = map $_.'s', @s;
```

(LISP hackers will recognize this as an incarnation of *mapcar*.) The general forms of `map` are

```
map expression, list;
```

and

```
map BLOCK list;
```

The function evaluates the expression or block for each element of `list`, temporarily setting $_ equal to the list element, and returns a list containing the values of each such evaluation. (Remember that the value returned by a block is the value of the last expression evaluated in the block.)

grep

In UNIX,

```
grep pattern file
```

prints (i.e. sends to STDOUT) all lines of the file *file* that contain an instance of *pattern*. In its simplest form, the Perl `grep` function takes a pattern and a list and returns a new list containing all the elements of the original list that match the pattern. For example, given

```
@things = (car, bus, cardigan, jumper, carrot);
```

then

```
grep /car/ @things;
```

returns the list

```
(car, cardigan, carrot)
```

In fact, the Perl `grep` is much more powerful than this. Its general form is `grep expression, list`; or `grep BLOCK list`. Like map, the function evaluates the expression or block for each element in the list, temporarily setting $_ to that value: it returns a list of those elements for which the evaluation returns true. It should be noted that if evaluation of the block changes $_, this change will be made in the original list: while this is undoubtedly useful, it may not be what you were expecting.

grep and map are closely related:

```
@a2 = grep expression @a1;
```

does the same as

```
@a2 = map (expression ? $_ : () ) @a1;
```

2.10 Working with hashes

2.10.1 Creating hashes

We have seen that we can assign a list to an array, so it is not surprising that we can assign a list of key–value pairs to a hash, as, for example,

```
%foo = (key1, value1, key2, value2,. . .);
```

This tends to become unreadable for more than a short list, and an alternative syntax is provided using the => operator to associate key–value pairs, thus:

```
%foo = (banana => 'yellow',
        apple => 'green',
        ... );
```

The => operator is more than just a synonym for a comma, since it forces a 'bare' identifier to its left to be quoted as a string in the same way that a bare identifier appearing in braces to identify a hash element is quoted.

2.10.2 Manipulating hashes

A hash can be 'unwound' into a list containing the key–value pairs by assigning it to an array, e.g.

```
@list = %foo;
```

However, this is not usually a useful thing to do, since the order in which the key–value pairs occur reflects the structure of the hash table in which they were stored, and so is unpredictable. Instead, Perl provides a number of built-in functions to facilitate manipulation of hashes. If we have a hash called magic,

```
keys %magic
```

returns a list of the keys of the elements in the hash, and

```
values %magic
```

returns a list of the values of the elements in the hash. These functions provide a convenient way to iterate over the elements of a hash using foreach:

```
foreach $key (keys %magic) {
 do something with $magic{$key}
}
```

Remember that the explicit loop variable can be omitted, in which case the anonymous variable $_ will be assumed:

```
foreach (keys %magic) {
 process $magic{$_}
}
```

An alternative approach is to use the each operator, which delivers successive key–value pairs from a hash, e.g.

```
while(($key,$value) = each %magic) {
 ...
}
```

Other useful operators for manipulating hashes are delete and exists:

```
delete $magic{$key}
```

removes the element whose key matches $key from the hash %magic, and

```
exists $magic{$key}
```

returns true if the hash %magic contains an element whose key matches $key. A common idiom is

```
exists($h{'key'}) && do{ statements }
```

to avoid using an if statement.

2.10.3 Inverting a hash

A hash would be a natural structure for a phonebook application, with the name as key and the associated phone number as value. Hashes map keys to values efficiently, and exists can be used to check that there is an entry with a particular key. Suppose, however, that we want to do the reverse, to find out if a hash contains an entry with a particular value, and to map it onto the associated key. The natural response of a programmer familiar with conventional languages is to iterate over the hash, e.g.

```
# looking for $number
$target = "NOT FOUND";
foreach (keys %phones) {
  if ($phones{$_} eq $number) {
    $target = $_;
    last;
  }
}
```

However, as Larry Wall has observed, 'doing linear scans over an associative array is like trying to club someone to death with a loaded Uzi', and a much better way is to invert the hash using reverse, thus:

```
%by_number = reverse %phones;
$target = exists $by_number{number} ?
    $by_number{number} : "NOT FOUND";
```

It is instructive to consider why this works. When a hash appears in a list context, as in reverse %phones it is unravelled into a list of alternating keys and values. When the reversed list appears as the target of an assignment to a hash, the now reversed key–value pairs produce the desired inverted hash, i.e. one that is keyed by number.

2.10.4 Mixed context

Finally, we present two examples of mixed context. A hash name such as %magic occurring on the right of an assignment is normally evaluated in a list context. If it is evaluated in a scalar context, e.g.

```
$test = %magic
```

it returns true if the hash contains any elements, and false if it is empty. (More precisely, if the hash table is populated, it returns a string summarizing the current state of the hash table (buckets used/buckets allocated), and if the hash table is empty it returns the string "0", which by convention means false.) If %magic appears on the left of an assignment, it establishes a list context, and expects a list on the right: if the right-hand side is a scalar value, the existing contents of the hash are silently discarded, leaving an empty hash. Contrast this with the behaviour of arrays, where

```
@an_array = "scalar_value";
```

is treated as

```
@an_array = ("scalar_value");
```

2.11 Simple input and output

We have already seen examples of simple output using the print function, and input from standard input using <STDIN> (or <IN>, where IN is a filehandle for an open file). Recall that

```
$line = <STDIN>;
```

assigns the next line of input to the variable $line as a string, complete with the trailing newline. Frequently we would prefer not to have the trailing newline included in the string: the chomp function removes it, so a common idiom is

```
$line = <STDIN>; chomp($line);
```

or more commonly

```
chomp($line = <STDIN>);
```

(Strictly, <STDIN> reads up to and including the next occurrence of the *input record separator* character as defined by the variable $/. This is initially set to a platform-specific default – "\n" for UNIX, "\r\n" for Windows, "\r" for Macintosh – but can be changed by the user. The chomp function removes the line-ending character(s) as defined in $/. The chop function removes the last character, whatever it is, and returns it.)

When used in a list context, <STDIN> delivers the whole of the file as an array of strings, one element per line, e.g.

```
$foo = <STDIN>;    #next line
@foo = <STDIN>;    #rest of file
```

In list context, chomp(@foo) removes the trailing line-ending character(s) from every element of the array. A trick used by experienced Perl hackers is to read a file in 'slurp mode' by setting the input record separator to undef, thus

```
{local $/; $f = <IN>;}
```

Since there are no recognizable line endings, the whole file is read as a single string: it can later be decomposed into lines using split. (The local declaration is explained later in this chapter. Here, its effect is to create a temporary version of $/ which has the value undef: the normal value is restored at the end of the block.)

The print function prints in a default format. Control over formatting is provided by the C-like printf function which expects to find a format string as the first item on its argument list, e.g.

```
printf "%10s %8.2f\n", $name, $value;
```

prints $name as a 10-character string, then a space, then $value as a decimal number with 2 digits after the decimal point in a total field width of 8 characters, then a newline.

2.12 Strings, patterns and regular expressions

We saw in Chapter 1 that a typical characteristic of a scripting language is enhanced functionality in certain areas. Perl is no exception: one such area is its string and text handling. In most conventional languages strings are a 'poor relation', with a very limited set of string manipulation operations being provided by a collection of library functions. Since the strings are stored as arrays of characters, most of the operations work in terms of numerical offsets within a string, and the length of the array limits the length of the string, making dynamic string manipulation very difficult. Perl provides very powerful dynamic string manipulation based on the use of regular expressions. These have long been a feature of text editors, but have not featured in conventional languages, where the power of regular expression matching can only be achieved by using an external package. AWK was the first language to make regular expressions a feature of the language (though SNOBOL has some claim to be the first language built round pattern matching), and Perl has extended this approach. Pattern matching with regular expressions and sub-string substitutions are an integral part of the language, making it particularly suitable for text manipulation.

2.12.1   Introduction to regular expressions

Regular expressions provide an extremely powerful way of defining patterns. Strictly, a regular expression is a notation for describing the strings produced by a *regular grammar*: it is thus a definition of a (possibly infinite) class of strings. (A better, though informal, definition of regular expressions is 'what wild cards want to be when they grow up'.) The first practical application of regular expressions in computer systems was in the text editors ed and sed in the UNIX system.

Readers who are familiar with regular expressions can omit this section, but should scan the next section to get the particular flavour of regular expressions in Perl.

The idea of a regular expression can be built up in stages.

1. The characters

    ```
    \ | ( ) [ { ^ $ * + ? .
    ```

    are *meta-characters* with special meanings in a regular expression. (If we think of the regular expression as a language for defining patterns, the meta-characters are operators.) To use a meta-character in a regular expression without a special meaning being attached, it must be escaped with a backslash. (] and } are also meta-characters in some circumstances.)

2. Apart from the meta-characters, any single character in a regular expression matches itself, so the regular expression /cat/ matches the string *cat*. (Regular expressions are conventionally written in the form /string/. The slashes are not part of the regular expression, just syntax for delimiting and identifying it. We describe a regular expression enclosed between slashes as a *pattern*.)

3. The meta-characters ^ and $ act as *anchors*: ^ matches the start of a line and $ matches the end of a line, so the regular expression /^cat/ matches the string *cat* only if it appears at the start of a line, and /cat$/ matches only at the end of a line. /^cat$/ matches lines which contain just the string *cat*, and /^$/ matches an empty line – a really empty line, not a line consisting only of whitespace characters. (This description is slightly simplified: see below for more information on anchors when matching multi-line strings.)

4. The meta-character dot (.) matches *any* single character except newline, so /c.t/ matches *cat*, *cot*, *cut*, etc.

5. The character class, a set of characters enclosed in square brackets, matches any single character from those listed, so /[aeiou]/ matches any vowel, and /[0123456789]/ matches any digit. This latter regular expression can be expressed more concisely as /[0-9]/. A character class of the form /[^ ...]/ matches any character *except* those listed, so /[^0-9]/ matches any non-digit. (Note that in a character class, the characters – and ^ take on the a restricted rôle as meta-characters: if we want to define a regular expression to match the arithmetic operators we have to write /[+\-*/]/ to remove the special meaning from the minus. Alternatively we could put the minus before the plus, since a minus as the first character cannot be part of a range.)

6. Repetition of characters within a regular expression can be specified by the quantifiers * (zero or more occurrences), + (one or more occurrences) and ? (zero or one occurrence). Thus /[0-9]+/ matches an unsigned decimal number, and /a.*b/ matches a sub-string starting with '*a*' and ending with '*b*', with an indefinite number of other characters in between. Note that the quantifiers are 'greedy' – they always match the *longest* string possible.

2.12.2 Regular expressions in Perl

Perl implements a very rich form of regular expressions, with many enhancements on the basic facilities described above. We present the most useful facilities here: for an exhaustive (and exhausting) account, the reader is referred to the Perl 'man pages'.

Alternations

If RE1, RE2 and RE3 are regular expressions, RE1|RE2|RE3 is a regular expression that will match any one of the components. For example, the pattern /^Date:|^From:|^To:|^Subject/ matches (some of) the header lines in a mail message.

Grouping

Round brackets can be used to group items: the example above could be written /^(Date:|From:|To:|Subject)/, thus 'factoring out' the start-of-line anchor. Further examples are

```
/Pitt the (elder|younger)/
/(([0-9][ ])|([a-z][ ]))+/
```

The first of these patterns matches *Pitt the elder* and *Pitt the younger*. The second matches a sequence of one or more items, each of which is either a sequence of digits followed by a space or a sequence of lower-case letters followed by a space.

Repetition counts

In addition to the quantifiers *, ? and +, explicit repetition counts can be added to a component of a regular expression, e.g. /(wet[ ]){2}wet/ matches 'wet wet wet'. The full list of possible count modifiers is:

{n}	must occur exactly n times
{n,}	must occur at least n times
{n,m}	must occur at least n times but no more than m times

Thus an Internet IP address is matched by the pattern

```
/([0-9]{1,3}\.){3}[0-9]{1,3}/
```

Non-greedy matching

A pattern including .* matches the longest string it can find. The pattern .*? can be used when the *shortest* match is required. (In fact, any of the quantifiers can be followed by a ? to specify the shortest match.). We shall see examples later where non-greedy matching is required.

Shorthand

Some character classes occur so often that a shorthand notation is provided: \d matches a digit, \w matches a 'word' character (upper-case letter, lower-case letter or digit), and \s matches a 'whitespace' character (space, tab, carriage return or newline). Capitalization reverses the sense, e.g. \D matches any non-digit character.

Anchors

We have seen the use of ^ and $ to 'anchor' the match at the start or end of the target string, respectively. Other anchors can be specified as \b (word boundary) and \B (not a word boundary). Thus if the target string contains *John* and *Johnathan* as space-separated words, /\bJohn/ will match both *John* and *Johnathan*, /\bJohn\b/ will only match *John*, while /\bJohn\B/ will only match *Johnathan*.

Back references

Round brackets serve another purpose besides grouping: they define a series of partial matches that are 'remembered' for use in subsequent processing (see Section 2.12.3) or in the regular expression itself. Thus, in a regular expression, \1, \2 etc. denote the sub-string that actually matched the first, second etc. sub-pattern, the numbering being determined by the sequence of opening brackets. Thus we can require that a particular sub-pattern occurs in identical form in two or more places in the target string. If we want the round brackets only to define a grouping without remembering the sub-string matches we can use the syntax (?:...).

2.12.3   Pattern matching

The 'match' operator

We saw an example of a simple pattern matching operation in Section 2.2.1, in the line of code

```
    print if /Shazzam!/
```

We now recognize /Shazzam!/ as a pattern containing a regular expression. Perl compares the pattern with the value of the anonymous variable, $_, and returns true if the pattern given matches a sub-string in that value, giving the desired effect. What is really happening is that the isolated pattern /Shazzam!/ is recognized as a convenient shorthand for the full form of a match operation m/Shazzam!/: this is an expression which in a scalar context, as here, returns a Boolean value recording success or failure of the matching operator. If the m operator is present we can use any character as the pattern delimiter, e.g.

```
print if m|Shazzam!|
```

The pattern behaves like a double-quoted string, so variable interpolation is permitted, e.g.

```
print if m/($word1|$word2)/;
```

Variable interpolation can, however, be suppressed by using single quotes as the pattern delimiter. An empty pattern, e.g. //, denotes the most recently used regular expression.

Setting a target

A match with a specific variable rather than the anonymous variable is denoted by the =~ operator. For example,

```
($a =~ /abc/)
```

is an expression which has the value true or false according as the pattern /abc/ matches or does not match the string held in $a.

Remembering what matched

If a pattern is matched successfully, the variable $& is set to the entire matched string, and the portions of the target string that matched sections of the regular expression in round brackets are assigned to the variables $1, $2, etc., the numbering being determined by the sequence of opening brackets. (Compare the back reference capability described earlier.) Thus

```
($url =~ m|(http|ftp)://(.*?/)(.*$)|)
```

will match a URL held in $url, setting $1, $2 and $3 to the protocol, site and path, respectively. Note the use of an explicit delimiter, since the regular expression contains slashes: note also the use of non-greedy matching to extract the site. If a match expression is evaluated in list context the 'remembered' strings are returned in an array, so we could decompose the URL with

```
($proto, $site, $path) =
    ($url =~ m!(http|ftp)://(.*?/)(.*$)!);
```

With the regular expression written as above, the first slash is included in the site, since it is remembered as part of $2 in the non-greedy match. We can avoid this by rewriting the regular expression thus:

```
($proto, $site, $path) =
    ($url =~ m!(http|ftp)://([^/]*)/(.*$)!);
```

This illustrates an idiom that can often be used to get the effect of a non-greedy match without using the non-greedy qualifier. The pattern [^/]*/ matches a string that consists of an arbitrary number of characters which are not slashes, followed by a single slash. So even if there are more slashes further on in the target string, the first slash will terminate the match on the pattern. Obviously, the general form is [^x]*x, where x is any character.

Lookahead assertions

A lookahead assertion is denoted by the syntax (?=...). This behaves like any other grouping in a regular expression, but if it matches the target string, the matching character(s) are not remembered. Thus an alternative way of parsing a URL without including a trailing slash in the site would be to change the pattern match operation to

```
m!(http|ftp)://(.*?(?=/))(.*$)!
```

Pattern matching modifiers

The operation of the pattern match operator can be modified by adding trailing qualifiers, thus:

m//i   Ignore case when pattern matching.

m//g   Find all occurrences. In a list context it returns a list of all the sub-strings matched by all the bracketed sections of the regular expression. In a scalar context it iterates through the target string returning true whenever it finds a match, and false when it runs out of matches (i.e. it remembers how far it got after each match, and starts at that position next time). This form is typically used in a while loop, e.g. we can count all occurrences of a sub-string with a loop of the form

```
$count = 0;
while ($target =~ m/$substring/g) {
    $count++
}
```

m//m   Treat a target string containing newline characters as multiple lines. In this case, the anchors ^ and $ are the start and end of a line: \A and \Z anchor to the start and end of the string, respectively.

m//s   Treat a target string containing newline characters as a single string, i.e. dot matches any character *including* newline.

m//x   Ignore whitespace characters in the regular expression unless they occur in a character class, or are escaped with a backslash. This modifier also makes # a meta-character introducing a comment running to the next end-of-line. Together, these facilities add greatly to the readability of complex regular expressions.

m//o   Compile regular expression once only. The regular expression 'engine' has to construct a non-deterministic finite automaton which is then used to perform a back-tracking match. This is called 'compiling the regular expression' and may be time consuming for a complex regular expression. The /o modifier ensures that the regular expression is compiled only once, when it is first encountered. If the regular expression includes variable substitution, using /o constitutes a promise that the values of the variables will not change – if they do, the change will have no effect.

Any number of qualifiers can be added, e.g.

```
$count = 0;
while ($target =~ m/$substring/gi) {
   $count++
}
```

will count substrings using case-insensitive matching.

2.12.4 Substitution

Instead of simply finding whether a pattern matches a string, we can additionally specify a substitution to be made when a match succeeds, e.g. given a file in which each line starts with a four-digit line number followed by a space,

The pattern could alternatively be written /^\d{4} /: putting the space in a character class makes the pattern more readable – the space might otherwise not be noticed.

```
while (<STDIN>)
 {s/^\d{4}[ ]//;
  print;
 }
```

will print the file without line numbers. The general syntax is

```
s/pattern/subst/
```

The substitution operator checks for a match between the pattern and the value held in $_, and if a match is found the matching sub-string in $_ is replaced by the string *subst*.

As with the match operator, the matched string is stored in $& and matches corresponding to parts if the regular expressions in round brackets are stored in $1, $2, etc. These variables can be interpolated in the substitution string. Thus to move the line numbers in the previous example to the end of the line, we would write

```
while (<STDIN>)
 {s/(^d{4}[ ])(.*$)/$2 $1/;
  print;
 }
```

Again as before, matching against an explicit named variable uses the =~ operator, e.g.

```
$a =~ s/pattern/subst/
```

Substitution modifiers

The i, g, m, o, s and x modifiers work with the substitution operator in the same way as they do for the match operator. In addition, the substitution operator has an additional, very powerful modifier, e. This modifier signifies that the substitution string is an expression that is to be evaluated at run-time if the pattern match is successful, to generate a new substitution string dynamically. Obviously this is only useful if the code includes references to the variables $&, $1, $2 etc. For example, if the target string contains one or more sequences of decimal digits, the following substitution operation will treat each digit string as an integer and add 1 to it:

```
s/\d+/$&+1/eg;
```

2.12.5   Other string operators

Perl has many other string operators besides matching and substitution. We describe the most useful of them here.

Character translation: tr

The syntax of the tr operator is

```
        tr/original/replacement/
$var =~ tr/original/replacement/
```

As should be obvious by now, the first form works on $_. In its simplest form, *original* and *replacement* are sequences of characters of the same length. The tr operator scans its target string from left to right, replacing occurrences of characters in *original* by the corresponding character in *replacement*: characters not included in *original* are left unchanged. Thus, for example

```
$line =~ tr/A-Z/a-z/;
```

forces the string in $line into lower case, leaving non-alphabetic characters unchanged. If *replacement* is shorter than *original*, its last character is replicated as many times as is necessary to fill it out. For example, on a UNIX system

```
$line =~ tr/.,:;!?/\012/;
```

will convert all punctuation characters in the string held in $line to newlines, thus generating a list of words, one to a line. (\012 is the octal code for linefeed, which is treated as newline in UNIX.)

The behaviour of tr can be influenced by trailing modifier characters as follows:

tr/ / /d   Do not replicate last character in *replacement*. Characters in *original* with no corresponding replacement characters are deleted.
tr/ / /c   Complement *original*, i.e. it includes all characters *except* those specified.
tr/ / /s   Condense ('squash') duplicate replaced characters to a single character.

Note that variable interpolation does not take place in *original* or *replacement*.

Everything in Perl returns a value: tr returns the number of replacements made. This leads to an idiom for counting occurrences of particular characters by providing identical search and replacement lists, e.g.

```
$digits = tr/0-9/0-9/
```

sets $digits to the number of digit characters in the target string. In fact, the true Perl idiom is

```
$digits = tr/0-9//
```

since an empty replacement string causes the search list to be replicated.

Split and join

Used in a list context, the split function scans a string looking for delimiters defined by a pattern (regular expression) and returns a list of the sub-strings so identified. (If used in a scalar context it returns a count of the sub-strings.) Thus if $line contains a string made up of words separated by arbitrary amounts of whitespace,

```
@words = split /\s+/, $line;
```

returns a list of the words in the array @words. If the second argument is omitted it defaults to $_; if both arguments are omitted the delimiter is assumed to be whitespace and the target is $_, thus making the common case easy. For example, given a file phones.txt in which each line consists of two space-separated fields (name and number), we can build a hash using the first field as a key and the second field as the corresponding value with

The meaning of these two lines is reasonably obvious. File operations are explained in detail in Chapter 3. <IN> behaves like <STDIN> in earlier examples.

```
$IN = "c:\phones.txt";
open IN or die "Can't open
    phones.txt";
while (<IN>) {
  ($name, $number) = split;
  $phones{$name} = $number;
}
```

The join function does the reverse of split, converting a list of strings into a single string, using a *separator string* provided as an argument. Thus

```
$line = join " ", @words;
```

puts the words from the array @words into $line, separated by spaces.

2.12.6 Putting it all together: CGI argument parsing

To illustrate how the features that we have met so far can work together, we show how Perl can be used in processing form input in a CGI script on a Web server.

Each component of a form is assigned a name using HTML tags, and if the 'GET' method is specified for form submission, the user's response is sent to the server as a single query string appended to the URL, which specifies the CGI program that is to process it. The query string takes the form "name=value&name=value& ..." but because certain characters are not allowed in URLs, it has to be 'URL encoded' as follows:

- space is replaced by +
- non-alphanumeric characters are replaced by a hex code %dd
- line breaks in multi-line data are replaced by %0D%0A.

The CGI script has to reverse this encoding and extract the key–value pairs for subsequent processing. The first stage is as follows:

```
@kv_pairs = split( /&/, $query);
```
Split the query string on & to obtain a list of key–value pairs which are placed in an array. $query contains the query string, obtained from an environment variable.

```
foreach $key_value (@kv_pairs) {
  ($key, $value) =
    split( /=/, $key_value);
  $value =~ tr/+/ /;
  $value =~ s/%([\dA-Fa-f]{2})/
            pack("C",
  hex($1))/eg;
$form_data{$key} = $value;}
```
Split each key–value pair on =.

Replace + by space.

Use a regular expression match with the e modifier to extract the hex codes.

Place the values in a hash, indexed by the key.

Here, hex is a built-in function that converts hexadecimal values to decimal, and the pack function converts this decimal code to a single ASCII character as described in Chapter 3.

We have in fact slightly oversimplified the problem: in practice the query string may contain repeated keys, e.g. from multiple selections in a listbox. To deal with this situation, before placing the value in the hash we test whether an entry with that key already exists. If there is such an entry, we join the new value onto the existing value with a null character (later processing will recover the multiple values by using split). The last line of the script, which places the value in the hash, is replaced by the following:

```
unless (defined form_data{$key}) {
   $form_data{$key} = $value;
}
else {
   $form_data{$key} =
   join("\0", $form_data{key}, $value);
```

It is instructive to compare this short script with the equivalent code in other languages, e.g. Java. The two statements which replace + by space and decode the hex-coded characters require 18 lines of Java:

For Java programmers only.

```
int len = value.length;
StringBuffer buf = new StringBuffer();
char[] c = value.to CharArray();
int i = 0;
while (i<len) {
  if (c[i] == '+') {
    buf.append(' ');
    i++;
```

```
    } else if (c[i] != '%') {
      buf.append(c[i]);
      i++;
    } else {
      String hex = new String(c, i+1, 2);
      buf.append((char) Integer.parseInt(hex, 16));
      i += 3;
    }
  }
  value = new String(buf);
```

In real life, the Perl version would be even simpler. The Perl community is devoted to the Open Source principle, and vast amounts of code are freely available in the form of modules provided by people who had a particular need and developed some Perl code to satisfy it. (Modules are described in Chapter 3.) Some modules are included in the standard Perl distribution, and the rest are readily downloaded from the CPAN (Comprehensive Perl Archive Network). Lincoln Stein's CGI.pm module makes CGI scripting simple: to decode the URL encoding and set up the hash of name–value pairs requires just a few lines:

```
use CGI qw/:standard/
...
foreach $name (param()) {
  $form_data{$name} = param($name)
}
```

(Don't worry about how this works: the idea is just to show you how Perl modules can make complicated tasks almost trivial.)

2.13 Subroutines

2.13.1 Defining subroutines

Subroutines (or *subs*) are named blocks of code, thus:

```
sub foobar {
  statements
}
```

Note that the subroutine definition does not include argument specifications: it just associates the name with the block. Subroutines are like everything else in Perl, in the sense that they return a value. The value returned is the value of the last expression evaluated in the block that forms the subroutine body, unless the `return` function is used to return a specific value, e.g.

```
sub foobar {
  ...
  return value;
}
```

2.13.2   Calling subroutines

Subroutines can be regarded as out-of-line code, but the semantics of a Perl subroutine are better captured by the 'textual substitution' model. If `foobar` is defined as a subroutine it can be called without arguments by

```
&foobar;
```

or equivalently (remember that there's more than one way to do it)

```
&foobar();
```

In either case, the effect is as if the block forming the body of `foobar` had been copied into the script at that point. The ampersand identifies `foobar` explicitly as the name of a subroutine, so this form of call can be used even if the subroutine definition occurs later in the script. If the subroutine has been defined earlier, the ampersand can be omitted: it is common to provide forward declarations of subroutines that are defined later in a script, so that the ampersand hardly ever needs to be used. A forward declaration takes the form

```
sub foobar;
```

i.e. it is a declaration without a subroutine body.

2.13.3   Subroutine arguments

If a subroutine expects arguments, the call takes the form

```
&foobar(arg1, arg2);
```

or in the likely case that the subroutine is already declared, we can omit the ampersand:

```
foobar(arg1, arg2);
```

In fact, for a pre-declared subroutine, the idiomatic form of call is

```
foobar arg1, arg2
```

The Perl subroutine model is based on the premise that subroutines are typically variadic, i.e. have a variable number of arguments, unlike conventional languages in which the number and type of the arguments are defined as part of the subroutine declaration. A subroutine expects to find its arguments as a single flat list of scalars in the anonymous array `@_`: they can be accessed in the body as `$_[0]`, `$_[1]` etc. Note that this has the effect that arguments that are variable names are called by reference. This is because the values stored in `@_` are implicit references to the actual scalar parameters. Thus if you assign to `$_[0]` the value of the corresponding actual parameter is changed. We shall see later how to achieve the effect of call-by-value.

A common idiom in a subroutine which is expecting a variable number of arguments is to structure the body as

```
foreach $arg @_ {
  ...
}
```

to process each argument in turn. Another common idiom is to use `shift` to peel off one argument at a time. For convenience, `shift` can be used without an argument in a subroutine body, and Perl will assume that you mean the argument array @_.

When a subroutine is called with arguments, e.g.

```
foobar arg1, arg2, arg3;
```

the effect is as if the assignment

```
@_ = (arg1, arg2, arg3);
```

is executed just before the text of the body of foobar is inserted in the script.

The value returned by a subroutine may be a scalar or a single flat list of scalars. It is important to note that in either case, the expression that determines the return value is evaluated in the context (scalar or list) in which the subroutine was called. Thus if we write

```
$x = foo($y, $z)
```

the return value will be evaluated in scalar context, but if we write

```
@x = foo($y, $z)
```

it will be evaluated in list context. This can lead to subtle errors if the expression is such that its value depends on the context in which it is evaluated. To deal with this the function `wantarray` is provided: this returns true if the subroutine was called in a list context, and false if it was called in a scalar context. A typical idiom is to use a conditional expression in the `return` statement:

```
return wantarray ? list_value : scalar_value;
```

In obscure circumstances it may be necessary to force evaluation in list context. This can be done using the construct @{foo($x, $y)}.

2.13.4 Local and global variables

The text-substitution model implies that variables used in a subroutine are global (strictly, global to the module in which the subroutine is defined – see Chapter 3). Thus if a variable $x appears in the body it will take the value of an existing $x if there is one: if not, a new variable will be created and initialized, and will be available for the rest of the script. This behaviour can be modified by using the my declaration, or the `local` declaration.

The my declaration establishes a lexical scope; that is to say, a variable so declared exists only in the block in which it is declared (and any blocks lexically enclosed by this block): a global variable with the same name becomes temporarily invisible. More than one variable can be declared in a my declaration by providing a list of variables enclosed in brackets, e.g.

```
sub s1 {
  my $foo; my $bar;
```

```
      my ($c, $m, $y, $k);
      ...
   }
```

The my declaration can also be used to initialize the local variables, e.g.

```
   sub s2 {
      my ($red, $green, $blue) = (255, 127, 0);
      ...
   }
```

A common idiom is to use initialized local variables for the formal arguments, neatly combining the effect of an explicit formal parameter list with call-by-value. For example, for a subroutine known to have exactly two arguments,

```
   sub compute {
      my ($m, $n) = @_;
      ...
   }
```

Although the my declaration has been described in the context of creating lexically scoped local (private) variables in a subroutine body, it can in fact appear anywhere, and the scope of the variable(s) declared extends from the point of declaration to the end of the innermost enclosing block. In particular, a my declaration can be used at the start of a script to declare global variables (and is the only way to declare variables).

The my declaration is a feature of Perl 5. In earlier versions of Perl, variables in a subroutine could be declared local with the local declaration, which is retained for backwards compatibility. The effect of local is to save the values of the variables specified, and to create new initialized variables of the same name. Values given to these variables are accessible in any subroutines subsequently called, and the original values are restored on exit from the subroutine in which the local declaration occurred. Thus these are not really local variables, but dynamically scoped global variables. As with the my declaration, local can appear anywhere, and the scope of the variable(s) declared extends from the point of declaration to the end of the inner-most enclosing block.

2.14   Scripts with arguments

We have seen that a Perl script can be invoked with arguments on the command line. These arguments are placed in an array @ARGV. A common idiom is to use a foreach loop to process each argument in turn:

```
   #!/usr/bin/perl
   foreach $arg @ARGV;
```

```
{... #process each argument in turn
     #as $arg
}
```

An alternative is to peel off the arguments one at a time using the `shift` operator:

```
#!/usr/bin/Perl
while ($arg = shift){
   ...
}
```

Process each argument in turn as $arg.

(In this context, `shift` used without an argument shifts `@ARGV`. This is a good example of Perl doing the obvious thing: recall that in a subroutine body the `shift` operator without an argument shifts `@_`.)

Frequently the command-line arguments given to a script are file names and we need to process the contents of each file in turn, line by line. This is achieved using the line input (angle) operator without a filehandle. Recall that when applied to a filehandle, as in `<STDIN>`, the line input delivers the lines of the file, one by one in scalar context and all at once in list context. When used without a file handle, it delivers the lines from all of the files listed on the command line that invoked the script, in the order in which they occur, so a common idiom is

```
while (<>) {
   ...    #process  $_
}
```

If the script was invoked without arguments, `<>` delivers lines from standard input: this magic is achieved as follows. If the `@ARGV` array is empty when `<>` is evaluated for the first time, `$ARGV[0]` is set to -, and, following a long UNIX tradition, an attempt to open a file called - opens standard input.

2.15 Conclusion

This has been a long chapter, and we have still only covered a small part of Perl. Some more advanced features are introduced in the next chapter, but it would take a book longer than this one to really do justice to the language. However, although it is a complex language, Perl has a very low entry fee, and it is possible to achieve a lot of useful work using only a small subset of Perl's capabilities. This is a great virtue in a language. Let Larry Wall have the last word:

> You're learning a new language . . . a language full of strange runes and ancient chants, some easy and some difficult, many of which sound familiar, and some of which don't. You may be tempted to become discouraged and quit. But think upon this: consider how long it took you to learn your native tongue. Was it worth it? I think so. And have you finished learning it? I think not. Then do not expect to learn all the mysteries of Perl in a moment.

2.16 Reference: operators and precedence

The Perl operators are listed here in precedence order, highest to lowest. The associativity is shown in brackets: (L) left associative, (R) right associative, (N) non-associative.

(L)	List operators (leftward)
(L)	->
(N)	++, --
(R)	**
(R)	!, ~, \, unary +, unary -
(L)	=~, !~
(L)	*, /, %, x
(L)	+, -, .
(L)	<<, >>
(N)	Named unary operators
(N)	<, >, <=, >, +, lt, gt, le, ge
(N)	==, !=, <=>, eq, ne, cmp
(L)	&
<L)	|, ^
(L)	&&
(L)	||
(N)	..
(R)	?:
(R)	=, +=, -=, etc.
(L)	comma, =>
(N)	List operators (rightward)
(R)	not
(L)	and
(L)	or, xor

Notes

[1]   The Digital Equipment Corporation (DEC) VAX computer, very popular at the time, was always referred to as 'a VAX'. 'VAXen' is the hackish plural of VAX.

[2]   The quotation comes from Chapter 10 of *Open Sources: Voices from the Open Source Revolution*, Chris DiBona, Sam Ockman and Mark Stone Eds., O'Reilly, 1999.

[3]   A dynamically typed language should not be confused with a *type-free* or *un-typed* language like BCPL, where the only kind of data is a bit pattern, and the operators +, -, *, and / are 'operations which work directly on bit patterns and just happen to be useful for working with integers'.

[4]   In certain obscure circumstances it is necessary to use a unary plus to prevent the syntax analyser drawing the wrong conclusions about the meaning of an expression. For example, f(...) denotes application of a function to an argument list: writing f +(...) makes it clear that the brackets are enclosing an expression that is not to be associated with the function f.

## Chapter 3

Advanced Perl

In this chapter we explore a number of additional features of Perl, further demonstrating the remarkable power of the language. In particular, we look at Perl's approach to data structures, its implementation of objects, its module structure, its interfaces to UNIX, Windows NT and the Internet, and its approach to security. Along the way we give a taste of the power that is provided by the extensive collection of Perl modules that have been contributed by the worldwide Perl community.

3.1 Finer points of looping

3.1.1 The continue block

A `while` loop can have an explicit `continue` block which is executed at the end of each normal iteration before control returns to re-test the condition, e.g.

```
while (...) {
  ...
}
continue {
  ...
}
```

A `last` command, if present, skips the remainder of the main block but then executes the continue block as if the main iteration had completed. The `continue` block is analogous to the third component in a `for` loop specification: indeed, the `for` loop can be defined in terms of a `while` loop with a continue block as follows.

```
for ($i = 1; $i < 10; $i++) {
  ...
}
```

is equivalent to

```
$i = 1;
while ($i < 10) {
  ...
}
continue {
 $i++
}
```

3.1.2   Multiple loop variables

A `for` loop can iterate over two or more variables simultaneously, e.g.

```
for ($m = 1, $n = 1; $m < 10; $m++, $n += 2) {
   ...
}
```

Here we have used the comma operator in a scalar context. In a list context the comma operator is a list constructor, but in a scalar context the comma operator evaluates its left-hand argument, throws away the value returned, then evaluates its right-hand argument. This is only useful if evaluation of the left-hand operand has a useful side effect, which is the case here where evaluation of the arguments sets or increments the values of $m and $n to achieve the desired effect.

3.1.3   Last, next and redo revisited

In Chapter 2 we referred to `last`, `next` and `redo` as *commands*, not statements. This is a subtle distinction: they are effectively unary operators which change the flow of control, and can therefore be included in expressions by Perl magicians of a high order. For example, although Perl does not have a case statement, we can easily construct something similar using `last` in an expression as shown in below.

```
SELECT: {
   $red += 1, last SELECT    if /red/;
   $green += 1, last SELECT if /green/;
   $blue += 1, last SELECT   if /blue/;
}
```

This construct increments $red, $blue or $green according as the anonymous variable $_ contains the string 'red', 'blue' or 'green'. The comma operator binds tightly, so that

```
$red += 1, last SELECT if /red/;
```

parses as

```
($red += 1, last SELECT) if /red/;
```

Here we are again using the comma operator for its side effect, and using `last` as an operator in an expression to cause exit from the labelled bare block.

3.2   Finer points of subroutines

3.2.1   Subroutine prototypes

Perhaps the most misunderstood feature of Perl is the *subroutine prototype*, introduced in Perl 5.003, which appears to allow you to specify the number of arguments a subroutine takes, and the type of the arguments. Thus, for example,

```
sub foo($);
```

specifies that `foo` is a subroutine that expects one scalar argument, and

```
sub bar();
```

specifies that `bar` is a subroutine that expects no arguments. The natural conclusion is that the prototype is there to enable compile-time checking of the number and type of arguments provided: that conclusion is mistaken. Let us explore these simple cases further before looking at other features of prototypes.

For scalar arguments, compile-time checking of the number of arguments takes place, and a mismatch results in compilation being aborted. However, type checking does not take place: rather, the `$` in `sub foo($);` tells the compiler that if the single argument is not a scalar, it should be converted into a scalar by fair means or foul. So what is the real purpose of the prototype? It is to allow us to define subroutines that behave like the built-in functions when called without brackets round the arguments. Suppose `bar` is a subroutine that takes no arguments and we write

```
$n = bar -1;
```

If a subroutine has been defined before it is called, it is legitimate to omit the brackets round its arguments, thus if `bar` had been defined without a prototype, `$n` would be assigned the value returned by `bar`, since the compiler would gobble up the `-1` as an argument. But with the prototype specifying no arguments, the compiler knows that the statement should be parsed as

```
$n = bar() -1;
```

Similar considerations apply to subroutines taking one scalar argument. Suppose we define `foo` without a prototype, as follows

```
sub foo {
  return shift
}
```

Then if we write

```
@s = (foo $w1, $w2, $w3);
```

the value of `@s` is a list of one element, whose value is that of `$w1`: `$w2` and `$w3` have been gobbled up as arguments, but ignored by `foo`. But if `foo` is defined with a prototype (`$`), the compiler knows to collect only one argument, and the value of `@s` is a list of three items, `foo($w1)`, `$w2` and `$w3`. However, this behaviour does not extrapolate to subroutines with more than one scalar arguments: if we define

```
sub foobar($$);
```

and write

```
@s = (foobar $w1, $w2, $w3);
```

we get a compile-time error, 'too many arguments supplied'. Prototypes can also include optional arguments:

```
sub foobar($;$)
```

is a subroutine that expects at least one scalar argument, but may additionally have another optional scalar argument. The compiler will complain if the call of foo has no arguments or more than two arguments: the argument(s) supplied will be coerced to scalars if they are not scalars already.

Let us now look at more complicated prototypes involving non-scalar arguments. A prototype can specify non-scalar arguments using @, % or &. The immediate reaction is 'array', 'hash' and 'subroutine', but beware – @ signifies a *list*, not an array. Thus a prototype

```
sub foobar(@);
```

specifies a subroutine that expects a variable number of arguments, i.e. it is just the normal Perl variadic subroutine. It can be called without any arguments, and the compiler will not complain: an empty list is still a list. The prototype

```
sub foobar($@);
```

appears to specify a subroutine with two arguments, the first a scalar and the second a list: in fact it just defines a subroutine with at least one argument, which will be coerced to a scalar if necessary. The prototype

```
sub foobar(%);
```

appears to specify a subroutine that expects a single argument that is a hash, but in practice you can call the subroutine with pretty well any kind of argument, and the compiler will not complain.

We return to prototypes later, after we have discussed references.

3.2.2   Determining the calling context

A subroutine can examine the call stack using the caller function. Used without an argument, this returns the package name, file name and line number that the currently executing subroutine was called from, e.g.

```
($pkge, $file, $line) = caller;
```

(Packages are described later in this chapter.) Used outside a named package, caller returns the package name as 'main'. An argument can be provided in the form of an expression which evaluates to a non-negative integer. The effect is to go back that number of stack frames from the current one, and also to return additional information: the subroutine name, the number of arguments and the calling context (as returned by wantarray). Thus to obtain the full set of information about the caller of the currently executing subroutine we would write:

```
($pkge, $file, $line, $name, $args, $context) =
    caller 0;
```

A simple stack trace can be generated with

```
$i = 0;
while (@trace = caller($i++)) {
  print "$trace[3]\n";
}
```

3.3 Using pack and unpack

The pack function resembles join, in that it combines a list of items into a string. However, it builds a binary structure described by a *template* which is given as an argument, and returns this as a string. A common use is for converting between ASCII codes and the corresponding characters. Thus if @codes is a list of 10 integers between 0 and 127,

```
pack "cccccccccc", @codes
```

or

```
pack "c10", @codes
```

produces a string containing the 10 corresponding ASCII characters. (c in a template denotes 'character'.) Since the template is a string, and therefore allows variable interpolation, we can generalize this to a list of any length:

```
$count = @codes;
pack "c$count", @codes;
```

The unpack function reverses the process, converting a string representing a data structure into a list. Like pack, it uses a template to define the order and type of the items in the data structure.

3.3.1 Simulating C structs with pack and unpack

As we have just seen, the pack function takes a list of values and packs them into a string. Since a string is just a sequence of bytes, we can equally well say that pack takes a list of values and packs them into a binary structure. To illustrate this, suppose we have an application that deals with chunks of data that are made up as follows:

- type identifier – a character
- descriptive identifier – a string of up to 32 characters, null padded
- payload – 16 long (32-bit) integers.

In C we would store such a data item in a *struct* with three fields: the C compiler stores these fields head-to-tail in memory, thus the struct occupies 69 bytes. In Perl we can pack the components into a 69 byte string as follows

```
@payload = (...);    #list of 16 integers
$s = pack "ca32N16", (chr(15),
  "Data for 20 September", @payload);
```

In the template, c is the code for a character, a32 denotes an ASCII string of length 32, and N16 denotes 16 long integers. (Note that the numerical qualifier is the length for a string, but a repetition factor for numbers.)

The unpack function performs the inverse operation, reconstructing a list of values from the packed string:

```
@chunk = unpack "ca32N16", $s;
```

Why should we want to do this? The answer is that a string is a convenient thing to pass around in a program: it can be passed as a subroutine argument, so this gives us a way of having subroutines that take 'structs' as arguments, and/or return 'structs' as values. Very commonly, packed data is stored in a binary file (see the next section): the recipient of such a file can then recover the structured data from the flattened version passed in the file (possibly over the network).

Clever (and useful) effects can be obtained by packing with one template and unpacking with another. In the example above, we used the code N for a long integer. Strictly, this denotes a long integer in 'network' or 'big-endian' order, i.e. most-significant byte first. Suppose we are sending our chunks to a VAX machine, which stores its integers least-significant byte first ('little-endian' order). All that is necessary is to change the unpacking template on the VAX to "ca32V16" to cause the integers to be unpacked in 'VAX order'. Another useful idiom is to use a call of pack as an argument of unpack, with different templates for the two operations. Thus

```
$n_in_binary = unpack "B32", (pack "N", $n);
```

will convert a Perl integer into its binary representation, a 32-bit string. In the real world we would probably strip off the leading zeros in the result with a regular-expression substitution:

```
$n_in_binary =~ s/^0+//;
```

3.4 Working with files

Perl scripts communicate with the outside world through a number of I/O channels. We have already met STDIN, STDOUT and STDERR, which are automatically opened when a script is started: in addition, channels can be linked to files, and can be linked to network sockets as described in Section 3.18. I/O channels are named by *filehandles*, which are names without any special character at the start, conventionally written using uppercase letters.

3.4.1 Filehandles

Filehandles are created by the open function:

```
open(IN,  "<filename");   # read
open(OUT, ">filename");   # write
open(LOG, ">>filename");  # append
```

```
open(FILE1, "+>filename"); # read and write
open(FILE2, "+<filename"); # read and write
```

(The < in the first example is not obligatory, but it is good practice to include it.) Note particularly the possible trap embodied in the two different forms of 'open for read and write'. Filehandles opened for writing overwrite an existing file of the same name: +> opens for reading and writing, but opens for writing first, so that an existing file of the same name is destroyed. Using +< opens for reading first and keeps the existing file, which is often the effect you intended.

If the open operation is unsuccessful no warning is given: input using the filehandle will return undef, and output will be silently discarded. It is therefore sensible to check success. The idiom is

```
open HANDLE, "filename" or die "Can't open\n";
```

die prints its argument on STDERR and kills the current process: the or operator ensures that die is only invoked if open fails, analogous to short-cut evaluation of Boolean expressions. (You may see an alternative form in older scripts:

```
open(HANDLE, "filename") || die "Can't open\n";
```

The brackets round the arguments of the open function are necessary because || has a higher precedence than comma.)

Rather than just say 'Can't open', you may also want to include the error code returned by the operating system, since this may be helpful to the expert user. The code is returned in the special variable $! (mnemonic: 'what went bang?'), so we can write

```
open HANDLE, "filename" or die "Can't open
  ($!)\n";
```

An alternative syntax for the open function allows the file name to be omitted: in this case the file name is taken from a variable with the same name as the filehandle, e.g.

```
$IN = "/home/users/dwb/books/WSL/chapter3";
open IN or die "Can't open $IN\n";
```

Once successfully opened, an input filehandle can be used in angle brackets like <STDIN> in the previous examples, and an output filehandle can appear immediately after print or printf, to specify the channel to be used, e.g.

```
open IN, "<$a" or die "cannot open $a";
open OUT,">$b" or die "cannot open $b";
while(<IN>) {
  print OUT
};
```

Good housekeeping suggests adding the line

```
close(IN); close(OUT);
```

Note the syntax when print has an explicit list of values to print, e.g.

```
print STDERR "Error is ", "$!\n"
```

There is no comma after STDERR: commas only occur as list-building operators, constructing the list of items to be given to print.

Filehandles have a somewhat equivocal status in Perl. They are not quite 'first class citizens' – you cannot assign them as values of variables, store them in data structures, or pass them as parameters to subroutines. There is a way round this restriction using a *typeglob*: see Section 3.6 for more details. Alternatively, we can use the IO::File package, which generates filehandle objects: we return to this later (in Section 3.13.1) after we have described Perl's modules and object facilities.

3.4.2 File status checks

In the UNIX shell a variant of the if statement allows the status of a file to be tested before attempting to open it. For example, to test whether a file foo in directory /tmp has write permission we can use the construct

```
if -w "/tmp/foo" ...
```

Perl generalizes this idea by providing a collection of unary file test operators, which take as an argument a file name or a filehandle and test the associated file to see if something is true about it.

The tests available depend on the capability of the underlying operating system, and therefore vary between platforms. Table 3.1 lists a collection of the more useful operators that are common to UNIX and Windows NT: for a full list of tests available consult the Perl documentation for the platform in question.

Table 3.1 File status checks

-e	file exists
-s	file has non-zero size
-z	file has zero size
-r	file is readable
-w	file is writeable
-x	file is executable
-f	file is a plain file, not a directory
-d	file is a directory
-t	'file' is a character device

Since the operators return Boolean values they can obviously be used in an if statement: they can however equally well be used in other constructs, e.g.

```
-w "c:\foo" or die "Can't write to c:\foo";
```

The -s operator deserves special mention. As noted, it returns true if the file has a non-zero size: in fact, it returns the actual size of the file, so that we can compare file sizes with (-s $f1 > -s $f2). In the same vein, if @files contains a list of file names,

```
@list = map {-s $_} @files);
```

lists the corresponding file sizes in the array @list.

The -t operator is most commonly used to check that standard input is connected to the keyboard:

```
-t STDIN or die "not reading from keyboard";
```

A similar syntax is used for operators which return information about the age of a file: –M returns the age in days since the last modification, and –A returns the age in days since the last access.

3.4.3 Pipes

On platforms that support pipes, the open function can also be used to attach the standard input or output of a command to a filehandle by placing a vertical bar at the start or end of the second argument. The rest of this argument is taken as a command line, to be executed in a new process. For example:

```
open(WHO,  "who|");
@who = <WHO>;
```

Here, the filehandle WHO is connected to the output of the *who* command, so the second line captures the list of logged-in users in the array @who. If the vertical bar appears at the beginning of the argument, the filehandle becomes a pipe into the command, e.g.

```
open(LPR,  "|lpr  -P  callahan");
print LPR  @bar;
```

In this example, LPR is a handle for input to the (UNIX) *lpr* command which runs in parallel with the Perl script unless forced to wait by close(LPR);.

Pipes are one-directional communication channels between processes. A pipe can be created explicitly by the pipe function, which returns two filehandles, one for the reading end and one for the writing end. This is only useful if you want to set up communication between two processes running in parallel, and we return to this subject in Section 3.15.5.

3.4.4 Binary data

As we have seen, Perl treats a byte in a string as just 8 bits, without ascribing any significance to the contents of the byte. Thus binary data can conveniently be represented as a string. There is one exception to this statement: built-in file-handling functions treat carriage return (\r) and linefeed (\n) specially. Perl adopts the UNIX convention that lines end with \n: DOS and Windows use \r\n as the line end, and the Macintosh uses \r. Perl's input–output system performs the necessary translations according to the platform on which it is running, unless instructed not to do so by the binmode function:

```
binmode BINFILE;
```

This ensures that in processing the file with filehandle BINFILE, bytes containing the code for \n or \r will be treated 'as-is', with no translations. binmode must be used after the open, and before the file is accessed for reading or writing. If your script handles binary data, it is a good idea to use binmode even though your platform may not require it, in order to guarantee portability.

Binary data (in a string) can be written to a file using the usual print function. However, it does not make sense to read binary data using the <*filehandle*> construct, since it does not have record separators. Instead, the read function is used. This takes as an argument the number of bytes to be read. For example,

```
$n_read = read BINFILE, $binstring, $n;
```

attempts to read $n bytes from the file opened with filehandle BINFILE, placing them as a string in variable $binstring and returning the number of bytes actually read (zero if the attempted read takes place at end-of-file). It is sensible always to check that the read has been successful: a common idiom is

```
(read BINFILE, $binstring, $n) == $n or
    die "reading past EOF";
```

As a refinement, read can take an optional argument to specify an offset in the target string variable at which the data is to be placed, thus

```
read BINFILE, $binstring, $n, length $binstring;
```

will append $n bytes to the current string in $binstring.

Once the binary data has been read into a string, it can be decomposed using unpack with a template that defines the structure of the data. Suppose, for example, that we are processing Internet messages at a low level. A UDP packet has an 8-byte header which contains the source and destination port numbers, the length of the packet and the checksum, all as 16-bit numbers. We can read and decode the header, assuming a filehandle has been set up, as follows:

```
read PACKETS, $header, 8;
($src_port, $dest_port, $length, $checksum)
    = unpack  "S4", $header;
```

Having extracted the length, the packet payload is then read with

```
read PACKETS, $data, $length;
```

3.4.5   sysread and syswrite

Experienced C programmers working in the UNIX environment can access the underlying UNIX I/O system calls by using the sysread and syswrite functions. Perl provides equivalent functions. Perl's sysread is used in exactly the same way as read to read a block of data of known length. syswrite makes it possible to write a block of data of known length, e.g.

UNIX gurus only!

```
$bytes_written =
    syswrite BINFILE, $binstring, $n;
```

The value returned is the number of bytes actually written.

These functions should only be used by experienced UNIX programmers, and you should never mix calls of `read` and `sysread`, or `print` and `syswrite`, on the same filehandle unless, to quote Larry Wall, 'you are into heavy wizardry (and/or pain)'.

3.4.6 Random access files

As we have seen, the angle operator, e.g. <STDIN>, reads the next line (record) from the file identified by the filehandle. Files of binary data have no record structure; however, we can define a point in the file in terms of an offset – the number of bytes from the start. When we use the `read` function to read a number of bytes from a file, the read normally starts where the previous `read` left off (at the start of the file for the first read after opening the file). The `seek` function can be used to set this 'file pointer' explicitly, allowing a read to start at a position in the file determined by some computation. Thus if we have opened a file with filehandle `BINFILE`,

```
seek BINFILE, $n, 0;
```

will set the file pointer to an offset (byte position) of $n from the start of the file (first byte is at offset zero). For convenience,

```
seek BINFILE, $n, 1;
```

sets an offset (positive or negative) relative to the current value of the file pointer, and

```
seek BINFILE, $n, 2;
```

sets an offset (positive or negative) relative to the end of the file. The `seek` function returns 1 if successful, 0 if the seek is impossible, and it is always wise to test the return value, e.g.

```
seek BINFILE, $n, 0 or
die "Seeking beyond end of file\n";
```

Since a file does not 'know' whether it contains binary data or text records, `seek` can be used on text files. This will normally only make sense if all lines are the same length, so that the offset of a desired line can be calculated easily.

The `tell` function is the inverse of `seek`, returning the current file pointer offset, e.g.

```
$position = tell BINFILE;
```

This is useful if you need to be able to go back to a particular position in a file. If `tell` is used without a filehandle argument, it returns the value of the file pointer offset of the file last read.

3.5 Navigating the file system

The preceding section has covered the business of getting information into and out of files, provided that you know the name of the file you want to work with. The other side of the coin is navigating the file system to find the file that you want. Perl makes this very straightforward.

3.5.1 Searching directories

In the same way that `open` gives you a filehandle to access an open file, `opendir` gives you a handle on a directory:

```
opendir(TEMPDIR, "/tmp");        # UNIX
opendir(TEMPDIR, "c:\temp");     # Windows
```

In practice, you would always protect yourself against failure:

```
$dir = "c:\temp";
opendir(TEMPDIR, $dir) or
    die "Cannot open $dir";
```

Having got the handle to the directory, you can read the directory contents with `readdir`, e.g.

```
@tempfiles = readdir TEMPDIR;
```

Like the angle operator, `readdir` delivers a list of all the directory entries if called in list context. In scalar context it delivers the next entry each time it is called, so the idiom is

```
opendir(TEMPDIR, $dir) or
    die "Cannot open $dir";
foreach $entry (readdir TEMPDIR) {
    ...   #process the entry
}
closedir TEMPDIR
```

3.5.2 File name globbing

In the UNIX shell, the process of expanding a * argument on the command line to a list of all the file names in the current directory is called *globbing*. Perl's angle operator, used with a wild-card pattern, e.g. `<*.c>` performs 'file name globbing', delivering the names of all the files in the current directory which match the wild-card pattern. In list context all the file names are delivered: in a scalar context the operator delivers the next file name each time it is called, assigning the name as the value of `$_` if not otherwise assigned. When there are no more names to deliver, it returns false, so it can be used in a `while` loop, e.g.

```
while <*.c> {
    chmod 0400 $_
}
```

(In UNIX this sets permissions of all `.c` files to 'read by owner only'.)

3.6 Typeglobs

The *typeglob* is a somewhat esoteric concept which crops up in a variety of contexts. It is necessary to understand how typeglobs work in order to make sense of a number of advanced features of Perl, especially the way that packages and modules manipulate namespaces, and we therefore describe them at this point.

A *typeglob* is a generic variable name which when evaluated produces a scalar value that represents all the variables of that name, so that `*foo` can represent `$foo`, `@foo`, `%foo`, `&foo` etc. The typeglob is a real data object: Perl's symbol table is organized as a hash that contains an entry for each unique identifier used in a program (strictly, each unique identifier in a package – packages are described later in this chapter). The key is the identifier – the variable name without an initial special character – and the associated value contains slots for each of the things that can share this name. Thus for a name `foo`, the value contains slots for `$foo`, `@foo`, `%foo`, `&foo` etc. (assuming that these exist). This hash entry is the typeglob, and can be referred to in a program as `*foo`. It can be assigned as the value of a variable, stored in an array and passed as a parameter to a subroutine, exactly like any other data item, and a typeglob in a subroutine body can be localized with the `local` declaration. (However, it doesn't make sense to try to use a my declaration to create a lexically scoped typeglob – the typeglob *is* the symbol table entry.)

3.6.1 Aliases

A typeglob assignment, e.g.

```
*bar = *foo;
```

makes `bar` an alias for `foo`, i.e. `$bar` is another name for `$foo`, `@bar` is another name for `@foo`, and so on. We can see how this works from the way the symbol table is organized. `*foo` is the typeglob that holds pointers to `$foo`, `@foo`, etc.; after the assignment the name `bar` in the symbol table is associated with the same typeglob, and therefore points to the same values.

Temporary aliases can be created using `local`. Suppose we have the following block:

```
{local *bar;
 *bar = *foo;
 ...
}
```

The `local` declaration copies the pointers in `*bar` and replaces them with `undef`. The typeglob assignment then makes `bar` an alias for `foo` as before. However, at the end of the block the original pointers in `*bar` are restored.

A common use of typeglob aliasing is to pass an array to a subroutine by reference. If we have a subroutine `asub` which expects one parameter as an array, we can call it with

```
&asub(@my_array);
```

which will cause the contents of the array `@my_array` to be copied into the argument array `@_`. For a large array this is inefficient, and prior to Perl 5 it was better to declare the subroutine to take a typeglob as a parameter, thus

```
sub asub {
  local *copy = shift;
  ... #use @copy in the body
}
```

If we now call the subroutine with

```
&asub(*my_array);
```

then in the subroutine body copy is an alias for my_array, and so @copy[] actually accesses an element of my_array. Because the typeglob *copy did not exist before the local declaration, it is discarded at the end of the block that forms the subroutine body. Perl 5 solves this problem more elegantly using references, as described later in this chapter.

Typeglobs can also be used to create a special form of alias: if a string value is assigned to a typeglob, Perl creates a variable whose name is the same as the string.

3.6.2 Filehandles and typeglobs

As we have noted earlier, filehandles are not quite 'first class citizens' in Perl. You cannot assign them as values of variables, store them in data structures, or pass them as parameters to subroutines (except for built-in functions like open). However, they do have their own namespace, and therefore they form a possible component of a typeglob: if you have a filehandle INFILE and a variable of the same name, the typeglob *INFILE represents them both. Recall that

```
$INFILE = "/tmp/foo";
open INFILE;
```

has the same effect as

```
open INFILE, "/tmp/foo";
```

If open is called with a single filehandle argument, Perl uses the typeglob to locate the file name as a value of the scalar variable of the same name. We can thus declare subroutines that take a typeglob as an argument as a way of passing filehandles: we declare

```
sub fileop {
  local *FILE = shift;
  while (<FILE>) {
    ...
  }
}
```

and call it with something like

```
open TESTFILE, "/tmp/test.txt" or
 die "Can't open file";
fileop(*TESTFILE);
```

We can use a similar technique to redirect output:

```
open LOG "log.txt" or die "Can't open logfile";
*STDOUT = *LOG;
print "$logmessage\n";
```

Here, `print` defaults to printing on `STDOUT`, and the typeglob assignment causes the redirection. This is of course an artificial example, since we could perfectly well have written

```
open LOG "log.txt" or die "Can't open logfile";
print LOG "$logmessage\n";
```

3.7 eval

The `eval` operator comes in two forms. In its simplest form it takes an arbitrary string as an operand and evaluates the string, at run-time, as a Perl script. It is executed in the current context, so that any variable settings remain afterwards. However, any variables declared local with `my` or `local` have a lifetime which ends when the `eval` is finished. The value returned is the value of the last expression evaluated, as with a subroutine: alternatively, `return` can be used to return a value from inside the `eval`. In the event of a syntax error or a run-time error, `eval` returns the value 'undefined' and places the error message in the variable `$@`. (If there is no error, the value of `$@` is an empty string.) A simple example of the use of this form of `eval` is to get the value of a variable whose name is to be computed, as a string, at run-time, e.g.

```
$myvar = '...';
...
$value = eval "\$$myvar";
```

Another example is a little shell, which allows you to type in a script which will be run when the end-of-file character (Ctrl-D in UNIX, Ctrl-Z in Windows) is entered:

Accumulate lines in @script as typed, convert to space-separated string and pass to eval.

```
my @script = <STDIN>;
chomp @script;
eval join ' ', @script;
```

The second form of `eval` is quite different. It takes a block as its argument, and the block is compiled only once, at the same time as the surrounding code. However, if there is an error at run-time, the error is still returned in `$@`, so that this form of `eval` provides a robust exception handling mechanism. The structure is reminiscent of the `try ...` `catch` structure in C++ (and JavaScript – see Chapter 9). Instead of `try` we use `eval`, and instead of `catch` we test `$@`, e.g.

```
eval {
   ... # code which might have errors
}
if ($@ ne '') {
   ... # clean up after error
}
```

3.8   References

3.8.1   References and pointers

The concept of the *pointer* is common in many languages, allowing indirect access to a piece of data – the value of a pointer variable tells us where we will find the data object. In C a pointer is just another data type: we can declare pointer variables, assign values to them and even do arithmetic on them: the value of a pointer variable is for all practical purposes a memory address. Indeed, pointers in C can be initialized using the 'address of' operator, e.g.

```
int x;        /* integer */
int *px;      /* pointer to integer */
px = &x;      /* "address of x" */
```

and the original documentation of C tells us that 'the unary operator * treats its operand as the address of the ultimate target'. (In most C programs pointers are mostly generated by a call to the memory allocation function `malloc()`, or by passing an array as a function argument – in C the name of an array is in fact a pointer to its first element.)

It is possible (but dangerous) to perform arithmetic on pointers in C. In other languages, e.g. Pascal, a pointer is more restricted, and is just a way of identifying a piece of data that has been created dynamically – an opaque *indirect address*. This kind of pointer is better called a *reference*, since it is a true abstraction of an address: its only use is to locate its referent.

3.8.2   Hard references and symbolic references

Perl provides a generalized version of this kind of reference in the form of the so-called *hard reference*, which locates an actual value in memory – a 'thingy' in Perl-speak. A hard reference should not be confused with the *symbolic reference*, which is a variable whose value is a string that happens to be the name of another variable. A reference (we will drop the adjective 'hard' from now on) is a scalar value, and can be used in any context that a scalar is valid (it doesn't make sense to print its value, though). The only operation that can be carried out on a reference is *dereferencing*, i.e. locating the referent.

A Perl variable is an association of an identifier in the symbol table with a reference to a value. If the identifier appears in an expression, dereferencing takes place to obtain the value: if it occurs on the left-hand side of an assignment, the reference is used to locate the value to be updated. An explicit reference to a value can be created: this may be a value that is associated with an identifier in the symbol table, or it may be an 'anonymous' value with no associated variable: in this case the only way to get to the value is via the reference.

3.8.3   Creating references

References to variables and subroutines

The backslash operator creates a reference to a named variable or subroutine, e.g.

```
$ref2foo  = \$foo;
$ref2args = \@ARGV;
$ref2sub  = \&initialize;
```

Note that by creating the reference we have two independent references to the *same* value: one associated with the name in the symbol table, and another which is the value of the reference variable. Neither reference 'knows' that the other exists. References to references can be created to any depth, e.g.

```
$ref2ref2foo = \\$foo;
```

References to anonymous values

An anonymous scalar is just a constant, and it is possible to create a reference to it, e.g.

```
$pi_ref = \3.145926536;
```

This appears at first sight to be rather pointless, but it can be used in combination with a typeglob to create a read-only variable, as described later.

More useful are references to anonymous arrays and hashes. A reference to an anonymous array is created by enclosing a list in square brackets. This *array composer* creates an anonymous array and returns a reference to it, thus

```
$ref2array = [255, 127, 0];
```

The square brackets give us a mnemonic association with array subscripts: the reference composing interpretation only takes place in a context where Perl is expecting a term in an expression, so there is no ambiguity with the use of square brackets to enclose subscripts. The square brackets can be nested:

```
$ref2array2 = [255, 127, 0, [255, 255, 255]];
```

Here we have a reference to an array with four elements, three integers and a reference to an array.

In the spirit of 'no surprises', a reference to an anonymous hash can be created using curly brackets (braces):

```
$ref2hash = {winter => 'cold',
             summer => 'hot'
            };
```

As with the array composer, nesting is possible: the values (but not, of course, the keys) can be anonymous hash composers (or, indeed, array composers).

A reference to an anonymous subroutine is created with the *anonymous subroutine composer*:

```
$ref2sub = sub{...};
```

This looks like the definition of a subroutine without a name, but it is in fact an expression, hence the semicolon after the closing brace.

3.8.4 Typeglobs and references

We can think of a typeglob as a hash with a fixed set of keys, SCALAR, ARRAY, HASH, etc., and associated values which are references to the scalar, array, hash etc. variables that share the name associated with the typeglob. Indeed, you can write `*foo{SCALAR}` instead of `\$foo` if you want to write obscure code.

This equivalence is put to practical effect in the capability to create selective aliases. We have seen that

```
*bar = *foo;
```

makes $bar the same as $foo, @bar the same as @foo, etc. If we write

```
*bar = \$foo;
```

then $bar is an alias for $foo, but @bar and @foo remain different arrays. In a similar vein,

```
*Pi = \3.1415926536;
```

creates a read-only variable: an attempt to assign to $Pi causes an error.

3.8.5 Using references

Is it a reference?

The ref function, given an expression as an argument, returns true if the value is a reference and false otherwise:

```
ref $n or die "Panic!! Expected a reference!";
```

What is it a reference to?

More precisely, the ref function returns an empty string if its argument is not a reference. If the argument is a reference, ref returns a string specifying what the argument is a reference to – REF, SCALAR, ARRAY, HASH, CODE, or GLOB.

Dereferencing

The operation of dereferencing applied to a reference delivers the referent, i.e. the thingy that is the 'target' of the referencing. Given a reference to a scalar variable, e.g.

```
$ref2foo = \$foo;
```

then an occurrence of $$ref2foo has the same meaning as $foo. Thus

```
print "$foo\n";
print "$$ref2foo\n";
```

both print the value of $foo. We can do dereferencing on the left-hand side of an assignment also, thus:

```
$ref2foo = \$foo;
$foo = 1;
$$ref2foo = 2;
```

The value of $foo is now 2, but what we have done is potentially dangerous, since we have two independent ways of referring to the same chunk of memory.

Perl interprets $$ref2foo as the name of a scalar variable (first dollar) in which the alphanumeric identifier has been replaced by the name of a scalar variable containing a reference of the appropriate type. Thus a reference to an array is dereferenced by @$ref_to_array and a reference to a subroutine is dereferenced by &$ref_to_sub. Multiple references to references are dereferenced by recursive use of this rule, e.g.

```
$refrefref = \\\$foo;
print "$$$refrefref\n";
```

has the same effect as print "$foo\n";. Advanced wizards can take advantage of the fact that the alphanumeric part of a variable name can be replaced by a block that returns a reference of the correct type. Thus if &bar is a subroutine that takes two arguments and returns a reference to a scalar, we can write something like

```
$foo = ${&bar($x, $y)};
```

If we attempt to dereference something that is not a (hard) reference, Perl will treat it as a symbolic reference. Thus if we have given a value to a variable $foo, e.g.

```
$foo = 'bar';
```

then $$foo will be interpreted as $bar, i.e. the value of $foo will be treated as an identifier name. This can be dangerous: if you intended $foo to be a hard reference there will be no warning that things have gone wrong. To avoid the danger you can use the statement

```
use strict 'refs'
```

to ensure that only hard references are allowed. The scope of the restriction extends to the end of the block in which it occurs: it is most usual to place the statement at the head of the script.

3.8.6 References to arrays and hashes

References to arrays and hashes are used in two main contexts, construction of data structures and passing arrays or hashes as arguments to subroutines. We describe this latter application first, returning to data structures later.

If a subroutine takes a single argument which is an array, there is an advantage in passing a reference, since this avoids making a copy of the (possibly large) array in @_. (Use of a typeglob as described earlier is an alternative, but is deprecated.) If a subroutine has more than one argument, and one or more of the arguments is an array, use of references is essential. For example, suppose we have a subroutine p which takes two arrays as arguments. The 'obvious' syntax for a call, &p(@a, @b); does not have the desired effect. The calling sequence effectively does an assignment @_ = (@a, @b); and this will produce a single flat list containing all the elements of @a followed by all the elements of @b. To get the effect of passing arrays, we have to pass references to arrays, and dereference within the body of the subroutine. This has the side benefit that we can also pass array 'constants' as parameters, since an array composer returns a reference to an anonymous array. Typical calls might be

```
p(\@a, \@b);
p(["cat", "kitten"], ["dog", "puppy"]);
```

and the skeleton of the body is

```
sub p {
 my ($arg1, $arg2) = @_;
 ...
}
```

Elements of args *are accessed as* $$arg1[0] *etc. in the body.*

Note particularly that when we write $$arg1[0], the sequence is first to dereference $$arg1, and then to apply the subscripting operation. An alternative way of dereferencing an array reference is to do it explicitly using the arrow operator: since arg1 in the above example is a reference to an array we can write $arg1->[0] in place of $$arg1[0] without change of meaning. The arrow operator is generally regarded as the clearest way of specifying dereferencing: we shall see more examples of its use later in this chapter.

Similar considerations apply to references to hashes: in particular, if $h is a reference to a hash we can access an element of the hash as %$h{'key'} or $h -> {'key'}.

3.8.7   References to subroutines

The most common use of a reference to a subroutine is to pass a subroutine as an argument to another subroutine. For example, a generic sort subroutine might be called with two arguments, the first a reference to a subroutine that determines the ordering of two items supplied to it as arguments, and the second the array to be sorted:

```
sub genericsort {
my $ordering = shift;
my @array = @_;
...
if &$ordering($array[i], $array[j]) ...
```

As with arrays and hashes, the arrow operator can be used for dereferencing, thus:

```
if ($ordering -> ($array[i], $array[j])) ...
```

(An experienced programmer would pass the array as a reference as described above.)

Anonymous subroutines

Suppose that we have a family of related subroutines, sub1, sub2 and sub3, and we wish to be able to call a particular subroutine depending on the outcome of a run-time computation. We can do this by creating an array of references to them, thus

```
@subs = (\&sub1, \&sub2, \&sub3);
```

A particular subroutine can then be selected at run-time as `&${$subs[i]}`. The names used for the subroutines are in fact completely arbitrary, and we could get the same effect with

```
@subs = ( sub {...}, sub {...}, sub {...} );
```

Callbacks

References to subroutines and anonymous subroutines are particularly useful in contexts where callbacks have to be associated with asynchronous events: for example, you may want your script to perform some special action when the user presses Ctrl-C, which would otherwise terminate the script. On UNIX systems Perl supports the UNIX method of inter-process communication using signals. On other platforms a subset of this facility is provided, depending on the capability of the underlying operating system. (NT4 provides most of the capabilities required, but on Windows 9x Perl just simulates the 'interrupt' signal when Ctrl-C is pressed.)

Signals are identified by reserved strings, e.g. `"INT"` (keyboard interrupt), `"ZERO"` (divide by zero), `"ALRM"` (timeout) and `"CHLD"` (child process terminated). The special hash `%SIG` has these signals as its keys, and a signal can be trapped by setting the corresponding value in the hash to be a reference to a subroutine, the *signal handler*. For example, if we have defined a subroutine `ctrl_C` to take appropriate action when the user interrupts execution with Ctrl-C, we can capture the signal with

```
$SIG{"INT"} = \&ctrl_C;
```

For reasons related to the C libraries used in the implementation of Perl, and too complicated to go into here, signal handlers should be as short as possible. This means that an anonymous subroutine constructor can often be used, e.g.

```
$SIG{"INT"} = sub {die "ctrl-c"};
```

This seems pointless at first sight, until we remember that we can catch errors that arise in an `eval` block (see Section 3.7). Thus we enclose the section of code for which we want to intercept Ctrl-C in an `eval` block: if the user presses Ctrl-C, execution of the block will be terminated and the special variable `$@` will contain the string `"ctrl-c"` on exit from the block.

We shall see more examples of callbacks when we come to Perl-Tk in Chapter 6.

3.8.8   References and subroutine prototypes

The calling sequence for a subroutine that expects references as parameters can be simplified by using a subroutine prototype. If we write the above declaration as

```
sub p (\@\@) {
  my ($arg1, $arg2) = @_;
  ...
}
```

Elements of args *are accessed as* $$arg1[0] *etc. in the body.*

the prototype (\@\@) specifies that the subroutine will be called with two arguments which are arrays, and that the arguments are to be passed as *references to the arrays*, allowing the user to use the natural calling sequence

```
p(@a, @b);
```

However, note that we cannot provide explicit lists as arguments, e.g.

```
p(("cat", "kitten"), ("dog", "puppy"));
```

since the prototype specifies *array* parameters. This generalizes to any kind of parameter, e.g. \$ in a prototype specifies a scalar as the actual argument, to be passed as a reference.

The symbol & in a prototype indicates that the parameter is an anonymous subroutine. Like most things related to prototypes, this is not as simple as it looks. If we declare a subroutine with such a prototype, e.g.

```
sub sort (&@) {
    ...
}
```

then when the subroutine is called the first argument must be an anonymous subroutine composer, e.g.

```
sort((sub {...}), @myarray);
```

You might think that you could call the subroutine with a reference to a subroutine as the first argument, but the compiler will reject this. If you want this style of calling the prototype must be ($@), since a reference is a scalar.

3.8.9 Closures

An important use for anonymous subroutines is in constructing *closures*. This is best illustrated by an example. Consider the following definition:

```
sub tricky {
  my $x = shift;
  return sub {print "$x and $_[0]"};
}
```

This somewhat esoteric topic can safely be omitted if you do not know what is meant by 'static locals'.

The subroutine `tricky` expects one argument, and returns a reference to an anonymous subroutine, which also expects one argument. The body of the anonymous subroutine includes a reference to $x, and as this occurred within the scope of the my declaration, the $x in the body of the anonymous subroutine is the *local* $x. Thus if we write

```
$sub = &tricky("green");
```

then the value of $sub is a reference to an anonymous subroutine whose body contains the 'frozen' value of `tricky`'s $x – in this case the string "green". If later in the script we have

```
$x = "yellow";
&$sub("red");
```

then the output is 'green and red', not 'yellow and red'. This is because the body of the anonymous subroutine has been executed in the environment in which it was declared, not the environment in which it is executed. It carries its declaration-time environment with it: this combination of code and environment is what computer scientists call a closure.

This looks like nothing more than clever trickery, but closures can be very useful, since they allow us to provide the equivalent of static local variables, i.e. local variables whose values are remembered between calls. To see why this is so, we need to consider what happens when a script runs. In the normal course of events, local variables declared with my are allocated memory at the time of declaration, and this memory is de-allocated at the end of the innermost enclosing block, What in fact happens is that Perl allocates the memory and assigns a reference count of 1, to indicate that there is one reference to this variable. At the end of a block, the reference counts of variables declared in the block are decremented by 1, and if the resulting count is zero the memory is de-allocated. However, if a subroutine defines a closure, and the body of the anonymous subroutine contains a variable that is currently in local scope, the reference count of that variable will be increased to 2. At the end of the block the reference count will fall to 1, but as it is not zero, the memory will not be de-allocated. Thus if in the body of the anonymous subroutine we assign a value to that variable that value will still be there when the anonymous subroutine is next called.

An example may make this clearer. Suppose we require a subroutine that will return the next value in a sequence each time it is called, e.g. the powers of 2. First define

```
sub p2gen {
   my $n = 1;
   return sub {
               $n *= 2;
            }
}
```

Now if we set

```
$powers_of_two = p2gen;
```

then the call

```
&$powers_of_two;
```

will return 2: subsequent calls will return 4, 8, 16 and so on.

3.9 Data structures

3.9.1 Arrays of arrays

In C, a two-dimensional array is constructed as an array of arrays, reflected in the syntax for accessing an element, e.g. a[0][1]. This technique does not work in Perl, since it is not possible to create a LISP-like list of lists. However, a similar effect can be obtained by creating an array of references to anonymous arrays. Suppose we write

```
@colours = ([42, 128, 244], [24, 255, 0],
            [0, 127, 127]);
```

The array composer converts each comma-separated list to an anonymous array in memory and returns a *reference* to it, so that @colours is in fact an array of references to anonymous arrays. When we write an expression like

```
$colours[0][1] = 64;
```

$colours[0] is a reference to an array, and applying a subscript to it forces dereferencing, returning the anonymous array from which an element is selected by the second subscript. (In fact, Perl inserts a dereferencing operator -> between an adjacent] and [.)

Prior to Perl 5 the only way to obtain the effect of an array of arrays was to construct an array containing the names of the component arrays:

```
@colours = ('colour1', 'colour2', 'colour3');
```

How do you change the value of an element in the array colour1? With great difficulty: it involves constructing a Perl statement and using eval to call the interpreter to evaluate it at run-time, as follows.

```
$colours = $colours[0];
eval "\$${colours}[1] = 64";
```

Here, the first $ is escaped: the second $ causes string substitution, giving $colour1[1].

An alternative way was to use a typeglob. Recall that if a string value is assigned to a typeglob, this creates a variable whose name is the same as the string. Thus, since $colours[0] is a name (stored as a string),

```
*colours = $colours[0];
$colours[1] = 64;
```

does the job. This technique is much more efficient, but no more readable.

A two-dimensional array can be created dynamically by repeatedly using the push operator to add a reference to an anonymous array to the top-level array. For example, if we have a rectangular table of data stored in a file as a series of lines in which fields are separated by whitespace, it can be converted into an apparent two-dimensional array by repeatedly using split to put the fields of a line into a list, making this an anonymous array, then using push to add the reference to an array, as follows:

```
while (<STDIN>) {
 push @table, [split]
}
```

3.9.2 Complex data structures

By analogy with the array of arrays, which is actually an array of references to arrays, we can create hashes of (references to) hashes. This is a very common data structure in Perl, since the anonymous hash provides a way of providing the capability of records (structs) in other languages. Likewise, we can create arrays of (references to) hashes and hashes of (references to) arrays. By combining all these possibilities, data structures of immense complexity can be created. As an example, we sketch out the implementation of a doubly-linked list.

Such a list can have a variety of representations (there's more than one way to do it): we choose to make each element of the array a hash containing three fields with keys 'L' (left neighbour), 'R' (right neighbour) and 'C' (content). The values associated with L and R are references to element hashes (or undef for non-existent neighbours): the value associated with C can be anything – scalar, array, hash or reference to some complex structure. Typically we will have two scalar variables containing references to element hashes: $head, a reference to the first element in the list, and $current, a reference to the element of current interest: the content of the current element is evidently accessed by $current->{'C'}.

We can move forwards along the list with

```
$current = $current->{'R'};
```

and backwards with

```
$current = $current->{'L'};
```

If we create a new element with

```
$new = {L=>undef, R=>undef, C=>...};
```

we can insert this element after the current element with

```
$new->{'R'} = $current->{'R'};
$current{'R'}->{'L'} = $new;
$current{'R'} = $new;
$new->{'L'} = $current;
```

Finally we can delete the current element with

```
$current->{'L'}->{'R'} = $current->{'R'};
$current->{'R'}->{'L'} = $current->{'L'};
```

(There are a few loose ends to tidy up, but the basic ideas should be apparent.)

3.10 Packages

A package is a unit of code with its own namespace (i.e. a separate symbol table), which determines bindings of names both at compile-time and run-time. (Run-time name lookup happens when symbolic references are de-referenced, and during execution of eval.) Initially, code runs in the default package main. Variables used in a package are global to that package, but invisible in any other package unless a 'fully qualified name' is used, thus $A::x$ is the variable x in package A, while $B::x$ is the (different) variable x in package B, and x is the variable x in the package main. The special punctuation-only variables like $_ belong to the main package, but are visible in other packages without a main:: qualifier. Note that locally-scoped variables declared in a my declaration are a lexical device, and are therefore not associated with a package: a declaration like

```
my $A::x;
```

is a compile-time error.

A package is introduced by the package declaration, and extends to the end of the innermost enclosing block, or until another package declaration is encountered. In this case the original package declaration is temporarily hidden. To understand this, remember that *all* a package declaration does is to switch to a different symbol table, so that if we write

```
package A;
$x = 0;
...
package B;
$x = 1;
...
package A;
print $x;
```

the value printed is zero. The package B declaration switches to a different symbol table, then the package A declaration reverts to the original symbol table in which $x has the value 0. An illusion of nested packages can be created by using package names of the form A::B. However, this is purely a syntactic device: package A::B has no necessary connection with package A, and all references to variables from outside the package (even from package A) must be of the fully qualified form, e.g. $A::B::x.

A package can have one or more BEGIN routines processed (in sequence) at *compile-time*, before the code of the package is interpreted, and one or more END routines, executed (in LIFO sequence) as late as possible, when the interpreter exits (even as a result of an exception). These allow initialization and tidying up, in much the same way as object constructors and destructors.

The package declaration is rarely used on its own. Packages are the basis for libraries, modules and objects, and we now describe these higher-level constructs.

3.11 Libraries and modules

Packages, as we have seen, provide elementary control over namespaces. Several package declarations can occur in a single file: alternatively, a single package can extend over multiple files. Libraries and modules, on the other hand, are packages contained within a single file, and are units of program reusability. The power of Perl is immensely enhanced by the existence of a large number of publicly available libraries and modules that provide functionality in specific application areas. Indeed, largely due to the wealth of modules available, Perl is moving away from its roots in 'throw-away' programming to being a serious language for major projects.

3.11.1 Libraries

A library is a collection of subroutines that can be used in some specific area, e.g. a collection of mathematical functions. Although libraries have been largely superseded by modules, described later, we give a brief account of the library mechanism here.

A library is usually declared as a package to give it a private namespace, and is stored in a separate file with an extension .pl. Thus we might have a library of mathematical functions in a library stored in a file Math.pl. These subroutines can be loaded into a program by placing the statement

```
require "Math.pl";
```

at the head of the program. If the library is declared as a package called Math, we can call its functions using fully qualified names, e.g.

```
$rootx = Math::sqrt($x);
```

(Recall that we can omit the ampersand from a subroutine name provided that the subroutine has been defined before we call it: by definition, subroutines in a package are predefined.)

3.11.2 Modules

Libraries have been largely superseded by modules, which provide enhanced functionality. Strictly speaking, a module is just a package that is contained in a separate file whose name is the same as the package name, with the extension .pm; however, modules follows certain specific conventions and take advantage of built-in support that makes them a powerful form of reusable software. From the user's point of view, the great thing about a module is that the names of the subroutines in the module are automatically imported into the namespace of the program using the package. Thus if the collection of mathematical routines in the library Math.pl are converted into a module Math.pm, the user merely writes

```
use Math;
```

at the start of a program, and the subroutines are available as if they were defined in the program. This transparent extendibility of the language is immensely powerful – members of the Perl community regularly contribute modules for a variety of application areas.

To be precise, the subroutine names imported are those defined in the *export list* of the math module. Selective importing of names is allowed, e.g.

```
use Math ('sin', 'cos', 'tan');
```

(Clearly, the names specified for import must be in the module's export list.) It is possible to suppress the import of names, e.g.

```
use Math ();
```

but this rather loses the point of the module.

Related modules are usually collected into a directory: for example

```
use IO::File;
```

indicates a requirement for the module `File.pm`, which will be found in a directory called `IO`, which is located using a system default path for module directories. Nowadays most modules are structured as collections of objects rather than subroutines. Before exploring this way of working we give a short account of the mechanics of modules for those who are interested.

3.11.3   The mechanics of modules

The 'use' statement

When you write `use Math;` at the head of a script, the effect is as if you had written

```
BEGIN {
    require "Math.pm";
    Math::import();
}
```

If you write

```
use Math ('sin', 'cos', 'tan');
```

the effect is as if you had written

```
BEGIN {
    require "Math.pm";
    Math::import('sin', 'cos', 'tan');
}
```

However, if you explicitly suppress name import with `use Math ();` this equates to

```
BEGIN {
    require "Math.pm";
}
```

Finding the module

The statement `require "Math.pm";` loads the module code if it is not already present. Remember that `BEGIN` blocks are processed at compile time, thus we can be assured that modules requested in `use` statements are successfully loaded before execution of our script starts. How does Perl find the module? It first looks in the current directory. If the module file is not found there, it next searches the directories listed in the array `@INC` which is set up when the Perl interpreter is installed, and contains a platform-specific list of directories.

Importing the names

The module names are imported by calling the import() method defined in the module. The package writer is free to define import() in any way: in practice, most modules inherit the import() method provided as part of the Exporter module. (Just don't ask why the import() method appears in the Exporter module!)

Suppose that our hypothetical Math module is written the standard way, using Exporter. The first few lines of the file Math.pm are

```
package Math;
require Exporter;
@ISA = 'Exporter';
@EXPORT = qw(...);
@EXPORT_OK = qw(...);
```

The second line ensures that the Exporter package is loaded. The significance of the third line will be apparent after we have explained Perl's object system in the next section: essentially it ensures that if the package calls any subroutines that are not declared within the package, Perl will look for them in (inherit them from) the Exporter package. This is how the default import() routine is found. The array @EXPORT contains the names of the subroutines that are to be exported by default, and the array @EXPORT_OK contains a list of variables (scalars, arrays and hashes) and subroutines that will be exported on request.

The import() routine first uses the built-in function caller to get the name of the package that has called it. If we start a program with

```
use Math;
```

then, as we have seen, the subroutine Math::import() is called. The inheritance ensures that Exporter::import() is called: its caller is main since the use statement occurred outside a named package. The import() routine then enters a loop: for each subroutine name in the @EXPORT array it sets up a selective alias in the caller's symbol table with a statement like

```
*{"main::sqrt"} = \&sqrt;
```

3.12 Objects

Objects in 'real' object-oriented programming (OOP) are encapsulations of data and methods, defined by classes. Important aspects of OOP technology are inheritance and polymorphism. Objects in Perl provide a similar functionality, but in a different way: they use the same terminology as OOP, but the words have different meanings, as demonstrated below.

- **Objects**   An object is an anonymous data structure (usually, but not necessarily, a hash) that is accessed by a reference, has been assigned to a class, and knows what class it belongs to. We have not defined classes yet: just remember that a Perl class is not the same thing as an OOP class. The object is said to be *blessed* into a class: this is done by calling the built-in function `bless` in a constructor.
- **Constructors**   There is no special syntax for constructors: a constructor is just a subroutine that returns a reference to an object.
- **Classes**   A class is a package that provides methods to deal with objects that belong to it. There is no special syntax for class definition.
- **Methods**   Finally, a method is a subroutine that expects an object reference as its first argument (or a package name for class methods).

To sum up, an object is just a chunk of referenced data, but the blessing operation ties it to a package that provides the methods to manipulate that data. Thus there is no encapsulation, but there is an association between data and methods.

3.12.1   Constructors

Objects are created by a constructor subroutine which is generally (but not necessarily) called new. For example:

```
package Animal;
sub new {
  my $ref = {};
  bless ref;
  return ref;
}
```

Remember that `{}` returns a reference to an anonymous hash. So the `new` constructor returns a reference to an object that is an empty hash, and knows (via the `bless` function) that it belongs to the package `Animal`. Note that a practised Perl hacker would write this constructor as

```
package Animal;
sub new {return bless {};}
```

The use of the term 'bless' is not very felicitous: the function might better be called 'tag', because that is exactly what it does. It attaches a tag to the anonymous data structure recording that it 'belongs' to a particular package. Indeed, if you use the `ref` operator on an object reference, it returns the name of the package to which the object belongs. This tagging is required in order to implement polymorphism, with late binding of method calls, as we shall see shortly.

3.12.2   Instances

With this constructor defined we can create instances of the object (strictly speaking, references to instances), e.g.

```
$Dougal = new Animal;
$Ermyntrude = new Animal;
```

This makes $Dougal and $Ermyntrude references to objects that are empty hashes, and 'know' that they belong to the class Animal. Note that although the right-hand side of the assignment, new Animal, looks superficially like a simple call of a subroutine new with one argument Animal, it is in fact a special syntax for calling the subroutine new in the *package* Animal. The package name is in fact made available to the constructor as an argument, but is ignored in straightforward cases like this since the constructor already knows what package it is in. (This will become clearer when we discuss 'class methods' in Section 3.12.4.)

3.12.3 Method invocation

Let's suppose that data for the animal object is a hash with entries keyed by properties, e.g. species, colour, weight. The package will contain instance methods for working on such objects: for the Animal class these might include methods to set and return the species of a particular animal. An instance method always has an object reference as its first argument, identifying the particular instance of the class that is the target for the operation, so our methods will be something like

```
sub get_species {
  my $self = shift;
  return $self->{'Species'};
  }
sub set_species {
  my $self = shift;
  $self->{'Species'} = shift;
  }
```

We could invoke these functions in the classic OO form:

```
$Dougal->set_species 'Dog';
$Dougal_is = $Dougal->get_species;
```

When the dereferencing (arrow) operator is used with a 'blessed' reference as its left argument, its right argument is recognized as a call of a subroutine in the package to which the object belongs, and that subroutine is called with the object reference inserted before the arguments supplied. Thus the first call above is dynamically resolved first to

```
set_species($Dougal, 'Dog');
```

and then, via the tag attached to $Dougal by the bless operation in the constructor, to

```
Animal::set_species($Dougal, 'Dog');
```

Note that the dynamic resolution of the method provides polymorphism: other objects can have their own set-species and get_species methods.

An alternative syntax for method invocation is the so-called 'indirect object' form (indirect object as in 'He gave the dog the bone'):

```
set_species $Dougal 'Dog';
$Dougal_is = get_species $Dougal;
```

Note particularly in the first call that there is no comma after the object reference: compare the syntax of a print statement with an explicit file handle:

```
print STDERR "Oops!"
```

These are just syntactic variations: both forms are provided because sometimes one is clearer than the other (and there's more than one way to do it).

3.12.4 Attributes

In our Animal class, Species is an item of *instance data*, otherwise known as an *attribute*. The set_species and get_species methods described above are a standard way of handling attributes, but an alternative approach favoured by some programmers is to combine the two into a single function:

```
sub species {
   my $self = shift;
   if (@a_) {$self->{'Species'} = shift;}
   return $self->{'Species'}
}
```

The trick here is to remember that the condition of an if statement is evaluated in a scalar context, so @_ returns the length of the argument array after the shift operation. If the function was originally called with an argument, this will still be there after the object reference has been shifted off, the condition will evaluate to true, and the assignment to the hash will take place: otherwise the current value is returned.

When this function is used to assign a new value, it trivially returns that value. It is sometimes useful for the function to return the previous value:

```
sub species {
   my $self = shift;
   my $was = $self->{'Species'};
   if (@a_) {$self->{'Species'} = shift;}
   return $was;
}
```

3.12.5 Class methods and attributes

In the examples we have seen so far, method calls are applied to a particular *instance* of the object class. There may be operations that are relevant to the class, but don't need to operate on a specific instance. Such operations are called class methods (or static methods). Likewise, there may be attributes (data) that are common to all instances of a class: we call these class attributes.

Class attributes are just package global variables: class methods are just subroutines that do not require an object reference as the first argument: the new constructor defined earlier is an example. However, Perl provides polymorphism though late binding for class methods as well as instance methods. The full definition of the new constructor for the Animal class is

```
package Animal;
sub new {
my $package = shift;
my $obj = {};
  bless $obj, $package;
  return $obj;
}
```

When the dereferencing operator finds a package name as its left argument, as in

```
$Dougal = Animal->new();
```

it locates the subroutine given as the right argument in the specified package, and passes the package name as the first argument of the subroutine call. The utility of this is illustrated in the next section.

3.12.6 Inheritance

Perl only provides method inheritance. Inheritance is realized by including a special array @ISA in the package that defines the derived class. For single inheritance, @ISA is an array of one element, the name of the base class. However, by making @ISA an array of more than one element, multiple inheritance can be realized. Each element in the array @ISA is the name of another package that is being used as a class. If a method cannot be found, the packages referenced in @ISA are recursively searched, depth first. The current class is the derived class: those referenced in @ISA are the base classes. Evidently, if the current package contains a method with the same name as a method in one of the base classes, the method in the current package will be called. This makes it possible to override a method inherited from a base class. If, in this situation, you want to invoke the method provided by the base class, you can use a pseudoclass provided by Perl called SUPER, e.g.

```
$s = SUPER::foo();
```

When using derived classes, we have to make sure that the constructor defines the package into which the object is blessed. As an illustration, suppose we have a derived class Stuffed_Animals, with base class Toy_Animals. Since the constructor is a class method it works in the context of the base class, and to generate instances of the derived class, we have to use the form of constructor described in the previous section. We create instances of Stuffed_Animals with

```
$obj = new Stuffed_Animals;
```

or

```
$obj = Stuffed_Animals->new();
```

3.12.7 Summing up

We see that the Perl realization of objects is based on maximum reuse of existing concepts and syntax. Although the Perl object system may seem confusing at first sight, familiarity comes with use, and it has been generally adopted as the vehicle of choice for writing modules.

3.13 Objects and modules in action

As we have remarked above, the modules contributed by the Perl community cover a wide range of applications, and whatever you want to do there is a good chance that you will find a module, or collection of modules, to do the job. Using this pre-written code gives you immense leverage, and we shall see some spectacular examples when we discuss the use of Perl in Web programming in Section 3.17. First we give some simpler examples of how useful modules can be.

3.13.1 Filehandles revisited

We have noted earlier that filehandles are second class citizens in Perl: we cannot store them in arrays or hashes, and we can only pass them as arguments to a subroutine with great difficulty, using typeglobs. The IO::File module wraps a filehandle in a filehandle object, effectively making them first class citizens – the object reference can be stored in an array or hash, and can be passed as a subroutine argument like any other scalar.

The filehandle object constructor replaces the open function, and supports all the variations supported by the open function, e.g.

```
use IO::File
$in = IO::File->new('<data.txt');
$out = IO::File->new('>results.txt');
$who = IO::File->new('who|');
```

If the operation is unsuccessful, new returns undef. If the object reference returned is used in a context where a filehandle is expected it will be automatically dereferenced, e.g.

```
print $out "Hello World!\n";
```

or

```
while (<$in>) {
 print
}
```

The filehandle object also has a close method, e.g.

```
$in->close;
```

Since a filehandle object reference is a scalar, it can be localized with a my declaration. In this case, the file will be closed automatically when the variable goes out of scope.

Note that `IO::File` is a slightly unusual use of modules, since it requires a modification to the core Perl system to accept object references in place of filehandles. The great majority of modules simply provide 'bolt-on' extensions to the functionality of the language.

3.13.2 Bar charts

Suppose that Scripts'r'Us Inc. has surveyed the use of different scripting languages within the organization, and has found the following percentage usage figures:

Perl	45%
Tcl	10%
JavaScript	20%
Visual Basic	25%

The information conveyed would clearly have more impact as a bar chart, as shown in Figure 3.1.

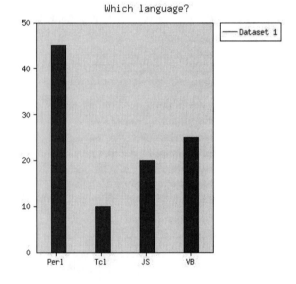

Figure 3.1 Bar chart representation of data

Using the `Chart` module, we can produce the bar chart with exactly eight lines of Perl:

```
use Chart::Bars;
@langs = qw/Perl Tcl JS VB/;
@use = qw/45 10 20 25/;
```

```
my $bar = Chart::Bars->new(400,400);
$bar->set('title', 'Which language?');
$bar->add_dataset(@langs);
$bar->add_dataset(@use);
$bar->gif('chart.gif');
```

The code is almost self-explanatory. Lines 2 and 3 set up two arrays, the labels for the bars and the sizes of the bars. Line 3 creates a bar-chart object: the arguments are the dimensions of the chart in pixels. The remaining lines construct the chart and specify a file in which to store the image. Note that this code could be used in a CGI script to create an image for a Web page on the fly.

The Chart module can produce a variety of chart formats: see the Perl documentation for details.

3.13.3   Text wrapping

If you are producing a formatted report, e.g. from a log file, you may need to wrap the text, i.e. force a line break at the end of the last word that will fit on a line. The Text::Wrap module makes this easy, as shown in the following example.

```
use Text::Wrap;
# create a very long string as an example
$a = "Now entertain conjecture of a time when" .
        "creeping murmur and the stilly night fill" .
        "the wide vessel of the universe. From" .
        "camp to camp the hum of either army" .
        "faintly sounds\n";
$Text::Wrap::columns = 40; #set line length
$in1 = "    ";
$in2 = "";
print "$a\n\n";
print Text::Wrap::wrap($in1, $in2, $a),
"\n\n";
```

Lines 3–7 assign a very long string to $a. Line 8 specifies the desired width of the output: note that here we are assigning a value to one of the module's variables, rather than calling a method. Lines 9 and 10 define the indent for the first line and subsequent lines of the output, and line 11 calls the wrap method of Text::Wrap to do the actual work. The output printed is as follows.

```
    Now entertain conjecture of a time
when creeping murmur and the stilly
night fill the wide vessel of the
universe. From camp to camp the hum of
either army faintly sounds
```

3.14 Tied variables

Another example of modules and objects can be found in so-called *tied variables*, which allow us to intercept access to a variable transparently – whenever the variable is used we in fact invoke methods in an associated object class. Thus if a hash has been tied, an attempt to read the value indexed by a given key is diverted to the FETCH method of the associated class, and updating an entry or adding a new entry is diverted to the STORE method. Similarly, use of exists() and delete() is diverted to the EXISTS and DELETE methods of the associated class. The class must also provide methods FIRSTKEY and NEXTKEY to support iterations over the hash. The tied hash is most commonly used to implement persistent hashes or to provide transparent access to a database – the FETCH and STORE methods might access an SQL database over the network, but to the user the data still appears to be in a hash. Scalars, arrays and filehandles can also be tied to objects, but the tied hash is the most common instance of the technique. As an example of a tied hash we present a script that was developed for a real-world UNIX system admin-istration task [1]. This example repays study not only as an illustration of a tied hash, but also as an example of the programming style that is typical of the experienced Perl hacker.

When the UNIX shell executes a command it creates a new process for the purpose. The problem is to kill all the processes that are running the 'sleep' command. As you might expect, this command does nothing for a specified length of time: don't ask why it was necessary to kill these processes. A running process is identified by a unique process identifier (pid), and information about running processes can be obtained using the ps (process state command), which displays one line per process giving the process number, assorted information about the status and the command string which started the process, e.g.

```
8453    1 S    0:43 xclock -geometry 75x75-1+0
```

So to solve our problem we divert this information into a tied hash in which the key is a process number, the value is the corresponding command string, and deleting an entry kills the process. If the tied hash is called %procs, then all we need is a simple loop:

```
while (($pid, $procname) = each %procs) {
    if ($procname =~ /sleep/) {
        delete $procs{$pid};
    }
}
```

The code follows. First we define a module Tieps: since this gets complicated at times, we have added a commentary to explain what is going on.

```
package Tieps;
use strict;
```

(Require declarations for all variables.)

```
sub TIEHASH {
  my $pkg = shift;
  my $obj = {};
```

```
    $obj->{procs} = [];
    bless($obj, $pkg);
}
```

(This is the constructor, which populates the anonymous hash with an empty anonymous array identified by key `procs`. As with all the methods involved in a tie, the name is prescribed by Perl, since it is used as an internal hook. The use of upper case for such variable names is a Perl convention.)

```
sub FETCH {
    my $obj = shift;
    my ($pid) = @_;
    my $procname = `/bin/ps h $pid`;
    chomp($procname);
    $procname =~ s/^.*\d:\d\d //;
    $procname;
}
```

(This method retrieves the program name for a process whose pid is given as an argument. Line 4 executes a shell command, which returns one line giving the status of the process whose pid is given as an argument: the h option suppresses the header line. Section 3.15.3 explains the mechanism. Referring to the example of output from *ps* on the preceding page, we see that the regular expression in line 6 matches the whole line up to the start of the command string, and the substitute operator deletes this. The final line returns the command string as the required value. In this example the tied hash is read only, so there is no STORE method.)

```
sub FIRSTKEY {
    my $obj = shift;
    my @procs = `/bin/ps ahx`;
    map { $_ = (/(\d+)/)[0] } @procs;
    $obj->{procs} = \@procs;
    shift(@{ $obj->{procs} });
}
```

(This bit of code is full of low cunning. Line 3 runs a shell command to return the process status for all running processes, which gets stored in the array @procs, one line per process. Note that this @procs is a local variable, not to be confused with the anonymous array stored in the object with the key 'procs'. The map statement in line 4 converts @procs into an array containing just the pids, one per element. The regular expression matches a digit string, and since map imposes a list context, matches with bracketed sub-expressions are returned as an array. Rather than assigning this to a variable, the writer has just subscripted the expression to get the first match, which is the desired pid. Within the block that specifies the mapping, $_ is set to each array element in turn. In fact, $_ becomes an alias for the array element, so by assigning to it we modify the array in place. Line 5 places a reference to this array of pids as the value of the element with key procs in the object. Since the *ps* command runs in a separate process it will report its own pid, and this is discarded in line 6. Note the use of the special syntax to ensure that the dereferencing happens in list context.)

```
sub NEXTKEY {
    my $obj = shift;
    shift(@{ $obj->{procs} });
}
```

(This is straightforward. Line 3 strips off the first pid in the array and returns it as the subroutine value, moving all the other elements up one place.)

```
sub DELETE {
    my $obj = shift;
    my ($pid) = @_;
    kill -9, $pid;
}
```

(This too is fairly straightforward. The first argument, which is always a reference to an object, is discarded, and the next argument is the pid of the process to be removed. The kill function is badly named, as it is in UNIX also: it does not of itself kill a process, but just sends a signal to it. In this case the argument -9, which matches the UNIX format, sends the 'sudden death' signal, which causes instant but clean termination of the process.)

```
1;
```

(By convention, module definitions always return true to signify successful completion.)

Having defined the Tieps module, and stored it in a file called Tieps.pm, we can now write a script to do the actual job of clearing out the sleeping processes.

```
#!/usr/bin/perl -w

use Tieps;
use strict;
```

(use Tieps makes the subroutines defined in the module available in the rest of the script. use strict enforces variable declarations as before.)

```
my %procs;
tie %procs, "Tieps";
```

(The tie function sets up the association of the hash with the object that is going to implement it. It implicitly calls the constructor TIEHASH and sets up hooks to the FETCH, FIRSTKEY, NEXTKEY and DELETE methods.)

```
my ($pid, $procname);
while (($pid, $procname) = each(%procs)) {
    if ($procname =~ /sleep/) {
        delete $procs{$pid};
        print $pid, "\t", $procname, " killed\n";
    }
}
```

(This is essentially the loop given earlier. The first time round the `while` loop, `each` will use `FIRSTKEY` to get a key, and `FETCH` to get the value associated with that key, returning them as values of `$pid` and `$procname` respectively. Subsequent iterations will use `NEXTKEY` and `FETCH`. The regular expression match in line 3 selects the sleeping processes, which are deleted in line 4. Here, the access to the hash will be diverted to `FETCH`, and the delete operation will be diverted to `DELETE`.)

3.15 Interfacing to the operating system

The original UNIX implementation of Perl mirrored the most used system calls as built-in functions, so that Perl could be used as an alternative to writing shell scripts. When Perl was ported to other platforms, an attempt was made to mirror the system calls of the host system, but with the same syntax as the calls in the UNIX version – recall the comment in Chapter 2 about 'a portable distillation of the UNIX environment'. The extent to which system calls can be replicated obviously depends critically on the capabilities of the host operating system. Windows NT is able to provide equivalents for most UNIX facilities, and in this section we describe a collection of facilities that are common to the UNIX and NT implementations of Perl. We conclude with a summary of NT-specific facilities. (The NT implementation that we describe is ActivePerl, produced by Active State Tool Corp.)

This section describes the operating system interface that is common to UNIX and Windows NT. Facilities described here may not be available on other platforms.

3.15.1 Environment variables

The current environment variables are stored in the special hash `%ENV`. A script can read them or change them by accessing this hash. A clever trick is to make a temporary change to an individual variable, taking advantage of the fact that the `local` operator can give just one element of an array or hash a temporary value, e.g.

```
{ local $ENV{"PATH"} = ...;
  ...
}
```

The commands inside the block are executed with the new `PATH` variable, which is replaced by the original one on exit from the block.

3.15.2 File system calls

All return a value indicating success or failure, so a typical idiom is

```
chdir $x or die "cannot chdir to $x\n";
```

Here we have used the ultra-low precedence `or` operator; we could equally well have written

```
chdir $x || die "cannot chdir";
```

since named unary operators like `chdir` have higher precedence than logical operators. (However, it is a good idea to stick to `or` in this context: you will get fewer nasty surprises that way.)

Examples of the more common calls for manipulating the file system are:

```
chdir $x                Change directory
unlink $x               Same as rm in UNIX or delete in NT
rename($x, $y)          Same as mv in UNIX
link($x, $y)            Same as ln in UNIX. Not in NT
symlink($x, $y)         Same as ln -s in UNIX. Not in NT
mkdir($x, 0755)         Create directory and set modes
rmdir $x                Remove directory
chmod(0644, $x)         Set file permissions
```

3.15.3 Shell commands

Perl allows execution of shell commands in two ways, by using the built-in `system` function or by 'quoted execution'.

The system function

A simple example of the system function is

```
system("date");
```

The string given as argument is treated as a shell command to be run by */bin/sh* on UNIX, and by *cmd.exe* on NT, with the existing STDIN, STDOUT and STDERR. Any of these can be redirected using Bourne shell notation, e.g.

```
system("date >datefile") && die
   "can't redirect";
```

Note particularly the use of && rather than || as the connector: this is because shell commands returns *zero* to denote success and a non-zero value to denote failure. The system function can be given a list of arguments, in which case the first argument is treated as the command to be run, and the remaining arguments are passed on as arguments to that command, without any interpretation of special shell characters. Alternatively, the argument may be a scalar whose value is a string containing the name of a program and its arguments as blank-separated words. In this case any shell meta-characters present will be processed before the command is passed to the shell. A rather trivial example is

```
system("echo textfiles: *.txt");
```

In this case the *.txt will be expanded to a list of all the files in the current directory with the .txt extension before the echo is executed.

Quoted execution

The output of a shell command can be captured using *quoted execution*, e.g.

```
$date = `date`;
```

Here, the output of the date command is assigned to the variable $date. The precise semantics are that the result of the command replaces the back-quoted string. Since this is a form of quoting, variable substitution can take place, and by analogy with the q, qq and qw operators, any character can be used as the quotation character, e.g.

        $date = qx/date/;   *qx: quoted execution.*

(The back-tick notation is used in the UNIX shell for a similar purpose, and is included in Perl to give UNIX hackers a feeling of warm familiarity.)

3.15.4   exec

The exec function terminates the current script and executes the program named as its argument, in the same process. Thus unlike system, exec never returns, and it is otiose to have any Perl statements following it, except possibly an or die clause, e.g.

        exec "sort $output" or die "Can't exec sort\n";

exec can be used to replace the current script with a new script:

        exec "perl -w scr2.pl" or die "Exec failed\n";

(We shall see a use for this when we discuss process control in the next section.) If the argument is a list, or is a string containing blank-separated words, argument processing is the same as for the system function.

3.15.5   Process control in UNIX

Perl implements the classic UNIX process mechanism: the fork function creates a *child process* as a clone of the current process (the *parent process*), which runs in parallel with its parent. The immediate reaction of most people is to wonder what is the use of having two identical processes running in parallel, and how do they know which is which? The answer to the second question is that the value returned by fork is different in the two processes: the value returned in the parent is the process identifier of the child, while the value returned in the child is zero. The answer to the first question follows on from this: we use the value returned by the fork function to control an if-then-else construct, providing one block of code to be executed in the parent process and another block of code to be executed in the child. It is common, but not universal, to follow the classic UNIX paradigm, where almost the first thing the child process does is to use exec to start a new program running in the same process resulting in two different programs running in separate processes. Note that a parent can create multiple child processes by repeated use of fork, and a child process can itself create its own children using fork.

   The child process inherits all open filehandles (including pipes), and therefore it is usual for it to do some tidying up by closing unwanted filehandles before doing anything else. Likewise, the parent process will tidy up the filehandles as well; otherwise, confusion is likely to arise if two separate processes operate on the same filehandle.

   A simple example may help. Suppose we want to create a child process that will send data to its parent, using a pipe. (Recall from Section 3.4.3 that the pipe function sets up a pipe, returning two filehandles, one for the reading end and one for the writing end.)

```
pipe(READHANDLE, WRITEHANDLE);
if ($pid = fork) {
# here we are in the parent process
close WRITEHANDLE;
...
} elsif ($pid == 0) {
# here we are in the child process
close READHANDLE;
...
exit;
} else {
# something went wrong
die "Can't fork\n"
}
```

The parent process is going to read from the pipe, so closes WRITEHANDLE: likewise the child process is going to write to the pipe, so it closes READHANDLE. This ensures that the pipe will indicate EOF to the parent process if the child process closes it. Note the need for an explicit exit at the end of the child procedure code. This terminates the child process and causes a 'CHLD' signal to be generated: this can be trapped by the parent, as described in Section 3.8.7, if the parent needs to know when the child terminates.

A common scenario is that a parent process will want to suspend execution until a child process has completed its job. The wait function waits for a child process to terminate and returns the process identifier (pid) of the child, or -1 if there are no child processes. The waitpid function waits for completion of a child process whose pid is given as an argument, returning true when the process is dead, or -1 if there are no child processes. In both cases the exit status of the child process is returned in the special variable $?.

Before leaving this topic, we return to consider the situation that arises if the fork function is unable to create a new process. In this case, the function returns -1, and in the example above this was caught by the else clause, which just invoked die. The most common reason for fork to fail is that the user has reached the limit imposed by the operating system, or possibly that the system's process table has filled up. In either case, given the dynamic nature of process creation in UNIX, it is likely that the fork will succeed if we try again after a short delay. We can do this by checking the error message returned when fork fails: if this is 'No more processes' we wait a while and try again using redo. The final version of the code is:

```
FORK: {
  pipe(READHANDLE, WRITEHANDLE);
  if ($pid = fork) {
    # here we are in the parent process
    close WRITEHANDLE;
    ...
  } elsif ($pid == 0) {
    # here we are in the child process
    close READHANDLE;
```

```
    . . .
    exit;
  } elsif ($! =~ /No more processes/) {
    # try again
    sleep 5
    redo FORK
  } else {
    # something went horribly wrong
    die "Can't fork\n"
    }
  }
}
```

3.15.6 Process control in Windows NT

Process control in Windows NT is the province of the `Win32::Process` module. A new process is created by calling the constructor:

```
Win32::Process::Create($child,
  "D:\\winnt\\system32\\notepad.exe",
  "notepad temp.txt",
  0, NORMAL_PRIORITY_CLASS, ".") or
die "Can't create process\n";
```

The first argument is a variable to hold the object reference created by the constructor. The second and third arguments are the full path of the executable and the shell command that the process is to run. The fourth argument is 1 if the new process is to inherit the open filehandles of its parent, and 0 if the filehandles are not to be inherited. The fifth argument is a constant defining the priority of the child process, and the final argument specifies the current directory for the child process.

The child process runs in parallel with the parent, but is subject to the parent's control, e.g.

```
$Child->Suspend();
$Child->Resume();
```

The parent can wait for the child to terminate:

```
$Child->Wait(INFINITE);
```

As a protection against rogue child processes, it is better to specify a maximum waiting time:

```
$Child->Wait($timeout);
```

If the waiting period is completed without the child process completing, it can be forcibly terminated:

```
$Child->Kill($exitcode);
```

3.15.7   Accessing the Windows Registry

The `Win32::TieRegistry` module provides full access to the Windows Registry, making it appear as a tied hash. The details are beyond the scope of this book: we just give the flavour with a single example from the module documentation.

```
$Registry->Delimiter("/");
$tip18 = $Registry->
{'HKEY_LOCAL_MACHINE/Software/Microsoft/' .
'Windows/CurrentVersion/Explorer/Tips//18'};
```

`$Registry` is a reference to a tied hash that mirrors the Registry. The first line specifies forward slash as a delimiter: the actual separator used in the Registry is backslash, but this makes for difficulty in reading in Perl, because every backslash has to be escaped with another one. The assignment statement illustrates how we can navigate through the registry structure until we reach the desired item: the tied hash returns the associated value, which in this case is assigned to a variable.

3.15.8   Controlling OLE Automation servers

OLE Automation servers are discussed in detail in Chapter 8. You may want to come back to this section later.

An OLE Automation server is a Windows application which provides an interface by which it can be controlled by other applications. The interface takes the form of a collection of objects (the object model) which have properties (instance variables) and methods. The `Win32::OLE` module makes it possible for a Perl script to control an Automation server. The importance of this is that all the components of Microsoft Office are implemented as automation servers, so that programs written in Visual Basic for Applications (VBA) can control them. VBA is thus a universal macro language for the Office suite, and `Win32::OLE` makes it possible to use Perl as an alternative macro language.

The constructor starts up an instance of an automation server and returns a reference that can be used to access the properties and methods of the objects implemented by the server:

```
xl = Win32:OLE->new("Excel.Application");
```

This statement starts a new instance of Excel, and the methods of the `Excel.Application` object are invoked in the usual way, e.g.

```
ok = xl.CheckSpelling($word);
```

Alternatively,

```
xl = Win32::OLE->
   GetActiveObject("Excel.Application");
```

will return a reference to a currently running version of Excel if there is one, otherwise it returns `undef`. Yet another variation is to start up Excel with a worksheet preloaded:

```
xl = Win32::OLE->
   GetObject('c:\\accounts\\sales.xls');
```

The properties of an automation object appear to Perl as a hash: for example we can find Excel's default file path with

```
$filepath = xl->{'DefaultFilePath'};
```

Unfortunately, a new value cannot be set by writing to the hash: instead we have to say

```
xl->LetProperty('DefaultFilePath', $newpath);
```

(Writing to the hash performs a 'by reference' assignment: we want a 'by value' assignment, which is what `LetProperty` does.)

The example of firing up Excel just to do a spellcheck is perhaps a little far-fetched: `Win32::OLE` comes into its own when used with Microsoft's 'Active Data Objects' to access remote databases.

3.16   Creating 'Internet-aware' applications

The Internet is a rich source of information, held on Web servers, FTP servers, POP/IMAP mail servers, News servers etc. A Web browser can access information on Web servers and FTP servers, and specialist clients access mail and News servers. However, this is not the only way of getting to the information: an 'Internet-aware' application can access a server and collect the information without manual intervention. For example, suppose that a Web site offers a 'lookup' facility in which the user specifies a query by filling in a form, then clicks the 'Submit' button. The data from the form is sent to a CGI program on the server (probably written in Perl!), which retrieves the information, formats it as a Web page, and returns the page to the browser. A Perl application can establish a connection to the server, send the request in the format that the browser would use, collect the returned HTML and then extract the required fields that form the answer to the query. In the same way, a Perl application can establish a connection to a POP3 mail server and send a request which will result in the server returning a message listing the number of currently unread messages.

Much of the power of scripting languages comes from the way in which they hide the complexity of operations, and this is particularly the case when we make use of specialized modules: tasks that might require pages of code in C are achieved in a few lines. The LWP (Library for WWW access in Perl) collection of modules is a very good case in point: it makes the kind of interaction described above almost trivial. We describe how it is used, then go on to consider the 'nuts and bolts' of Internet programming in Perl.

3.16.1   Web access using LWP::Simple

The `LWP::Simple` module provides a simple interface to Web servers. We do not attempt to give a full account of the module: our purpose is just to illustrate the leverage that can be achieved by exploiting modules. Using `LWP::Simple` we can retrieve the contents of a Web page in a single statement:

```
use LWP::Simple
```

```
$url = "http://www.somesite.com/index.html";
$page = get($url);
```

(Note that LWP::Simple does not use objects: it provides a procedural interface for Web access.)

The get function retrieves the page content and stores it as a character string: if anything goes wrong, it returns undef. This is not particularly helpful, since lots of things can go wrong – the host may be down or busy, or the page may not exist any more. For this reason it is better to use an alternative function that has associated error checking:

```
$rc = getstore($url, "page.html");
```

retrieves that page and stores its contents in the file page.html. Analogously,

```
$rc = getprint($url);
```

sends the page content to STDOUT. The response returned in $rc is the actual code returned by the http server, e.g. 200 for success, 404 if the page is not found, etc. The is_success() and is_error() functions provided by LWP::Simple take this code as an argument and return a Boolean value. If it is required to test for particular outcomes we can use the 'constants' defined in the HTTP::Status package, which are imported by LWP::Simple. For example,

```
use LWP::Simple

$url = "http://www.somesite.com/index.html";
$rc = getstore($url, "page.html");
die "page not found" if $rc == RC_NOT_FOUND;
```

These so-called constants are in fact functions defined in HTTP::Status with definitions like.

```
sub RC_NOT_FOUND () {404}
```

This technique provides a feature equivalent to 'hash-define' constants (macros) in C, and enumerations in Visual Basic.

We often wish to fetch a page only if it has been modified since we last fetched it. This is done by the mirror() method:

```
use LWP::Simple

$url = "http://www.somesite.com/index.html";
$rc = mirror($url, "page.html");
```

If the page has not been modified this will just set $rc to RC_NOT_MODIFIED: if the page has been modified $rc will be set to RC_OK, and the new version of the page stored in the file page.html.

Another useful function in LWP::Simple is head(). This returns an array containing the content type, document length, modification time, expiry time and server name. Thus we can discover the content type of a given page with

```
print "Content type is ", (head($url))[0], "\n";
```

A complete example

Before leaving `LWP::Simple` we present a complete example showing how easy it is to create Web-aware scripts.

Many Web sites provide a simple staff lookup facility: you enter a name in a form, and a CGI script returns a page containing a line for each entry in the staff database that matches the name. Suppose we have a simple system that simply returns a line containing the name and telephone extension, e.g.

```
Firefly, Rufus. T  2789
```

When the user enters 'Firefly' as the search name and clicks on the 'Submit' button, the browser sends a 'GET' request with the query data appended to the URL thus

```
http://www.shyster.com/cgi-bin/lookup?Firefly
```

A Perl script can imitate this, and then pick out the relevant lines from the HTML page that is returned:

```
use LWP::Simple

# suppose the desired name is in $name
$url = "http://www.shyster.com/cgi-bin/lookup?" .
       "$name";
$rc = getstore($url, "c:\temp\page.html");
die "page not found" if $rc == RC_NOT_FOUND;
open HTML, "<c:\temp\page.html";
while <HTML> {
  print if /dddd/
}
```

We construct the URL including the query, and use `getstore()` to read the page into a file. Then we print out any lines in the file that contain a four-digit string, i.e. a telephone extension. This script would require a certain amount of refinement in practice, but the basic ideas are very simple.

3.16.2   Web access using LWP::UserAgent

There are some requirements that are not met by `LWP::Simple`. For example, suppose we attempt to retrieve a page:

```
use LWP::Simple

$url = "http://www.somesite.com/index.html";
$rc = getstore($url, "page.html");
```

If the page has been moved, and a good webmaster has recorded this fact, the attempt will fail, with the $rc set to RC_MOVED_PERMANENTLY or RC_MOVED_TEMPORARILY. We would like our request to be redirected automatically to the new location: this is the kind of thing `LWP::UserAgent` can do. `LWP::UserAgent` is a high-powered module, and we can only touch on its capabilities here.

The module uses an object approach, and implements a user–agent object, which makes use of the classes HTTP::Request and HTTP::Response which act as envelopes for an HTTP request and the corresponding response from the server. Thus a simple page fetch is performed as follows

```
use LWP::UserAgent
$agent = LWP::UserAgent->new()
$url = "http://www.somesite.com/index.html";
$request = HTTP::Request->new('GET',$url);
$response = $agent->request($request);
...
```

Here we have created an Agent object, and set up the Request object, then used the Request method of the Agent object to do the business.

The advantage of this over using LWP::Simple is that the request method performs automatic redirection if required. Another advantage is that we can request pages using the 'POST' method: LWP::Simple is restricted to request using the 'GET' method.

The response object has five commonly-used methods:

- content()   the actual contents of the page fetched
- is_success()   Boolean denoting success
- is_error()   Boolean denoting error
- code()   the code returned by the HTTP server
- message()   a human-readable string corresponding to the code,
                 e.g. 'OK' for 200, 'NOT FOUND' for 404.

The request() method is polymorphic. If it is given a second scalar argument, this is treated as a file path, and the content will be stored in this file, just like getstore() in LWP::Simple, e.g.

```
$response = $agent->request($request,
                            'page.html');
```

There is yet another form, which allows you to process data before the whole page is loaded:

```
$response = $agent->request($request,
                \&process, $blocksize);
```

Each time a chunk of the size specified by the third argument is read, the subroutine referenced by the second argument is called to process it. This can be very useful when loading large pages, especially over a slow connection.

LWP::UserAgent has many other features that we do not describe here. As before, the aim is just to illustrate the power of modules.

3.17 'Dirty hands' Internet programming

Modules like LWP::Simple and LWP::UserAgent meet the needs of most programmers requiring Web access, and there are numerous other modules for other types of

Internet access, e.g. Net::FTP for access to FTP servers. However, some tasks may require a lower level of access to the network, and this is provided by Perl both in the form of modules (e.g. IO::Socket) and at an even lower level by built-in functions. Support for network programming in Perl is so complete that you can use the language to write any conceivable Internet application.

Access to the Internet at this level involves the use of sockets, and we explain what a socket is before getting down to details of the programming.

3.17.1 Sockets

Sockets are network communication channels, providing a bi-directional channel between processes on different machines [2]. Sockets were originally a feature of Berkeley UNIX: later, other UNIX systems adopted them and the socket became the de facto mechanism of network communication in the UNIX world. The popular Winsock package provided similar functionality for Windows, allowing Windows systems to communicate over the network with UNIX systems, and sockets are a built-in feature of Windows 9x and Windows NT4.

From the Perl programmer's point of view, a network socket can be treated like an open file – it is identified by a filehandle, you write to it with print, and read from it with the angle operator. The socket interface is based on the TCP/IP protocol suite, so that all routing information is handled automatically. In addition, TCP provides a reliable channel, with automatic recovery from data loss or corruption: for this reason a TCP connection is often described as a *virtual circuit*. The socket implementation in Perl is an exact mirror of the UNIX facility, and also permits connections using UDP (Unreliable Datagram Protocol).

Servers and server sockets

The typical network scenario has a number of client systems seeking services from servers: a server is a long-running process that controls access to a resource. Examples are HTTP servers, which provide access to Web pages, FTP servers, which allow retrieval of files using the File Transfer Protocol, and POP/IMAP servers, which provide access to electronic mail. Every socket has an associated *port number*: mostly these are allocated dynamically by the system software, but servers listen for connections on 'well-known ports', which the client specifies when creating a socket. Thus if we want to communicate with a Web server we establish a connection on port 80 (usually).

A server socket has to cater for multiple connections. Typically, the server socket is initially set up with its associated well-known port number and listens for requests. When a connection is made to the well-known port the server spawns a new instance of itself running in a separate thread or process to handle the request, and the original version listens for further requests.

3.17.2 Creating and using sockets

As we have already observed, much of the power of scripting languages comes from the way in which they hide the complexity of operations, and there can be few better example of this than socket programming. Perl mirrors exactly the UNIX socket implementation, so it can be used to write both client-side and server-side socket code, using either the TCP or the UDP protocol. We confine ourselves to a simple example of a client-side TCP socket.

Suppose we want to set up a socket to communicate with a remote server. Following the UNIX model, the steps required are:

- Create a socket and give it a name
- Connect the socket to the remote host on a specified port.

Following a successful connect operation, the socket identifier can be used just like a filehandle: we write to the remote host using print, and read the response using the angle bracket operator. (Note, however, that some non-UNIX implementations do not provide this equivalence between sockets and filehandles. On such systems you have to use the send and recv functions – see the Perl man pages for further details.) Creating a socket requires us to provide a variety of constants for protocol numbers etc.: these may be platform dependent, but the Socket module provides the correct values for any particular platform.

As an example, we present a simple script to access a POP3 server and determine if there is any mail waiting for collection. A POP3 client retrieves mail from the POP3 server in a simple client–server interaction. When contact is first established with the server, a response indicates availability: the server then engages in a dialogue in which user name and password are sent, and if all is well the server responds with a message indicating how many new messages are available. In the following dialogue, client commands are in normal type and server responses are in bold.

establish connection
+OK POP3 penelope v6.50 server ready
USER dwb
+OK User name accepted, password please
PASS 12345678
+OK Mailbox open, 1 messages

Note that successful operations always result in a reply starting +OK. This dialogue can be automated with a Perl script: the code is fairly straightforward.

```
use Socket;
my ($host, $port, $ip, $proto, $reply);
$host = "penelope.ecs.soton.ac.uk";
$port = 110; #"well known" port
# use DNS to convert host name to IP address
$ip = inet_aton $host
    or die "DNS lookup failed\n";
# Get code for TCP protocol
$proto = getprotobyname 'tcp';

socket MAILCHECK, PF_INET, SOCK_STREAM, $proto;
connect MAILCHECK, sockaddr_in($port, $ip) or
    die "Connect failed: $!\n";
```

```
BODY: {
$| = 1; # set socket to auto-flush on output

# Get server response:
# premature exit from block if bad reply
$reply = <MAILCHECK>;
unless ($reply =~ /\+OK/) {
    print STDERR
    "Unexpected response from server\n";
  last BODY
  }
print MAILCHECK "USER dwb";
$reply = <MAILCHECK>;
  unless ($reply =~ /\+OK/) {
    print STDERR
    "Unexpected response from server\n";
  last BODY
  }
print MAILCHECK "pass 12345678\n";
$reply = <MAILCHECK>;
} unless ($reply =~ /\+OK/) {
    print STDERR
    "Bad password\n";
  last BODY
  }
$reply =~ s/^.*,//;
print "You have$reply\n";
}
close MAILCHECK;
```

Send USER command, premature exit from block if bad reply.

Send PASS command, premature exit from block if bad reply.

Extract number of messages from reply.

Note the way in which error conditions are dealt with by premature exit from the block, rather than by calling exit. This ensures that the socket is always closed, whatever happens.

3.17.3 Using IO::Socket

The IO::Socket package provides an object-oriented wrapper for the low-level socket functions. A socket reference is created by the new function:

```
$remote = IO::Socket::INET->new(Proto => 'tcp',
 PeerAddr => $host, PeerPort => $port ) or die
"cannot connect to $host:($port)\n";
```

The new function creates the socket and performs the connect operation. The object reference returned can be used in any place where a filehandle is valid (like the filehandle references in IO::File described in Section 3.13.1).

All the socket functions are available as methods of the object, e.g. if we want to use the `recv` function we can call it as `$remote->recv(...)`.

3.18 Security issues

Languages which provide full access to the underlying operating system open up possibilities for malicious actions. For example, a badly written script might use a string derived from user input as a shell command: in UNIX passing the string `rm -r *` in this context will cause the entire file system to be erased, and mistaken trust in a file name might cause the password file to be modified. Such possibilities are even greater when scripts make network access to untrusted sources, and Perl therefore provides an effective way of maintaining control by a process called *taint checking*.

3.18.1 Taint checking

The Perl approach to security is based on the premise that data coming from outside is untrustworthy, or 'tainted' [3], and that such data coming from outside a program cannot be used to affect something else outside the program without some deliberate action on the program's part. Taint checking is automatically invoked in the UNIX environment when a script is running with more privileges than the owner of the script normally enjoys (a so-called `setuid` or `setgid` script), and it can also be invoked explicitly by invoking the Perl interpreter with the `-T` option. (CGI scripts are usually run with taint checking enabled in this way.)

When taint checking is active, command-line arguments, environment variables and file (socket) input are marked as tainted. Perl then performs a flow analysis so that any value derived from a tainted variable is itself marked as tainted. Such data may not be used (directly or indirectly) in any command that invokes a sub-shell, or in any command that modifies files, directories or processes: such use will generate an error (which may of course be trapped in a block `eval` as described earlier). The only way to bypass the taint checks is to reference a pattern variable set by a regular expression match. The presumption is that if you have constructed a regular expression with bracketed sub-expressions, you have thought about the problem, and written the regular expression to weed out dangerous strings.

3.18.2 The 'Safe' module

Taint checking provides security for code you have written which uses potentially unsafe data from outside. A different situation arises if you have to execute code that comes from an unknown or untrusted source. The `Safe` module allows you to set up 'Safe objects': each of these is a compartment (or 'sand box') in which untrusted code can be executed in isolation from the rest of your program. A `Safe` object has a namespace which is rooted at a specified level in the package hierarchy, so the code executed cannot access variables declared and used at a higher level in the hierarchy. (UNIX gurus will recognize the analogy with the UNIX *chroot* function, which is used, for example, to restrict a user of anonymous FTP to a sub-tree of the file system.) In addition, a `Safe` object can be set up to make specified Perl operators unavailable, thus adding another level of security.

Notes

[1] This script was written by Jon Hallett, whose permission to use it is gratefully acknowledged.

[2] In UNIX systems sockets can also be used as a method of inter-process communication between processes running on the same machine. Although Perl supports this capability, we do not pursue it further in this book.

[3] The *Oxford English Dictionary* gives a number of definitions for 'taint' as a verb. Two relevant ones are 'to touch, tinge, imbue slightly (usually with some bad or undesirable quality)' and 'to infect with pernicious, noxious, corrupting or deleterious qualities; to touch with putrefaction; to corrupt, contaminate, deprave'.

## Chapter 4

Tcl

Tcl is two things. First, it is a reuseable command language, a simple language for issuing commands to a variety of interactive tools, combined with sufficient programmability to allow users to define procedures for more powerful commands than those on the tool's base set. Second, it is an interpreter which can be embedded in an application to provide it with a command-line interface The original philosophy of Tcl was that application development is best accomplished using a combination of two languages: a conventional programming language such as C or C++ for manipulating the complex internal data structures where performance is key, and a scripting language to 'glue' these components together. However, in many modern applications the whole application is written in Tcl, the components themselves being Tcl scripts. Tcl is an unusual language – it has little syntax and no inherent semantics – and in this chapter we discover the power of this novel approach to scripting.

4.1 The Tcl phenomenon

Like Perl, Tcl (Tool command language) is another example of a software package developed to solve the author's individual problem and made freely available to the community over the Internet, which has attracted an enthusiastic band of supporters and a wide range of applications because the problem turns out to be a common one. Also like Perl, though originally developed in the UNIX environment it has been ported to most major platforms, including Windows and the Macintosh. First distributed in 1989, by 1993 Tcl had garnered tens of thousands of users, and estimates of the number of Tcl developers today range from half a million to a million. It is used for a wide range of applications: to give but two examples, the National Broadcasting Company (NBC) uses Tcl for its master control for distribution of programming, which operates 19 hours a day, 7 days a week, and Cisco uses it for its Automated Test System, which checks router configuration.

4.2 The Tcl philosophy

John Ousterhout, the original author of Tcl, believes strongly that application development is best accomplished using a combination of two languages: 'one, such as C or C++, for manipulating the complex internal data structures where performance is key, and another, such as Tcl, for writing smallish scripts that tie together the C pieces and are used for extensions'. Thus Tcl (as seen by its inventor) is not so much a language – it has little syntax and no inherent semantics – as an interpreter which can be embedded in an application to provide a simple command-line interface, making it a universal command language. Alternatively it can be used to implement a graphical user interface (GUI) by associating Tcl scripts with the events (mouse clicks, key presses etc.) recognized by the underlying operating system: this is the basis of the Tk toolkit described at length in the next chapter. However, a measure of the success of a language design is the extent to which it is used for purposes not intended, or envisaged, by its designer, and on this measure Tcl is an enormous success: many large applications are written entirely in Tcl, with no C code at all.

Tcl has a large band of devoted followers, and the newsgroups frequently carry heated arguments about the relative merits of Tcl and Perl for scripting – one extreme statement is that 'Tcl is a mistake that should never have happened'. As we have remarked in the Preface, such religious wars are outside the scope of this text.

4.3 Tcl structure

Tcl implements a command-line syntax that will be familiar to users of the UNIX shell, or DOS on a PC. Each command consists of one or more 'words' separated by whitespace: the first word is the *command word* (or *verb*), and the remaining words (if any) are arguments. The command word may identify an in-built command, a user-written Tcl procedure, or a user-supplied external function written in C: either way, the interpreter passes control to the command/procedure/function, making the argument words available to it for it to treat as it pleases. It follows that Tcl has no inherent semantics: all the 'meaning' is provided by the code associated with the command word.

Tcl was conceived as an embedded interpreter which would provide a command-line interface for its host application: the interaction between the Tcl interpreter and the application is illustrated in Figure 4.1. User input is passed by the application to the Tcl *parser*, which breaks it into words and identifies the command word. The parser then passes control as described above. This is the 'classic' Tcl structure, but more recently, many applications have been written purely in Tcl. In this scenario the 'application' in Figure 4.1 becomes a simple shell, which just reads lines of input from the keyboard (or a

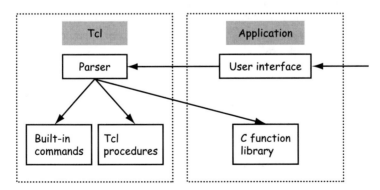

Figure 4.1 Tcl as an embedded system

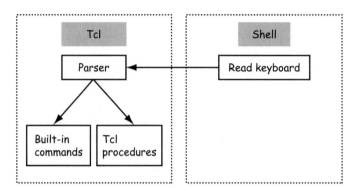

Figure 4.2   Structure of a pure Tcl application

file) and passes them to the Tcl parser as shown in Figure 4.2. Such a shell, *tclsh*, comes as part of the Tcl distribution.

'Pure Tcl' applications have become so common that the recently released 'TclPro' product includes a wrapper that creates a single executable file containing everything needed to run a Tcl application. This makes it easy for developers to distribute Tcl applications to users. Tcl scripts can also run as embedded components ('Tclets') in a Web browser – see Chapter 11.

4.4   Tcl syntax

As we have already seen, a Tcl command is formed by words separated by whitespace. The first word is the name of the command (the command word), and the remaining words are arguments to the command. In its simplest form a 'word' is just a sequence of characters not including space or tabs: within a word the dollar sign ($) substitutes the value of a variable, and backslash can be used to introduce special characters, e.g. \n for newline. Note particularly that the dollar sign is a *substitution operator*, not part of the variable name as it is in Perl.

Words containing spaces may be enclosed in double quotes or braces (curly brackets). The value (i.e. the argument passed to the command procedure) of a word enclosed in double quotes comprises the characters between the quotes after any substitutions have been made. A word that starts with an opening brace { extends to the *matching* closing brace }: *no* substitutions are made, and the value passed as an argument is the entire word with the outer braces stripped off. A 'word' enclosed in square brackets denotes a script to be evaluated immediately: the argument passed corresponding to such a word is the output of the script.

4.5   Understanding Tcl: the parser

The rules given above describe the grammar that determines valid statements in Tcl. However, the key to understanding the language is to look at what the interpreter actually does.

4.5.1 The main loop

The Tcl interpreter reads a *script* from a file (or standard input). The operations of the main loop are as follows.

- The first stage of processing is to assemble a complete command. The interpreter reads characters up to the next command terminator – a non-hidden semicolon or newline – which is discarded. Command terminators are hidden if they appear in a quoted string or in a string bounded by opening and closing braces. A semicolon can also be hidden by escaping it with a backslash, but a backslash followed by a newline, together with any whitespace at the start of the next physical line, is replaced by a single space. This allows long commands to be broken over several physical lines in a readable manner.
- The next stage of processing is to remove comments. If the first character of the command is a hash, the command is ignored.
- Next, the command is scanned from left to right and broken into a sequence of sub-strings called *words* as described below; this process is described as *parsing*. The first word of a command must be the name of a *command procedure* – a built-in Tcl command, a Tcl procedure or C function registered by the application. At the end of parsing Tcl calls the appropriate command procedure, passing the remaining words of the command as string arguments. The interpretation of these words is entirely up to the command procedure.
- When the command procedure returns control, the main loop starts again to process the next command.

4.5.2 Words

A *word* is a string of visible characters bounded on the left by the start of the command or whitespace, and on the right by whitespace or command terminator, except that

- if the first character following whitespace is an opening brace (curly bracket) the word is terminated by the *matching* closing brace. The word consists of the characters between the outer braces, not including the braces themselves, and no processing is carried out on those characters. (Remember that a backslash–newline combination appearing within braces is converted to a space before the parsing starts.)
- if the first character following whitespace is an opening square bracket, text up to and including the matching closing square bracket is processed specially as described in *command substitution* below.
- If the first character following whitespace is a double quote, the word is terminated by the next double quote. The word consists of the characters between the double quotes, not including the quotes themselves, possibly modified by one or more *substitutions* (see below). Semicolons, newlines and whitespace appearing within the quotes are treated as ordinary characters and included in the word.

4.5.3 Substitutions

During the left-to-right scan by the parser, various substitutions can occur, except for text enclosed in matching braces. Possible substitutions are discussed in the following sub-sections.

Command substitution

If a word starts with an opening square bracket, the interpreter is called recursively to process subsequent characters as a Tcl script, with the closing square bracket acting as the script terminator. The result of the last statement of the script replaces the square brackets and the text between them as the next word. (The same idea of command substitution has already been seen in the backtick and qx operators in Perl, and is also a feature of the UNIX shells.)

Variable substitution

If a word contains a dollar sign, variable substitution takes place. There are three forms:

$name   Characters following the dollar sign up to the first character which is not a letter, digit or underscore are taken as the name of a scalar variable. The characters $name are replaced by the value of the variable.

${name}   The characters between the braces (any character except closing brace being allowed) are taken as the name of a scalar variable, whose value replaces the characters ${name}. This notation allows very unusual variable names, e.g. a variable called **?@!!!%$.

$name(index)   The characters between the dollar and the opening bracket, which can include only letters, digits and underscores, give the name of an (associative) array, and the value in the array associated with index as a key replaces the construct. The string index can be almost any string, but strings with embedded spaces can cause trouble if the spaces are not escaped or enclosed in quotes: they are best avoided. The string index is itself subject to substitutions.

Backslash substitution

If a backslash appears in a word, then except as provided below, it is discarded and the following character is not ascribed any special meaning. Thus to include a literal dollar sign in a string it must be escaped as \$, and a literal backslash is included with \\. The exceptions, where actual substitution occurs, are:

\b	Backspace	\t	Tab
\n	Newline	\0dd	Character with octal code dd
\r	Carriage return	\xhh	Character with hex code hh

Only one substitution

It is important to note that each character is processed exactly once by the interpreter, e.g. if variable substitution is performed and the value substituted includes a dollar character, this will not cause another variable substitution. (There are ways of making this happen, as we shall see later.)

4.5.4   Examples of parsing

We illustrate the rules given above with a few examples.

Using braces

```
set a {dog cat {horse cow mule} bear}
```

This command consists of three words:

```
| set | a | dog cat {horse cow mule} bear |
```

Command substitution

```
set a [format {I am %s years old} 99]
```

The first stage of parsing finds three words:

```
| set | a | [format {I am %s years old} 99] |
```

The third word starts with an opening square bracket, so command substitution is invoked. The command in square brackets is parsed into three words

```
| format | I am %s years old | 99 |
```

The command word is `format`: when invoked with the second and third words as arguments the format function returns the string

```
I am 99 years old
```

so the final parse is three words:

```
set | a | I am 99 years old |
```

Variable and command substitution

```
set age 99
set a [format {I am %s years old} $age]
```

The first line is parsed into three words

```
| set | age | 99 |
```

and the `set` command procedure sets variable `age` to 99. The second line parses as before:

```
| set | a | [format {I am %s years old} $age] |
```

Command substitution is invoked on the third word:

```
| format {I am %s years old} | $age |
```

The third word of this parse includes a dollar sign, so variable substitution takes place:

```
| format | {I am %s years old} | 99 |
```

leading to the final parse as before:

```
| set | a | I am 99 years old |
```

4.5.5 Comments

We have seen that a command is ignored if it starts with a hash, thus providing a full-line comment:

```
# Procedure to munge the data
# Version 2.5
# 12 September 1998
```

Note that C-style 'block' comments can be used

```
# procedure to munge the data #
# version 2.5                  #
# 12 September 1998            #
```

The trailing hash on each line is ignored along with the rest of the 'statement'. Note also that end-of-line comments can be used with a simple artifice:

```
set a $b; # temporary copy
```

The semicolon terminates the `set` statement, so the hash is at the start of a new statement.

4.5.6 That's it!

This description of the parsing process defines the language: everything else is a matter of the definitions of the built-in and user-supplied command words, to which we now turn our attention.

4.6 Variables and data in Tcl

4.6.1 Everything is a string

When faced with a new language, we usually start by looking at the data types and data structures that it provides. This is easy in Tcl: everything is a string [1], and the only data structure is an array (which must be associative, given that the only scalar data type is the string). Using strings as the universal data type makes communication between scripts and command procedures simpler, especially if they are C functions. Remember that the command procedure can interpret the words it receives in any way, and where appropriate a command procedure may convert strings to numbers.

In particular, the `expr` command which evaluates expressions (see Section 4.6.3) recognizes character sequences that represent numbers and converts them into numbers. A string of decimal digits is treated as decimal integer unless it starts with a zero, in which case it is treated specially: if the next character is a digit the string is treated as an octal number, and a string starting 0x is treated as a hexadecimal number. Other 'numbers' – those including decimal point or in scientific notation – are converted to floating point.

In a context where a Boolean value is required, a number must be supplied: zero is treated as false, and anything else is treated as true.

4.6.2 Assignment

Assignment is done by the built-in command procedure set, e.g.

```
set x 3;
set y "Hello World!\n";
```

The set command expects to be given two words (and will complain if you give it more or fewer than two words): the first is the name of the variable to be assigned, and the second is the value to be assigned. Because the variable name is just a word, unusual variable names are possible, e.g.

```
set {a very long name including spaces}  3
set {aaarrrggghhh!!!} "System all fouled up\n"
```

Another form of assignment is the append command, which adds text to the end of a variable's (string) contents. Thus

```
set a "Hello"
append a " World!"
```

sets a to "Hello" and then adds " World!" to give the new value "Hello World!".

4.6.3 Expressions

The expr command

Expressions are evaluated by the built-in command procedure expr, e.g.

```
expr ($a + $b/5.5) * 5.14159
```

The expr command first concatenates all its argument words into a single string, performing variable and command substitution. (Variable and command substitution may already have been done by the parser, unless the operand was protected by braces to prevent substitutions when first encountered, e.g.

```
expr {($a + $b/5.5) * 5.14159}
```

It is generally sensible to do this, to prevent nasty surprises. However, we see here an example of a powerful Tcl concept: the ability for the programmer to control the precise point at which a script gets interpreted.) The resulting string is then evaluated, recognizing brackets in the usual way and applying operator precedence rules. Tcl provides all the common operators: details can be found in Section 4.15.1 at the end of the chapter. By default, floating point expressions are evaluated with 12 significant figures in Tcl 8.0 and 6 significant digits in earlier versions. The default can be changed by setting the value of a special variable, `Tcl_precision`.

The `expr` command is most commonly used in the context of command substitution. For example, given

```
set a [expr $b * ($c + 2)]
```

command substitution will call `expr` to evaluate the expression `"$b*($c+2)"`, the resulting value being assigned to a. A common special case is

```
set a [expr $a + $b]
```

which adds a to b and assigns the result back to a. This incrementing operation can be expressed more concisely as

```
incr a $b
```

If the second argument is omitted, it defaults to 1 (so `[incr a]` is equivalent to Perl's a++).

As noted earlier, strings representing numbers are converted to numbers by `expr`. This conversion is aggressive: any string that could represent a number will be converted to a number, and later converted back into a string if the context requires this. Thus if we have variables a and b which have string values, and we check for equality with `expr $a==$b`, mysterious things can happen. For example, if a happens to have the value `"0xa"` and b happens to have the value `"10"`, `'expr $a==$b'` will return the value 1 (true), although the strings are clearly not the same. This is because when converted to numbers, both strings give the value 10. For this reason it is wise not to use the comparison operators on strings: an alternative and reliable method is available, as described in Section 4.11.1.

Conditional expressions

The *choice* operator (?) provides a conditional expression facility, e.g.

```
expr ($x < 0 ? 0 : 1)
```

evaluates to zero if x is negative, and 1 otherwise. The syntax is clearly borrowed from C and Perl.

4.7 Control flow

Tcl built-in command procedures provide a full range of control flow commands, including `while`, `for`, `foreach`, `break`, `continue`, `if` and `switch`. Control flow commands are made up of conditions and scripts whose execution is dependent on the outcome of the evaluation of the condition: the conditions and scripts are enclosed in braces to prevent evaluation when first encountered. The control flow command procedures call `expr` internally to evaluate the condition, at which time variable and command substitutions will take place.

4.7.1   Loops

while loop

```
while {$p > 0} {
  set result [expr $result*$base]
  set p [expr $p-1]
}
```

(Note the placement of the opening curly bracket, to hide the newline that would otherwise terminate the command prematurely. Alternatively, the newline could be escaped with a backslash.)

for loop

```
for {set i 0} {$i < 10} {incr i 3} {
  set a [expr $a + $b(i)]
}
```

Note the similarity to C syntax.

foreach

```
foreach i {0 3 6 9} {
  set a [expr $a + $b(i)]
}
```

4.7.2   Branching

if

```
if {$a < 0} {set a -1} \
elseif {$a > 0} {set a 1} \
else {set a 0}
```

switch

This command provides flow control based on pattern matching. It is described in Section 4.12.3.

4.8   Data structures

4.8.1   Lists

Tcl scripts frequently use *lists*. Although a list has many of the properties of a data structure, in Tcl it is just a string consisting of the list elements separated by whitespace.

Braces and double quotes can be used to group elements into sub-lists: as with commands, braces provide strict quoting, while double quotes allow substitutions using $. For example, given the list of three items

```
apple {orange $a} "orange $a"
```

if the variable a has the value "lemon", the second item in the list is the string "orange $a", and the third item is the string "orange lemon".

Tcl provides a number of commands for manipulating lists: we give a brief description here, with reference details in Section 4.15.2.

Building lists

The list command constructs a list from its arguments, e.g.

```
list $x apple pear banana
```

If any argument contains special characters the command performs automatic quoting to ensure that the argument appears as a single list element. Thus in the above example, since the value of the variable x may itself be a list, the list command encloses the value in braces. The linsert command inserts its arguments into an existing list at a specified point; lappend adds its arguments at the end of a list, and concat joins multiple lists into a single list.

The split command provides a useful way of converting input lines into a list. For example, a departmental index might be held in a file in which each line records an individual's name, building, room and telephone number in the following format, e.g.

```
David Barron#B16#1011#2386
```

If this line has been read into the variable line, then

```
split $line #
```

returns a list of four items:

```
{David Barron} B16 1011 2386
```

Alternative splitting characters can be specified. Thus

```
split $line {# }
```

will split on hash or space, returning the list of five items

```
David Barron B16 1011 2386
```

By specifying an empty string as the split character you can convert each character of a string into a list element: sometimes useful, but probably not the best way of doing the job – see Section 4.11 for a discussion of efficient string processing in Tcl.

Working with lists

The llength command returns the number of elements in a list. lindex returns an element of a list identified by an index supplied as an argument (elements are numbered from zero); lrange returns a specified range of elements from a list, e.g.

```
lrange L 4 14
```

returns elements 4 to 14 of the list L, and lreplace returns a new list in which a range of elements in a target list have been replaced by new elements supplied as arguments. The lsearch command returns the index of the element in a list which matches a given pattern (with the option of using regular expression matching). The lsort command can be used to sort the elements of a list in a variety of ways. The join command is (almost) the inverse of the split command described above: if the variable list contains the list

```
{{David Barron} B16 1011 2386}
```

then join $list # returns the original hash-separated string. A multi-character 'glue' string can be specified: join $list {::} would return

```
David Barron::B16::1011::2386
```

Lists and arrays

The lindex, lrange and lreplace commands allow you to treat a list as if it were an array. However, a list is just a string with a special interpretation, and the string therefore has to be parsed on each list access: this can slow down processing. In particular, prior to Tcl 8.0 large lists were very inefficient: for example, locating a specified element required a left-to-right scan, counting or checking elements until the specified one was found. The only way to determine the number of elements in the list was to scan the entire list and count the elements. Tcl 8.0 uses an internal format (an array of pointers to the start of each list item) which requires constant time to access any element: it also records the length of the list.

4.8.2 Arrays

The Tcl interpreter recognizes one-dimensional associative arrays, e.g.

```
set a $b(foo)
set b(bar) 4
```

We can obtain the effect of a two-dimensional array by using an index, which is two comma-separated items, e.g.

```
set a $b(2,1)
```

Care has to be exercised in using this facility: if we attempt to improve readability by adding a space after the comma

```
set a $b(2, 1)
```

then we have changed the string that will be used as the key for lookup in the associative array. It is important to be consistent in the use of spaces, and if they are employed, it is best to quote the whole array reference thus:

```
set a {b(2, 1)}
```

One of the problems of the command-line style is that since every command must have a unique word to identify it, a large number of command words are needed. A technique widely used in Tcl is to group commands into families: the first word (the command word) identifies the family, and the next word identifies a particular command within the family. Remaining words (if any) are arguments. Thus the command procedure associated with the command word is just a multi-way branch which uses the first argument supplied (the second word of the command) to locate the real command procedure. This technique is illustrated by the `array` command, which provides array operations that are very reminiscent of the way Perl deals with hashes.

An array can be initialized in one step by providing a list in which keys and values alternate, using the `array set` command, e.g.

```
array set fruits {apple red banana yellow \
                  grape green}
```

The converse of this is `array get`, which delivers a list of alternating keys and values. This can be used in conjunction with a variant of the `foreach` loop which allows multiple loop variables. The skeleton of the code is:

```
foreach {key value} [array get A] {
...
}
```

Each time round the loop, `key` is set to the next element of the array, and `value` is set to the following element.

More usefully, the `array names` command delivers a list containing the keys: this can be used to iterate over the elements of the array:

```
foreach key [array names fruits] {
...
}
```

The function of `array exists` and `array size` should be obvious. A complete list of the operations provided by the `array` command is given in Section 4.15.3.

4.9 Simple input/output

Since everything is a string, Tcl I/O is built round strings. Tcl talks to the outside world through *streams*: it will come as no surprise to learn that the three streams, `stdin`, `stdout` and `stderr` are predefined. More generally, a stream can be associated with a file: see Section 4.13.

4.9.1 Output

Basic output is performed by `puts` ('put string'). This outputs a string, by default to `stdout`, with a newline appended. The option `-nonewline` causes the newline to be omitted. An explicit destination can be specified, e.g. `stderr`. Note that if this option is used it must be the first word after `puts`. Examples:

```
puts "Hello World!"
puts stderr "oops!"
puts -nonewline "Enter your name: "
```

4.9.2 Input

There are two commands for input: `gets` and `read`.

gets

In its simplest form, `gets` is almost the inverse of `puts`: it reads a line from a stream and returns the line as a string with the trailing newline removed.

```
set answer [gets stdin];
```

Note particularly that the stream specifier is always required: it does not default to `stdin` as you might reasonably expect. An alternative form specifies the destination variable as an additional argument:

```
gets stdin answer
```

In this form the string is assigned as the value of the variable given as an argument, and `gets` returns the number of bytes read, e.g.

```
set n [gets stdin answer]
```

If end-of-file is reached, `gets` in its first form returns an empty string, and in its second form returns a value of −1. Thus a common idiom is

```
while {[gets stdin line] >= 0} \
        {... process $line ... }
```

(See also `eof` below.)

read

`read` provides a block-read facility (more efficient than line input for large volumes of input) from the specified stream. Thus

```
read stdin
```

reads the remainder of the stream and returns it as a string, including the final newline. The string that is delivered by `read` can be separated into lines using the `split` command described earlier. The `-nonewline` option causes the final newline to be discarded:

```
read -nonewline stdin
```

A byte-count argument can be supplied:

```
read stdin 4096
```

In this case `read` reads that number of bytes from the stream, or as much as there is if there is not enough data in the stream. Note that the optional byte-count argument and the `-nonewline` option cannot both be present at the same time.

eof

The `eof` command returns 1 if the stream is at end-of-file, and 0 otherwise, leading to the idiom

```
while {![eof stdin] } {
...
}
```

4.10 Procedures

4.10.1 Defining and using procedures

Procedures are introduced by the `proc` command, which takes the form

```
proc name {argumentlist} {body}
```

The `argumentlist` is a list of formal parameters: when the procedure is invoked the variables in the list will be assigned the values given in the call, left to right (with a complaint if there are too many or too few values provided). Each element of the `argumentlist` is either a variable name or a list containing a variable name and a default value to be used if a value is not supplied when the procedure is called. An example of the use of default parameters is given later. The result of a procedure is the result returned by the last statement in the body, unless the `return` command is used to return a specific value. Variables introduced in the body are local to the procedure unless specified by use of the `global` command. (Full details on scope and parameter passing, in particular the ability to use call by reference, are given in Section 4.10.2.)

To illustrate procedure definition, consider the following examples.

A local variable.

```
proc power {base p} {
     set result 1
      while {$p > 0} {
        set result [expr $result*$base]
        set p [expr $p-1]
     }
     return $result
}
```

This is a function procedure, since it returns a value: if it is called, e.g. by

```
puts [power 2 5]
```

it will return a value of 32 as the second word of the `puts` command: the variables `base`, `result` and `p` will not be visible on exit. Alternatively, we could have made the procedure set a global variable:

```
proc power2 {base p} {
    global result
    while {$p > 0} {
        set result [expr $result*$base]
        set p [expr $p-1]
    }
}
```

A global variable.

With this definition we could write

```
set result 1
power2 2 5
puts $result
```

and the global variable `result` would be printed as 35. Finally, parameters can be given default values, as illustrated in the next example.

```
proc power3 {p {base 2}} {
  set result 1
  while {$p > 0} {
    set result [expr $result*$base]
  set p [expr $p-1]
  }
  return $result
}
```

If this procedure is called by

```
power3 5
```

it will return 32, since the default value of `base` will be used. Note that parameters with default values must come to the right of required parameters in the parameter list. More than one parameter can be specified with a default value, e.g.

```
proc p {a {b 3} {c no}}
```

This procedure can be called with one, two or three arguments. The arguments provided are associated with the formal parameters from left to right, thus if p is called with one argument, this is associated with a; b and c take their default values. If the procedure is called with two arguments, these are assigned to a and b, leaving c to take its default value.

A variadic procedure (one with a varying number of arguments) can be defined by using the keyword `args` as the last entry in the argument list. When the procedure is called, the value of `args` is assigned as a list of all the actual arguments that have not been associated with formal arguments.

4.10.2   Scope issues and call-by-reference

We saw earlier that procedure parameters are called by value, and that variables introduced in a procedure body are local unless explicitly specified as global. The `upvar`
command allows us to determine scopes more precisely. In its simplest form with two
arguments, `upvar` makes a local variable an alias for variable in the stack frame of the
calling procedure. Thus the declaration

```
upvar foo myfoo
```

at the start of a procedure body creates a local variable `myfoo` which is an alias for the
calling procedure's variable `foo`.

This technique allows us to obtain the effect of call-by-reference as opposed to the
usual call-by-value. Suppose we want to pass an array to a procedure. Tcl syntax only
caters for array elements, so we cannot pass the array in the normal way. Instead we have
to pass its name as the actual parameter, and then use `upvar` to reference the array
elements in the context of the calling procedure using a local name for the array:

```
proc  P arrayname {
  upvar $arrayname a

  ...

}
```

In the more general form with three arguments, e.g.

```
upvar 2 foo myfoo
```

the additional argument specifies how many stack frames to go back from the current
frame – the ultimate in extreme cleverness or dirty tricks. An absolute stack frame can be
specified using the syntax `#n`, with `#0` being the global frame, thus

```
upvar #0 foo foo
```

has the same effect as `global foo`.

4.10.3   'On the fly' command creation

Procedure names are global, and exist in their own namespace, which is separate from the
namespace for global variables. (Thus it is possible to have a procedure with the same
name as a variable, which may cause confusion but can be very useful.) It follows that if a
procedure a contains a `proc` command in its body defining a procedure b, that procedure
will come into existence when a is called. Thus we can have a command that creates other
commands. This capability is used extensively in the Tk toolkit: as we shall see in the next
chapter, if we create an instance of a 'button' widget named `.B1` thus

```
button .B1 -text "OK" ...
```

then as a side effect of the action, the `button` command creates a command named `.B1`
which can be used later to change properties of the button, e.g.

```
.B1 configure -text "Cancel"
```

Note that the desired method is provided as an argument to the command named after the object: there is a close parallel here with the Smalltalk paradigm of invoking methods on an object by sending a message to the object. An example showing how this kind of behaviour is created will be found in Section 4.14.2.

4.11 Working with strings

4.11.1 The string command

Many operations on strings in Tcl are carried out by the generic `string` command. The first argument to `string` defines the operation to be performed, the second is the string to be operated on, and there are additional arguments for some operations. A complete account of the operations available is given in Section 4.15.4.

Characters in a string are indexed from zero: the special keyword `end` can be used to refer to the last character in a string. The most useful operations are as follows.

- `string compare` – lexicographic comparison.

  ```
  string compare $S1 $S2
  ```

  returns 0 if strings S1 and S2 are identical, −1 if S1 sorts lexicographically before S2, and +1 if S1 sorts after S2. Always use this method to order strings – do not be tempted to use the arithmetic comparison operators (`==`, `!=`, `>`, `>=`, `<` and `<=`). Although these operators will often work, provided that you remember to put the string in quotes and then enclose the whole expression in braces to stop the parser stripping off the quotes, mysterious things can happen, as we have already seen in Section 4.6.3.
- `string match` – pattern matching, see Section 4.12.
- `string trim`, `string trimleft`, `string trimright` – useful for tidying up strings. For example

  ```
  string trim $S
  ```

  will remove leading and trailing whitespace characters from string S. `string trimleft` and `string trimright` have obvious meanings. Other characters can be trimmed by providing a further argument. Thus

  ```
  string trimright $S 0123456789
  ```

  will trim trailing digits from string S.
- `string tolower`, `string toupper` – case conversion.
  Note also that although commands like `string range`, `string wordstart` and `string wordend` provide the ability to decompose strings in various ways, this is invariably better done using regular expressions, as described in Section 4.12.2.

4.11.2 Other string operations

Other string commands include `append`, `format`, `split` and `subst`.

■ append takes a variable name as its first argument and concatenates the remaining arguments onto the end of the current value of the variable, e.g.

```
set message {Hello World}
append $message ", have a nice day\n"
```

■ format formats a string in the same way that the C *printf* function does: if a has the value 1234567.89,

```
puts [format "%10.2f %10.8e" $a $a]
```

prints the value of a in decimal form (total width of 10 characters with two digits after the decimal point) and in scientific notation (mantissa comprising 10 characters with 8 digits after the decimal point, plus exponent), thus:

```
1234567.89    1.23456789e+06
```

Since the format specifier is a string, there are many opportunities for demonstrating cleverness by invoking variable substitution (or even command substitution) in the string. One example would be to compute the field width dynamically.

■ We have already met the split command, which turns a string into a list by breaking it at specified characters, and seen how it is often used as a way of turning a sequence of input lines into a list. Another example of its utility is in processing CGI query strings, which we met in Chapter 2. It will be recalled that they take the form

```
name1=value1&name2=value2&name3=value3&...
```

We can use split to create a list containing alternate names and values, and then use the extended foreach loop to store the value in an array, which we will call query with the name as the key. Thus (assuming the query string is in the variable qstr)

```
foreach {name, value} [split $qsrt &=] {
set query($name) $value
}
```

■ The subst command takes a string and performs variable substitution and command substitution as if the string were a command, returning a string in which the substitutions have been performed. We shall see an example of its use later.

4.12 Working with patterns

Tcl provides two varieties of pattern matching, the so-called 'glob matching', which is a simple wild card technique, and more sophisticated regular expression matching.

4.12.1 Glob matching

Simple pattern matching is accomplished by string match. This performs glob matching using just three patterns: * matches any number of characters, ? matches a single character, and [abc] matches any one of the set of characters enclosed in the brackets. (Remember that if you use a choice-of-alternatives pattern it must be hidden within braces or stored as the value of a variable, otherwise the interpreter will try to do a command substitution.) Thus

```
string match {[A-z][a-z]*} $name
```

will return true if the value of $name is a string of alphabetic characters with the first character capitalized.

4.12.2 Regular expression matching

More complex matching using regular expressions is done using the regexp command, e.g.

```
regexp {[a-zA-Z]*}  $foo
regexp {[a-zA-Z]*}  $foo  bar
```

In these examples, the pattern is a regular expression that matches any sequence of upper- or lower-case letters. (If this is not obvious, you may find it useful to go over the explanation of Perl regular expressions in Section 2.12.) In both cases the command returns 1 if a match is found in the value of the variable foo: in the second case, as well as returning a value, the string that was recognized by the match will be stored in the variable bar. (It is legitimate to specify the same variable as source and destination if you don't want to keep the original value.) Note particularly that in this case we require the *value* of foo, which is the string to be matched, but the *name* of a variable to hold the match. If the regular expression includes groups, then the strings matching the groups are stored in the variables match1, match2 etc. from left to right (analogous to the $1, $2 etc. in Perl).

The behaviour of regexp can be modified by including flags, e.g.

```
regexp -indices {[a-zA-Z]*} $foo bar
```

Here bar will contain not the actual matching string but a pair of integers denoting the indices within foo of the start and end of the matching string. Other flags include -nocase to make the matching case insensitive. A pattern starting with a minus will be incorrectly recognized as a flag: to protect against this, the flag -- marks the end of the flags.

The regsub command combines regular expression matching with replacement of the matching string (like the Perl substitution operator). In its simplest case

```
n = regsub -all {abc} $foo {xyz} bar
```

it will copy the value of foo into the variable bar with all occurrences of the string abc replaced by the string xyz, returning the number of substitutions made. If the -all flag is not present, only the first match will be substituted. The first argument can be a regular expression, in which case any sub-string that matches the pattern will be replaced. In the replacement string, $ stands for the string that was matched, and \1 to \9 stand for the strings that matched sub-strings in the pattern. Flags -nocase and -- can be used as in the regexp command.

Regular expression syntax in Tcl 8.0 and before

Versions of Tcl up to and including version 8.0 support a very simple regular expression syntax which provides the capabilities described in Section 2.12.1. The syntax provides for matching, repetition, alternation and sub-patterns enclosed in parentheses, but no more. The syntax supported is summarized here:

- . matches any character
- * zero or more occurrences of the previous pattern
- + one or more occurrences of the previous pattern
- ? zero or one occurrence of the previous pattern
- | alternation
- [ ] character set or range
- ^ anchor pattern to start of string
- $ anchor pattern to end of string
- ( ) grouped sub-pattern

The special meaning of these meta-characters can be switched off by escaping them with a backslash. Thus \[.*\] will match an arbitrary string of characters enclosed in square brackets. Other characters can be 'backslash escaped' and retain their identity. Thus \n in a regular expression matches the letter n: this is likely to confuse a programmer who wants to match a newline character. To enable this, the regular expression must be enclosed in double quotes so that the Tcl parser recognizes the \n before the regular expression is passed to the regular expression engine. Things get even messier if the newline escape is inside a character set enclosed in square brackets: in this case the square brackets must be escaped to prevent the Tcl parser from doing command substitution. (This messiness is resolved in Tcl 8.1.)

Regular expression syntax in Tcl 8.1 and later

Version 8.1 of Tcl introduced a much more powerful regular expression syntax which supports, inter alia, back references, lookahead, non-greedy matching, shorthand and repetition counts, as described in Section 2.12.2. Indeed, the extended regular expressions of Tcl 8.1 are almost identical with those of Perl 5. A feature provided in Tcl 8.1 that is not available in Perl is the named character class. Thus, while \d matches a decimal digit in Tcl 8.1 (as in Perl), this can also be written [:digit:]. Here digit is a classname: other classnames are

alpha	a letter (*warning*: includes many non-ASCII characters).
upper	an upper-case letter.
lower	a lower-case letter.
digit	a decimal digit.
xdigit	a hexadecimal digit.
alnum	an alphanumeric (letter or digit).

print   an alphanumeric. (Same as `alnum`.)
blank   a space or tab character.
punct   a punctuation character.
graph   a character with a visible representation.
cntrl   a control character.

Named character classes can be mixed with ranges and single characters, e.g. `[[:digit:]a-cx-z]` matches a digit (0–9), a, b, c, x, y or z.

In Tcl 8.1, backslash substitution is done by the regular expression engine, so that `\n` in a regular expression matches a newline character.

An example

To round off the discussion it is instructive to see how Tcl can decode a URL-encoded string, and compare it with the way Perl does it, as described in Section 2.12.6. Suppose the URL-encoded string is in a variable S. The first step is to replace any occurrence of + by a space, an easy job for `regsub`:

```
regsub -all {\+} $S { } S
```

(The + is escaped because it is a special character in regular expression syntax.) The next step is to locate the escape patterns of the form %dd and replace them with the character whose hex code is dd. Finding the patterns is easy:

```
regsub -all {%([0-9a-hA-H] [0-9a-hA-H])} $S ...
```

The problem is to recover the character, and the trick is to make the substitution string a Tcl command that will do the conversion, and use `subst` to perform command substitution. The part of the regular expression that matches the two hex digits is enclosed in brackets, so the matching string will be remembered and can be referenced in the replacement string as `\1`. Converting a hex string into a character is a job for `format`, so the Tcl command we want is

```
format %c 0x\1
```

(The `%c` tells `format` to generate a character from a numerical code, and the `0x` forces interpretation as a hexadecimal number.) So the final code is

```
regsub -all {%([0-9a-hA-H] [0-9a-hA-H])} $S \
    {[ format %c 0x\1]} S
set S [subst $S]
```

4.12.3   Switch

Having described pattern matching, we are now able to return to the `switch` command, the Tcl version of a case statement. This compares the value of an expression with each of a sequence of patterns in turn, and when a match is found executes the body associated with the matching pattern. The style of matching is determined by an option: `-glob` performs glob-style matching, -regexp does a regular expression match, while -exact requires an exact match (which is also the default). For example,

```
switch -regexp -- $value \
    \t###   {body1} \
    {[a-z]*} {body2}
```

As before, the -- flag denotes the end of the flags, in case the value starts with a minus. If the patterns do not involve substitutions, the need for backslashes at the end of each line can be avoided by grouping all the pattern–body pairs in a single set of braces, e.g.

```
switch $case {
    0 {...}
    1 {...}
    2 {...}
}
```

If the last pattern is the special word default, the associated body is executed if no earlier pattern has matched. However, if default appears as a pattern earlier in the sequence, it will only match the literal string 'default'.

It is often helpful to use comments to identify each case in the switch. However, care is needed: since the hash that introduces a comment must appear at a point where the interpreter is expecting a command, whole-line comments cannot be used – the hash would appear where the interpreter was expecting a pattern. The usual approach is to use end-of-line comments, e.g.

```
switch -regexp -- $value \
    \t###   {proc1;   #special marker} \
    {[a-z]*} {proc2; #normal word}
```

4.13 Working with files and pipes

4.13.1 Associating a stream with a file or pipe

So far we have encountered the predefined streams stdin, stdout and stderr for input and output. A stream is associated with a file by the open command, e.g.

```
set myfile [open /tmp/foo w 0600]
puts $myfile "This goes to foo"
```

(The name assigned to a stream is also referred to as a 'file descriptor'.) The *mode* and *permissions* arguments are optional. The mode determines *how* the file can be accessed, the default being read only. The permissions determine *who* can access the file, and are expressed in the standard UNIX format: the default is 0666. Possible forms of access are listed in Section 4.15.5. (Note that the use of permissions in this style in non-UNIX implementations of Tcl may or may not work, depending on the capabilities of the underlying operating system: consult the local manual.)

As in Perl, a stream can also be associated with either end of a pipeline: however, there are subtle differences. Writing to a pipeline uses a similar syntax to Perl:

```
set pipeto [open |foo w]
```

opens a stream for writing: anything sent by `puts` to this stream will be piped into the standard input of command `foo`, and the standard output of `foo` will be sent to the standard output of the Tcl application. However, whereas Perl indicates reading from a pipe by putting the bar *after* a process name, in Tcl the bar remains in front, to signify 'pipe', and the stream is opened for reading, as in

```
set pipefrom [open |foo r ]
```

which attaches the stream to the standard output of `foo`. If we open a 'pipe' stream for reading and writing, as in

```
set pipe [open |foo r+ ]
```

two pipes are set up: `puts $pipe ...` will write to `foo`'s standard input, and `gets $pipe ...` will read from `foo`'s standard output.

4.13.2 End of line markers

Moving textual data between different platforms can be complicated by the different conventions used to mark the end of a line. UNIX uses a newline character (\n), Windows uses a carriage return-linefeed pair (\r\n), while the Macintosh uses just a carriage return (\r). The `gets` command converts the native platform line ending to a newline, and on output `puts` converts the newline to the native platform line ending. This facilitates portability, and is usually what you want, but it is possible to force a specific behaviour for `gets` and `puts` using the `fconfigure` command. (This is a command that configures various aspects of file behaviour: we shall see further uses for `fconfigure` in the next chapter.) Thus

```
fconfigure $myfile -translation cr
```

specifies Macintosh-style files: on input \r is translated to \n, with the reverse translation on output.

```
fconfigure $myfile -translation crlf
```

specifies Windows-style files: on input \r\n is translated to \n, with the reverse translation on output.

```
fconfigure $myfile -translation lf
```

specifies UNIX-style files, i.e. no translation. Default behaviour is restored with

```
fconfigure $myfile -translation auto
```

4.14 Putting it all together: some example code

4.14.1 A phonebook

A file phones.txt contains a simple telephone directory in which each line has two tab-separated fields, which are a user id and a telephone number, e.g.

```
ajgh    2748
dder    2418
dwb     2386
...
```

The first step is to read this information into an associative array, where the user ids are the keys. This array can then be used for a variety of lookup functions. The 'obvious' way of doing this is to follow a C-like paradigm of reading a line at a time until end-of-file is reached:

```
set in [open {d:\phones.txt} r]
while {![eof $in]} \
  {set line [gets $in]
    set phones([lindex $line 0]) [lindex $line 1]
  }
```

The first line opens the file for reading. The body of the while loop reads a line as a string then treats it as a list, using lindex to extract the two fields, and setting up the array. However, the following is a more idiomatic piece of Tcl code to do the same job:

```
array set phones \
    [split [read -nonewline $in] "\n\t"]
```

Here we have used the read command to do a block read of the whole file: this returns a string containing all the lines of the file separated by newline characters. (The -nonewline option suppresses the final newline.) We then use split to convert this to a list using tab and newline as the separator characters: this yields a string of whitespace-separated words which are key–value pairs, and finally the array set command converts this into the desired array. Note that this also works with a more complicated input format, where user ids are replaced by names that can include spaces, e.g.

```
Barron, David   2386
DeRoure, Dave   2418
Hey, Tony       2748
...
```

If the variable name holds a user id or name, the corresponding telephone number is $phones($name). However, if the name is not in the array, this will lead to an error message, so it is better to check for this error situation:

Be sure you understand why we write phones in lines 2 and 3, but $phones in line 5.

```
#procedure to look up by name
proc look_up_by_name {name} {
  global phones
  if {[info exists phones($name)]}\
```

```
        {return $phones($name)} \
    else \
        {return "NO INFO"}
```

If we require to do a reverse lookup, to ascertain the user id or name corresponding to a given number, a little more work is required, as we have to search the array:

```
#procedure to look up by number
proc look_up_by_number {phone} {
 global phones
 set name "NO INFO"
 foreach key [array names phones] \
{if {$phonebook($key) == $phone} \
        {set name $key; break} \
   }
 return $name
 }
```

This should be self-explanatory.

4.14.2   Modelling objects

There are many object-oriented extensions to Tcl, one of the most popular being [incr Tcl] [2]. However, it is possible to implement an object-based flavour using basic Tcl commands, as we illustrate in this example [3]. The idiom is to provide a constructor which creates an instance of an object, and at the same time defines a command with the same name as the instance, which can be used to invoke methods on the object, as illustrated in Section 4.10.3.

Suppose we want to work with a class of objects called Snark. A Snark object has properties Boojum and visible, which take Boolean values, and two methods, visible to set the visible property, and is_visible to return the current value of the property. (The apparent ambiguity of using 'visible' both as a property and a method does not cause any problems.) A constructor Snark creates a new instance: this constructor has one obligatory argument, the name of the instance, and two optional arguments to define the values of the properties Boojum and visible: if not set explicitly these default to false. (Readers familiar with Lewis Carroll's poem *The Hunting of the Snark* will appreciate the significance of these defaults.) Thus we can create a new invisible Snark with

```
Snark snark1
```

and then make it visible with

```
snark1 visible true
```

Information about Snark objects will be held in an array called snark_data: an object named snark1 will have two entries in the array, identified by the keys snark1-boojum and snark1-visible. Methods are implemented by a private command doSnark, which takes the name of the object as its first argument and the name of the method as the second argument. This command takes the form

```
proc doSnark {name method arg} {
  global snark_data
  switch -exact -- $method {
    visible {set snark_data{$name-visible} $arg}
    is_visible {return $snark_data{$name-visible}}
  }
}
```

(We have not made any use of the Boojum property. *The Hunting of the Snark* suggests that if the visible method sets the property true, it should then check the value of Boojum: if this is also true the method should raise a fatal exception and terminate the script.)

The constructor is fairly straightforward:

```
proc Snark {name {visible false} {Boojum false}} {
  global snark_data
  set snark_data{$name-boojum} $Boojum
  set snark_data{$name-visible} $visible
  proc $name {method arg} \
    "doSnark $name \$method \$arg"
  return $name
}
```

The only tricky bit is the definition of the command named after the object: note carefully how its body is constructed, with substitution of the value of name taking place at procedure definition time.

4.15 Reference material

4.15.1 Operators and precedence

	–	Unary minus
12	!	Not
	~	Bitwise complement
	*	Multiply
11	/	Divide
	%	Remainder
10	+	Add
	–	Subtract
9	<<	Left shift
	>>	Right shift

8	<	Less than
	>	Greater than
	<=	Less than or equal
	>=	Greater than or equal

7	==	Equals
	!=	Not equals

6	&	Bitwise and
5	^	Bitwise xor
4	|	Bitwise or
3	&&	And
2	||	Or
1	?	Choice

Operators are listed in precedence order, highest first. Operators with the same precedence associate to the left.

4.15.2 List-related commands

list *arg1 arg2* ...	Create a list from args
llength *list*	Number of elements in list
lindex *list i*	*i*th element of list
lrange *list i j*	Slice from *i*th to *j*th element of list
lappend *var arg1 arg2* ...	Append args to value of var
linsert *list index arg1 arg2* ...	insert args before element at index, returning a new list
lsearch *mode list value*	Return index of element in list that matches value. Mode is -exact, -glob or -regexp. Returns −1 if no match
lreplace *list i j args*	Replace *i*th to *j*th elements with args, returning new list
lsort *switches list*	Sort according to switches: -ascii, -integer, -real, -increasing or -decreasing
concat *arg1 arg2 arg3* ...	Join multiple lists at same level, returning new list
join *list glue*	Convert a list into a string, using glue characters
split *string chars*	Convert string into a list, splitting on chars

4.15.3 The array command

array exists	True if argument is an array variable
array size *array*	Returns number of indices defined for array
array set *array list*	Set array array from index/value list
array get *array pattern*	Convert array to index/value list. If pattern is present, return only keys that (glob) match

array names *array pattern*	Return list of indices. If pattern present, only those that (glob) match
array *startsearch array*	Return a search token for the search
array donesearch *array id*	End search defined by token id
array nextelement *array id*	Next element in array in search defined by id
array anymore *array id*	True if search not finished

4.15.4 The string command

string compare *str1 str2*	Lexicographic comparison. 0 if equal,. −1 if *str1* before *str2*, 1 if *str1* after *str2*
string match *pattern str*	1 if *str* matches pattern; 'glob' matching
string length *str*	Number of characters in *str*
string first *str1 str2*	Index in *str2* of first occurrence of *str1*, −1 if *str1* not found
string last *str1 str2*	Index in *str2* of last occurrence of *str1*, −1 if *str1* not found
string index *str index*	Character at specified index
string range *str i j*	Range of characters in *str* from *i* to *j*
string trim *str chars*	Trim characters in *chars* from both ends of *str*. *chars* defaults to whitespace
string trimleft *str chars*	Same, but trim at start only
string trimright *str chars*	Same, but trim at end only
string wordstart *str i*	Index in *str* of character after the word containing the character at index *i*
string wordend *str i*	Index in *str* of first character in the word containing the character at index *i*
string tolower *str*	Convert to lower case
string toupper *str*	Convert to upper case

4.15.5 File access modes

r	Open for reading: file must exist
r+	Open for reading and writing: file must exist
w	Open for writing: 'rewind' if file exists, create if file does not exist
w+	Open for reading and writing: 'rewind' if file exists, create if file does not exist
a	Open for writing at end: file must exist
a+	Open for reading and writing at end: file must exist

Notes

[1] The statement that 'everything is a string' was true in earlier versions of Tcl. In Tcl 8.0 strings are replaced with structures ('objects') that can hold both a string value and an internal form such as a

binary integer. This makes it possible to store information in efficient internal forms and avoid the constant translations to and from strings that occurred with the old interpreter. However, to the programmer it still appears that everything is a string.

[2] A dreadful pun – as a Tcl expression, `[incr Tcl]` increments the value of the variable `Tcl`, in the same way that the C expression `C++` increments the value of the variable `C`.

[3] This is a simplified version of a program written by Will Duquette and circulated on the Web (http://www.cogent.net/~duquette/tcl/objects.html). Permission to use the material is gratefully acknowledged.

## Chapter 5

Advanced Tcl

In this chapter we review a number of more advanced Tcl features including mechanisms for executing code 'on the fly', the organization of libraries and packages, namespaces, error trapping, network programming and security issues. We also describe the interfaces between Tcl and C, and Tcl and Java.

5.1 The eval, source, exec and uplevel commands

5.1.1 eval

The eval command takes any number of arguments, concatenates them with a separating space, then calls the interpreter recursively to execute the resulting string as a Tcl script. Thus it is possible to construct a Tcl command as the value of a variable, which can later be passed as an argument to eval. This may sound trivial, but in practice complex scripts may be constructed, their form depending on the execution of other scripts, and/or user input. Probably the most common use of eval, though, is to force a second parsing of part of a script. Recall that although a dollar sign causes variable substitution, if the value substituted starts with a dollar sign, this will not cause a second substitution. If this is the effect desired, then eval can be used.

Problems can arise from the way eval concatenates its arguments. Suppose we want to construct a command to be evaluated later. The simple case is straightforward, e.g. we construct a command

```
set cmd {set a 5}
...
```

and later we call eval to execute the command:

```
eval $cmd
```

However, it is likely that the command will include variables, e.g.

```
set cmd {set a $b}
...
eval $cmd
```

Here, the value of $b will be substituted when eval constructs its argument. If $b has the value "hello", eval will construct its argument as the string set a hello which is fine. But if the value of $b is "Hello World", eval will construct the argument string set a hello world, and the interpreter will raise an error because the set command has too many arguments. To avoid this pitfall it is sensible to use the list command to construct the argument list for eval:

```
set cmd [list set a $b]
```

The list command ensures that a substituted argument consisting of multiple words is bracketed as a single list item, so that if the value of $b is "Hello world", the value assigned to cmd is set a {Hello world}.

5.1.2 source

The source command takes a single argument which is the name of a file: it calls the interpreter to execute the contents of the file as a Tcl script. (Readers familiar with the UNIX C-shell will recognize the origin of this command.)

5.1.3 exec

The exec command is a feature of Tcl implementations on systems that support process creation, e.g. UNIX and Windows NT. It looks for an executable file with a name identical to its first argument and executes that file in a separate child process, waiting for the process to complete. (Note the difference from the Perl exec, which terminates the current program and runs the new command in the same process.) Any further arguments to exec are passed on as arguments for the executable file. Thus as a simple example,

```
set today [exec date]
```

will set the value of the variable today by executing the system's date command. Note that exec will run any executable file: it is not limited to system commands.

5.1.4 uplevel

The uplevel command combines eval and upvar (which was described in Section 4.10.2), allowing a script to be interpreted in a specified context. As with upvar, the level can be a relative or absolute stack-frame number, and defaults to 1 (the context of the caller) if omitted.

5.2 Libraries and packages

Developers using Tcl soon reach a stage where they have collections of scripts that define procedures that are useful in more than one application, and it is convenient to make these readily available as libraries from which procedure definitions can be loaded automatically as required. A simple way of doing this is provided by the *autoload* feature, which we describe in Section 5.2.1. Version 7.5 of Tcl introduced a more sophisticated package mechanism, which supports version numbers and works using the common 'provide/require' paradigm. This is described in Section 5.2.2.

5.2.1 Autoloading

The 'unknown' command

When the Tcl interpreter encounters a command that does not exist, it invokes the command unknown (if that exists) passing the name and arguments of the original command to it. Thus if we write

```
html2pdf {c:\docs\tcl.html}
```

and there is no command html2pdf, the interpreter invokes

```
unknown html2pdf {c:\docs\tcl.html}
```

instead. (If the arguments of the original command include substitutions, the substituted form is passed to the unknown command.) The user can provide a custom unknown command, but more commonly will use the default version provided by the Tcl system. This performs the following operations, in order:

1. If the command is a procedure defined in a library file, autoload it and execute it, as described in the next section.
2. If there exists a program with the name of the command, exec it, redirecting its standard input, standard output and standard error to the corresponding Tcl channels. Thus a Tcl script running under UNIX can use any of the UNIX shell commands as if they were Tcl commands. The same is true of Windows NT; however, this facility is intended as a convenience for programmers working in interactive mode. Within a script, system commands should be invoked with an explicit exec.
3. If the command name supplied is a unique abbreviation for an existing command, expand the name and call the interpreter recursively to execute the command. (Here we see why uplevel is useful: the command must be invoked in its original environment, which is one stack frame back from the environment in which unknown is executing.)

The autoloader

The key to the autoloading process is to make it possible for the unknown command to be aware of the library files. If this is achieved, then the first time a library procedure is used, the unknown command can locate the library file, source it, and then re-invoke the original command. Next time the command is used, it will be defined, so autoloading will not be necessary.

Libraries

A library consists of one or more directories each containing some procedure definitions. Having created the directories, the next stage is to run the command

```
auto_mkindex . *.tcl
```

for each directory in turn. This creates a file called `tclIndex` in the directory, containing the names of the procedures defined in the directory. Finally, applications which want to use the library must set a variable `auto_path` to contain a list of the directory names. When a non-existent procedure is first used, the `unknown` command consults `auto_path` and searches each directory in turn, looking in its `tclIndex` file for the procedure name required.

5.2.2 Packages

The package mechanism is basically the same as the autoloader, but with some refinements. The most significant is that it supports versioning: a package can exist in multiple versions, and a script can specify constraints on the version it requires. The second refinement is that a package can be composed of a mixture of Tcl procedure definitions and commands implemented in C. (Commands implemented in C are described later, in Section 5.9.)

Creating packages

As with the autoloading mechanism, script files are contained in one or more directories. Each file declares the package that it implements, using the `package provide` command, e.g.

```
package provide utils 2.1
```

This specifies that this library file implements version 2.1 of the package `utils`. The version number is in 'major.minor' format: following convention, a change in the minor version number signifies backwards compatibility: a change to the major version number denotes a substantive change to the package. Note that more than one library file can contribute to the same package: a package is thus an abstract concept sitting on top of a physical file structure. As with the autoloader, a package must have an index listing the procedures provided by the package: this is generated by the Tcl procedure `pkg_mkIndex`, e.g.

```
pkg_mkIndex {c:\tcl\lib\utils} *.tcl
```

Finally, as with the autoloader, the `auto_path` variable must be set to list the directories containing the library files.

Using packages

An application which uses packages specifies the packages it requires using the `package require` command, e.g.

```
package require utils
```

In this case the highest available version of the package will be used. If we specify

```
package require utils 2.1
```

then no version prior to 2.1 will be used, though a later version may be used if it exists. The `package require` command does not actually load the procedures immediately: they are autoloaded as required when first called.

5.3 Namespaces

Tcl as originally designed, and as described in the previous chapter, has two scopes for variables: global scope for variables used outside procedure bodies, and local scope for variables used within a procedure body, unless declared global. In addition, procedure names occupy a global namespace separate from variable names. This simple model is adequate for short scripts, but presents increasing problems as scripts become larger. In particular, it becomes increasingly difficult to avoid name clashes when using libraries. Prior to Tcl 8.0 the problem was addressed by using strict naming conventions, but this is not an ideal solution [1], and therefore Tcl 8.0 introduced the concept of *namespaces* to provide independent naming contexts within the global scope for variables and procedure names. Be warned that namespaces can be confusing: if you get the impression of a facility that was grafted on to the language at a late stage, you are not far wrong.

5.3.1 Using namespaces

A namespace is set up and populated by the `namespace eval` command., e.g.

```
set x 0
namespace eval utils {
variable x
...
set x 10
...
}
```

The argument following `namespace eval` identifies the namespace, and the next argument is an arbitrary script to be evaluated in that namespace. If the namespace does not exist, it is created. (Thus `namespace eval` can be used to create and populate a new namespace, or to add further definitions to an existing namespace.) Since a namespace defines a new naming context, the x defined by the `variable` command inside the namespace block in the example above is distinct from the x used outside. We can refer to the 'inner' x from outside the namespace as `utils::x`, and the 'outer' x can be referenced inside the namespace as `::x`. This notation is reminiscent of the way path names are used in a hierarchical file system – this is no coincidence: the namespace `utils` is nested inside the global namespace, whose name is `::` (c.f. / for the root of a file system in UNIX). Thus `utils::x` is a relative name, resolved from the current (global) namespace, while `::x` and `::utils::x` are absolute (or 'fully qualified') names. This nesting can be continued, e.g.

```
set x 0
namespace eval utils {
variable x
...
set x 10
  namespace eval file_utils {
  variable x
  ...
  set x 20
  }
}
```

Now the innermost `x` can be referenced anywhere by the fully qualified name `::utils::file_utils::x`, but can be accessed from the `utils` namespace using the relative name `file_utils::x`. Whether nested namespaces are a benefit is a moot point.

The `variable` command used outside a procedure body introduces a variable that is global to all the procedures in the namespace, or more commonly a list of such variables with initial values, e.g.

```
namespace eval utils {
 variable x 0 y 1
 ...
}
```

If the `variable` command is used inside a procedure body it makes a namespace-global variable available in the body, in the same way as the `global` command used outside a namespace, e.g.

```
namespace eval utils {
 variable x 0 y 1
 proc do_this {x} {
  variable y
  ...
 }
}
```

5.3.2 Namespaces and libraries

One of the most common uses of a namespace is when implementing a library containing procedures which need to share data. If these data items are made global, then they are accessible throughout the script: we want them to be accessible only to the family of procedures. Also, we don't want to have to worry about potential name clashes. A namespace solves the problem (almost):

```
namespace eval utils {
 variable x 0
 proc p1 {a b} {
  variable x
  . . .
 }
proc p2 {a} {
  variable x
  . . .
 }
}
```

Recall that the variable x can still be accessed outside the namespace by using a fully qualified name, ::foo::x. Thus it is not completely hidden, as private data is in languages like Java, but it is only possible to access the variable from outside by a deliberate action: using a namespace protects programmers against accidentally changing the variables from outside.

Although we want the shared variable not to be directly accessible outside the namespace, the opposite is true of the library procedures, which should be accessible without the use of fully qualified names. To make this possible, the namespace export command can be used: this customarily appears before any procedures are defined in the namespace, and lists the names of procedures that are allowed to be visible outside the namespace, e.g.

```
namespace eval utils {
 variable x 0
 namespace export p1 p2
 proc p1 {a b} {
  variable x
  . . .
 }
proc p2 {a} {
  variable x
  . . .
 }
}
```

To make the names available in another namespace (including the global namespace) the namespace import command is used. The arguments are the fully qualified names of the procedures to be imported, e.g.

```
namespace import  foo::p1 foo::p2
```

Wild cards can be used:

```
namespace import foo::*
```

If the name of an imported procedure clashes with a local procedure, an error is raised unless the -force option is used, in which case the imported procedure overrides the local procedure.

5.3.3 Namespaces and packages

A common idiom is to enclose the code of a package in a namespace which has the same name as the package, e.g.

```
package provide utils 1.0
namespace eval ::utils {
 variable x 0
 namespace export p1 p2
 proc p1 {a b} {
  variable x
  ...
 }
proc p2 {a} {
  variable x
  ...
 }
}
```

5.3.4 Callbacks

Event-driven applications like Tk require us to provide scripts that will be executed at some later time in response to an event such as a mouse click on a button. By default, such *callbacks* are executed in the global scope: however the namespace code command can be used to ensure that they are executed in a particular namespace context. For example, anticipating the next chapter, in Tk we can define a button with an associated script to be executed when the button is 'pressed':

```
button .B1 -command {puts $x}
```

If this command occurs in a namespace that defines a variable x, we can ensure that it is that x which is used, and not an x in the global scope, by changing the command to

```
button .B1 -command [namespace code {puts $x}]
```

5.4 Trapping errors

The Tcl interpreter is unforgiving: unless you take special steps it will exit on any error condition. The catch command is provided to allow error trapping: in its simplest form

```
catch {script}
```

it executes the script supplied as an argument, returning 1 if the script terminates prematurely because of an error, and 0 otherwise. We can thus use a construction like

```
if [catch {set myfile [open /tmp/foo w 0600]}] {
    puts stderr "cannot open $myfile"
```

```
} else {
...
}
```

When used in its second form,

```
catch {script} variable
```

in the event of normal termination of the script the variable will hold the result returned by the script, while in the event of premature termination it will hold whatever error message was generated by the fault. Thus the idiom is

```
if [catch {command args} result] {
  puts stderr $result
} else {
...
#return value is $result
}
```

A possible 'gotcha' is that if the catch script contains return, break or continue commands, executing any of these will cause catch to return a non-zero value (2, 3 or 4 respectively). Thus a robust use of catch will check the error code actually returned in a switch:

```
switch [catch {script} result] {
  0 {...; #normal exit}
  1 {...; #system error}
  2 {return $result; #return from procedure}
  3 {break}
  4 {continue}
  default {...; #user-defined errors}
}
```

5.5 Event-driven programs

Although Tcl was originally designed as a command-line system, it also supports event-driven programming (providing that you are using version 7.5 or later – prior to this, event-driven programming was only implemented within Tk). The Tcl event model is very straightforward: a script can register events and associated commands, and, providing that the event loop is active, the system will execute the commands when the event occurs. (The event loop is always running in Tk: if you are using pure Tcl you need to start it explicitly, as described later.)

Tk, described in the next chapter, provides a full event-driven GUI that handles window events (keystrokes and button clicks). Outside Tk there are three classes of events:

- Timer events, which are raised after a specified time has elapsed
- File events, e.g. data becoming available on a channel
- Idle events, which are raised when the system has nothing else to do.

Timer events and file events are described in more detail in the following sections: idle events are self-explanatory.

5.5.1 Starting and stopping the event loop

The event loop is controlled by the vwait command. This is called with a variable as an argument, e.g.

```
set ev 0
vwait ev
```

This starts the event loop, and vwait immediately blocks. Events are processed until some event handler changes the value of the variable ev, at which point vwait returns.

5.5.2 Timer events and idle events

Timer events are registered by the after command, e.g.

```
after 1000 [list someprog arg1 arg2]
```

This causes the procedure someproc to be called with arguments arg1 and arg2 after 1 second (1000 milliseconds). If called with only one (numerical) argument, e.g.

```
after 500
```

the application pauses for that number of milliseconds.

A command can be run at the next idle moment by specifying idle as the first argument of an after command.

Cancelling pending timer events

The after command returns a value which identifies the event, e.g.

```
set ev1 [after 1000 [list someproc arg1 arg2]]
```

This identifier can be used to cancel the pending event by a variant of the after command, e.g.

```
after cancel ev1
```

5.5.3 File events

File events are registered by the fileevent command, which can specify a read handler and a write handler for a specified channel. These handlers are called when the channel is ready for reading or writing: the main use is with pipes and network sockets. We describe how the system works for pipes here, since there is a more wide-ranging discussion of socket programming in the next section.

If we try to read from a pipe and there is no data available, the request will block. By using file events we can avoid this, making it possible for our application to get on with something else useful until data is available from the pipe, at which point the read handler will be called. For example,

```
set p [open "|cmd1"]
#register read handler
fileevent $p readable [list read_handler $p]
...
```

Structure of a read event handler

To avoid the danger of blocking because no data is available, the event handler should read only one line with `gets` (or one block with read if the pipe generates data in fixed size blocks). If more than one line or block is available the handler will be called again as soon as it exits. The second important thing is to check for end-of-file inside the handler, and to close the channel if end-of-file occurs. This is necessary because end-of-file makes a channel readable, and therefore causes the handler to be called. Closing the channel automatically unregisters the handler: if you don't do this, the handler will be called repeatedly. Thus the `read_handler` registered in the example above will have the following form.

```
proc read_handler {pipe} {
global line
  if [eof $pipe] {
    close $pipe
    return
  }
gets $pipe line
...; #read a line and do something with it
}
```

If we are indulging in really defensive programming, we have to take account of the fact that the close operation might fail: if it does, we should explicitly cancel the handler by registering an empty string as the new handler, thus:

```
if [eof $pipe] {
  if [catch {close $pipe} {
    fileevent $pipe readable ""
  }
  return
}
```

Non-blocking I/O

Even though we have set up an event-driven model for reading the pipe, there is still a possibility that our application will block. The 'pipe readable' event fires as soon as there is some data to read. If there is only a partial line, the `gets` in `read_handler` will block until the rest of the line is available. We can avoid this situation by setting the pipe into 'non-blocking' mode, thus:

```
set p [open "|cmd1"]
fconfigure $p -blocking 0
# register read handler
...
```

When `gets` is called on a non-blocking channel it always returns immediately: if no data was available it returns −1. Thus our `read_handler` procedure must be modified to recognize this possibility, returning without taking any action if `gets` returns −1.

Blocking on a write operation is much less common, but can happen unless the channel is a non-blocking channel. In this case the data written by `puts` is buffered internally and sent to the channel when it unblocks.

5.6 Making applications 'Internet-aware'

The Internet is a rich source of information, held on Web servers, FTP servers, POP/IMAP mail servers, News servers etc. A Web browser can access information on Web servers and FTP servers, and specialist clients access mail and News servers. However, this is not the only way of getting to the information: an 'Internet-aware' application can access a server and collect the information without manual intervention. For example, suppose that a Web site offers a 'lookup' facility in which the user specifies a query by filling in a form, then clicks the 'Submit' button. The data from the form is sent to a CGI program on the server, which retrieves the information, formats it as a Web page, and returns the page to the browser. A Tcl application can establish a connection to the server, send the request in the format that the browser would use, collect the returned HTML and then extract the required fields that form the answer to the query. In the same way, a Tcl application can establish a connection to a POP3 mail server and send a request which will result in the server returning a message listing the number of currently unread messages.

Much of the power of scripting languages comes from the way in which they hide the complexity of operations, and this is particularly the case when we make use of libraries and packages: as in Perl, tasks that might require pages of code in C are achieved in a few lines. The `http` package that comes with the standard Tcl distribution is a very good case in point: it makes the kind of interaction described above almost trivial. We describe how it is used, then go on to consider the 'nuts and bolts' of Internet programming in Tcl.

5.6.1 The 'http' package

Retrieving a Web page could not be simpler:

```
package require http 2.0
set token [::http::geturl www.flub.com/]
```

will retrieve the 'welcome page' from the server `www.flub.com`. The value of `token` is a token identifying an array – the 'state array' – that contains the result of the transaction: it can be converted into an array name by

```
upvar #0 $token state
```

Having done this, the body of the page is available as `state(body)`. The `state` array has eight other elements:

`currentsize`	number of bytes transferred
`error`	error code for an aborted transfer
`http`	HTTP reply status
`meta`	list of keys and values from <META> tags in reply header
`status`	ok, eof or reset
`totalsize`	expected size of returned data
`type`	content type of returned data
`url`	URL of the request

For convenience, the most commonly used elements of the state array can be retrieved by individual functions:

```
::http::data $token
```

returns the `body` element (i.e. the URL data) of the state array.

```
::http::status $token
```

returns the `status` element of the state array.

```
::http::code $token
```

returns the `http` element of the state array.

```
::http::size $token
```

returns the `currentsize` element of the state array.

Asynchronous operation

Used as above, `::http::geturl` blocks until the transfer is completed. A cautious programmer will probably want to specify a timeout to prevent the application from hanging indefinitely:

```
set token \
    [::http::geturl www.flub.com/ -timeout 60000]
```

will time out after 1 minute (60 000 ms). Alternatively, the page can be retrieved asynchronously by providing a callback procedure to be called on completion:

```
set token \
    [::http::geturl www.flub.com/ -command done]
::http::wait token
```

The call of `::http::wait` starts the Tcl event loop. The callback procedure is given an argument that is the token returned by `::http::geturl`, and takes the form

```
proc done {token} {
    upvar #0 $token state
    # Access state as a Tcl array as before
}
```

While the transfer is in progress, the `currentsize` field of the state array records the number of bytes transferred so far, and the `status` field is set to 'pending'.

Feedback to the user can be provided by using the `-progress` option:

```
set token \
  [::http::geturl www.flub.com/ -command done \
   -progress progress]
```

The procedure `progress` is called after each transfer of data from the URL. It is given three additional arguments: the token from `::http::geturl`, the expected total size of the contents from the 'Content-Length' meta-data, and the current number of bytes transferred so far. It is thus possible to display an animated record of the progress, e.g. a bar representing the percentage completion of the transfer. A simpler approach, borrowed from FTP servers, is just to output a dot each time the procedure is called, to reassure the user that something is happening:

```
proc progress {token, finalsize currentsize} {
  puts -nonewline "."
}
```

Saving to a file

If the page being retrieved is a large graphic, it may be desirable to store it in a file rather than in the state array in memory. This too is straightforward:

```
set imgf [open "c:\\temp\image1.jpg" w 0600]
set token \
  [::http::geturl www.flub.com/ -channel $imgf]
```

5.7 'Nuts-and-bolts' Internet programming

The `::http` package is by far the easiest way to program Web applications in Tcl, and you should think very carefully before doing the job yourself using the low-level facilities provided by core Tcl. This section goes into a modest amount of detail for the interested reader: when you have seen what is involved you will appreciate even more the advice to use packages.

Network programming is based on the use of sockets. These were introduced in Chapter 3, but we repeat the introduction here. Those who have read Chapter 3 should note that, unlike Perl, Tcl implements only a subset of the complete socket capability — but a very useful subset.

5.7.1 Sockets in Tcl

Sockets are network communication channels, providing a bi-directional channel between processes on different machines [2]. Sockets were originally a feature of Berkeley UNIX: later, other UNIX systems adopted them and the socket became the de facto mechanism of network communication in the UNIX world. The popular Winsock package provided similar functionality for Windows, allowing Windows systems to communicate over the network with UNIX systems, and sockets are a built-in feature of Windows 9x and Windows NT4.

From the Tcl programmer's point of view, a network socket can be treated like an open file – you write to it with `puts`, and read from it with `gets`. The socket interface is based on the TCP/IP protocol suite, so that all routing information is handled automatically. In addition, TCP provides a reliable channel, with automatic recovery from data loss or corruption: for this reason a TCP connection is often described as a *virtual circuit*. (The full socket specification also permits connections using UDP (Unreliable Datagram Protocol) but this feature is not supported in Tcl.)

Servers and server sockets

The typical network scenario has a number of client systems seeking services from servers: a server is a long-running process that controls access to a resource. Examples are HTTP servers, which provide access to Web pages, FTP servers, which allow retrieval of files using the File Transfer Protocol, and POP/IMAP servers which provide access to electronic mail. Every socket has an associated *port number*: mostly these are allocated dynamically by the system software, but servers listen for connections on 'well-known ports', which the client specifies when creating a socket. Thus if we want to communicate with a Web server we establish a connection on port 80 (usually).

A server socket has to cater for multiple connections. In the Tcl implementation, the server socket is initially set up with its associated well-known port number and a callback procedure to actually handle requests. When a connection is made to the well-known port a new socket is created for subsequent communication, so that the server socket can listen for further requests. Data from the client that initiated the request is automatically re-routed to the new socket, and the channel descriptor of the new socket is passed as an argument to the callback procedure, along with the client's address and port number.

Tcl can be used to implement both clients and servers, but in the remainder of this section we concentrate on client-side programming, to give an idea of the flavour of network programming in Tcl.

5.7.2 Creating and using sockets

As we have already observed, much of the power of scripting languages comes from the way in which they hide the complexity of operations, and there can be few better example of this than socket programming. Because Tcl implements only a subset of the socket functionality, it can conceal almost all of the details that had to be specified when creating a socket in Perl (Section 3.17): a single Tcl statement sets up a socket and connects to a server, doing the job which in C requires around thirty lines of code:

```
set mysock [socket www.somesite.com 80]
```

The first argument for the `socket` command specifies the server: we usually use a domain-style name, as here, but a numeric IP address is also acceptable. The second argument is the port number. The socket command returns when the connection is established. We can now use mysock as a channel identifier as if we had opened a file, thus

```
puts $mysock $line
```

sends a line of text to the Web server, and

```
gets $mysock line
```

reads a line from the server.

As an example of socket programming, we present a simple script to access a POP3 server and determine if there is any mail waiting for collection. A POP3 client retrieves mail from the POP3 server in a simple client–server interaction. When contact is first established with the server, a response indicates availability: the server then engages in a dialogue in which user name and password are sent, and if all is well the server responds with a message indicating how many new messages are available. In the following dialogue, client commands are in normal type and server responses are in bold.

establish connection
+OK POP3 penelope v6.50 server ready
USER dwb
+OK User name accepted, password please
PASS 12345678
+OK Mailbox open, 1 messages

Note that successful operations always result in a reply starting +OK. This dialogue is readily replicated with a Tcl script:

```
set pop [socket pop.ecs.soton.ac.uk 110]
set reply [gets $pop]
if {[string first "+OK" $reply] != 0} {
  puts "Unexpected response from server:"
  puts $reply
  exit
}

puts $pop "user dwb"
flush $pop
set reply [gets $pop]
if {[string first "+OK" $reply] != 0} {
  puts "Unexpected response from server:"
  puts $reply
  exit
}

puts $pop "pass 12345678"
flush $pop
set message [gets $pop]
if {[string first "+OK" $message] != 0} {
```

Open socket on well-known port 110 and check response.

Send USER command and flush buffered output: get reply and check it.

Send PASS command and flush buffered output: get reply and check it.

```
        puts "Unexpected response from server:"
        puts $reply
        exit
    }
```

Extract message about new mail.

```
    puts [string range $message 4 end]
    close $pop
```

5.7.3 Complications

Skip this section unless you are interested in the arcane minutiae of network programming.

Of course, it isn't really as simple as that. In the real world there are numerous complications that we need to take care of.

Failed connections

The socket command may fail immediately, e.g. if we specify a non-existent host. This possibility is easily dealt with using catch:

```
    if [catch {socket www.somesite.com 80} result] {
      puts stderr $result
    } else {
    set mysock $result
    }
```

Connection timeout

If the server is busy it may leave our request waiting in a queue or refuse to accept the connection, and for the sake of the user we ought to abandon the attempt if no connection is established within a reasonable time. This can be achieved by employing some low cunning. If we use the socket command with the -async option, it returns immediately without waiting for the connection to be established. The socket becomes writable when the connection is established, or fails, and we can use a fileevent to recognize this:

```
        set mysock [socket -async www.somesite.com 80]
        fileevent $mysock writable {set connected 1}
        vwait connected
        ...
```

The vwait will block, leaving the event loop running, until the fileevent sets the value of connected to 1. The low cunning is to have a timer event that will also change the value of the variable connected after a certain time:

```
        after 120000 {set connected 0}; # 2 minutes
        set mysock [socket -async www.somesite.com 80]
        fileevent $mysock writable {set connected 1}
        vwait connected
```

```
if !connected {
  puts stderr "Server not responding"
  exit
}
...
```

If connected *is zero when* vwait *returns, connection timed out.*

(We are writing this code as if it were running at top level, hence the `exit` on timeout. In practice, the connection operation would be encapsulated in a procedure, and we would return with a return code signifying the nature of the error.)

Finally, we need to incorporate the `catch` to detect immediate failure due to a bad address. (Even with the `-async` option, the `socket` command checks that the address is valid before returning.) The code follows.

```
after 120000 {set connected 0}; # 2 minutes
if [catch {socket -async www.somesite.com 80} \
    result] {
  puts "Connection failed"
  puts "$result"
  exit
} else {
  set mysock $result
  fileevent $mysock writable {set connected 1}
  vwait connected
  if !connected {
    puts stderr "Not responding"
    exit
  }
}
...
```

If connected *is zero when* vwait *returns, connection has timed out.*

The astute reader will have noted the significance of the statement that the socket becomes writable when the connection completes *or fails*. Thus if `connected` has the value 1 when `vwait` returns, all we can conclude is that the connection did not time out: we cannot guarantee that a connection has been established. We shall show later how to deal with this contingency.

Non-blocking I/O

Network connections are subject to arbitrary delays, and it may be desirable that an application should not freeze while waiting for responses. To achieve this, the socket channel should be set to non-blocking mode, with reading delegated to a `fileevent` handler as explained in the previous section.

Protection against sudden disconnection

If our application is interacting with a server, there is a structured exchange of messages: we send some text to the server, and the server sends some text in reply. However, the nature of the Internet is such that the connection may be broken by a failure at one of numerous staging posts: equally, the server may go down at any time. To protect against this possibility, whenever we send a message to a server we should set a timeout for receipt of a reply. (If we are using a non-blocking channel the message will always appear to go, since Tcl will, if necessary, buffer it internally until the channel is writable.) Setting a timeout also protects us against the situation encountered earlier, where a socket generates a 'writable' event even if the connection failed.

5.8   Security issues: running untrusted code

The largely platform-independent nature of Tcl makes it a natural medium for mobile code – code which is sent over the network to be executed on a remote system. The code might be sent as an e-mail attachment or via a socket connection. However, running code from an unknown or untrusted source using eval or source has grave security implications. The code has access to the interpreter's namespace(s), including the procedure namespace, thus it can accidentally change the value of any variable. There are many possibilities for a malicious script: it could redefine a procedure as a basis for a trojan attack, or change the destination of a socket as a basis for spoofing. The remote script also has access to the underlying system so that, for example, files and directories can be modified or deleted, whether by accident or malice.

The solution is to run untrusted code in a 'sand box' which isolates it as far as possible from the environment [3]. On platforms which support multiple processes (UNIX, Windows NT) Tcl provides this capability in the form of *slave interpreters* and *safe interpreters* which implement a restricted language called Safe Tcl.

5.8.1   Slave interpreters

A slave interpreter is a Tcl interpreter that runs as a separate process under the control of a master interpreter. Since it is a new instance of the interpreter in a separate process, it has its own global namespace (which is the root for the tree of defined namespaces), and its own procedure namespace. Thus the slave does not have access to the variables or procedures of the master: the only data shared between master and slave are the environment variables in the variable env. The master and slave also have separate namespaces for open files, though explicit commands are provided to share files and to transfer references to open files from one interpreter to another.

The significance of the term *slave* derives from the fact that the master can control the operation of the slave by creating *command aliases*. A command alias defines a procedure in the master that is obeyed in place of the aliased command whenever that command is invoked by the slave: an example of this is given later in this section.

A master can create any number of slaves: for example, a multi-file editor might be implemented as a master script which sets up a separate slave interpreter for each new file to be edited. A slave interpreter can itself create additional slaves for which it is master, resulting in a hierarchy of interpreters. Also, command aliases can be set up between slaves anywhere in the hierarchy. However, we will not explore these complications further.

The interp command

Slave interpreters are created and controlled using the `interp` command. A slave interpreter named `foobar` is created by

```
interp create foobar
```

The interpreter `foobar` starts up in a separate process and waits for a script to interpret, which is provided by its master with a command like

```
interp eval foobar {puts "I'm a slave!\n"}
```

As a shorthand, this can be abbreviated to

```
foobar eval {puts "I'm a slave!\n"}
```

Either of these commands returns a value which is the value of the last expression evaluated in the slave: this provides a primitive communication method between slave and master. Having evaluated the script, the slave waits for another script: this continues until the master kills the slave with

```
interp delete foobar
```

As with the simple `eval` command discussed earlier, the argument given to `interp eval foobar` or `foobar eval` is converted to a space-separated string of words, and to avoid problems with substitutions it is safest to use the `list` command, e.g.

```
interp eval foobar [list puts "I'm a slave!\n"]
```

File descriptors

File descriptors can be passed between master and slave in two ways. A file descriptor created by the master can be shared between master and slave, so that both can use it, or it can be transferred to the slave for the slave's exclusive use. Thus if we open a file for writing in the master with

```
set myfile [open /tmp/foo w 0600]
```

then the file descriptor can be shared with a slave by

```
interp share {} $myfile foobar
```

(Note the use of { } to denote the current interpreter.) The channel will not be closed until both interpreters have issued a `close` command for it either explicitly or implicitly – I/O channels accessible in an interpreter are automatically closed when an interpreter is destroyed. Alternatively,

```
interp transfer {} $myfile foobar
```

transfers the file descriptor to the slave, implicitly closing it in the master.

We now show how this can be combined with command aliases to provide a degree of control over the slave's access to the file system. Suppose we want to allow the slave foobar to have read access to files, but to deny write access. We can do this by aliasing the open command to a command in the master that will force the mode to read-only before opening the file, and then transfer the descriptor to foobar, thus:

```
proc safeopen {path mode permissions} {
global foobar
set chan [open $path r $permissions]
interp transfer {} $chan foobar
return $chan
}
foobar alias open safeopen
```

5.8.2 Safe Tcl

The degree of control by a master over a slave is greatly enhanced if the slave is created with the -safe option, becoming a so-called safe interpreter, e.g.

```
interp create -safe foobar
```

This creates a slave interpreter that implements Safe Tcl, a cut down language that does not have commands to access or manipulate the file system, access the network or to run other programs or scripts. The full list of commands that are not available in safe Tcl is as follows:

```
cd      exec   exit   fconfigure   file     glob
load    open   pwd    socket                source   vwait
```

In addition, the slave interpreter does not share environment variables with its master: it runs scripts in isolation from the outside world except for the ability to return a string to the master. (The ability to return a string may appear harmless, but a malicious script running in the slave might compute a very long string, hoping to provoke a buffer overflow, or might take a very long time to compute the string as a form of denial-of-service attack. When it comes to considering security risks, you have to be paranoid.)

The techniques of aliasing commands, described above, can be used with safe interpreters, provided that care is taken never to evaluate, or perform substitutions on, values passed from the slave; this avoids the danger of executing arbitrary code planted by a malicious slave. However, a further degree of control is provided by the fact that the commands listed above as not available in Safe Tcl are not actually removed from the safe interpreter: they are in fact hidden, and can be invoked in the slave by an explicit command in the master. For example, if we want to execute a script from a file in a safe interpreter, the master can invoke the hidden source command to read the script:

```
interp create -safe foobar
interp invokehidden foobar source $file
```

The master can choose to make a hidden command permanently visible in the slave, e.g.

```
interp expose foobar pwd
```

makes the pwd command available to the slave foobar. (This is unlikely to be useful, since cd is still hidden, but it illustrates the point.) Similarly, the master can hide commands that are not on the default hidden list, e.g.

```
interp hide foobar after
```

hides the after command, making it impossible for scripts executed in foobar to execute a command after a time delay. (This is quite a sensible thing to do. The command after $time delays execution of the current script for a time (in milliseconds) determined by the value of $time, and is therefore the basis for a possible denial-of-service attack.) If you are totally paranoid, you can remove commands entirely, e.g.

```
interp eval foobar [list rename after {}]
```

removes the after command from foobar.

5.8.3   The Safe Base

The *Safe Base*, implemented in the ::safe module, allows a master interpreter to create safe interpreters that contain a set of predefined aliases for the source, load, file and exit commands and are able to use the autoloading and package mechanisms. (The interpreters created using the Safe Base also include an alias for the encoding command. This command is used when handling data that uses a special encoding, e.g. the euc-jp encoding, which represents ASCII characters as single bytes and Japanese characters as two bytes.) All the commands provided in the master interpreter by the Safe Base reside in the safe namespace. The aliases for source and load only work for files that occur in a list of directories provided by the master when the safe interpreter is created. The exit alias causes the slave interpreter to be terminated.

The file alias provides access to a safe subset of the subcommands of the file command. Because the source, load and file commands access the local file system, there is a potential for information leakage about its directory structure. To prevent this, commands that take file names as arguments in the safe interpreter use tokens instead of the real directory names; these tokens are translated to the real directory name while a request to, for example, source a file is mediated by the master interpreter. This virtual path system is maintained in the master interpreter for each safe interpreter created, and the path maps tokens accessible in the safe interpreter into real path names on the local file system thus preventing safe interpreters from gaining knowledge about the structure of the file system of the host on which the interpreter is executing.

5.9   The C interface

Tcl was originally envisaged as a command-line interpreter which could be embedded in a C application. The application created a new instance of an interpreter, and then registered the application-specific commands (written in C) with the interpreter, so that they could be used in scripts alongside the Tcl built-in commands. Nowadays, many Tcl applications are 'pure Tcl', hosted by a simple shell such as the wish shell. However, it

This section requires some knowledge of C programming.

may still be necessary to create commands coded in C, either in the interests of efficiency, or because the command requires facilities not available in Tcl, e.g. low-level access to the operating system or hardware. In this section we present a brief and somewhat oversimplified account of the interface between Tcl and C.

5.9.1 Integrating Tcl into an existing application

Integrating Tcl into an application is just a matter of including the Tcl header files, and calling Tcl_CreateInterp:

```
#include <tcl.h>
Tcl_interp *interp
...
interp = Tcl_CreateInterp()
```

This function returns a pointer to a Tcl_Interp structure, which is used as an argument to other functions to identify the interpreter involved. (Remember that an application can invoke multiple interpreters.)

Calling the intepreter in versions before Tcl 8.0

Once the interpreter is set up, we can invoke it with Tcl_Eval, e.g.

```
char script[] = "puts {Hello World!}";
result_code = Tcl_Eval(interp, script);
```

The result_code variable is set to TCL_OK if interpretation is successful, and TCL_ERROR if the interpreter reports an error. A pointer to the result string (or error message) is left in interp->result.

There are several variants on TclEval: Tcl_EvalFile has a file name as its second argument, and treats the file contents as a script to be evaluated. Tcl_VarEval can have an arbitrary number of string arguments after the interpreter argument, and concatenates them into a single string to be evaluated as a script. The last argument must be NULL.

Calling the interpreter in Tcl 8.0

Tcl 8.0 introduced the Tcl_Obj structure. These structures are used to store all internal values in Tcl: the fields of the structure comprise *reference count, type, string value, length* and *internal representation*. Thus, for example, a string that represents a decimal number will be stored in a Tcl_Obj object with its value as the *string* field: the first time it is used in a numerical context, the string-to-number conversion will be performed, and the resulting binary form of the number stored in the *internal representation* field. On subsequent occasions the numerical conversion will not be required.

Tcl 8.0 also introduced the technique of compiling scripts into a byte-code form. The Tcl_Eval function is replaced by Tcl_EvalObjEx, which takes a pointer to a Tcl_Obj structure as its second argument rather than a string. The *string* field contains the script, and the first time it is used, the script is compiled into bytecode format, which is stored in the *internal representation* field. Next time `Tcl_EvalObjEx` is called with this structure, the bytecode version of the script will be used. A result code, `Tcl_OK` or `Tcl_ERROR` is returned, and the result string or error message is packaged into a `Tcl_Obj` structure, which can be retrieved with `Tcl_GetObjResult`.

5.9.2   Creating new commands in C

Structure of a command procedure before Tcl 8.0

The Tcl interpreter parses a command into a series of words. If the first word is recognized as being a C-coded command (by a mechanism to be described shortly), these argument words have to be passed to the C program. In versions of Tcl prior to Tcl 8.0, this was done using the same mechanism as is used in the shell for passing arguments to a C command. A C function that is to be used from the command line conventionally starts with the line

```
main(int argc char *argv[])
```

argc is a count of the number of arguments, and argv is a pointer to an array of (pointers to) strings, which are the arguments supplied. The value of argv[0] is the name by which the function was called. The interface to a Tcl command procedure is very similar, being defined by a procedure prototype:

```
typedef int Tcl_CmdProc(ClientData clientData,
    Tcl_Interp *interp, int argc, char *argv[0]);
```

Here argc and argv behave in exactly the same way as in a main function. The second argument is a pointer to the interpreter: the significance of the first argument will emerge later. A Tcl command procedure returns a value, TCL_OK or TCL_ERROR and places its result in interp->result, like Tcl_Eval.

Structure of a command procedure in Tcl 8.0

As we have just seen, in Tcl 8.0 all values are held in `Tcl_Obj` structures. A command procedure is passed an array of pointers to these structures rather than an array of pointers to strings. The procedure prototype is

```
typedef int Tcl_OCmdProc(ClientData clientData,
    Tcl_Interp *interp, int objc,
    Tcl_Obj *CONST objv[]);
```

As before, the command procedure returns TCL_OK or TCL_Error: it uses `Tcl_SetObjResult` to set its result as a `Tcl_Obj` structure, which can later be retrieved using `Tcl_GetObjResult`.

Registering a new command: versions before Tcl 8.0

A new command is registered with the interpreter using the function `Tcl_CreateCommand`. This takes five arguments:

- A pointer to the interpreter with which the command is to be registered: this will be passed to the command procedure whenever it is called
- The name of the command as it will be used in Tcl
- The name of the C command procedure that implements the command
- The 'client data': a one-word argument (typically an integer or a pointer) which will be passed to the associated command procedure as its first argument whenever it is called
- The 'delete' procedure.

The first three of these are self-explanatory, but the other two require some explanation. The client data argument is useful if a single command procedure is provided to implement a number of related commands. As each command is registered, the client data argument can be used to identify the particular member of the family so that when the procedure is called it can use its client data argument to control a switch to control command-specific actions. For example, in a robot control application we could define Tcl commands forward, back, left and right which all call the same C procedure with a numerical parameter as client data to indicate the motion required. The delete procedure, if specified, will be called when the Tcl command is deleted with Tcl_DeleteCommand. Here we are entering the realms of high magic, beyond the scope of this text.

As an example, suppose we want to add a Tcl command 'wibble', and we have written a C command procedure, WibbleCmd to implement it. The necessary call is

```
Tcl_CreateCommand(interp, "wibble", WibbleCmd,
    (ClientData) NULL,(Tcl_CmdDeleteProc *) NULL);
```

Registering a new command in Tcl 8.0

In Tcl 8.0, if the command procedure has been written to use the object interface, the command is registered using Tcl_CreateObjCommand in the place of Tcl_CreateCommand. Everything else remains the same.

5.9.3 Dynamically loadable packages

The Tcl package mechanism has been described earlier in Section 5.2. A package can be defined in C by creating a shared library (.so file in UNIX, DLL in Windows) that will be dynamically loaded in response to a package require command. Suppose we want to create a package 'wibble' which is to provide a Tcl command 'makewib'. The skeleton of the necessary file is as follows. (The actual mechanics of creating shared library files are beyond the scope of this discussion.)

```
/* wibble.c */
#include <tcl.h>
/* declare command procedure */
int makewibCmd(ClientData clientData,
            TclInterp *interp,
            int objc,
            Tcl_Obj *CONST objv[]);
/* Declare function to be called when */
```

```
/* package is loaded */
int Wibble_Init(Tcl_Interp *interp {
  Tcl_CreateObjCommand(interp, "wib_a",
      makewibCmd, (ClientData) NULL,
      (Tcl_CmdDeleteProc *) NULL);
Tcl_PkgProvide(interp, "Wibble", 1.0);
  return TCL_OK;
}
```

When the compiled package has been placed in a suitable directory (i.e. one listed in the auto_path variable), we run pkg_mkIndex in that directory. This creates index entries so that when we say

```
package require Wibble
```

the function Wibble_Init will be called. This creates the new command, and the Tcl_PkgProvide function creates the pkgIndex.tcl file which will be consulted by the autoloader the first time a command defined in the package is used.

5.10 The Java interface

'TclJava' began as a research project at Sun Microsystems. It included two projects, *TclBlend* and *Jacl* (Java Application Control Language). TclBlend was designed to bridge the Java environment to the C-based Tcl implementation, while Jacl was to be a pure Java implementation of the Tcl interpreter and environment. Thus TclBlend would make it possible to interface legacy Tcl code to Java, while Jacl was to be a 100% pure Java implementation of Tcl, which would run on any system that incorporated a Java Virtual Machine, i.e. any Web browser. The original developers created version 1.0 of Jacl and TclBlend, and released them early in 1998. The first versions worked well and were used by a number of people. However, when the Tcl group left Sun to form Scriptics Corporation, development was halted due to a lack of programmers available to work on the project. Development was continued by a couple of enthusiasts from the academic community, one working on TclBlend and the other on Jacl. One of them has since moved on to other things, so support for TclJava now depends on a single enthusiast.

This section requires some knowledge of Java programming.

The current version of both TclBlend and of Jacl, at the time of writing, is version 1.1.1. Unfortunately, the Jacl implementation is far from a complete port of Tcl, though it includes all of the control structures and a majority of core Tcl commands. There are plans to implement namespaces and sockets but they have not been implemented as yet. In particular, Tk has not yet been implemented. There are also complications between platforms; for example, Microsoft's Java implementation does not properly implement I/O features that Jacl depends on. For these reasons we will not discuss Jacl further.

5.10.1 TclBlend

TclBlend is an extension of the C implementation of the Tcl interpreter which allows the interpreter to be dynamically loaded into a Java Virtual Machine (JVM), and conversely allows a Tcl interpreter to dynamically load a JVM. This means that Tcl extensions can be written in Java rather than in C, with the consequent benefits of platform independence.

The Java package

The Java package, invoked by

```
package require java
```

is at the heart of TclBlend. It uses the Java Reflection API to create and interact with Java objects from a Tcl script. A trivial example is

```
set f [java::new java.awt.frame]
$f setTitle "Hello World!"
```

The java::new command creates an instance of the Java class provided as an argument, in this case java.awt.frame, and returns an identifier for the object which is stored in the variable f. A side effect of this operation is that $f becomes a command that can be used to invoke the methods of the object, in this case the setTitle method. Another side effect is that the Java object is associated with the Tcl object, and will not be garbage-collected until the Tcl object is freed.

The things we can do using the Java package include:

- Create new instances of any public class
- Call methods on objects or static methods for a class
- Access or set any public field of an object (or class if field is static)
- Discover the class, base class or super class of an object
- Discover the public methods and fields for a given object or class
- Load new Java classes from a path specified in Tcl
- Define new Java classes from a byte stream in Tcl.

Defining Tcl commands in Java

Tcl Blend includes a number of Java classes which expose the internals of the Tcl interpreter to allow Java classes to provide extensions to a running interpreter. This capability is provided by the Java package tcl.lang. which uses the Java Native Interface (JNI) to interact with the C-based Tcl interpreter. The interfaces are quite similar to the C interfaces provided by the C implementation.

A Tcl interpreter is represented by the class Interp. A Java class may register a new command in a Tcl interpreter using the createCommand method of the Interp class. When the Tcl script running in the Tcl interpreter invokes the command, the Java class registered for the command is called. The Java code to create one (or more) Tcl commands can be collected together into a Tcl extension.

In the C version we provided a command procedure to implement the Tcl command: in TclBlend we have to provide a Java class to implement the command. Thus for the 'makewib' command of the 'Wibble' class, we would define a class as follows

```
import tcl.lang.*;
class makewibCmd implements Command {
  public void cmdProc( Interp interp,
    TclObject argv[])
  throws TclException {
  ...
  }
}
```

The `cmdProc` method has a Tcl interpreter object as its first argument and an array of `TclObject` objects as its second argument. Notice that unlike the C function prototype, the number of arguments is not passed because Java has bounded arrays. As before, `argv[0]` is the name of the Tcl command, and all of the other elements are the arguments specified on the Tcl command line. The class processes its arguments and returns a result, which is passed back to the Tcl interpreter via the `interp` object, using the `setResult` method:

```
interp.setResult(...);
```

Having defined the class we can now register the new command as follows.

```
import tcl.lang.*;
public class WibbleExtension extends Extension{
public void init( Interp interp) {
   interp.createCommand("makewib",
                new makewibCmd());
  }
}
```

To complete the job we have to ensure that the extension is loaded in our Tcl script:

```
package require java
java::load WibbleExtension
```

Notes

[1] Building large programs without namespaces is difficult, but not impossible. The exmh mail user interface has grown to over 25 000 lines of Tcl, at least half of this coming from the user community. Strict adherence to naming conventions made this possible without the use of namespaces.

[2] In UNIX systems sockets can also be used as a method of inter-process communication between processes running on the same machine. Although Perl supports this capability, Tcl does not.

[3] For example, if suitable browser plug-ins are installed, Tcl scripts can also be incorporated in Web pages as Tcl applets or *Tclets*. It is essential that these are not allowed unrestricted access to the system. See Chapter 11 for more on this topic.

## Chapter 6

Tk

Visual interfaces are usually implemented using a library of functions that implement a collection of building blocks: menus, dialog boxes, buttons etc. This is notoriously difficult in languages like C++. Tk originated as a toolkit using Tcl as the glue for such a collection of functions in the X Window system for UNIX. It has since been ported to the Windows environment, so providing a system-independent visual model. The functionality of Tk can also be accessed from Perl, demonstrating that it is language-independent as well. In this chapter we see how the combination of Tcl and Tk can be used to proto-type graphical user interfaces without the need for complicated program-ming, and give a brief account of the similar facilities provided by Perl-Tk.

6.1 Visual toolkits

Low-level programming of visual interfaces is exceedingly tedious, basically because every pixel on the screen has to be specified. The operating system provides a simple level of abstraction away from pixels: for example, the X Window System library Xlib contains functions to

- create an empty window
- draw dots, lines rectangles, polygons and arcs
- fill rectangles, polygons and arcs
- draw text strings.

Even with this level of assistance the programmer is working at a very low level. Consider the simple window shown in Figure 6.1, which has the usual title bar, menu bar and scrollbars. To create this, the programmer must write code for the following sequence of actions:

- create the parent window
- draw lines to create a border
- draw rectangles for the title bar, menu bar and client area
- fill these with appropriate colours
- draw text in the title bar
- draw rectangles for the control buttons
- draw patterns on the control buttons
- draw text in the title bar and menu bar
- draw rectangles for the scrollbars
- draw rectangles for the scrolling buttons
- draw patterns on the scrolling buttons to create the arrows.

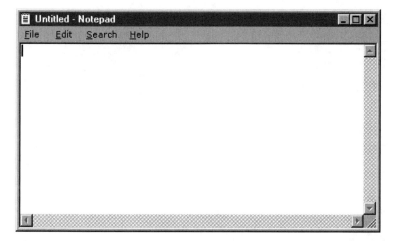

Figure 6.1 A simple window

This is just the start. The application has to include code to respond to external events created by the user: for example, a mouse-down event when the mouse coordinates lie within one of the scroll buttons requires redrawing of the client area to scroll the contents: this has to be done repeatedly until a mouse-up event is received.

The answer, of course, is to move to a higher level of abstraction. Systems like the X Window System and Microsoft Windows include toolkits to provide canned procedures for the 'building bricks' from which visual interfaces can be constructed: these are called *widgets* in X and *controls* in the Microsoft world. While the use of a toolkit and a widget library is an improvement, programming at this level is still highly complex, requiring substantial expertise in C or C++, together with an understanding of the internal working of the underlying operating system to handle the external events. Systems like Tk and Visual Basic provide dramatic illustrations of the leverage that can be achieved with scripting languages, making it possible to do in a few lines of readable code what previously required pages of impenetrable C or C++ code.

6.2 Fundamental concepts of Tk

Tk uses Tcl to provide a command language to build graphical user interfaces based on a collection of widgets. In the original implementation the underlying system was the X Window System: widgets were implemented in C using the X toolkit, and Tcl had a dual rôle: it was used to implement a command language for creating and positioning widgets, and as the language used to describe the effects of external events like mouse clicks. Tcl/Tk has since been ported to the Windows (Win32) and Macintosh environments, so providing a system-independent visual model. An alternative view of Tk is that it defines a set of graphical objects (widgets) and a collection of methods for manipulating those widgets: the Perl-Tk system takes this view, allowing the functionality of Tk to be accessed from Perl. In this chapter we describe the Tcl-Tk combination as implemented for Windows, concluding with a brief look at Perl-Tk.

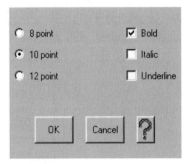

Figure 6.2(a) Tk widgets: buttons

Figure 6.2(b) Tk widgets: listbox and scrollbar

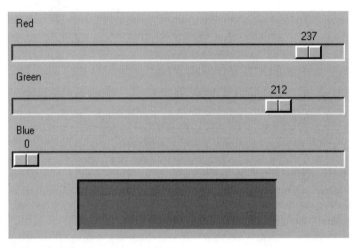

Figure 6.2(c) Tk widgets: scales

Figure 6.2(d) Tk widgets: menu

6.2.1 Widgets

Widget classes

Tk provides many kinds of widget: some of them are illustrated in Figures 6.2(a) to 6.2(d). Many of these widgets are introduced in the examples that follow in Section 6.3. Major widget classes are described briefly here, but space does not permit a complete description of all the widgets: as always, our intention is to convey the flavour and power of the language, not all the detail. The Tk documentation should be consulted for a full account. Important widget classes are

- *Frame*: a rectangular area forming a container for widgets. A frame may be invisible, or may have borders and '3-D effects', e.g. appearing raised or sunken.
- *Label*: a frame that contain a line of text.
- *Message*: a frame that contains a multi-line text message.
- *Entry*: a box into which users can type an editable line of text.
- *Button*: a plain button can be seen as a label that responds to mouse clicks. Check buttons and radio buttons are also provided.
- *Listbox*: a box which displays multiple lines of text and allow the user to select a particular line.
- *Scrollbar*: interacts with other widgets, e.g. listboxes, to determine exactly what is displayed.
- *Scale*: allows the user to change an integral value by dragging a pointer along a horizontal or vertical bar.
- *Text*: a widget that allows you to display and edit multiple lines of text.
- *Canvas*: General purpose container for drawings and images.
- *Menu*: including drop-down menus, pop-up menus and cascading menus.

Widget names

Every widget has a name, which is assigned when the widget is first created. The name must be unique among the widgets at the same level in the hierarchy (see below).

Widget creation

The name of a widget class is also the name of a command that will create an instance of the class, e.g. button .b creates an instance of a button and assign the name .b to it. (The significance of the dot in the name will become apparent shortly.) Note that widget names must start with a lower-case letter after the dot.

Widget properties

Widgets have *properties* (or *attributes*) that determine their appearance, e.g. their colour, the font to be used for text, etc. Properties can be set when the widget is first created, and can be changed subsequently: when a widget is created, a command of the same name is automatically defined for later use in configuring the properties [1], e.g.

```
button .b -text Go
...
.b configure -text Stop
```

Widgets have a very large number of attributes – even a simple button widget has 37 attributes – but many widgets share a common set of attributes: these include size, orientation, colour and appearance.

Widget hierarchies

The widgets that make up an interface form a hierarchy: Tk uses a notation reminiscent of file system paths to represent this hierarchy, so that a fully qualified name determines the exact position of the named widget in the hierarchy. The hierarchy is based in the 'top-level window', which is normally the application's main window, created at the time the Tk application starts by calling the `Tk_Main` function from the application's C code. This function sets up the main window, performs various initializations, then initiates the event loop by calling `Tk_MainLoop`. (An application can have more than one top-level window, as described later.) This top-level window is an implicit frame named `.`, and each successive level in the hierarchy is denoted by another dot. Consider, for example, the display shown in Figure 6.3: this is made up of a number of widgets, which are arranged in a hierarchy as shown in Figure 6.4.

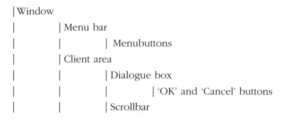

Figure 6.3   Nesting of Tk widgets

```
| Window
|          | Menu bar
|          |          | Menubuttons
|          | Client area
|          |          | Dialogue box
|          |          |          | 'OK' and 'Cancel' buttons
|          |          | Scrollbar
```

Figure 6.4   Tk widget naming hierarchy

Thus the fully qualified name of the OK button in Figure 6.3 might be given as `.clientarea.dialog.Okbutton`.

6.2.2   Geometry management

Widgets are invisible when first created: they become visible when they are located on the screen to meet the requirements of the interface designer by a geometry manager, which controls the positioning of widgets. (Not for the Tk user the ease of drag-and-drop design as found in Visual Basic.) A geometry manager positions widgets within a frame, and complex layouts can be achieved by placing frames within frames.

Tk provides three geometry managers.

1.   The *pack* geometry manager is constraint-based: the user specifies constraints on the location of widgets, e.g. stacking vertically or horizontally, and the manager works

out for itself the exact locations. *Pack* was the only geometry manager in the original version of Tk.

2. The *grid* geometry manager allows widgets to be placed on a grid with variable sized rows and columns. The user specifies the rows and columns to be occupied by a widget, and the geometry manager adjusts the size of the grid to fit.

3. The *place* geometry manager allows widgets to be positioned precisely in term of absolute or relative x and y coordinates.

Any particular widget can only be controlled by one geometry manager, but since the geometry manager controls widgets in a frame, different frames can be controlled by different geometry managers.

The three geometry managers are called by the commands `pack`, `grid` and `place`, respectively. Each command takes as an argument a list of widgets to be displayed, with options to fine-tune the positioning. The *pack* and *grid* geometry managers are introduced in the examples which follow; a more detailed account of all three geometry managers is given in Section 6.5.

A top-level window is a frame which occupies its own window. As we have seen, an application starts with one top-level window: subsequent top-level windows can be created in the same way as widgets, using the `toplevel` command as shown in the following example.

```
label .l -text "Original window"
toplevel .new_window
label .new_window.l -text "New window"
pack .l
pack .new_window.l
```

6.2.3 Events

Many widgets respond to user input (events) in the form of mouse operations and key presses. The programmer must provide a callback script which will be executed when the event occurs: these scripts will typically change the display to reflect the outcome of some computation. The callback is defined by *binding* events to Tcl scripts, either by an explicit command or, in the case of buttons, as an option to the command that creates the widget, e.g.

```
button .b -text Finish -command {exit}
```

is a shorthand for

```
button .b -text Finish
bind .b <Button-1> {exit}
```

See Section 6.4 for a full account of events and binding.

6.3 Tk by example

In this section we present some examples of Tk, which illustrate many of the features of the language, including the working of the *pack* and *grid* geometry managers. In each case we present the example using *pack*, then describe how to achieve the same effect using *grid*. The examples use the *wish* interactive shell, which is provided as part of Tk: this provides a 'console' window in which the user types code, and a second window which displays the results of executing the code.

6.3.1 Example 1: A button

```
button .b1 -text "Press Me" \
   -command {.b1 configure -text "You did!"}
pack .b1
```

When this code is typed into the console window it generates an interface with a button labelled 'Press Me'. When the button is 'pressed' by clicking the mouse on it, the display changes, as shown in Figures 6.5(a) and 6.5(b).

Figure 6.5(a) A simple button,
initial state

Figure 6.5(b) A simple button,
after mouse click

Notes

- The first line creates a button widget: it includes a `-text` option to specify what is to appear on the button, and also a `-command` option. Since the most common user interaction with a button is to 'press' it by clicking the mouse, Tk includes the command option to specify a script to be executed when the button is pressed. This shortcuts the more general mechanism of binding events to scripts.
- The script that is invoked when the button is pressed uses the `configure` option to change the text on the button.
- The default behaviour of the *pack* geometry manager is to place the first widget at the top of the window, and then to shrink the client area to an exact fit round the widget(s) it has placed. In this case the area shrinks vertically to match the size of the button: the horizontal size is constrained by the minimum size for the *wish* shell's title bar.

Using grid

Clearly, since we are only placing one widget we could use the grid geometry manager. Replacing the line `pack .b1` by `grid .b1` would produce exactly the same display, with the parent frame shrinking to fit the widget – the grid is elastic.

6.3.2   Example 2: Delayed action

Events are not limited to external user actions: timer events can be used, as illustrated in this example.

```
button .b1 -text "Press Me" -command {
  .b1 configure -text "You did!";
  after 2000 {bell; exit}
  }
pack .b1
```

This example behaves in the same way as the previous one, with the addition that 2 seconds after the button has been pressed and the text has changed, there is a 'beep' and the *wish* window disappears.

Notes

- The script bound to the `press` event now contains two commands.
- The `after` command returns immediately having set up a delayed action event: the script given as its second argument is executed after a number of milliseconds given as the first argument.
- The `bell` command 'rings the terminal bell' – an expression dating back to the early days of UNIX and hard-copy Teletype terminals. In practice it generates a 'beep' from the PC's speaker.

6.3.3   Example 3: A phonebook

Figure 6.6 shows a simple visual front-end to the phonebook discussed in Section 4.14.1. In Figure 6.6(a) the user has typed in a user id: pressing Return causes the matching phone number to be displayed as in Figure 6.6(b).

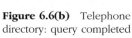

Figure 6.6(a)   Telephone
directory: query entered

Figure 6.6(b)   Telephone
directory: query completed

This example makes use of *entry* widgets. An *entry* provides a box in which a line of text can be typed and edited. The widget has an associated variable called its 'textvariable' which is specified by the `-textvariable` option of the entry command, e.g.:

```
entry .e -width 15 -textvariable t1
```

(The option can be abbreviated to -textvar.) The value of this variable is the text currently in the entry widget, and by assigning to this variable new text can be displayed in the entry widget.

Most of the code is concerned with building and accessing the array: this is virtually the same as the code used in the Tcl version presented in Chapter 5, the only difference being that we have made a small addition to provide a warning 'bell' if the lookup fails.

```
#set up array from file
set in [open {d:\phones.txt} r]
array set phones [split [read $in nonewline] "\n\t"]
#procedure to look up by name
proc look_up_by_name {name} {
  global phones
  if {[info exists phones($name)]}{
      return $phones($name)
    } else {
        bell; return "NO INFO"}
}

#procedure to look up by number
proc look_up_by_number {phone} {
global phones
 set name "NO INFO"
 foreach key [array names phones] {
    if {$phonebook($key) == $phone} {
       set name $key; break
    }
  }
 if {$name == "NO INFO"} {bell}
 return $name
}

#now set up the visual interface
label .label1 -text "Name: "
entry .name -width 10 -relief sunken \
 -textvariable Ename
label .label2 -text "Phone: "
entry .phone -width 10 -relief sunken \
 -textvariable Ephone
button .exit -text EXIT -command exit
pack .label1 .name .label2 \
 .phone .exit -side top -pady 2
bind .name <Return> {set Ephone \
 [look_up_by_name $Ename]}
bind .phone <Return> {set Ename \
 [look_up_by_number $Ephone]}
```

Set up entry widgets with labels and display them, stacked vertically.

Bind Return keypress event to the code.

Notes

- The `entry` commands have options to set the width (in characters), the appearance and the variable that holds the text from the entry, and the button is given `exit` as its command.
- The widgets are packed vertically (`-side top`) with a small amount of padding in the vertical (`-pady`) direction. Padding is expressed here in pixels.
- Actions (callbacks) are associated with the *entry* widgets using the `bind` command, which takes as arguments the name of the widget, the action in question and a callback script to associate with the action. We have chosen to use a press of the Return key (denoted by the syntax `<Return>`), and the associated action is to set the `textvariable` for the appropriate entry to the text returned by the relevant lookup procedure.
- If we wish to allow a click of the right mouse button as an alternative to pressing Return, it requires just two more commands:

```
bind .name <Button-3> {
  set Ephone [look_up_by_name $Ename]}
bind .phone <Button-3> {
  set EName [look_up_by_number $Ephone]}
```

(Tk, having originated in the X Window System world, assumes a three-button mouse. In the Windows version the two mouse buttons are `Button-1` and `Button-3`.)

Using grid

A simple vertical top-to-bottom stacking of widgets is achieved by a single *pack* command specifying `-side top`. The same display would require five calls to the grid geometry manager, since each `grid configure ...` command starts a new row in the grid. Thus we would replace the pack command by

```
grid configure .label1 -pady 2
grid configure .name   -pady 2
grid configure .label2 -pady 2
grid configure .phone  -pady 2
grid configure .exit   -pady 2
```

6.3.4 Example 4: Listboxes and scrollbars

Figure 6.7 shows a listbox containing part of the telephone directory used in the previous example. The code that created it is as follows:

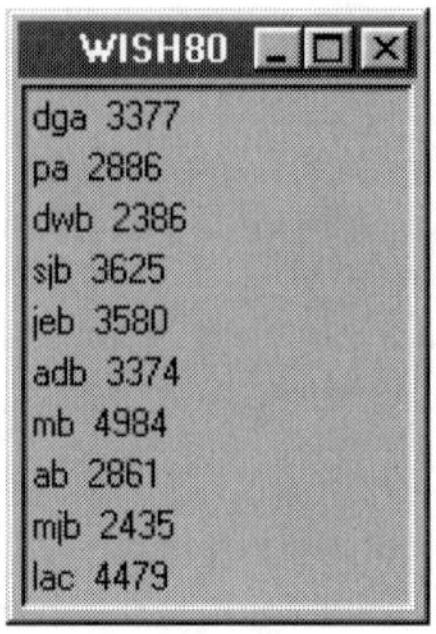

Figure 6.7 Listbox

```
listbox .phones
pack .phones
set f [open {d:\phones.txt} r]
while {[gets $f line] >= 0} {
    .phones insert end $line
}
```

The while loop reads a line at a time from the file phones.txt and places it in the variable line. This is then inserted in the listbox .phones, at the end. The default size of a listbox is 10 items, so only the first ten items entered are visible.

Clearly, for the listbox to be useful, we also need to be able to scroll through it with a scrollbar, which is available as another Tk widget. A listbox and scrollbar combination is shown in Figure 6.8.

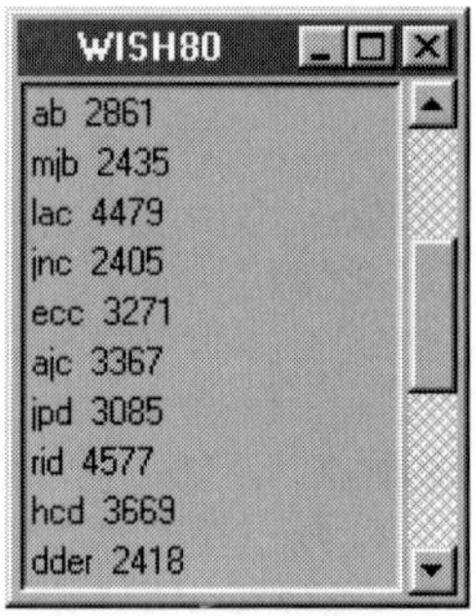

Figure 6.8 Listbox with scrollbar

The code to generate this display is as follows.

```
listbox .phones -yscrollcommand ".scroll set"
pack .phones -side left
scrollbar .scroll -command ".phones yview"
pack .scroll -side left -fill y
set f [open {d:\work\teaching\cm300_98\phones4.txt} r]
while {[gets $f line] >= 0} {
    .phones insert end $line
}
```

Interaction of scrollbar and listbox

This code requires some explanation. The Tk scrollbar is modelled on the X Window system: the solid bar indicates by its size the proportion of the total list that is actually displayed, and by its position the relative position within the total list of the information displayed. Clicking on the arrows scrolls up or down one line, clicking in the scrollbar shifts the display to that approximate relative position, and dragging the solid bar causes continuous scrolling. All this behaviour is built into the widget.

There is a two-way interaction between the scrollbar and the listbox. When the scrollbar is created it has a -command option: this specifies a partial command that will be invoked when the user clicks or drags on the scrollbar. The command is completed by arguments added by the widget. Likewise, the listbox is created with a -command option which specifies a partial command to be obeyed whenever the contents of the listbox change: again, the partial command is completed with arguments supplied by the listbox widget. The command to be executed when the scrollbar is used was specified as .phones yview, which changes the display in the listbox. The full form of the yview command option (which can be used independently of scrollbars to scroll any scrollable widget) is

```
widget yview scroll num units
```

which causes the display in the listbox to scroll by *num* units (lines, pages etc.). Scrolling is down if *num* is positive, up if *num* is negative. The scrollbar widget works out the number of lines that should be scrolled, depending on the user's actions, and adds the string scroll *num* lines to the partial command specified when the scrollbar was created.

The partial command associated with the listbox is .scroll set, which redraws the scrollbar. The full form is

```
widget set first last
```

where *first* and *last* are floating point values between 0 and 1 that specify the relative position of the top and bottom of the material displayed. When the listbox contents are changed, the widget computes new values for *first* and *last* and appends them to the .scroll set command, which causes the scrollbar to be redisplayed with the solid block in the appropriate position.

Notes

- The listbox was aligned with the left-hand edge of the window by the command

  ```
  pack .phones -side left
  ```

- The scrollbar widget was then aligned against the right edge of the listbox with the command

  ```
  pack .scroll -side right -fill y
  ```

- The option -fill y is necessary because the default scrollbar occupies less vertical space than the listbox, and would be centred in the vertical space occupied by the listbox. The -fill y option ensures that the widget is stretched in the *y* (vertical) direction to occupy all the available space.

Using grid

Using the *grid* geometry manager, we have a simple layout of one row and two columns. The command

```
grid configure .listbox .scroll
```

will create this layout, but we still have the problem of the default size of the scrollbar widget. The grid command places widgets in the centre of the available space unless an option -sticky is specified. If the value given for this option is one of n, s, e or w the widget is aligned against the specified edge of its cell in the grid. If we specify a value ns or ew the widget is stretched to meet both of the specified edges. So we need to change our grid command to

```
grid configure .listbox .scroll -sticky ns
```

6.3.5 Example 5: A history list for notepad

Notepad is a handy editor for short text files, but lacks any history mechanism. This Tk application provides such a mechanism. The initial display is shown in Figure 6.9. After entering a directory name and hitting return the display changes to confirm the directory setting, and we enter a file name, as shown in Figure 6.10. When we hit Return, Notepad opens up in a separate window to edit the file, and the history window changes as shown in Figure 6.11: the entry box for the file name is cleared, and a button appears labelled with the name of the file we have chosen to edit. Clicking this button in future will open Notepad to edit the file again.

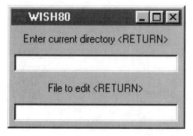

Figure 6.9   Notepad history: initial screen

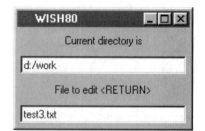

Figure 6.10   Notepad history: first filename entered

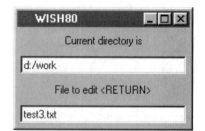

Figure 6.11   Notepad history, one file edited

Each time we edit a file another button is created until five files have been edited: the
next file causes the oldest button to be removed (Figures 6.12 and 6.13).

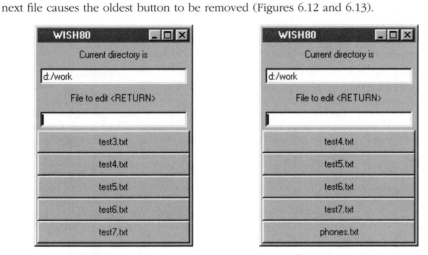

Figure 6.12 Notepad history:
five files edited

Figure 6.13 Notepad history: six
files edited

The code to achieve all this is remarkably compact – another example of the leverage
we get from a scripting language. It introduces a number of features that we have not met
hitherto, including dynamic creation and removal of widgets, use of the exec command
to launch an application, the event generate command which allows a script to 'press'
a button by remote control, and the cd and pwd commands for changing directories and
determining the current directory. Here is the code.

```
label .dir -text "Enter current
                 directory <RETURN>"
entry .dirname -width 30 -relief sunken \
              -textvariable dirname
label .file -text "File to edit <RETURN>"
entry .filename -width 30 -relief sunken \
              -textvariable filename
pack .dir .dirname .file .filename -side top \
-pady 1m

set id 0
bind .dirname <Return> {
cd $dirname
 .dir configure \
   -text "Current directory is"
 set dirname [pwd]
}
bind .filename <Return> {
incr id
 if {$id > 5} {
```

*Set up text boxes with
labels.*

Initialize button count.

```
  destroy .b[expr $id -5]
}
button .b$id -text $filename
bind .b$id <Button-1> {exec notepad $filename}
pack .b$id -fill x
event generate .b$id <Button-1>
.filename delete 0 end
}
```

The work is done in the bindings for the <Return> keypress. <Return> in the directory box changes directory, remembers the new value, and changes the box label to confirm the action. <Return> in the file name box removes the oldest button if necessary, creates a new button to launch Notepad for the named file, presses it by remote control and clears the file name from the box.

Notes

- In the first pack instruction we have specified packing as one millimetre (1m) rather than using the default pixels.
- We use .b$id to generate a widget name dynamically. (This works because the parser replaces $id by its value before it is used as an argument of the button command. (More generally, one might define an argument as .b[expr ...].)
- The callback for the button is defined by an explicit bind command, rather than the customary -command option of the button command. This is because the event generate command, which generates an event as if it had come from the outside world, only works with explicit bindings.
- We use -fill x to stretch buttons to a uniform width.
- In the last line (which deletes the filename), 0 is the index of the first character, end is the index of the last character.

Using grid

This simple vertical layout is easily generated using the grid manager. The first pack command is replaced by

```
grid configure .dir -pady 1m
grid configure .dirname -pady 1m
grid configure .file -pady 1m
grid configure .filename -pady 1m
```

and the second one by

```
grid configure .b$id -sticky ew
```

6.3.6   Example 6: A more elaborate front end for Notepad

In this example we develop the code for a more elaborate graphical front end to Notepad. When the program starts up the user is presented with a window as shown in Figure 6.14.

To edit a file the user can type the file name into the entry box at the top, then click the OK button or hit Return to start Notepad running with the file loaded. The listbox on the left maintains a cyclic list of the last five files to be edited, and instead of typing a name the user can double click one of these entries (Figure 6.15).

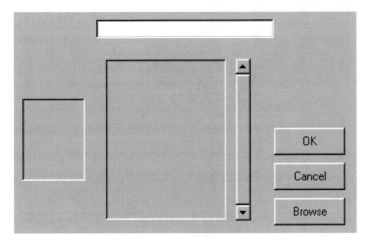

Figure 6.14   Notepad interface: initial view

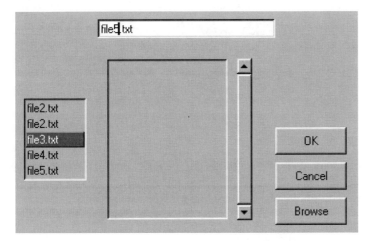

Figure 6.15   Notepad interface: history list

Clicking the Browse button produces a listing of the current directory in the scrollable listbox in the centre of the window (Figure 6.16).

Double-clicking a file name in this window fires up Notepad on that file as before, and also adds the file name to the cyclic list. However, a double-click on a directory name causes the contents of that directory to be displayed instead (Figure 6.17).

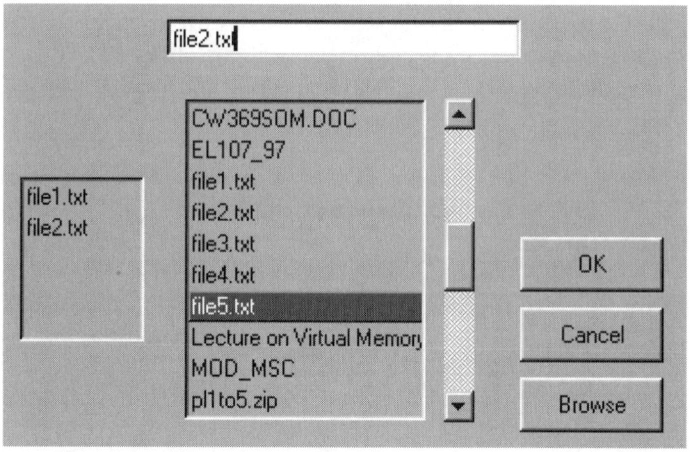

Figure 6.16 Notepad interface: directory listing

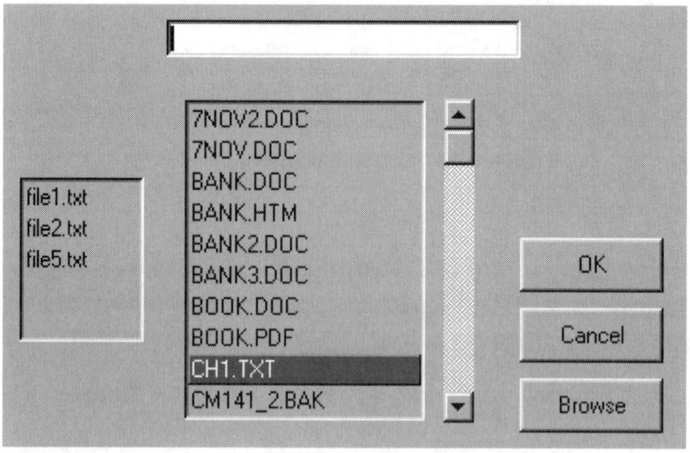

Figure 6.17 Notepad interface: sub-directory listing

(There is no provision for returning to the parent directory: this can be regarded as a bug or a feature, as you choose.) Clicking the Cancel button terminates the application.

The code is built up in stages. The first stage, if we are using the `pack` geometry manager, is to set up the physical layout as a set of empty frames.

Note the use of `-in` *to specify which frame widgets are to be placed in.*

```
frame .top -height 1c -width 10c
frame .bottom -height 5c -width 10c
pack .top .bottom -side top -pady 1m
frame .left -height 5c -width 4c
frame .middle -height 5c -width 4c
frame .right -height 5c -width 2c
pack .left .middle .right \
  -side left -padx 2m -in .bottom
frame .fill -height 2c -width 2c
```

```
frame .buttons -height 3c -width 2c
pack .fill .buttons -side top -in .right
```

This creates a hierarchical division of the space available: first we split the top-level window into *top* and *bottom*, then we split *bottom* into *left*, *middle* and *right*, then we split *right* into *fill* and *buttons*, partitioning the window as shown in Figure 6.18. (Empty frames without 3-D effects are not normally visible: we have used shading to identify the frames.)

Figure 6.18 'Skeleton' for display

Now we can start placing the widgets in the frames: first the entry box, then the buttons, and finally the listboxes:

```
entry .entry -width 30 -relief sunken \
  -textvariable file
pack .entry -side left -padx 1c -pady 1m \
  -in .top

button .ok -width 10 -height 1 \
  -text "OK" -command Go!
button .cancel -width 10 -height 1 \
  -text "Cancel" -command exit
button .browse -width 10 -height 1 \
  -text "Browse" -command dirlist
pack .ok .cancel .browse \
  -padx 1m -pady 1m -side top -in .buttons

listbox .oldfiles -relief sunken \
  -borderwidth 2 -height 5 -width 10
listbox .dirfiles -relief sunken \
  -borderwidth 2 \
  -yscrollcommand ".scroll set"
```

Scrollbar and listbox interact as described earlier.

```
scrollbar .scroll \
  -command ".dirfiles yview"

pack .oldfiles -side left -in .left
pack .dirfiles .scroll -side left \
  -padx 1m -fill y -in .middle
```

Next we set up the event bindings for the entry box and the listbox. (Bindings for the buttons were set up as part of their definition.) <Return> in the entry box and the OK button are both bound to a yet to be defined procedure, Go. This procedure updates the cyclic list of files edited and execs an instance of Notepad to edit the file whose name is retrieved from the entry box. The Cancel button is bound to the exit command, and the Browse button is bound to a procedure dirlist, also to be defined later, which writes the file names into the .dirlist listbox. A double-click in the history box clears the entry box, copies the selection into it and then calls the Go procedure. A double-click on a file name in the directory listing has the same effect, but if the target is a directory name we do a cd to change directories and call dirlist again.

```
bind .entry <Return> Go
bind .oldfiles <Double-Button-1> {
 .entry delete 0 end
 .entry insert 0 [selection get]
 Go
}

bind .dirfiles <Double-Button-1> {
 set sel [selection get]
 if {[file isdirectory $sel]} {
   .dirfiles delete 0 end
   .entry delete 0 end
   cd $sel; dirlist
 }
 if {[file isfile $sel]} {
   .entry delete 0 end
   .entry insert 0 $sel
   Go
 }
}
```

Finally, we define the procedures Go and dirlist, and initialize the variable numfiles.

Update the cyclic history list and perform an exec to launch Notepad. (numfiles counts from zero, so passes 3 when the fifth file is processed).

```
proc Go {} {
 global file numfiles
incr numfiles
if {$numfiles > 3} {
    set numfiles 0
  .oldfiles delete 0
 }
```

```
 .oldfiles insert end $file
 exec notepad $file
}

proc dirlist {} {
 foreach file [lsort -dictionary [glob *]] {
  .dirfiles insert end $file
 }
}
set numfiles 0
```

Although short, the procedure `dirlist` is rather cryptic. The built-in command `glob` produces a list of file names from the current directory which match a specified pattern: since * matches zero or more characters, the command `glob *` will produce a list of all the names in the directory. This is sorted in dictionary order (fold case, treat digit characters as numbers), and a `foreach` loop picks the list elements one by one and adds them to the `.dirlist` list box.

Using grid

We can create an almost identical layout with the *grid* geometry manager by using a grid of five rows and four columns as follows.

Row 0:   file name entry, spanning all columns
Row 1:   listbox in column 1 spanning rows 1–4,
         scrollbar in column 2 spanning rows 1–4
Row 2:   listbox in column 0 spanning rows 2–4
         OK button in column 3
Row 3   Cancel button in column 3
Row 4:   Browse button in column 3

The first part of the code is rewritten as follows:

```
entry .entry \
   -width 30 -relief sunken -textvariable file
grid configure .entry \
   -columnspan 4 -pady 1

listbox .oldfiles -relief sunken \
   -borderwidth 2 -height 5 -width 10
listbox .dirfiles -relief sunken \
   -borderwidth 2 \
   -yscrollcommand ".scroll set"
scrollbar .scroll \
   -command ".dirfiles yview"

grid configure .oldfiles \
   -row 2 -column 0 \
   -rowspan 3 -padx 1
```

```
grid configure .dirfiles \
  -column 1 -row 1 -rowspan 4 \
  -padx 1m -sticky ns
grid configure .scroll \
  -column 2 -row 1 -rowspan 4 \
  -padx 1m -sticky ns
grid rowconfigure . 1 -minsize 80

button .ok -width 10 -height 1 \
  -text "OK" -command Go!
button .cancel -width 10 -height 1 \
  -text "Cancel" -command exit
button .browse -width 10 -height 1 \
  -text "Browse" -command dirlist
grid configure .ok \
  -padx 1m -pady 1m -row 2 -column 3
grid configure .cancel \
  -padx 1m -pady 1m -row 3 -column 3
grid configure .browse \
  -padx 1m -pady 1m -row 4 -column 3
```

This is all fairly obvious except perhaps for the line

```
grid rowconfigure . 1 -minsize 80
```

When we configure a widget that spans several rows, the grid manager makes them of equal size. In our case we want to push the buttons down towards the bottom of the display, and we therefore have to specify an adequate minimum size for row 1. When `grid` places the central listbox it will honour this request for the first row, and divide the remaining space up equally for the other three spanned rows, thus ensuring that the buttons are evenly spaced. The value 80 for the minimum size was arrived at by experiment.

6.3.7   Example 7: Menus

Tk makes it very easy to create menus. The first stage is to create a menu bar and populate it with buttons. The following code creates the window shown in Figure 6.19.

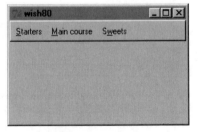

Figure 6.19   Menu bar

```
frame .mb -relief raised -bd 2
frame .dummy -height 3c
pack .mb .dummy -side top
```

```
menubutton .mb.starters \
  -text Starters -underline 0 -menu .mb.m1
menubutton .mb.maincourse \
  -text "Main course" -underline 0 \
  -menu .mb.maincourse.m1
menubutton .mb.sweet \
  -text Sweets -underline 1 \
  -menu .mb.m3
frame .mb.filler -width 2c
pack .mb.starters .mb.maincourse .mb.sweet \
  .mb.filler -side left
```

We create a frame to hold the menu bar, and pack it with another frame below it to give us some real estate [2]. Each menu button command has a text argument and a menu argument that identifies the menu that will be associated with it. Note that the menu must be a child of the menu button in the widget hierarchy. The underline option causes a letter (the first letter is character 0) of the text to be underlined to indicate a keyboard shortcut.

The next stage is to construct the menu contents by adding items – commands, cascading sub-menus, check buttons or radio buttons – to a named menu. We give the 'Main course' menu one command and two cascading menus (Figure 6.20): this is done with a handful of Tk commands:

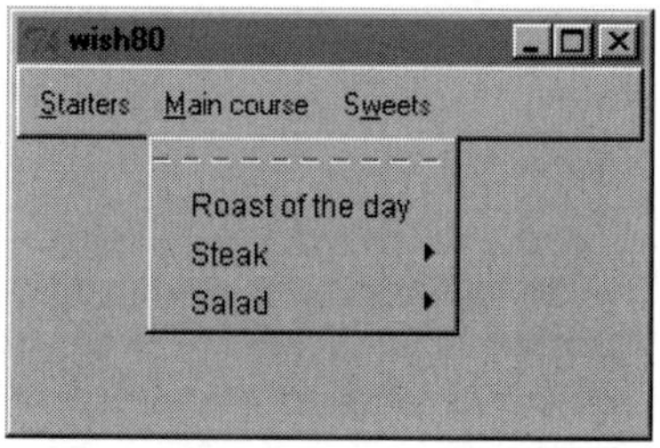

Figure 6.20 Drop-down menu

```
set m [menu .mb.maincourse.m1]
$m add command -label "Roast of the day" \
  -command {set main roast}
$m add cascade -label Steak -menu $m.sub1
$m add cascade -label Salad -menu $m.sub2
set m2 [menu $m.sub1]
set m3 [menu $m.sub2]
```

A command item has a command argument to define the script that will be executed when this item is selected: here we have just set a variable to record the choice. A cascading menu item has a menu option to define the menu as a child of the current menu.

Finally, we populate one of the cascading menus (Figure 6.21). The code should be self-explanatory.

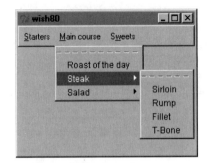

Figure 6.21 Cascading menus

```
$m2 add command -label Sirloin \
  -command {set main "sirloin steak"}
$m2 add command -label Rump \
  -command {set main "rump steak"}
$m2 add command -label Fillet \
  -command {set main "fillet steak"}
$m2 add command -label T-Bone \
  -command {set main "T-bone steak"}
```

New menu facilities in Tk 8.0

Tk 8.0 provides a new facility for placing a menu bar at the top of a top-level window: the menu bar shown in Figure 6.19 can be created as follows:

```
menu .menubar
. config -menu .menubar
menu .menubar.starters
menu .menubar.maincourse
menu .menubar.sweets

.menubar add cascade -label Starters \
  -menu .menubar.starters -underline 0
.menubar add cascade -label "Main course" \
  -menu .menubar.maincourse -underline 0
.menubar add cascade -label Sweets \
  -menu .menubar.sweets -underline 1
```

The menus and sub-menus are then populated with entries as before.

The Tk 8.0 menu implementation for Windows can also add entries to the Windows System menu (activated by clicking the icon at the left of the title bar) and to the Help menu by using the special names `.menubar.system` and `.menubar.help`. (Similar facilities are provided for the Macintosh: you can add entries to the 'Apple' menu with `.menubar.apple` and to the Help menu as in Windows.)

6.4 Events and bindings

We have seen in the examples how a callback script can be associated with a widget to enable it to respond to specified external events. The `button` command takes a

`-command` option to specify its response to a mouse click. More generally, the `bind` command registers a callback script for a widget, to be executed in response to specified events. The most common external events are associated with the mouse and the keyboard, but other events that can be captured include the mouse entering or leaving a window, a window receiving or losing focus, and changes in window size or position, and many others. 'Virtual events' can be defined to provide platform-independent code. For example, the paste operation in Windows occurs in response to Ctrl-V or Shift-Insert: in UNIX (X Window System) the sequences are Ctrl-V or F18. These options and differences can be encapsulated in a single virtual 'paste' event as described later. Events can be raised within a script to simulate user actions: again, we describe this later.

6.4.1 The bind command

The `bind` command registers a callback script to be executed when a sequence of one or more events (the *sequence*) occurs in one or more specified windows: the list of windows is called the *tag*. The form of the bind command to achieve this is

```
bind tag sequence script
```

The tag determines the widget(s) in which the event is to be recognized, the sequence defines the user action(s) that raise the event, and the script is an arbitrary Tcl script, protected from immediate evaluation by braces. If the script is preceded by a + it is added (without the +) to any existing bindings for the tag, otherwise it replaces the existing binding(s). A binding can be removed by specifying a null script, `{}`.

Binding tags

Usually we want to specify a binding for a single widget (window), e.g. a particular button. Suppose we have a top-level frame `.f` containing two buttons, `.f.b1` and `.f.b2`. Then

```
bind .f.b1 ...
```

defines a binding that is specific to the specified widget, `.f.b1`. The command

```
bind .f ...
```

defines a binding that is effective in the frame `.f` and all its child windows, i.e. it will apply to the frame and both buttons (unless it is later replaced by a more specific binding for a particular button). Bindings can be specified for all members of a widget class, e.g. the command

```
bind Button ...
```

defines a binding that is effective for all button widgets. This is commonly used to set up a default behaviour for a class of widgets, which can later be overridden or extended by specific bindings for individual widgets. (This is how Tk sets up default bindings.) Finally,

```
    bind all ...
```

defines a binding that is effective in all windows (widgets).

The `bindtags` command allows you to associate an arbitrary collection of binding tags for a widget. For example, the command

```
    bindtags .f.b1 [list .f .f1.b1]
```

specifies that if an event occurs in the button `.f1.b1` the scripts bound to that event in both `.f` and `.f1.b1` are to be executed, in that order. The order can later be reversed with another `bindtags` command.

6.4.2   Event specifications

Events are denoted by a specification enclosed in angle brackets, e.g.

```
    bind .w1 <Button-1> {...}
    bind .w1 <Key-space> {...}
```

A sequence of events can be specified:

```
    bind .w2 <Key-space><Key-space> {...}
```

An event specification can include modifiers that specify another key or button that must also be down to raise the event, e.g.

```
    bind .w1 <Control-Key-c> {...}
    bind .w1 <Shift-Control-Key-c> {...}
```

Keyboard events

Keyboard events are of two kinds, `KeyPress` and `KeyRelease`, e.g.

```
    bind .b1 <KeyPress-x> {...}
    bind .b1 <KeyRelease-x> {...}
```

`KeyPress` can be abbreviated to `Key` or omitted entirely, so that `<Key-a>` and `<a>` are alternative specifications for the event generated when the 'a' key is pressed. (This event can also be specified by the character a, without the angle brackets. However, it is good style always to enclose events in angle brackets so that they stand out within the `bind` command.) For non-printing and punctuation characters special *keysyms* are defined. These are dependent on the platform, but usually include `Return`, `Escape`, `Tab`, `BackSpace`, `comma`, `period`, `exclam` and `dollar`. The arrow keys are identified by `Up`, `Down`, `Left` and `Right`. All keysyms are case sensitive: the lack of consistency in capitalization (e.g. `space` but `BackSpace`) is a fertile source of errors.

Mouse events

Basic mouse events are `ButtonPress` (which can be abbreviated to `Button`), `ButtonRelease`, `MouseWheel` (wheel motion), `Enter` (mouse has entered the window) and Leave (mouse has left the window). Button events are qualified by a button number to identify the button, e.g.

```
bind .w1 <Button-1> {...}
```

(Following the X Window System, Tk recognizes buttons 1–5, though a five-button mouse is unusual. In Windows applications, the right-hand button is Button-3.) In the same way that <Key-a> can be abbreviated to <a>, so <Button-1> can be abbreviated to <1>. This can lead to confusion, since if the angle brackets are omitted the event is a KeyPress event, not a mouse event. It is good style always to use an explicit Key or Button in an event specification. A double mouse click is specified in an obvious way:

```
bind .b1 <Double-Button-1> {...}
```

Other external events

The remaining external events are somewhat esoteric. Possibly useful ones include:

Map	Window has been opened
Unmap	Window has been closed (iconified)
Destroy	Window has been destroyed
FocusIn	Window has gained focus
FocusOut	Window has lost focus
Configure	Window has changes size, position or stacking order.

6.4.3 Generating events from a script

The event generate command causes an event to be processed as if it had been reported by the operating system. Thus

```
event generate .b1 <Button-1>
```

causes the event handler for a mouse click on button .b1 to be invoked as if the user had actually clicked the button. The event specification must be a single event: sequences are not allowed.

6.4.4 Virtual events

The need for virtual events has already been explained. A virtual event is associated with multiple event sequences, and fires when any one of those sequences occurs. For example in a Windows application we can create a virtual 'paste' event that will fire on Ctrl-V or Shift-Insert:

```
event add <<Paste>> <Control-Key-v> \
                   <Shift-Key-Insert>
```

Note that virtual events are distinguished by double angle brackets. Once defined, a virtual event can be used in a bind command like any other event:

```
bind Entry <<Paste>> {%W insert
  [selection get]}
```

(As described below, in a callback script %W is replaced by the name of the widget that raised the event.) Virtual events can be raised within a script by event generate.

6.4.5 Callback scripts

The callback is a Tcl script, protected from evaluation by braces. In the interests of readable programs it is usually just a call of a procedure defined elsewhere. The script has access to a number of special variables which convey information about attributes associated with the event. Thus for mouse events, %b contains the button number, and %x and %y contain the mouse coordinates at the time of the event. For a MouseWheel event %D gives the 'delta' for the wheel movement, a signed integer that can be used to scroll the display by an appropriate amount. For KeyPress and KeyRelease events %k contains the keycode and %K contains the keysym. For all events %W contains the widget name. Thus if we wanted to turn buttons red when the mouse enters, and restore the default colour when it leaves, the commands would be

```
bind Button <Enter> {%W configure \
  -background red}
bind Button <Leave> {%W configure \
  -background grey}
```

If an event is raised within a script with event generate, arguments can be added to provide the information that is returned in the 'percent' variables, e.g.

```
event generate .f1 <Button-1> -x 10 -y 20
```

Here we are assuming that .f1 is a frame, and generating the mouse click event at coordinates (10, 20). The values of these 'percent' variables are substituted before the callback script is evaluated, so it is possible to use them as procedure arguments, e.g.

```
bind Button <Button-1> {btn1_click %W}
```

There are many other event variables: see the documentation of the bind command in the Tcl documentation for details.

It is important to remember that when an event occurs, the callback is evaluated in the global scope; this is outside any procedure, and therefore may not be the scope in which the bind command created the binding. Problems can arise if a callback is defined within a procedure and uses variables local to the procedure, since these variables will not be available when the callback is evaluated. This is another reason for making the callback a procedure call.

6.5 Geometry managers

We have seen examples of the *pack* and *grid* geometry managers. In this section we explore the working of these managers in more detail, and present a brief account of the *place* manager. For full details of all the possibilities of geometry management, the Tk documentation should be consulted.

6.5.1   Pack

Basic principles of packing

We have seen some of the behaviour of the *pack* geometry manager in the examples above. It employs a space filling algorithm, filling a target area from the edges to the middle. The direction of fill can be determined using the -side option, e.g.

```
pack .w1 .w2 .w3 -side bottom
```

will pack the widgets vertically, starting at the bottom of the unoccupied space. The widgets will be packed abutting on to each other: intervening space can be inserted using the -padx and -pady options, e.g.

```
pack .w1 .w2 .w3 -pady 2m -side bottom
```

These widgets are children of the top-level window, so the target area for packing is that window. If we create widgets as children of a frame, e.g.

```
frame .f
pack .f
entry .f.e1 -width 10 -relief sunken
entry .f.e2 -width 10 -relief sunken
entry .f.e3 -width 10 -relief sunken
```

then a pack command like

```
pack .f.e1 .f.e2 .f.e3 -pady 2m -side bottom
```

will use the frame as its target area. An alternative is to create the widgets apparently at top level, then use the -in option of the pack command:

```
frame .f
pack .f
entry.e1 -width 10 -relief sunken
entry.e2 -width 10 -relief sunken
entry.e3 -width 10 -relief sunken
pack .e1.e2.e3 -pady 2m -side bottom -in .f
```

Geometry propagation

Pack treats its target space as elastic, expanding or shrinking the client area to be an exact fit round the widget(s) it has placed. Widgets can be defined with a specified size, which is honoured except in the case of the containing frame, where the requested size may be ignored. This *geometry propagation* is illustrated in the following examples.

We first create three equal sized frames and pack them horizontally.

```
frame .r -width 6c -height 2c
```

```
pack .r
frame .r.c1 -width 2c -height 2c
frame .r.c2 -width 2c -height 2c
frame .r.c3 -width 2c -height 2c
pack .r.c1 .r.c2 .r.c3 -side left
.r.c1 configure -bg red
.r.c2 configure -bg yellow
.r.c3 configure -bg green
```

(The colouring is done so that the different frames can be identified in the figures.) When the frames are packed, the top-level window expands to accommodate them (Figure 6.22).

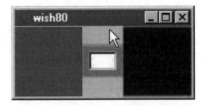

Figure 6.22   Initial frame configuration (three frames, each 2cm × 2 cm)

We next create a small widget and pack it in the centre frame:

```
entry .e -width 4 -relief sunken
pack .e -padx 2m -pady 2m -in .r.c2
```

We see from Figure 6.23 that pack has placed it in the middle of the frame, then shrunk the frame to fit round it with a default amount of padding.

Figure 6.23   Small widget packed

Geometry propagation can be controlled by the pack propagate command. If we turn off propagation (value zero) then the parent frame retains its requested size, as shown in Figure 6.24.

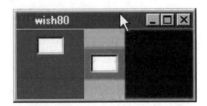

Figure 6.24   Small widget packed without propagation

```
entry .f -width 4 -relief sunken
pack propagate .r.c1 0
pack .f -padx 2m -pady 2m -in .r.c1
```

6.5.2 Grid

While there is a certain intellectual satisfaction to be gained by achieving a desired layout against the wishes of the *pack* geometry manager, it is often much simpler to use *grid*, as we have seen in the examples. This section summarizes the main features of the *grid* geometry manager: for full details the Tk documentation should be consulted.

Populating a grid

In its simplest form the `grid configure` command is given a list of widgets, which it places in a new row in the grid immediately below the previous row, e.g.

```
# assume widgets w1, w2 and w3
# have been defined
grid configure .w1 .w2 .w3
```

The grid is elastic, so that the height of the row adjusts to the height of the largest of the widgets being placed: column width increases if necessary to accommodate the widget being placed: when the dimensions have been determined each widget is centred in its cell. Additional spacing around widgets can be specified by the -padx and -pady options and the 'natural' size of a widget can be increased with internal padding using the -ipadx and -ipady options. Explicit row and column positioning is available, e.g.

```
grid configure .w5 -row 1 -column 2
```

(Row and column numbers start at zero.) A widget can be made to span multiple rows and columns using the -rowspan and -columnspan options, as illustrated in earlier examples.

Positioning widgets in cells

As noted above, by default a widget is centred in its cell. This behaviour can be over-ridden using the -sticky option. The edges of a cell are denoted by the points of the compass, i.e. n, s, e and w. A widget can be aligned with the top of its cell, for example, by specifying the option -sticky n. To align a widget in the top left-hand corner of its cell we specify -sticky nw. If we specify -sticky ns or -sticky ew the widget will be stretched in the appropriate direction to occupy the full height or width of the cell, respectively.

Fine tuning the appearance

We can adjust the size of whole rows and columns using the grid rowconfigure and grid columnconfigure commands. The arguments of these commands specify the frame concerned (in the simplest case, . for the top-level window), the row or column to be configured, and the attributes to be applied. These attributes either specify padding (-pad) to increase a row or column size, or specify a minimum size for the row or column (-minsize).

As with the pack manager, the master frame adjusts so that the grid just fits: if the master frame is larger than the required size of the grid, it shrinks to fit. This is called 'grid propagation'. The default behaviour can be modified by switching grid propagation off, e.g.

```
grid propagate . 0
```

Now, if the master frame is larger than the grid, the grid will be centred in it. However, if the grid becomes larger than the frame, it is anchored to the top left-hand corner of the frame, and clipped on the bottom right.

If the size of the master frame is increased by external action, by default the rows and columns do not resize. This behaviour can be changed: for example, if we specify

```
grid columnconfigure . 0 -weight 1
```

then column 0 will increase linearly as the master frame increases. By specifying different weights for different columns we can make them change at different rates: a column with a weight of 2 will grow (or shrink) at twice the rate as a column with a weight of 1. The same applies to rows. Thus elaborate behaviours can be obtained, but there are many pitfalls, and the results may well turn out to be not what you intended.

6.5.3 Place

At first sight, *place* is the most intuitive of the geometry managers: you locate widgets in a window using absolute or relative coordinates. Usually, you will set an absolute size for a window before using *place*, e.g.

```
. configure -width 200 -height 150
```

(Measurements are in pixels.) A widget can now be placed in an absolute position, e.g.

```
place .b1 -x 10 -y 10
```

or in a relative position, expressed as a fraction of the side of the rectangle, e.g.

```
place .b2 -relx .2 -rely .8
```

The coordinates specify the position of the widget's anchor: by default this is the top left-hand corner of the widget, but we can specify the coordinates of its centre if we wish, e.g.

```
place .b1 -x 10 -y 10 -anchor center
```

Other values for the -anchor option are n, s, e, w, ne, nw, se and sw, with obvious meanings.

Although this is simple and intuitive, the work involved in creating a moderately complex layout with *place* will soon convince you of the merits of the other geometry managers. The *place* manager does have some uses, however. For example, we can use it to position a frame exactly in the centre of a window:

```
frame .f -width 150 -height 100
place .f -relx 0.5 -rely 0.5 -anchor center
```

Having precisely positioned the frame, we can then use *pack* or *grid* to position widgets inside it.

6.6 Perl-Tk

Perl-Tk [3] provides the functionality of Tk in the Perl environment, making it possible to add a graphical user interface (GUI) to Perl scripts. The implementation approach is completely different from Tcl/Tk, which is a command language written in Tcl that allows us to create and manipulate a collection of visual items called widgets. In contrast, Perl-Tk implements widgets as objects with a collection of methods to manipulate them. Thus whereas in Tcl/Tk you associate an event with a callback using the `bind` command with the widget name, the event and the callback script as arguments, in Perl-Tk you invoke the widget's `bind` method with the event and the callback script as arguments. Despite this fundamental difference, Perl-Tk is designed in such a way that a user familiar with Tcl/Tk can soon adapt. For example, consider a trivial program that creates a button which when pressed causes the program to terminate:

You need to be familiar with Perl objects and references, which are described in Chapter 3, to make sense of this section.

```
button .b1 -text "Press Me" \
           -command {exit}
pack .b1
```

The equivalent Perl-Tk program is as follows:

```
use Tk;
$mw = new MainWindow;
$b1 = $mw->Button(-text=>"Press Me",
   -command=>sub {exit});
$b1 -> pack;
MainLoop;
```

or more idiomatically as

```
use Tk;
$mw = new MainWindow;
$b1 = $mw->
     Button(-text=>"Press Me",
            -command=>sub {exit})
     ->pack;
MainLoop;
```

This little example shows us quite a lot about Perl-Tk. The first line invokes the `Tk` package. The second line creates a top-level main window, and the next line invokes the window's `button` method to create an instance of a button as a child of the main window. (In Tcl/Tk we name the button `.b1` to indicate that it is a child of the top-level window.) Note the similarity of the argument list for the `button` method to the arguments of the Tcl/Tk button command: here it is a list of key–value pairs to be placed in the anonymous hash. Next we call the button's pack method to invoke the *pack* geometry manager, and finally we start the main event loop, which watches for a mouse click on the button. Note the use of an anonymous subroutine composer in the -command option.

Widgets in Tcl/Tk have many of the characteristics of objects. If we define a button with

```
button .b1 -text "Press Me" -command {exit}
```

we can regard the options as instance variables which are assigned values, and if we later change one of these values, as in

```
.b1 configure -text "You did!"
```

we can see this as an invocation of the configure method of the object .b1. However, the analogy breaks down when we come to the geometry managers, which have a purely procedural interface. In Perl-Tk, however, the widgets are true objects. All widget objects are derived from a base class which implements pack, grid and place as class methods. Thus when we refer to 'the widget's pack method', this is an inherited method. (The base class also defines a configure method that is inherited by all widgets.)

To complete our discussion of Perl-Tk we present the code for the phonebook example of Section 6.3.3.

```
use Tk;
```

Look up by name. Ename and Ephone are global variables that contain the text from the entry widgets 'name' and 'phone'.

```
sub by_name {
    $Enumber = exists $phones{$Ename} ?
        $phones{$Ename} : 'NOT FOUND';
}
```

Look up by number (code taken from Chapter 2).

```
sub by_number {
my %by_number = reverse %phones;
$Ename = exists $by_number{$Ephone} ?
    $by_number{$Ephone} : "NOT FOUND";
}
```

Read data into array and thence construct the hash.

```
open IN, 'd:\temp\phones.txt';
@g = <IN>;
close IN;
chomp @g;
%phones = split "\t", join "\t", @g;

$mw = new MainWindow;
$mw->Label(-text=>'Name: ')->
    pack(-side=>'top', -pady=>2);
$name = $mw->Entry(-width=>10,
    -relief=>'sunken', -textvariable=>\$Ename)->
    pack(-pady=>2);
$mw->Label(-text=>'Phone: ')->
    pack(-pady=>2);
$phone = $mw->Entry(-width=>10,
```

```
    -relief=>'sunken', -textvariable=>\$Ephone)->
    pack(-pady=>2);
$mw->Button(-text=>'Exit',
    -command=>sub{exit})->pack(-pady=>2);

$name->bind("<Return>", \&by_name);
$phone->bind("<Return>", \&by_number);
MainLoop;
```

It is interesting to note how closely the Tk code resembles the code in the Tcl/Tk version. Comparison of Figure 6.6(b) with Figure 6.25 shows that the 'look and feel' of the visual interface is identical in both versions.

Figure 6.25   Phonebook in Perl-Tk

The code is pretty straightforward, though the line which assigns the value of the hash %phones deserves study. The original input file contained a number of lines each containing two tab-separated fields, so each element of the array @g contains two tab-separated fields. The join operation combines these elements into a string using tab as the 'glue' character, giving us a string of tab-separated words, and the split operator converts this into a list of words. Since these are the key–value pairs we can assign this list to the hash with the desired effect. The cunning precedence rules for the list-forming comma operator ensure that the expression parses correctly without the use of brackets.

Notes

[1] We can say that the Tk programming style is *object-oriented*: the command specifies an object, and the first argument specifies a method to be invoked on that argument. Contrast this with the *action-oriented* style of Tcl programming, where the command specifies the action and the first argument specifies the object to be acted on.

[2] Tk allows cascading menus to spread outside the parent window. However, the mechanics of screen grabbing used to produce these figures require that the menus are entirely contained in the parent window, hence the extra real estate.

[3] Perl-Tk should not be confused with TkPerl, which was a (now unsupported) Perl 4 package that linked the Tk X toolkit with Perl. This was superseded by a Tcl module for Perl 5 that has a Tcl::Tk module extension. That module allows the use of Tcl within a Perl script, which means that you must know both languages to get your widgets to work.

## Chapter 7

Visual Basic and VBA

'Visual Basic' is both the name of a shrink-wrap application and the name of a language. In this chapter we describe the language, which is a modern version of BASIC, extended to include many object-oriented features. Its importance is that in its latest version it can be seen as a scripting language ('glue language') for ActiveX components, i.e. components that conform to Microsoft's Component Object Model (COM), and therefore provides an alternative to C++ for the development of component-based applications. We describe the language, concentrating in particular on the object-oriented aspects, and the way it interfaces to libraries of external objects.

7.1 The Visual Basic family

7.1.1 The original Visual Basic

Much confusion arises from the fact that the name 'Visual Basic' is used both as the name for a 'shrink-wrap' application and as the name of a language. The name was originally used for an innovative Microsoft product, the first tool for visual scripting – building up a visual interface from pre-built components. Following the introduction of Windows 3 in 1990, there was a serious dearth of native Windows applications. (Indeed, the attraction of Windows 3 to many users was that it provided a way of multi-tasking DOS applications.) Developing native Windows applications was very difficult, requiring a competence in C programming and an in-depth understanding of the Windows API as documented in the impenetrable System Development Kit (SDK). If Windows was to survive, there had to be a way of generating applications that was accessible to a wider range of programmers. Enter Visual Basic.

*BASIC is traditionally capitalized because it is an acronym – **B**eginner's **A**ll-purpose **S**ymbolic **I**nstruction **C**ode. However, modern versions of the language do not capitalize the name, reflecting the move away from its beginner's orientation.*

Visual Basic introduced a ground-breaking approach to application development. The user first determines the *appearance* of the interface by choosing items from a pre-built collection of visual components – menus, dialog boxes, buttons, scrollbars etc. – and positioning them on the screen, at the same time determining the size, background colour etc. The second stage is to use a glue language to connect the components together and describe the intended *behaviour* of the interface by associating scripts written in the language with the various external *events* – mouse clicks and mouse movements, key-presses etc. – that can be generated by the user. The language chosen for these scripts was Visual Basic, a powerful version of the BASIC language with modern control structures and structure declarations, augmented by support for accessing the methods and properties of the visual controls that made up the user interface. No distinction was made between the language and the product. There was no need: it was a closed product, and the controls conformed to an internal specification that was released to the public so that new 'custom controls' could be written in C. These controls were called Visual Basic Extensions or VBXs, following the file extension, .vbx, used to identify them.

7.1.2 Visual Basic for Applications

The confusion between the application and the language first arose in 1993, when the Excel development team recognized that the language within the Visual Basic application was being used as glue to connect a collection of objects, and decided to use a modified version of the Visual Basic language as the macro language for Excel 5: they chose the name Visual Basic for Applications (VBA). The distinction between language and application was very clear: VBA provided the glue to connect a collection of COM automation objects comprising the Excel object model. Clearly, the language could be used with any object model you cared to define.

For a while, Visual Basic and VBA followed separate development paths, with VBA being embedded in more of the Office applications. At the same time Visual Basic was changing, with the 16-bit VBX controls being replaced by 32-bit 'OCX' controls, which were in fact COM automation objects and are nowadays called ActiveX controls [1]. When Visual Basic 4.0 was launched in 1996 it adopted VBA as the underlying language, replacing the previous 'Visual Basic' language, and adopted the Excel model of using VBA to connect objects defined in an object model.

Thus we have a single language with two names: for historical reasons it is called Visual Basic within the Visual Basic development environment, and VBA when it is embedded in an application. To avoid confusion, in this chapter we will always refer to the application explicitly, as 'the Visual Basic application' or 'Visual Basic (the application)', allowing us to use 'Visual Basic' (or VB, or VBA) for the language. The application of VBA in the Office applications is covered in Chapter 13, but it is necessary to have read this chapter (and the next) first to learn the details of the language.

Visual Basic has evolved into a language with substantial facilities for object-oriented programming, and it provides an interface to the complete Windows API. At the same time, the tight coupling between language and object model has been removed from the Visual Basic application: its object model is just one of many object models to which the programmer has access. We can say that Visual Basic (the application) is on the same footing as Word, Excel and the other Office 97 applications: they are all applications that support multiple object models which can be scripted in Visual Basic. The only difference is that in the Office (and other) applications, the language is processed by an interpreter embedded in the application, whereas Visual Basic (the application) incorporates a compiler that can generate free-standing EXEs and DLLs. An alternative view is that Visual Basic is a language for scripting components that conform to Microsoft's Component Object Model and support the so-called *automation interface*, thus providing a scripting language alternative to C++ for the development of component-based applications. In this view, Visual Basic (the application) is a collection of ActiveX controls, together with a container framework in which the controls can be hosted.

7.1.3 VBScript

The latest product to overload the Visual Basic name is Visual Basic Scripting Edition, more commonly referred to as VBScript. This started life as a very much cut-down version of Visual Basic, best regarded as a separate language, but the latest version incorporates much of the functionality of VB. It was at first used mainly for client-side Web page scripting in Internet Explorer, but is now more widely used as a component of Microsoft's ActiveX Scripting Architecture. The language is described in detail in Chapter 10, and its applications are covered in the subsequent chapters.

7.1.4 Evolution of Visual Basic

The vision of the original designers of Visual Basic (the application) was to develop a tool that would bring Windows-based application development to the masses, making it possible for people to build graphical Windows-based applications rapidly and efficiently. They succeeded: a program to display a window with a single button which, when pressed, displays the message 'Hello World!' requires nigh on a hundred lines of C code, but in Visual Basic it just requires a drag-and-drop operation to select a command button from the palette and place it in the required position, and one line of Visual Basic code. It can all be done in a few minutes.

It was expected that in the professional development market the tool would be used for developing prototypes of applications prior to coding production versions in C++. Developers rapidly discovered that Visual Basic offered the performance and scalability of a C++ development tool in a rapid application development (RAD) environment, and it became widely used for application development. In response to this, Microsoft evolved the language away from its 'enthusiast' roots towards the needs of professional developers. Version 3 introduced a very restricted form of support for objects: this was greatly extended in Version 4 (which was a complete rewrite) by the ability to define object classes. Major extensions in Version 5 included the ability to create ActiveX controls, and a native-mode compiler to produce binary executable files – earlier versions had compiled to byte code that was interpreted at run-time. Version 6 extends the areas of application by providing extensive new support for database access and integration with Web browsers and servers: as is increasingly common in the Microsoft world, most of the additional functionality is provided in the form of new or extended object models. Version 6 does not change the core language greatly: in this chapter and the next we describe the core language and object models that are common to Version 5 and Version 6 (VBA in the Office suite is still at Version 5 at the time of writing). We also draw attention to some of the significant additions in Version 6.

Because of its origins in BASIC, most computer scientists mistakenly dismiss Visual Basic as a 'toy' language. It is far from a toy, having some claim to be the world's most popular language – in a recent survey of developers, 53% of respondents listed Visual Basic as their first language. (The survey was commissioned by Microsoft, so the outcome is perhaps not surprising.) It has over 3 million users, and nobody knows how many users of the Office suite have used VBA to write macros. And, as another author (Dan Appleman) has observed,

> It's interesting stuff. After all, aside from being the easiest, most efficient and cost-effective Windows development environment around, VB is widely reputed to also be the most fun.

(This is no doubt true for developers of Windows applications. But not nearly so much fun as Perl.)

7.2   Visual Basic: the core language

Apart from its object manipulation facilities, Visual Basic is a fairly straightforward language: here we highlight its main features. Most of the functionality is in the associated object models: we introduce aspects of the base object model as we go along to aid description of the language.

Facilities described in this chapter are provided in Version 5 and later. Facilities new in Version 6 will be flagged by a marginal note.

7.2.1   Variables, types and values

Variables

Variable names follow the usual rules: the permitted characters are letters, digits and underscore, and the first character must be a letter. Earlier versions of the language limited variable names to 40 characters, but this restriction is relaxed in later versions: the current version allows identifiers of up to 255 characters. Microsoft literature adopts the convention that variable names have an initial capital, and long names are made more readable by internal capitals, e.g.

```
TimeOfTheYear = "Summer"
```

However, this is pure convention, since in the long tradition of BASIC, Visual Basic is not case-sensitive.

Types

In 'traditional' BASIC, the only types are number and string. Visual Basic provides a rich assortment of types: `Byte`, `Boolean`, `Integer`, `Long`, `Single`, `Double`, `Currency`, `Date`, `String` and `Object`. Types `Integer` and `Long` are 16-bit and 32-bit integers, respectively: `Single` and `Double` are 32-bit and 64-bit floating point numbers, respectively. `Currency` is a scaled integer, xxxxx.yyyy, with 15 digits to the left of the point, and four to the right. Values of `Date` type variables are stored as IEEE 64-bit (8-byte) floating-point numbers that represent dates ranging from 1 January 100 to 31 December 9999 and times from 0:00:00 to 23:59:59. Note that there is no problem here with roll-over to the year 2000 (though there is nothing to stop programmers using two-digit dates if they choose to ignore the `Date` type, unfortunately). Strings are variable size by default, but can be declared fixed size.

Variants and sub-types

Visual Basic can be a static-typed language or a dynamically typed language: the programmer has the option of declaring variables with explicit types, or declaring them as type Variant. (There is a third option of not declaring variables at all: in this case they will be implicitly declared as variants on first use.) The Variant type provides dynamic typing: at run-time the value has an associated tag to record the type of the value currently stored (sometimes called the *sub-type*): this tag can be interrogated by the VarType() and TypeName() functions: VarType() returns a numeric code to identify the sub-type, while TypeName() returns the sub-type name as a string. There are four special values that a variant can have: Empty, Null, Error and Nothing: the values Empty and Null can be tested with the functions IsEmpty() and IsNull(). When a variant is first declared it is given the value Empty, to indicate that no value has been assigned to it (c.f. undef in Perl and undefined in JavaScript). The Null and Error values can be assigned by the user to indicate that the variable contains no useful data, or that an error condition has arisen. Nothing is used in connection with objects (see later).

Although the variant type might appear to be just a convenience, its real purpose is for use with 'automation objects' that are accessed through an interface which requires all arguments to be packaged as variants. (See Section 8.2.2 for a full treatment of object interfaces.)

Declarations

Variables can be declared implicitly or explicitly. (Implicit declaration is permitted by default, but declarations can be made obligatory with the statement Option Explicit.) The first use of a new variable name constitutes an implicit declaration of the variable: it is assigned the type variant by default, but types can be associated with implicit declarations by using a 'type character' (see below) or setting an alternative default with a 'DefType' statement: for example

```
DefInt I-N
```

causes variables with initial letter in the range I-N to be declared as type Integer. (The DefInt statement is included in the language for reasons of backward compatibility and sentimental attraction to the old days. Old-time FORTRAN programmers will find it familiar.)

Explicit declaration takes one of two forms, e.g.

```
Dim A
Dim B As Integer
Dim C As String
Dim D As String*10
```

The first style of declaration declares the variable as a variant. The notation String*10 in the declaration of D denotes a fixed-length string: C is a variable-length string. The use of Dim to introduce variable declarations may puzzle newcomers to the language: it is a throwback from early versions of BASIC, in which scalars were implicitly declared by use, and array variables had to be 'dimensioned'. A trap to watch out for is that if you write

```
Dim A, B, C As Integer
```

this does not declare three integers: A and B will be declared as variants since the As Integer only applies to the immediately preceding variable. Instead, it is necessary to write

```
Dim A As Integer, B As Integer, C As Integer
```

For reasons of backward compatibility only, 'type characters' can be used in explicit declarations, e.g. Dim Name$ declares variable Name with type String. (In the early versions of BASIC, string variables were distinguished from numeric variables by appending a $ character to the name. In later versions this technique was extended to other types – % for integer variables, ! for single-length floating point, # for double-length floating point and @ for currency. This convention is still honoured by Visual Basic, but note that there are no type characters for the types Byte, Boolean, Date and Object. The use of type characters is a deprecated feature, except that a type character is used to distinguish two kinds of built-in string functions – see Section 7.2.3.)

Variables can be declared as constants, e.g.

```
Const pi = 3.1415926536
```

(Keywords are customarily given an initial upper-case letter, but this is pure convention, since the language is not case-sensitive.)

Literal constants

Numerics and strings have the 'obvious' forms. Date literals are enclosed within number signs (#), and can be written in a variety of formats, e.g.

```
#2-Apr-98#
#April 2, 1998
#April 2, 1998 1:20 pm#
```

(A purely numerical date like #2-4-99# will be interpreted according to the locale set for Windows, 2 April in the UK, 4 February in the US.) Note that 2-digit year dates less than 30 have 2000 added to them, while dates of 30 or greater have 1900 added to them: Visual Basic programs have a potential Year 2030 problem!

Enumerations

Enumerations provide a convenient way of mapping a collection of meaningful names on to a sequence of integers, e.g. associating the days of the week with the integers 0–6, thus making code easier to read. An enumeration is declared using the keyword Enum, e.g.

```
Enum DayOfWeek
    Sunday
    Monday
    Tuesday
    Wednesday
    Thursday
```

```
        Friday
        Saturday
    End Enum
```

The first constant in the list is assigned the value zero, and each successive constant has a value one greater than its predecessor. A value can be assigned explicitly: thus if we want the days of the week numbered 1 to 7 instead of 0 to 6 we could define the enumeration

```
    Enum DayOfWeek
      Sunday = 1
      Monday
      Tuesday
      Wednesday
      Thursday
      Friday
      Saturday
    End Enum
```

Having declared an enumeration, variables of that type can be declared, e.g.

```
    Dim Today As DayOfWeek
```

A common idiom is to assign a negative value to an error condition, e.g.

```
    Enum Fruit
      Apple
      Pear
      Orange
      Banana
      Invalid = -1
    End Enum
```

The members of the enumeration can then be used to make code more readable, e.g.

```
    if Today = Monday Then
    . . .
```

The object models imported by Visual Basic in its various environments provide a large number of built-in enumerations to make life easier for the programmer. For example, if you want to check whether a variant currently has a string value, you can remember that the sub-type for string is '8' and write

```
    if VarType(myVar) = 8 Then
    . . .
```

However, it is much less error-prone, and more readable, to use an 'intrisic constant' from a built-in enumeration and write

```
    if VarType(myVar) = vbString Then
    . . .
```

Intrinsic constants use a naming convention in which the first two letters indicate the source of the enumeration, thus vbString comes from the Visual Basic object library, wdPaperA4 comes from the Word object library, xlValidateDate comes from the Excel object library, and so on.

7.2.2 Operators and expressions

All the common operators are present: a full table is given in Section 7.9, together with the precedence rules. Points to notice regarding operators are:

■ The Like operator performs a restricted form of regular expression matching:

> *string* Like *pattern*

returns true if *pattern* is matched in *string*. A very restricted regular expression syntax is supported: in a pattern,

*	matches zero or more characters
?	matches any single character
#	matches any single digit (0 through 9)
[abc]	matches a or b or c
[!abc]	matches any character except a or b or c

■ If the + operator is given two string arguments, it acts as a string concatenation operator. The string concatenation operator & converts non-string arguments to strings (strictly string variants).
■ The equivalence operator compares two logical values and returns true if both are true or both are false.
■ The implication operator is an obscure thing of interest only to mathematicians: how it got into Visual Basic is a mystery.

Type conversion

When expressions are evaluated, any reasonable type-conversion takes place silently and unobtrusively, e.g. if a floating point value is assigned to an integer variable, the fractional part is discarded, and if a string is a valid representation of a number it will be auto-matically converted if used in a numeric context. The function IsNumeric() can be used to test whether an expression can be converted to a number, and IsDate() can be used to test whether an expression is a date or can be converted to a date. Explicit type-conversion functions are also provided: these take a numeric or string expression and coerce it (if possible) into a value of a particular type. The target type is included (in abbreviated form) in the function name, e.g CDbl() converts a numeric (or valid string) value to a double. A full list of functions is

```
Cbool()   CByte()   CCur()   CDate()   CDbl()
Cint()    CLng()    CSng()   CStr()    CVar()
```

When other numeric types are converted to Date, values to the left of the decimal represent date information while values to the right of the decimal represent time.

Midnight is 0 and midday is 0.5. Negative whole numbers represent dates before 30 December 1899.

Conditional expressions

Many other languages provide a syntax for conditional expressions (an expression with two possible values, one of which is chosen at run-time depending on the outcome of a test), usually based on the C model. Thus in Perl we can write

```
$a = ($a < 0) ? 0 : $a;
```

to replace a negative value of a variable by zero. Although Visual Basic does not provide syntax for conditional expressions, the same effect can be obtained using the IIf function:

```
a = IIf(a < 0, 0, a)
```

However, there are hidden traps. Perl (and C) use 'shortcut' evaluation, so in Perl we can safely write

```
$y = ($x == 0) ? 0 : 1/$x;
```

but in Visual Basic

```
y = IIf(x = 0, 0, 1/x)
```

will cause a run-time error if x is zero: IIf is a function, and all its arguments are evaluated before the function is applied.

7.2.3 Built-in functions

We have already encountered some built-in functions, and we shall introduce more as we explore the language. Built-in functions that are not mentioned elsewhere are outlined in the following subsections.

Mathematical functions

The usual collection of trigonometrical and mathematical functions – Sin(), Cos(), Exp() etc.

Rounding

Functions to round fractional numbers – Int() and Fix(). For positive arguments these are identical, and round down. For negative arguments, Int() rounds to the nearest integer less than the argument, so that Int(-2.7) rounds to –3, while Fix() rounds the other way, so that Fix(-2.7) returns –2. In Visual Basic 6, Round(e, n) rounds the value of expression e to n decimal places.

Character conversion

Functions to convert characters to ASCII code equivalents and vice versa – `Asc()` and `Chr()`. Note that `Asc()` takes a *string* argument, and returns the ASCII value of the first character. On systems that support Unicode, `AscW()` and `ChrW()` perform Unicode conversions.

String manipulation (Visual Basic 5 and later)

A collection of functions for string manipulation, including

```
Len(S)              returns length of S
InStr(S1,S2)        returns position of S2 in S1 (index of first character)
Left(S,n)           returns leftmost n characters of S
Right(S,n)          returns rightmost n characters of S
Mid(S,n,m)          returns m characters starting at index n in S
```

(See the Visual Basic documentation for full specifications of these functions.)

String manipulation (Visual Basic 6)

Visual Basic 6 provides further string manipulation functions, including:

```
Join (A, c)             joins strings in array A using character c as separator and
                        returns result. If c is omitted, space is used
Split(S, c, 1)          splits string S using character c as separator: returns sub-
                        strings in an array. c defaults to space
StrReverse(S)           returns a string which is the reverse of S
InstrRev(S1, S2, n)     like InStr(), but starts search at character n. If n is omitted,
                        search starts at end of string
Replace(S1, S2, S3)     returns a string in which all occurrences of S2 in S1 have
                        been replaced by S3
Filter(A, S)            returns an array containing all strings in A that match S.
                        Filter(A, S, False) returns strings that don't match
```

(See the Visual Basic 6 documentation for full specifications of these functions, including additional optional arguments.)

Remarks on string manipulation functions

An odd feature of the functions that return a string is that they expect the target string argument to be a variant, and return a variant. This behaviour can be suppressed by appending a 'string' type character to the function name, e.g.

```
Dim S as String
...
S = Mid$("Abracadabra!", 4, 4)
```

Corresponding to the `Mid` function, there is a `Mid` statement: essentially, this is an application of the `Mid` function in a left-hand context, i.e. it replaces a sub-string rather than returning one.

Date and time

`Day()`, `Month()` and `Year()`, a collection of functions for manipulating dates and times, take an expression or variable of type date, and return the appropriate component as a variant of sub-type integer. `DateAdd()` adds or subtracts an interval to a date: the nature of the interval – day, month, year, hour, minute, second – being specified by one of the arguments. Thus if d is a date,

```
d = DateAdd("m", -1, d)
```

subtracts one month. `DateDiff()` returns the difference between two dates in units specified by an argument, e.g.

```
DaysLeft = DateDiff("d", EndOfSemester, Now)
```

Formatting

A compendious function `Format()` converts values into strings according to a predefined or user-defined format. For example, suppose that we assign values as follows

```
Dim Today as Date, Now As Date
Today = #November 17, 1998#
Now = #13:09:32#
```

then

```
Format$(Now, "hh:mm:ss: AMPM")
```

returns `"01:09:32 PM"` and

```
Format$(Today, "dddd, mmm d yyyy"
```

returns `"Tuesday, Nov 17 1998"`. User-defined formats can give precise control over conversion of numeric values to strings, e.g. suppressing non-significant zeros, thus

```
Format$(5459.4 "##,##0.00")
```

returns `"5,459.40"`. Visual Basic 6 provides a collection of specific formatting functions, e.g. `FormatCurrency()`, `FormatNumber()` etc. For more information on formats, see the Visual Basic reference documentation.

7.2.4   Data structures

The available data structures are arrays and 'user-defined types': the latter is a most inappropriate name for what is in fact the equivalent of a C *struct* or a Pascal *record*. We shall refer to this structure as a UDT. The scope rules are the same as for scalars.

Arrays

As in the early versions of BASIC, a fixed-size array can be declared with a `Dim` statement:

```
Dim A(10) As String
Dim B(10,15) As Double
```

The lower bound for subscripts is zero, unless the programmer sets it to 1 using `Option Base 1`. Doing this provides a fertile source for subsequent errors and misunderstandings: it is much better to specify the lower bound explicitly in the declaration:

```
Dim C(1 To 10) As Variant
Dim D(1 To 10, 1 To 10 ) As Currency
```

The functions `Lbound()` and `Ubound()` take an array name as an argument, with an optional second argument to specify the dimension to be queried (1 for first, 2 for second etc.) and return the lower (upper) bound for that dimension. Thus with the declarations of A and B given above, `LBound(A)` returns 0 and `Ubound(B, 2)` returns 15.

As well as declaring an array of variants, a variant array can be created, e.g.

```
Dim colours As Variant
...
colours = Array ("Red", "Green", "Blue")
```

Note that after obeying the above code, the variable `Colours` is a variable of type `Variant` whose value is of sub-type `Array`: the elements of the array are themselves of type `Variant` with sub-type `String`. The `Array` sub-type can be tested with the function `IsArray()`.

Dynamic arrays

Dynamic arrays can be declared e.g.

```
Dim B( ) As String
```

In this case the actual size of the array must be set before use by, e.g.

```
ReDim B(20)
```

(Note that `ReDim` is an executable statement, not a declaration.) The size of the array can be changed again later in the program by another `ReDim`. This has the effect of destroying the current contents of the array unless the `Preserve` keyword is used, e.g.

```
ReDim Preserve B(30)
```

However, if the `Preserve` keyword is used, only the *last* dimension can be changed. Thus a one-dimensional array can always be re-dimensioned preserving the contents, but if we have a two-dimensional array we can change the number of columns, but not the number of rows.

In Visual Basic 6 a dynamic array can occur on the left of an assignment.

UDTs

Visual Basic provides the equivalent of the C struct (or the Pascal record) in the form of a 'user-defined type'. This term is reflected in the declaration syntax, e.g.

```
Type SystemInfo
    CPU As Variant
    Memory As long
    VideoColours As Integer
End Type
```

Once declared, instances of the structure can be created in variable declarations:

```
Dim MySystem As SystemInfo, YourSystem As SystemInfo
```

Fields are accessed by the usual dot notation, e.g.

```
MySystem.cpu = "P233"
```

Structures of identical type can be assigned, e.g.

```
YourSystem = MySystem
```

However, a UDT cannot be stored in a variant.

7.2.5 Statements

Statements are normally terminated by end-of-line: a statement can be continued on the next line by placing an underscore immediately before the end of the first line. Multiple statements can be placed on a single line, separated by a colon, e.g.

```
X = 1: Y = 2: Z = 3
```

(The choice of the colon as a separator seems bizarre, given the otherwise almost universal use of a semicolon as a statement terminator/separator. It is another inheritance from the early days of BASIC.) 'End of line' comments are introduced by a single quote (apostrophe), e.g.

```
Const WM_USER = 1024 'Const for Win32 API call
```

(For backwards compatibility, comments can also be introduced with REM. However, since REM introduces a *statement*, these are whole-line comments, and are uncommon in VBA programs.)

7.2.6 Control structures

Visual Basic has all the usual control structures, though sometimes with a slightly unfamiliar syntax. A particular feature to note is that every structure has a closing 'bracket', e.g.

```
If ... End If
Do ... Loop
For ... Next
```

(A single statement If is an exception, as we shall see.) The explicit close means that there is no need for begin/end or curly brackets to delimit the scope of groups of repeated/conditional statements.

Conditionals

In an If statement, the condition that follows the If can be a comparison that yields a Boolean result, or an expression that evaluates to a numeric value: zero is false and anything else is true. Unlike other languages, there are no obligatory brackets round the expression. Conditional execution of a single statement is a 'one liner', e.g.

```
If Flag Then Flag = Not Flag
```

Points to note about the more general 'block if' statement are

- Then must be the last thing on the line (except for a comment)
- Else, ElseIf and End If must be the first thing on a line (except for a line number – an unlikely occurrence in modern Basic)
- End If is two words, but ElseIf is a single word.

In addition to the If statement there is a multi-way selection statement, the Select Case statement, e.g.

```
Select Case MyVar
  Case "red" document.bgColor = "red"
  Case "green" document.bgColor = "green"
  Case "blue" document.bgColor = "blue"
  Case Else MsgBox "pick another color"
End Select
```

A common idiom is to use a variable of some enumeration type as the Case expression, with constants from the enumeration forming the value lists in the arms of the case statement. For example, using the DaysOfWeek enumeration described earlier, we might write

```
Dim Today As DaysOfWeek
...
Select Case Today
Case Monday, Friday
  HoursWorked = 8
Case Tuesday To Thursday
  HoursWorked = 7.5
Case Else
  HoursWorked = 0
End Select
```

Repetition and loops

There are two repetition statements, Do and For. (There is also a While statement, but this is only included for backward compatibility, and its use is deprecated.) The Do statement comes in two forms:

```
Do While condition
   ...
Loop
```

can be a zero-trip loop, while

```
Do
   ...
Loop While condition
```

guarantees that the body will be executed at least once. In both cases, While can be replaced by Until to negate the condition.

The simple For loop is straightforward, e.g.

```
For I = 1 To 100 Step 2
   A(I) = 0
Next I
```

If the increment is 1 the Step can be omitted. Appending the counter variable to the Next statement helps readability of nested loops, but is optional.

The For Each statement can be used to iterate over the elements of an array (or the members of a collection object, as described later). It has an obvious use in iterating over the elements of a dynamic array, e.g.

```
Dim A()
... 'computation to decide size of array
ReDim A(N)
...
ReDim Preserve A(N+10)
...
For Each Item in A
Print Item
Next
```

Populate the array and add some more elements: no need to remember size.

Note, however, that the elements of the array are assigned to Item by value, i.e. they are local copies, thus you cannot change the contents of an array in a For Each loop. Another pitfall to watch out for is that For Each is not guaranteed to iterate over the array in index order.

Loops can be terminated prematurely using Exit Do and Exit For.

```
For I = 1 To N
   ...
   If A(I) < 0 Then Exit For
   ...
Next I
```

7.2.7 Procedures and functions

Visual Basic provides procedures and functions, but as a consequence of its ancestry, procedures are called 'subs' in the actual code. The term 'procedure' is used to mean 'procedure or function' when the context is unambiguous. In Office applications the term 'macro' is frequently used: strictly an Office macro is a global procedure that takes no arguments.

Procedure and function declaration and call

In declarations the type of the formal parameters can be specified optionally, as can the type of value returned by a function. Untyped formal parameters are variants: a function declared without a return type returns a variant. Examples:

```
Sub Scream (s As String, n As Integer)
  ...
End Sub
Function Foo (s As String) As Integer
  ...
End Function
```

The body of a function must contain an assignment to the name of the function to define the return value. In Visual Basic 5 the return value must be a scalar, i.e. not an array or UDT, though it is permitted to return a variant containing an array. These restrictions are lifted in Visual Basic 6. Execution of a procedure or function body normally terminates by 'dropping off the end', but exit from within the body is possible using the `Exit Sub` and `Exit Function` statements.

Procedure call takes the usual form, except that the arguments are *not* enclosed in brackets, e.g.

```
Scream "aaarrrgghhh!", 42
```

Note particularly that the space after the comma is obligatory. The same syntax is used for a function call if the value returned by the function is to be discarded. However, if the value returned is to be used, the normal parenthesis notation *is* used, e.g.

```
n = Foo("aaaarrrggghh!")
```

For backwards compatibility, the `Call` statement can be used for a procedure call, e.g.

```
Call Scream("aaarrrggghh!", 42)
```

In this case too the arguments are enclosed in brackets. (Yes, this *is* confusing.)

Call by reference and call by value

The default is to call arguments by reference, but value calling can be specified in the declaration by adding the qualifier `ByVal` *before* the parameter specification, e.g.

```
Sub foo (ByVal n as Integer)
...
```

Optional parameters

Optional parameters can be declared using the `Optional` keyword:

```
Sub foo (x As String, Optional y As Variant)
...
End Sub
```

Note that if an optional argument is declared, all subsequent arguments must also be declared optional. If there is no actual parameter corresponding to an optional formal parameter, the parameter is assigned as a variant, with the value `empty`. This can be tested with the function `IsMissing`, e.g.

```
Sub foo (x As String, Optional y As Variant)
If Not IsMissing(y) Then
   ... ' process y
End If
...
End Sub
```

An optional argument can be given a default value to be used if no actual argument is provided, e.g.

```
Sub foo (x As String, _
   Optional y As Integer = 0)
```

Finally, a procedure with an unknown number of parameters can be declared using the `ParamArray` keyword. This is followed by a 'formal parameter' which is an array: when the procedure is called, however many arguments are provided will be collected into the array as variants, e.g.

```
Sub foo (ParamArray args( ))
   For Each x in args
      ...
   Next x
   ...
End Sub
```

Keyword parameters

Keyword parameters can be used as an alternative to positional parameters: for example, the three procedure calls following are identical in effect.

```
Scream "aaaarrrgghhhh!", 42
Scream s := "aaaarrrgghhhh!", n := 42
Scream n := 42, s := "aaaarrrgghhhh!"
```

This facility is particularly useful if a procedure has a large number of optional arguments, all with default values, and it is required to set just one or two arguments to non-default values.

7.2.8 Program structure, variable scoping and lifetime

Terminology here may be confusing. Visual Basic (the application) has the concept of a *project*, which is more or less what we would otherwise call an application. A project consists of one or more *forms*, and may also include one or more *modules*. A form is a collection of visual objects (controls) and associated code, while a module consists of a possibly empty set of variable declarations, followed by one or more procedure or function declarations. For the purpose of determining variable scope, the code in a form is treated as a separate module (a 'form module'). The scoping rules are expressed in terms of modules, and are as follows:

1. Variables declared using `Dim` and constants declared using `Const` at the start of a module (before any procedure or function declarations) are global to the procedures and functions in the module, but invisible outside the module.
2. Variables declared using `Public` (instead of `Dim`) and constants declared using `Public Const` at the start of a module (before any procedure or function declarations) are global to the project, and visible in all modules.
3. Procedures and functions declared in a module are visible in all other modules unless they are declared by `Private Sub` or `Private Function`.
4. Variables and constants declared inside a procedure or function (explicitly or implicitly) are local to the procedure or function.
5. Local variables lose their value on exit unless either they are declared using `Static` instead of `Dim`, or the procedure declaration was preceded by the `Static` keyword, which makes all local variables static. Values of static variables are retained between calls.

7.2.9 Files and I/O

File input/output in Visual Basic 5 and earlier versions is straight out of 'classic' BASIC. Visual Basic 6 provides an alternative way of accessing text files through the methods of the File System Object Model, and this capability is also available to users of Visual Basic 5 if they download the Microsoft Scripting Runtime Library. This is described in Chapter 15: in the remainder of this section we describe the older form of I/O.

Text files

A text file (or *sequential character file*) is opened with the `Open` command, e.g.

```
Open "c:\myfiles\file1" For Input As #1
Open "c:\myfiles\file2" For Output As #2
Open "c:\myfiles\file3" For Append As #3
```

Once opened for input, a file can be read a line at a time using the `Line Input` command, e.g.

```
Line Input #1 TheLine
```

assigns the next line, as a `String`, to the variable `TheLine`. The newline character or characters are discarded. The `EOF()` function returns `True` at the end of the file, so a common idiom is

```
Open "C:\data.txt" For Input As #1
Do
Line Input #1 TheLine
... ' process TheLine
Loop Until EOF(1)
```

A Visual Basic program is unlikely to need to write to a file – most file access is to databases, for which special features are provided, as described in Chapter 8. If output to a sequential character file is required, for historical reasons the `Print` command is used, e.g.

```
Print #3 S1; S2; S3
```

Visual Basic regards the line as made up of *zones*, and including `Tab` in the print list moves the 'print' position to the start of the next zone. Alternatively, `Tab(n)` moves to absolute column n, and `Spc(n)` inserts n spaces in the line. This is likely to be overly restrictive. A better approach is to build up the whole line as a string, using the `Format$()` function as required, then give the string as a single argument to `Print`.

Random access files

A random access file is made up of records that are all of the same length. Typically, each record will be the contents of a variable declared as a UDT. For example, suppose we are maintaining staff records: and set up the following declarations.

```
Type Employee
    ID As Integer
    Salary As Currency
    StartDate As Date
    LastName As String*15
    FirstName As String*15
    Department As String*15
End Type
Dim anEmployee As Employee
```

To create a random access file we need to know the length of each record in bytes. It is best to let Visual Basic compute this, since the consequences of getting it wrong are likely to be catastrophic. (One trap for the unwary is that strings are stored internally in Unicode, so characters and bytes are no longer the same thing.) We open the file as follows:

```
Dim RecLength As Long
Reclength = LenB(anEmployee)
Open "C:\staff.fil" For Random As #1 Len =
RecLength
```

(The `LenB()` function applied to a user-defined type returns the in-memory size, including any padding between elements.) We can now write an arbitrary record in the file

```
Dim Position As Long
...
Position = ...
Put #1, Position, anEmployee
```

and we can read an arbitrary record in an analogous way:

```
Position = ...
Get #1, Position, anEmployee
```

Binary files

A binary file is made up of records of varying size. It is opened by a statement like

```
Open "C:\stuff.bin" For Binary As #1
```

A record can be appended to the file by

```
Put #1, theData
```

and the records can be read sequentially by repeated use of

```
Get #1, theData
```

(You can seek to an absolute byte offset, but given that the records are of variable length, such an action is likely to be perverse.)

Working with files and directories

Visual Basic provides a number of mechanisms for navigating and manipulating the file system. These include `CurDir`, `ChDrive`, `ChDir`, `MkDir` and `RmDir`. `CurDir` returns the path of the current directory on the current drive: with an argument, e.g. `CurDir("D:")`, it returns the current directory on that drive. The meaning of the other statements should be obvious. In addition `Name` can be used to rename a file, or move it to another drive, and `Kill` can be used to delete a file.

The File System Object Model, described in Chapter 15, provides a more comprehensive set of methods for working with files and folders.

7.3   The Visual Basic way of objects

7.3.1   Evolution of object handling in Visual Basic

The way Visual Basic treats objects reflects the way in which the language has evolved. When first introduced, Visual Basic was an *object-based* language rather than a traditional object-oriented language. It had the ability to access properties and methods of predefined objects, both those built in to the application and externally supplied 'custom controls', but that was all.

Version 3 of Visual Basic introduced some limited capabilities for handling objects, but it remained object-based – there was no ability to define classes with inheritance or to create instances from classes, and no polymorphism. Version 3 introduced an `object` data type that could hold a reference to an object: however, objects that could be referenced were limited to forms created using the GUI building function of the application and controls like dialog boxes, scrollbars etc. Thus having created a form called `MyForm` by dragging controls into the desired places on the screen, one could write

```
Dim AnotherForm As New MyForm
```

to create another instance of the form, which would spring into existence automagically when one of its properties or methods was accessed. Likewise,

```
Dim message As TextBox
```

declared a variable that could hold a reference to any `TextBox` control. Generic object variables could also be used:

```
Dim AnotherForm As Object
...
Set AnotherForm = new MyForm
```

Version 4 of Visual Basic took a major step towards object orientation by providing the ability to define classes (in the form of *class modules*): once a class had been defined, new instances of it could be created using the `New` keyword. However, sub-classing is not supported: instead, inheritance is achieved by the use of *interfaces* (see below). The limitation was that classes were restricted to being non-visual: the only way to generate a new instance of a visual object was to create a form using the GUI, and then make a clone from this *form class* using `New`. This restriction was removed in the so-called Version 5 Control Creation Edition (the CCE), which preceded the release of Version 5 proper. The CCE, as its name implies, provided a way of making ActiveX controls, and Version 5 extends this to creating ActiveX documents as well. It also incorporates *ActiveX Designers*, which make possible the visual design of visual classes.

7.3.2   Properties

The idea of a property is a unique Microsoft contribution to object-oriented programming (OOP). In classic OOP, objects have instance variables that are by default hidden from the outside world, and can be exposed by providing the object with methods to read or write values of particular instance variables. For example, a `Button` object might have an instance variable `Text`, containing the string that is to appear on the button. This variable would be private to the object, which would provide methods to set and read its value. For example, with a button called `B1` we might write

```
B1.Text_set("Exit")
```

to set the text, and

```
text = B1.Text_get( )
```

to read the current value. This is part of the encapsulation process: access to the button text is controlled; for example, the method that sets the value can perform validation of the text supplied, perhaps imposing a limit on the length of the string.

In Microsoft OOP, an instance variable that is exposed by an object is called a *property*, and Visual Basic makes it appear as a directly accessed variable, though in fact it is accessed by hidden methods. Thus in Visual Basic we would write

```
B1.Text = "Exit"
```

to change the text on the button, and

```
text = Button1.Text
```

to read the value. Although these look like simple assignment statements, in both cases a hidden method is invoked to perform the action.

7.4 Object models and type libraries

Modern Visual Basic has the concepts of objects and properties, and the syntax for referencing them, but has no in-built object model. Instead it can interface to any application that exposes a collection of objects (actually COM automation objects) which form the *object model* and are described in a *type library*. The type library defines the properties and methods of a collection of related objects, much as a header file in C describes a collection of functions in a library: the entries in the type library are in many ways the equivalent of a set of abstract base class definitions in Java. The user specifies which type library (or type libraries) is (are) to be imported at start-up, or more commonly accepts the default type libraries that the application designer has specified. Thus Visual Basic (the application) has its own type library describing the in-built controls, and most ActiveX controls have an associated type library.

The user can import other type libraries, so that a Visual Basic application that needs spreadsheet facilities can import the Excel type library. The development environment includes an object browser, so that the user can explore type libraries to find out what objects are available: this is essential, since the object models supported by an application such as Word or Excel are very large. Fortunately, it is not necessary for the Visual Basic programmer to understand the mechanics of automation objects: a brief account is given in Chapter 8 for the interested reader.

7.5 Working with objects

We describe here the facilities that Visual Basic provides for working with built-in or imported objects. In Chapter 8 we describe how it is possible to define new object classes.

7.5.1 Object categories

The objects that are used in Visual Basic fall into four distinct categories, which we summarize here.

Forms

The form is a fundamental concept in the Visual Basic application: it is a window into which controls can be placed. Each such window has an associated Form object. Forms have methods and properties like any other object, but in addition they can respond to events such as a mouse click if an event-handler method has been provided (see Section 7.7).

Controls

Controls are components that are embedded in a container. Controls can be placed in any *container application* that supports ActiveX controls: the Visual Basic application is an example of a container application, and other examples include Internet Explorer, Word and Excel. The term 'control' originated in the first version of Visual Basic, and meant the collection of built-in visual building bricks: nowadays a control can be an intrisic (built-in) control or an ActiveX control (an external component). Intrinsic controls provide some interactive user-controlled functionality: originally, ActiveX controls were exclusively visual components, providing further interactive functionality, but it is now common to find non-visual ActiveX controls. Controls have properties and methods, and, like forms, will respond to an external event if an event-handler method for that event has been provided. Things such as dialog boxes and listboxes are simple examples of controls and are included in the Visual Basic application as the *intrinsic controls*: at the other extreme an ActiveX control can be a very complex thing – HTML documents in Internet Explorer are displayed using an ActiveX control, so it is possible to embed an HTML viewer in another application, e.g. an 'HTML Help' facility.

Component objects

Component objects are objects (automation objects, in fact) that an application makes visible to other applications. For example, a range of cells in the worksheet currently active in Excel is exposed to other applications as an object, e.g. `ActiveWorkSheet. Cells(B1:B10)`. Such an object can be manipulated within Excel under the control of a VBA program running in Excel or in a different application (see Chapter 13). Component objects, and the mechanisms used to create them, are discussed in detail in Chapter 8.

System objects

The Visual Basic application object model includes some *system objects* that allow a program to interact with the host system. These are described in Section 7.6.

7.5.2 Properties

The syntax for referring to a property is

```
object_id.property_name
```

e.g.

```
ActiveCell.Value = "Annual Totals"
v = ActiveCell.Value
```

If several properties are to be interrogated or changed, the `With` statement can be used:

```
With ActiveSheet.Cells(1, 1)
   .Font.Name = "Arial"
   .Font.Bold = True
   .Font.Size = 8
End With
```

Many objects have a default property, which is used when the object name appears in a context where a property name is required. For example, a `TextBox` control has a property `Text`, whose value is the string currently displayed in the `TextBox`. Since `Text` is the default property, if we have created a `TextBox` called `FaxNumber`, we can write

```
FaxNumber = "2865"
```

as a shorthand for

```
FaxNumber.Text = "2865"
```

7.5.3 Objects as containers

A property of an object can have a value from any of the types supported by Visual Basic. In particular, the value can be an object reference, thus an object can act as a container that contains other objects. (Such a *container object* should not be confused with *container applications*.) For example, in Windows, the `Selection` object (the object representing the text currently selected on the screen) contains a `Find` object, which in turn has properties that define the search and an `Execute` method to start the search. Thus we might write code like

```
Selection.Find.Text = "Scripting Languages"
Selection.Find.Execute
```

to do a search in selected text. Note the way in which the syntax for denoting such contained objects resembles a path name in a hierarchical file system.

7.5.4 Methods

The `Execute` method used above takes no arguments. In general, the syntax for referring to a method is

```
object_name.method args
```

if the method is a strict procedure (returning no result), and

```
v = object_name(args)
```

if the method is a function returning a result. Keyword parameters are often used, e.g.

```
Application.PrintOut FileName :="", _
Range := wdPrintAllDocument, _
   Item := _wdPrintDocumentContent, _
   Copies := 1, Pages := "", _
   PageType := wdPrintAllPages, _
   Collate := True, _
   Background := True, _
   PrintToFile := False
```

Application is an object in the Word object model: Printout is one of its methods. See Chapter 13 for a full explanation.

7.5.5 Object variables

Many useful things can be done just by reading and setting the properties, and invoking the methods, of predefined objects. Sooner or later we want to do more complicated things, and this is where *object variables* are needed.

Generic object variables

An object variable is a variable whose value is a reference to an object. Clearly, a variant can hold an object reference, but we are concerned here with variables declared with explicit types. We have already seen (Section 7.2.1) that `Object` is a data type in Visual Basic, and so the 'obvious' way to get an object variable is with a declaration like

```
Dim Obj1 As Object
Dim Obj2 As Object
```

This declares generic object variables, i.e. variables that can hold a reference to an object of any class. Once we have declared `Obj1` we can assign an object reference to it using the keyword `Set`, e.g.

```
Set Obj1 = Form1
```

(`Set` was probably chosen because in the original BASIC, all assignment statements had to start with the keyword `Let`.) Once the reference is created, the object variable can be used in any context where the object itself could have appeared, thus `Obj1` appears to have all the properties and methods of the `Form1` object. Thus we can write

```
Obj1.BackColor = vbRed
```

to change the background colour of `Form1`. The correspondence between object variable and object is complete, even down to default properties. Thus if we have a `TextBox` called `FaxNumber`, we can write

```
Dim Fax as Object
Set Fax = FaxNumber
...
Fax = "3031"
```

and the default method (`Text`) of a `TextBox` will be used in the assignment to `Fax`.

Using `Set` distinguishes object reference assignments from assignments of other data types: it reminds us that we are assigning a reference, not a value. To elaborate this point, suppose we declare three integer variables `A`, `B` and `C`. If we then write

```
A = 100
B = A
C = A
```

`B` and `C` are each assigned a *copy* of the value of `A`: subsequent changes to the value of `A` do not affect `B` and `C`. Contrast this with the behaviour of object variables: if after setting the value of `Obj1` as shown above, we write

```
Set Obj2 = Obj1
```

then both `Obj1` and `Obj2` refer to the *same* object, and any changes in that object will be 'seen' by both `Obj1` and `Obj2`. Thus setting a property for `Obj1`, e.g.

```
Obj1.prop1 = True
```

means that `Obj2.prop1` will also have the value `True`. It is sometimes important to determine whether two object variables are referring to the same object: the `Is` operator tests for equivalence between two object references, i.e. returns true if two object variables are references to the same object. It can also be used to test for the value `Nothing`. The object reference `Me` can be used as a self-reference in order to distinguish between multiple instances of an object. Thus if there are multiple instances of a form object visible, you can say `Me.Hide` to hide the currently active instance (i.e. the one in which code is currently executing).

Within an `If` statement, but nowhere else, the `TypeOf( )` function can be used to report the specific object type of the object to which a generic object variable currently refers, e.g.

```
if TypeOf(Object1) = TextBox Then ...
```

Type-specific object variables

The disadvantage of generic object variables is that they are just that: generic. This means that the kind of object to which they refer cannot be determined until run-time, which means that late binding has to be used, with a consequent performance hit. For this reason, we try wherever possible to use early binding. We can do this whenever we are working with objects derived from a class that is described in a type library, since the properties and methods of the class are known at compile time, and the compiler can therefore perform type checking on method arguments. For example, the type library for the Visual Basic application includes a `Form` object, so we can declare a Form-object variable:

```
Dim Obj3 As Form
```

`Obj3` can now hold a reference to any `Form`, but not to any other class of object. When we build a Visual Basic project, the project has its own type library containing the form objects of the project. If a project incorporates a user-designed form called `MyForm`, Visual Basic automatically generates a class called `MyForm` in the project's type library, so we can declare an even more specific object variable that holds references only to `MyForm` objects:

```
Dim Obj4 As MyForm
```

7.5.6 Creating new instances

To create an instance of an object we use the `New` keyword:

```
Set Obj5 = New MyForm
```

The `New` keyword can create a new instance of local objects, including objects belonging to a user-defined class (see Chapter 8). However, the new instance is not initialized – Visual Basic does not have constructor functions. Since an uninitialized object is not much use, the new instance created by `New` is not actually loaded until one of its properties or methods is accessed (presumably as part of the initialization). Until this happens, the variable declared has the special value `Nothing`.

7.5.7 Controls as objects

The Visual Basic application provides a number of visual 'controls' which are represented by objects in the object model. We can therefore declare object variables to refer to them, e.g.

```
Dim C1 As Control
```

makes C1 a variable that can refer to any control:

```
Dim C2 As TextBox
```

makes C2 a variable that can refer to any textbox control. Unfortunately, while a form defines a class from which new instances can be derived, we cannot use the `New` keyword to create new instances of a specific control at run-time. However, this restriction applies only to the intrinsic (built-in) controls of the Visual Basic application: ActiveX controls are fully-fledged objects, so if we are using an ActiveX control called `YoYo` which has an associated type library, it is quite legitimate to write

```
Dim AnotherYoYo As YoYo
Set AnotherYoYo = New YoYo
```

7.5.8 Arrays of object variables and control arrays

An array of object variables can be declared just like an array of any other type, e.g.

```
Dim Things(1 To 10) As Object
```

This gives us an array of 10 generic objects. Since we try to avoid generic objects where possible, it would be more common to write something like

```
Dim MyForms(1 To 10) As Form
```

to get an array of references to `Form` objects. If we have created a form at design stage, `MyForm1` say, we can use the `New` keyword to create an array of references to instances of the form, thus

```
Dim MyForms(1 To 10) As New MyForm1
```

(The new instances will be created when the elements of the array are first used.)

Arrays of controls

Since controls are objects, we can create arrays of them, either generic or specific, e.g.

```
Dim TheControls(1 To 100) As Control
Dim Entries(1 To 5) As TextBox
```

The first array could be used to hold references to 100 controls of any type. The second array holds references to five `TextBox` controls: these must have been defined at design time, but can come from different forms. Arrays of controls are of very limited use, because as we have already seen, we cannot use the `New` keyword to create a new instance of a control at run-time. For this reason we more commonly use *control arrays*, as described in the next section, since they do make it possible to create new instances of an existing control. (Visual Basic 6 provides a more sophisticated way of creating controls dynamically: this too is described later.)

Control arrays

Many beginners discover control arrays by accident, when they inadvertently use the name of an existing control for another control of the same type, and provoke a dialog box like the one in Figure 7.1.

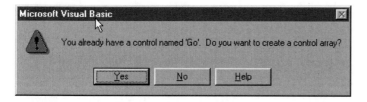

Figure 7.1 Response to duplicate naming of a control

Controls of the same type are grouped into a control array by giving them the same `Name` property and assigning a value to their `Index` property. (The Visual Basic application assigns consecutive integers as the controls are created, but the user can assign arbitrary integers for the Index property.) The controls in a control array are accessed using the normal array notation. Thus if the user had responded 'Yes' in the dialog box in Figure 7.1, the controls would be accessible as Go(1), Go(2), etc. Control arrays are used when it is desired to make the response to events such as a mouse click more or less uniform for all the controls in the array – see Section 7.7 for more details.

Control arrays can only be created at design time, but once created it is possible to add controls at run-time using the Load statement. For example, suppose we create a TextBox control called Entry at design time, and assign zero to its Index property, thus creating a control array. Then at run-time we can create more instances with a simple loop:

```
For I = 1 To 5
   Load Entry(I)
Next I
```

The new instances have the Visible property set to False, but otherwise inherit all the property values of the original TextBox control (strictly, the control with the lowest index in the array. This means that if made visible they will all be stacked on top of each other. Real-life code would use the Move method to place them in different positions, e.g.

The first argument of Move is the position of the left edge, the second argument is the position of the top edge. This code stacks the controls vertically.

```
For I = 1 To 5
   Load Entry(I)
   Entry(I).Move 600, I*600
   Entry(I).Visible = True
Next I
```

7.5.9 Collection objects

In practice, we rarely use arrays of objects: instead we use a *collection object*. A prime example is found in the object models exposed by applications which provide an object for some significant component, and also a collection object containing all the instances of that component. Thus the Excel object model has a Worksheet object and a Worksheets collection. Visual Basic provides three built-in collection objects: Forms, Controls and Printers. Thus to print the captions of all the loaded forms in a project, we might write

```
Dim TheForm As Form
For Each TheForm In Forms
   Debug.Print TheForm.Caption
Next
```

Note that when iterating over a collection of objects with a For Each loop, an implicit Set statement is executed each time round the loop. Thus the above loop is equivalent to

```
For I = 0 To Forms.Count-1
   Set TheForm = Forms.Item(I)
   Debug.Print TheForm.Caption
Next I
```

A collection object is not, however, restricted to collections of objects: it provides a convenient way to refer to a related group of items as a single object. (An alternative way of referring to a related group of items is to use the `Dictionary` object, which is built into Visual Basic 6, and can be used in Visual Basic 5 by downloading the Microsoft Scripting Runtime Library. The `Dictionary` object is described in Chapter 14.)

The items, or members, in a collection need only be related by the fact that they exist in the collection, and members of a collection do not have to share the same data type since the members of a collection are stored as variants: this makes the collection a useful alternative to an array. (It has been remarked that the collection object is the grown-up form of the array in the object-oriented world.) Note that since that UDTs are not a valid sub-type of a variant, they cannot be members of a collection. A further benefit of using a collection object is that collections are 'elastic', resizing themselves as required, unlike dynamic arrays which require an explicit `ReDim` statement to change their size.

A user-defined collection can be declared using the `New` keyword, e.g.

```
Dim C As New Collection
```

Once a collection is declared, members can be added using the `Add` method and removed using the `Remove` method. Specific members can be retrieved from the collection using the `Item` method. The number of items in the collection can be obtained from the `Count` property. The simplest form of the `Add` method is

```
C.Add item
```

where *item* is the item to be added: it will be added at the end of the collection. More commonly, a collection is treated as an associative array (hash), with items identified by a string that forms the *key*, e.g.

```
C.add TextBox1, "Name"
C.add TextBox2, "PostCode"
```

The placing of the item in the collection can be influenced by two further optional arguments, e.g.

```
C.Add TextBox3, "Town", "PostCode", "Name"
```

This causes the item to be added *before* the item with key `"PostCode"` and after the item with key `"Name"`. (The 'before' and 'after' arguments can be numeric expressions, determining the constraint on positioning in terms of ordinal positions in the collection, with the items numbered from 1 to `C.Count`. However, using such a numeric index is error-prone, and not recommended. An added complication is that while user-defined collections are indexed from 1, built-in collections like `Forms` are indexed starting from 0.)

The `Item` method returns an item from the collection, identified by key or numerical ordinal position, e.g.

```
Town = C.Item("Town")
PostCode = C.Item(3)
```

`Item` is the default method for a collection, so the above lines of code could be shortened to

```
Town = C("Town")
PostCode = C(3)
```

A neat shorthand allows the first of these to be written

```
Town = C!Town
```

However, good coding style deprecates the use of default methods and properties.

The number of items in a collection can be determined using its count property. This could be used to iterate over the collection, e.g.

```
Dim Item As Variant
For I = 1 To C.Count
  Item = C(I)
  ...
Next I
```

However, this is not recommended: the preferred way of iterating over the items in a collection is to use a For Each loop, e.g.

```
For Each Item In C
  ...
Next
```

7.5.10 Creating controls dynamically in Visual Basic 6

Now that we know about collections, we can see how Visual Basic 6 allows dynamic creation of controls. All the controls in a form are accessible via the Controls collection, and a new control can be created dynamically by invoking the Add method of the Controls collection, e.g. to create a command button dynamically we first declare a variable of type CommandButton:

```
Dim WithEvents OKBtn As CommandButton
```

and at the relevant place in our program we can instantiate it with

```
Set OKBtn = _
Form1.Controls.Add("VB.CommandButton",_
                   "OKButton")
```

The new control can be accessed via its object reference returned by the Add method, e.g. we can make it visible with

```
OKBtn.Visible = True
```

Alternatively, it can be accessed as a member of the Controls collection, e.g.

```
Me.Controls("OKBtn").Visible = True
```

The first argument to the Add method is the 'progID' (programmatic identifier) of the control as defined in the Registry. Visual Basic makes these identifiers available as constants with mnemonic names, e.g. "VB.Label", "VB.TextBox" etc. The second argument is the name to be assigned to the new control. An optional third argument can be used to specify a different container for the new control. The variable OKBtn must be declared with the WithEvents qualifier to ensure that the Visual Basic engine redirects events that occur in the button to the associated event handlers, if these have been defined.

7.6 System objects

Visual Basic provides a number of built-in system objects: Clipboard, Printer, Screen and Window allow access to aspects of the host environment; Err provides information about run-time errors, and the Debug object provides assistance in debugging code during the design phase.

7.6.1 The Clipboard object

The Clipboard object mirrors the Windows clipboard, which at any time holds not more than one text item and not more than one graphics item. The object has methods equivalent to the cut and paste operations of the Windows GUI: setText (send text), getText (retrieve text), setData (send graphics item) and getData (retrieve graphics item). The setText and setData methods have a required first argument which is the item to be sent: they may also take a second argument to describe the format, as described below. The getText and getData methods can be given an optional argument to specify a particular format. (Note that since these methods return values, the argument, if present, must be enclosed in round brackets.) The clipboard can be cleared by the Clear method.

Clipboard formats

Windows uses an internal code to record the format of an item on the clipboard: these code values are available as intrinsic constants:

vbCFRTF	richtext format
vbCFText	text
vbCFBitmap	bitmap (.bmp files)
vbCFMetafile	metafile (.wmf files)
vbCFDIB	device-independent bitmap (DIB)

The setText and getText methods assume plain text by default: rich text format can be specified by using the optional second argument, e.g.

```
Clipboard.setText someText, vbCFRTF
```

If getText is used with an explicit format specified and there is nothing on the clipboard that matches the format, an empty string is returned. Similarly, setData and getData discover the format automatically by default. An explicit format can be supplied: if there is nothing on the clipboard in that format, getData returns nothing.

The existence of an item in a particular format can be checked with the `getFormat` method: e.g. to test whether there is a Windows metafile graphic on the clipboard we would write

```
If Clipboard.getFormat(vbCFMetafile) Then
   Image = Clipboard.getData(vbCFMetafile)
Else
   Image = DefaultImage
End If
```

7.6.2   The Printer object and the Printers collection

The `Printer` object represents the default system printer: the `Printers()` collection is a collection of objects each of which represents a printer attached to the system. The default printer can be set to be any of the available printers by assigning a new value to the printer object, e.g. to make the printer called 'Research_3' the default printer we could write

```
Dim P As Printer
For Each P In Printers
   If P.DeviceName = "Research_3" Then
      Set Printer = P
      Exit For
   End If
Next I
```

The `Printer` object is in fact a device-independent drawing space in Windows terms, and graphics can be created on the printer by drawing directly on the printer object using methods such as `circle` and `line`. However, this is a complex operation, and the `Printer` object is more commonly used for determining the capabilities of the default printer, e.g. ability to print duplex, and setting options such as resolution and print quality, or selecting a particular paper tray.

Printer object properties

With one exception, the properties of the `Printer` object correspond to the properties available for the default printer in the Windows Control Panel, and include `ColorMode`, `Duplex`, `DeviceName`, `Fonts`, `Orientation`, `PaperBin`, `PaperSize`, `PrintQuality` etc. The exception is `TrackDefault`. If this is set to `True` the properties of the `Printer` object will be updated automatically if the user changes the default printer from the control panel. Options are set by assigning values to these properties, e.g.

```
Printer.Duplex = vbPRDPHorizontal
```

(The constant on the right-hand side is an intrinsic constant, in fact specifying the style of duplex printing as 'flip on horizontal edge'. You had better be sure that the printer is capable of duplex printing before setting this property!)

Each object in the `Printers` collection represents a system printer, and has the same properties as the `Printer` object. However, these properties are read-only: you can only write to the properties of the default printer. The most common use of the `Printers` collection is to find a printer with specific capabilities. For example, the following code finds a printer capable of colour printing and sets it as the default printer:

```
Dim P As Printer
For Each P In Printers
   If P.ColorMode = vbPRCMColor Then
      Set Printer = P
      Exit For
   End If
Next I
```

7.6.3 The Screen and Window objects

The `Screen` object abstracts some of the physical properties of the screen, and provides some information about the windows being displayed. The `Window` object and the `Windows` collection provide some control over these windows.

The Screen object

The `Screen` object provides information about the physical display through its `Font`, `FontCount`, `Height` and `Width` properties. The first two allow us to find out what fonts are supported by the screen: the following code would place the names of the supported fonts in a listbox control called `FontList`:

```
For I = 0 To Screen.FontCount - 1
FontList.AddItem Screen.Fonts(I)
Next I
```

The latter two give us basic information required to position windows and forms on the screen: for example, the following event handler for `Form1`'s `Load` event ensures that the form is positioned in the centre of the screen:

```
Private Sub Form_Load
Dim WW As Long, WH As Long
Dim FW As Long, FH As Long
WW = Screen.Width
WH = Screen.Height
FW = Form1.Width
FH = Form1.Height
Form1.Left = (WW - FW) \ 2
Form1.Top = (WH - FH) \ 2
End Sub
```

Backslash is the integer division operator.

The `MousePointer` property gives us control over the mouse pointer: for example, if a lengthy process has been started,

```
Screen.MousePointer = vbHourglass
```

changes the mouse pointer to an hourglass. The `ActiveControl` property returns a reference to the control that currently has focus, and if more than one form is being displayed, the `ActiveForm` property returns a reference to the currently active form.

The Window object

The `Window` object is used to show, hide or position windows, and to control focus. It has two self-explanatory methods, `Close` and `SetFocus`. The properties of the `Window` object include `Visible`, `Left`, `Top`, `Width` and `Height`. Again, these are almost self-explanatory. You can use the `Visible` property to return or set the visibility of a window. `Left` and `Top` return or set the current position of the window, while `Width` and `Height` return or set the current size of the window.

7.6.4 The Err object

The `Err` object provides information about a run-time error for an enabled error handler. An error handler is enabled within a procedure or function by the `On Error` statement, and remains in force until the procedure or function exit. For example

```
Sub someProc
On Error GoTo ProcessError
... ' code that might cause a run-time error
Exit Sub
ProcessError:
... ' code to deal with run-time errors
End Sub
```

If no errors arise, the procedure exits normally via the `Exit Sub` statement. If errors occur control is transferred to `ProcessError`. The code in this section can take remedial action, then resume execution at an appropriate point in the main code using the `Resume` statement, or more likely can cause the script to die gracefully with a helpful error message. (If you wish to live dangerously you can ignore all run-time errors with the statement `On Error GoTo 0`.)

When a run-time error occurs, details of the error are available to the error handler as properties of the `Err` object:

- `Number`: the error number.
- `Source`: the name of the current project.
- `Description`: a string corresponding to the return of the `Error` function for the specified `Number`, if this string exists. If the string does not, `Description` contains the string 'Application-defined or object-defined error'.
- `HelpFile`: the path name of the Visual Basic Help file.
- `HelpContext`: the Visual Basic Help file context ID for the error corresponding to the `Number` property.

The information returned in these properties can be used by the error handling code. A minimal response might be to display a message box, e.g.

```
ProcessError:
MsgBox Err.Description & vbCrLf & _
    "Error number: " & Err.Number
```

If the application has a Help file, we can display a message box which describes the error and has two buttons, OK and Help. Clicking OK will dismiss the message box, but clicking Help will display the relevant entry from the Help file. The code for this user-friendly action is as follows:

```
ProcessError:
MsgBox Err.Description, vbMsgBoxHelpButton, _
    "An error occurred", Err.HelpFile, _
    Err.HelpContext
```

Since the default property of the `Err` object is `Number`, writing `Err` alone is equivalent to writing `Err.Number`. This provides a convenient backward compatibility with earlier version of Visual Basic where the error number was returned in a *variable* called `Err`. The properties of the `Err` object are reset to zero or zero-length strings after execution of a `Resume` statement and after an `Exit Sub` or `Exit Function` statement within the error-handling code. The properties can be explicitly reset by the method `Err.Clear`.

A run-time error can be generated from within a program by invoking the `Raise` method of the `Err` object. This method takes the error number as an argument, so

```
Err.Raise 24
```

will trigger an error handler as if error number 24 had occurred naturally. This technique is often used to 'bounce' an error from one error handler to another.

7.6.5   The Debug object

The `Debug` object has two methods, `Print` and `Assert`. `Print` takes a list of one or more expressions, and prints their values in the 'immediate execution' window that forms part of the development environment, e.g.

```
Debug.Print "Count = " Count
```

`Assert` takes a Boolean expression as an argument; if this evaluates to false execution is stopped with the line highlighted. (This only works at development time: when a project is compiled, any instances of `Assert` are removed.)

7.7   Event-driven programming

Graphical interfaces are *event driven*: the application sits waiting for the user to use the mouse or keyboard, and then responds in an appropriate manner. In Windows, each running application has an associated *message queue*: as external events occur they are notified to the relevant application by placing a message in the message queue of the application that 'owns' the currently active window. An application runs in an apparently endless loop, taking messages from its message queue in sequence and processing them. If the message queue is empty, the application waits for a message to appear. (In practice, of course, multi-tasking between the applications is taking place.)

An application written in Visual Basic operates in a similar event-driven manner: the Visual Basic run-time appears as the 'application' as far as Windows is concerned, and whenever one of the components of the application (form or control) is active, Windows sends message events to the Visual Basic run-time, which effectively acts as a proxy for all the components. It keeps track of which control is currently active, and dispatches the appropriate *event handler* as described below. As a consequence, the developer has no need to be concerned with event loops and event queues: all the developer needs to do is provide the code to respond to each event. At design time the control advertises the events that will be passed on to the Visual Basic program: the user provides event handlers in the form of *event procedures* to handle any or all of these events. If no procedure is defined for an event, that event will be ignored.

Some events may be handled internally by the control. In this case, it is up to the designer of the control to decide whether the event should also be made visible in the Visual Basic environment. For example, consider a `TextBox` control. We can select text in the box by dragging the mouse, and this will also generate mouse events to which event handlers will respond if they have been defined. More usefully, as the user types text into the textbox, each keypress generates keyboard events: if handlers have been defined, these events are processed *before* the character is placed in the textbox. This makes it possible to validate input text as it is typed: an example is given in Chapter 8. Automation objects are a special case: by default all the external events are handled by the server application, but we shall see in Chapter 8 how it is possible for the events to be passed to Visual Basic.

Not all events are generated by external user actions. Events can be raised by programs, as described in Chapter 8, and also by controls. A case in point is the `Timer` control. This is an invisible control which fires a `Timer` event at regular intervals, determined by its `Interval` property as long as it is enabled (`Enabled` property). If an event handler is defined for the `Timer` event, the program's foreground process can be interrupted at regular intervals to perform some background task. Thus, suppose we have placed a `Timer` control on a form, named it `Timer1` and set its `Enabled` property to false at design time. A program can activate the timer with

```
Timer1.Interval = 60000 ' 1 minute:
                        ' units are msec
Timer1.Enabled = True
```

The background task is incorporated in the event handler

```
Private Sub Timer1_Timer()
   ...
End Sub
```

7.7.1 Event handlers

Event handlers are normal Visual Basic 'sub' procedures, distinguished by a special naming convention. The procedure identifier for a Visual Basic (application) event handler is made up of the name of the control and the name of the event, joined by an underscore, e.g. the event procedure for the `Click` event of a button called `ActionButton` has the header:

```
Private Sub ActionButton_Click
```

These names are recognized at compile-time: a procedure declaration like the one above causes the Visual Basic system to register this procedure as the event-handler for the `Click` event in the control `ActionButton`, so that if the button is clicked at run-time, the event dispatcher will pass control to the procedure.

When an event occurs in a control that is a member of a control array, the index of the control in the array is passed as an argument to the event procedure. Thus the event handler for the `Click` event of the family of controls named `Go` would start

```
Private Sub Go_Click(Index As Integer)
```

Within the body of the event handler, `Index` can be tested to give different behaviour to different instances of the button: however, control arrays are mainly used where there is a large degree of commonality in the behaviour over the instances – if the event handler does not discriminate by the value of `Index`, all the controls in the array exhibit the same behaviour when the event occurs.

If required, the Visual Basic harness can pass arguments to the event procedure. For example, when responding to a `MouseMove` event, we need to know not only the current coordinates of the mouse, but also which buttons were down during the move, and whether any of the Alt, Ctrl and Shift keys were down at the same time. This information will be passed to the event procedure through arguments, thus the event procedure for the `MouseMove` event in a form has four arguments:

```
Private Sub Go_MouseMove( _
    Button As Integer, Shift As Integer, _
    X As Single, Y As Single)
```

It should be noted that since an event procedure is just an ordinary procedure that has been bound to an event, it can be called in the normal way from within a program, thus an arbitrary piece of Visual Basic code can cause processing to happen as if another event had actually occurred. More information about event processing will be found in Chapter 8.

7.8   Working with Visual Basic (the application)

In this section we present three complete examples of Visual Basic in action. The examples were also coded in Tcl/Tk in Chapter 6, and it is instructive to compare the two versions. Of course, the Visual Basic code does not include any geometry management, since the application provides a visual tool for placing the controls.

7.8.1   Example 1: A phonebook

The source material for the phonebook is in a text file: each line contains two tab-separated fields, being the name and the phone number, e.g.

```
Firefly, Rufus T    2380
Hackenbush, Hugo Z 2748
Driftwood, Otis B   3069
...
```

The data is read into an array with two columns and as many rows as it takes. The user interface is shown in Figure 7.2: it consists of a `TextBox` control named `QueryBox` and a `Button` control named `QButton`. Entering a name in the textbox and clicking the query button causes the matching number to be displayed: entering a number and clicking the button causes the corresponding name to be displayed.

Figure 7.2 Phonebook interface

The code is straightforward: it is given below, annotated with explanatory comment.

```
Dim Phones(1 To 200, 1 To 2) As String
Dim NumEntries As Integer

Private Sub Form_Load
' initialization on form load
Dim s As String
Dim Sep As String
Dim i As Integer, Last As Integer
' Open file
ChDir "D:\book\examples"
Open "phones.txt" For Input As #1

' Put names and numbers in array. This is
' messy: Visual Basic has very poor string
' handling. We use InStr to find the index
' of the tab(Chr 9) and Mid to extract the
' sub-strings on either side of the tab
' character.
i = 0
Do
  Line Input #1, s
  i = i + 1
  Sep = InStr(s, Chr(9))
  Last = Len(s)
  Phones(i, 1) = _
    Mid(s, 1, Sep-1)
```

```
      Phones(i, 2) = _
         Mid(s, Sep+1, Last-Sep)
Loop Until EOF(1)
NumEntries = i

' We have to make the form visible before
' we can give focus to the text box
Form1.Show
QueryBox.SetFocus
End Sub

Private Sub QButton_Click
' Respond to the Click event for QButton
Dim Query As String
Dim LookUpColumn As Integer,
Dim ResultColumn As Integer
Dim i As Integer
Dim Found As Boolean

' Grab the user's text. if it's a number,
' lookup in column 2 and return value from
' column 1. Vice versa if not
s = QueryBox.Text
If IsNumeric(s) Then
  LookUpColumn = 2
  ResultColumn = 1
Else
  LookUpColumn = 1
  ResultColumn = 2
End If

' Do the search
Found = False
For i = 1 To NumEntries
  If s = Phones(i, LookUpColumn) Then
    s = Phones(i, ResultColumn)
    Found = True
    Exit For
  End If
Next I

' Complain if not found, then display the result
If Not Found Then
    s = "NO INFORMATION"
    Beep
End If
QueryBox.Text = s
End Sub
```

7.8.2   Example 2: History list for Notepad

Notepad is a handy editor for short text files, but lacks any history mechanism. This Visual Basic application provides such a mechanism. The initial window is shown in Figure 7.3(a) After entering a directory name and hitting Return, the caption above the textbox changes to confirm the directory setting, and we enter a file name, as shown in Figure 7.3(b). When we hit return, Notepad opens up in a separate window to edit the file, and the history window changes as shown in Figure 7.3(c). The filename entry is clear, and a button has been created labelled with the name of the file just edited. Clicking this button at a later time will start Notepad to edit that file. Each time we edit a file another button is created until five files have been edited (Figures 7.3(d) and 7.3(e)). The next file causes the oldest button to be removed (Figure 7.3(f)). This application with its multiple buttons is a good illustration of the use of control arrays.

Figure 7.3(a)   History list for Notepad: initial screen

Figure 7.3(b)   History list for Notepad: first filename entered

Figure 7.3(c)   History list for Notepad: one file edited

Figure 7.3(d)   History list for Notepad: three files edited

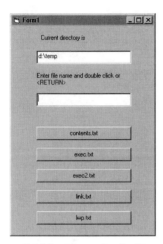

Figure 7.3(e) History list for Notepad: five files edited

Figure 7.3(f) History list for Notepad: six files edited

Here is the code

```
Dim CurrentDir As String, _
    CurrentFile As String, _
    CurrButton As Integer

Private Sub Initialize
' Set up the initial form
' with buttons invisible.
' The buttons form a control array

  Dim i As Integer
  Label1.Caption = _
    "Enter current directory and _
    double click or <RETURN>"
  Label2.Caption = "Enter file name _
  and double click or <RETURN>"
  For i = 0 To 4
    FileBn(i).Visible = False
  Next i
  CurrButton = -1
End Sub

Private Sub Form_Load
' Initialize and give focus to
' directory box
Initialize
Form1.Show
Dir.SetFocus
End Sub

Private Sub Dir_DblClick
```

```
' Double click in Dir textbox calls SetDir
SetDir
End Sub

Private Sub Dir_KeyPress(KeyAscii _
  As Integer)
' So does the RETURN key
If KeyAscii = 13 Then SetDir
End Sub

Private Sub SetDir
' Record directory and change caption to
' confirm. Pass focus to File textbox
CurrentDir = Dir.Text
Label1.Caption = _
   "Current directory is"
File.SetFocus
End Sub

Private Sub File_DblClick
' Double click in File textbox calls SetFile
SetFile
End Sub

Private Sub File_KeyPress(KeyAscii _
  As Integer)
' So does the RETURN key
If KeyAscii = 13 Then SetFile
End Sub

Private Sub SetFile
' Record file name and change caption to
' confirm. If all 5 buttons visible, discard
' earliest and make button 4 current
Dim i As Integer
CurrentFile = File.Text
File.Text = ""
CurrButton = CurrButton + 1
If CurrButton = 5 Then
 For i = 0 To 3
   FileBn(i).Caption = _
     FileBn(i + 1).Caption
 Next i
 CurrButton = 4
End If

' Make button visible (it will be already
' after 5 files), and put current file name
' as caption. Then spoof a click on it.
```

```
FileBn(CurrButton).Visible = True
FileBn(CurrButton).Caption = CurrentFile
FileBn_Click CurrButton
End Sub

Private Sub FileBn_Click(Index As Integer)
' Construct full path name then use Shell
' to start Notepad
Dim EditFile As String
EditFile = CurrentDir + "\" + FileBn(Index).Caption
Shell "c:\windows\notepad.exe " & _
    EditFile, vbNormalNoFocus
End Sub
```

7.8.3 Example 3: A front end for Notepad

This example is a reworking of the front end for Notepad, which was coded for Tcl/Tk in Section 6.3.6. It does not reproduce the precise interface of the Tcl/Tk version, which had a Browse button to bring up a list of files in the current directory. In this version we use the familiar Windows paradigm of a drive window, a directory window and a file window, as shown in Figure 7.4. (Given the built-in support for this interface in Visual Basic using the Drive Listbox, Directory Listbox and File Listbox controls, it would be madness to follow the interface style of the Tcl/Tk version. In real life, we would actually use the FileOpen Windows Common Dialog which does everything behind the scenes, but this would have less educational value.)

As before, the user can enter an explicit file name (or path) and invoke Notepad by clicking OK or hitting Return. Alternatively, the user can select a file in the file listbox with a single click, then click OK or press Return, or double-click a file in the file listbox. The history window records the details of the last five files edited: these can be re-edited by double-clicking the name, or be selecting a file and using the OK button or the Return key.

The code follows.

```
Dim Numfiles As Integer
Dim Path As String

Private Sub Form_Load()
' Initialization. Note that the form has
' to be visible (hence the Show) before
' focus can be given to the FileBox,
ChDir "d:\docs"
Form1.Show
FileBox.SetFocus
Numfiles = 0
End Sub

Private Sub CancelBtn_Click()
' Cancel terminates the application in
' the approved way
```

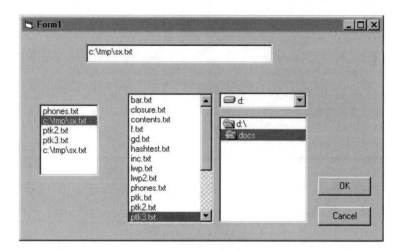

Figure 7.4 Front end for Notepad, Visual Basic style

```
Unload Me
End Sub

Private Sub Drive1_Change()
' Track change of drive, and update
' directory list
ChDrive Drive1.Drive
Dir1.Path = Drive1.Drive
End Sub

Private Sub Dir1_Change()
' Keep file listing in sync with directory
File1.Path = Dir1.Path
End Sub

Private Sub Dir1_Click()
File1.Path = Dir1.Path
End Sub

Private Sub EditFile()
' Procedure to launch Notepad and maintain
' history list
If Numfiles = 5 Then
  List1.RemoveItem 0
  Numfiles = 4
End If

Path = FileBox.Text
Shell "notepad.exe " & Path, vbNormalFocus
List1.AddItem Path
Numfiles = Numfiles + 1
End Sub
```

```
Private Sub History_Click()
FileBox.Text = History.filename
End Sub

Private Sub History_DblClick()
History_Click
EditFile
End Sub

Private Sub History_KeyPress(KeyAscii As Integer)
If KeyAscii = 13 Then EditFile
End Sub

Private Sub List1_Click()
FileBox.Text = List1.Text
End Sub

Private Sub List1_DblClick()
List1_Click
EditFile
End Sub

Private Sub List1_KeyPress(KeyAscii As Integer)
If KeyAscii = 13 Then EditFile
End Sub
Private Sub FileBox_KeyPress(KeyAscii As Integer)
If KeyAscii = 13 Then EditFile
End Sub

Private Sub OKBtn_Click()
EditFile
End Sub
```

Event handlers for click, double-click, Return (ASCII code 13) and OK.

7.9 Reference: operators and operator precedence

Arithmetic operators		Comparison operators	
+	Add	=	Equal
–	Subtract	<>	Not equal
*	Multiply	>	Greater than
/	Divide	>=	Greater or equal
^	Exponentiate	<	Less than
\	Quotient	<=	Less or equal
Mod	Remainder		

Logical operators		String operators	
Not	Logical negation	&	Concatenate
And	And	Like	Regexp match
Or	Or		
Xor	Exclusive or		
Eqv	Equivalence		
Imp	Implication		

Precedence rules are as follows:

- Arithmetic operators are evaluated first, string comparisons are done next, comparison operators are evaluated next, and logical operators are evaluated last.
- Arithmetic operators associate to the left, and have precedence among themselves as follows (highest first): exponentiation, negation, multiplication and division, integer division, modulus arithmetic, addition and subtraction.
- Comparison operators associate to the left and have equal precedence.
- Logical operators associate to the left and have precedence among themselves as follows (highest first): Not, And, Or, Xor, Eqv, Imp.
- The string concatenation operator (&) follows all arithmetic operators and precedes all comparison operators. The Like operator is equal in precedence to the comparison operators, although it is in fact a string operator.

Notes

[1] ActiveX controls are lightweight automation servers: we delve further into this murky area in Chapter 8.
[2] At first sight it appears that it would be more perspicuous to use a Find method whose arguments define the search. The reason why it's done the way it is will become apparent in Chapter 13.

Advanced Visual Basic

In this chapter we explore a number of advanced features of Visual Basic, including Internet-aware applications, COM and automation objects, class modules, the event model, the implementation of user-controlled drag-and-drop, how to create your own ActiveX controls, how a Visual Basic program can use the Windows API, and finally the facilities Visual Basic provides for accessing databases.

8.1 Developing Internet-aware applications

We have seen in earlier chapters how Perl and Tcl applications can be made Internet aware, and how the leverage provided by a scripting language with a rich collection of modules/packages can make a potentially complex operation very easy to achieve. A similar capability to access the Internet in a very easy way is provided in Visual Basic by the Internet Transfer Control (INet control) and the Winsock control. At first encounter, the idea of a control for Internet access or winsock programming seems strange: surely controls are visual objects that are positioned in a form? The resolution of the difficulty comes from the observation that a control does not always have to have an associated window visible on screen – remember the Timer control described in the previous chapter. The important thing is that a control has properties and methods, and can respond to events. This is just what we need for Internet access. For example if we want to retrieve a Web page we can set the site and file path as properties of the INet control, invoke one of the control's methods to initiate the transfer, and wait for the event that is generated when the transfer is complete.

The Internet Transfer Control

The Internet Transfer Control, usually abbreviated to INet, is a client control which implements the HTTP and FTP protocols. Its function is limited to transferring byte streams, so if you use it to access a Web page you will get the raw HTML. You would do this when you wanted your application to extract some particular information from the HTML, e.g. the result of a search.

This section assumes a modest familiarity with the way Web clients and servers interact using the HTTP and FTP protocols. It can be skipped if you don't have that background.

Simple access to the Web is trivially easy: if we have placed an INet control on the form and named it Client, (or, in Visual Basic 6, created the control dynamically), then

```
URL = "http://www.somesite.com/index.html"
HTMLStuff = Client.OpenURL(URL, icString)
```

will retrieve the content of the specified page and set HTMLStuff to be a variant containing the data as a string. Similarly,

```
URL = _
"ftp://www.somesite.com/downloads/thing.zip"
ZipFile = Client.OpenURL(URL, icByteArray)
```

will retrieve the zip file by anonymous FTP, and return it in ZipFile as a variant containing a byte array. OpenURL provides a simple synchronous transfer, i.e. the method does not return until the transfer is complete, or timeout occurs. (Default timeout is 60 seconds, but another value can be specified by setting the INet control's Request-Timeout property.)

For more complex operations we can use the Execute method to initiate an asynchronous transfer. This method takes up to four arguments:

- *url*: a string containing a URL
- *operation*: a string to describe the operation to be performed
- *data*: (HTTP only, optional): location of data to be sent with a POST request
- *requestHeaders*: (HTTP only, optional): additional HTTP headers to be sent with the request.

For HTTP transfers, the *operation* parameter is "GET" to submit a request using the GET method, "POST" to submit a request using the POST method, and "HEADER" to submit a request using the HEADER method (to return the HTTP response header(s) but not the body). If the POST method is specified, *data* must be set to provide a data source. For FTP transfers the *operation* can be any of the commands that an interactive user might type, e.g. "GET", "PUT", "CD", "DIR" etc.

The Execute method returns immediately. The INet control's Boolean property StillExecuting can be interrogated to find out if the request is still being processed, but more generally progress is tracked by providing a handler for the StateChanged event. The event handler is passed a single argument which can take any of the following values (defined as constants by the system):

```
icNone
icResolvingHost          icHostResolved
icConnecting             icConnected
icRequesting             icRequestSent
icReceivingResponse      icResponseReceived
icDisconnecting          icDisconnected
icError
icResponseCompleted
```

Of these, the most important is of course icResponseCompleted. When the StateChanged event handler gets this value it can proceed to retrieve the downloaded data, which has been written to a buffer by the Execute method. The INet control provides two methods to this end, GetChunk and GetHeader. For HTTP transfers, GetChunk retrieves some or all of the HTTP response body, and the response header is retrieved by GetHeader. For FTP transfers GetChunk retrieves the information returned by the server other than status information and data transferred in response to a GET request, which is written directly to file following normal FTP conventions.

GetChunk takes two arguments, size and datatype. The size argument specifies the maximum number of bytes to be retrieved, and datatype is icString or icByteArray. When collecting a complete response, GetChunk will be called repeatedly until it returns a string of zero length. GetHeader without an argument retrieves all the headers: it can be given a single argument, which is a string containing the name of a particular header to be retrieved. To avoid overloading system resources when transferring a large page, the icResponseReceived event can be trapped by the event handler, which can call GetChunk to transfer some of the data without waiting for completion.

If an error occurs, the StateChanged event handler receives the argument icError. The actual error can be identified by interrogating the properties ResponseCode (numeric error code) and ResponseInfo (textual description).

As an alternative to specifying a URL as an argument of OpenURL or Execute, the Internet resource to be accessed can be specified by four inter-dependent properties of the INet control:

- URL: a string containing the complete URL to be retrieved.
- Protocol: the protocol to be used, defined by in-built constants icDefault, icFTP, icHTTP, icHTTPS, icFile.
- RemoteHost: a string containing a fully qualified domain name or an IP address.
- Document: a string containing the complete path to the resource.

As noted, these are inter-dependent: for example, if the URL property is changed the other three properties will be updated to reflect the change. Once the resource has been specified, the transfer is initiated by calling the OpenURL or Execute method.

The Winsock control

The INet control gives us access to Web and FTP servers: to access other servers we need a lower level means of Internet access. This is provided by the Winsock control, which implements the TCP and UDP protocols.

Using the Winsock control is very simple. (Although the Winsock control can be used to set up server sockets, we restrict our discussion to client sockets.) The control is placed in a form at design time (it will be invisible at run-time), and if need be properties are set, e.g. changing the default protocol, sckTCPProtocol, to sckUDPProtocol. Suppose the control has been named Sock. Opening a connection is simply a matter of specifying the host and the port:

```
Sock.Connect "pop.ecs.soton.ac.uk", 110
```

(Alternatively, the host and port could be specified by setting the properties RemoteHost and RemotePort.) When the connection is established, the connect event is raised, which can be processed by an event handler

```
Sub Sock_Connect
...
End Sub
```

Data can be sent to the remote host using the `SendData` method, e.g. if `Message` is a string variable,

```
Sock.SendData Message
```

will send the string to the remote host. When data is received from the host, the `DataArrival` event is raised, and the data is processed within the event handler using the `GetData` method, e.g.

```
Private Sub Sock_DataArrival(ByVal bytesTotal As Long)
Sock.GetData Response, vbString
End Sub
```

Here, the data that arrives is stored in the variable `Response` as a string. At the end of processing the socket is closed with

```
Sock.Close
```

All the foregoing has assumed that nothing goes wrong. In practice, things always go wrong with net connections, and the `Winsock` control provides an error event, which traps almost 40 different errors. Some errors can be avoided by keeping a careful check on the current state of the socket – starting some new operation before a socket has completed the current operation is a sure recipe for disaster. The `state` property has possible values

```
sckClosed
sckOpen
sckConnectionPending
sckResolvingHost
sckHostResolved
sckConnecting
sckConnected
sckClosing
sckError.
```

The names of these constants are self-explanatory

As an illustration of the `Winsock` control we present a simple Visual Basic application that will check for incoming mail: this is the same application that was coded in Tcl in Section 5.7.2. The user clicks a button, and receives a single-line response (Figure 8.1). At design time we place a textbox and two command buttons on the form. The associated code is straightforward.

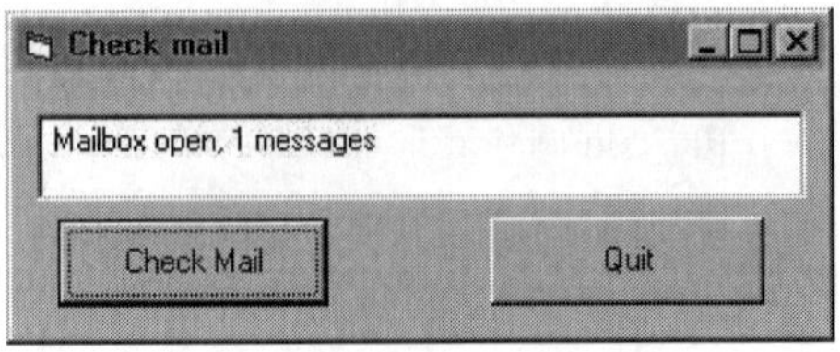

Figure 8.1 Mailbox checker

```
      Dim Response As String
      Dim State As Integer

      Private Sub Form_Load()
      State = 0
      End Sub

      Private Sub Command1_Click()
      Sock.Connect "pop.ecs.soton.ac.uk", 110
      End Sub

      Private Sub Command2_Click()
      Sock.Close
      Unload Form1
      End Sub

      Private Sub Sock_DataArrival(ByVal bytesTotal _
        As Long)
      Sock.GetData Response, vbString
      If StrComp("+OK", Left(Response, 3),_
        vbTextCompare) = 0 Then
        Select Case State
        Case 0
          Sock.SendData "USER DWB" & vbNewLine          Send USER command
          State = 1                                     with UNIX line
        Case 1                                          terminator.
          Sock.SendData "PASS 12345678" & vbNewLine
          State = 2                                     Send PASS command
        Case 2                                          with UNIX line
          Text1.Text = Right(Response,                 terminator.
          Len(Response) - 3)
        Case 3
          Exit Sub
        End Select
      Else
        MsgBox "Unexpected response: " & vbCrLf & _
      Response, vbOKOnly
        State = 3
      End If
      End Sub
```

Note that in this example we do not need to trap the connect event, since the POP server sends a response as soon as a connection is made. (We ought to check for timeout, though.) All the real work is done in the DataArrival event handler. We get the response as a string, and if it doesn't start with "+OK" we display an error message and exit. Otherwise the action depends on the current state – 0 for first response, 1 for response after USER command is sent, 2 for response after PASS is sent. Note that an error causes state 3 to be set, which ensures that any further response from the server is discarded.

8.2   COM objects

Although the Component Object Model (COM) is an essential underpinning of Visual Basic, prior to Version 5 this was hidden from the user. Although the user of Version 5 or 6 can continue in ignorance of COM in the old fashioned way, these versions expose many aspects of COM, in particular *multiple interfaces*.

A COM object is a chunk of compiled code providing an encapsulation of data and procedures: it is defined solely by its interface(s). Procedures that are made visible outside the object are called the *methods* of the object as in traditional object-oriented systems. The data (the *instance variables* in traditional object-speak) is separated into two parts: internal data manipulated by the methods, and externally visible data items. These items could just be global variables, but this would be dangerous, and directly contrary to the principles of encapsulation. COM-based applications such as Visual Basic therefore make them appear as *properties* that can be explicitly queried and set within Visual Basic as variables, but are actually accessed by hidden procedures, as described in the previous chapter. This collection of methods and properties is called an *interface*: as noted above, an object may have multiple interfaces. (In fact, every object has as least two interfaces, the internal *IUnknown* interface required by COM, and at least one user interface. When we refer to multiple interfaces we mean multiple *user* interfaces, which are discussed in detail later in this chapter.)

8.2.1   Automation objects

An automation object (alternatively called an *ActiveX component object* or just an *ActiveX component*) is a COM object that is made available by one application for use by other applications. The application that provides the object is called an 'automation server', and the application that uses the object is called an 'automation controller', since it is using the automation interface to control the operation of another application remotely. Applications like Word and Excel are both automation servers and automation controllers, since they make their functionality and data available as automation objects, and can control objects exposed by another application as automation objects. Although automation objects are just another form of COM object, the distinction is useful in reminding us that the objects manipulated in an application are of two kinds, internal objects and those provided by external servers. ActiveX controls and ActiveX documents are common examples of automation objects.

8.2.2   COM interfaces

The 'glue' that links Visual Basic to an application is provided by the Component Object Model (COM). As we have seen, a COM object has one or more interfaces, an interface being a collection of methods, which are functions or procedures. (COM literature describes them as functions: this is because until recently most COM applications were built in C++ which does not use the term 'procedure', preferring to use the term 'void function'.) The basic COM interface is a pointer to a table of pointers to functions, called a *vtable*: clearly, access to an object method by this method is very efficient. Early versions of Visual Basic were unable to navigate through vtables, and an alternative type of interface was developed for the benefit of Visual Basic, the 'dispatch interface' or *dispinterface*. The dispinterface assigns an integer identifier (the DispID) to each method (function) exposed by the object, and allows a client to invoke that method by calling the interface with the DispID of the required function as the first argument, followed by the actual function arguments. We can think of the dispinterface as using a multi-way switch to route the call to the desired function.

The other important feature of the dispinterface is the way it handles the arguments to the method calls. A COM object is a piece of code running in some application called a *server*, which is typically running out-of-process with respect to the code that is calling it. Part of the COM glue is to convert the arguments, which may be any data type, into a linear byte stream that can be sent to the object using Windows inter-process communication, and to reconstruct the arguments before calling the object's method in its address space. This is the operation of *marshalling* and *un-marshalling*, and for a vtable interface it is entirely transparent. However, a problem arises when Visual Basic wants to invoke a method outside Visual Basic, or vice versa, since the types used by the non-VB object may not have equivalents in Visual Basic. The dispinterface therefore places the onus of marshalling and un-marshalling on the client and server. All arguments have to be packaged into variants by the client, and results unpacked if necessary by the server.

Now that we know about dispinterfaces, we can give a precise definition of an automation object: it is an object that implements a dispinterface. The dispinterface, and the related automation concepts, were developed by the Visual Basic team separately from the mainline development of COM, and Microsoft applications that exported functionality did so entirely through dispinterfaces, so as to be compatible with Visual Basic and to allow interworking though VBA scripts. More recently, applications have begun to exhibit dual interfaces, so that they appear as automation objects to Visual Basic but as conventional COM objects with a vtable interface to other COM objects. With the introduction of Version 5, the dependence on the dispinterface was partially removed: the Visual Basic application (though not embedded VBA) will use a vtable interface if it is available, and a dispinterface if not. This is purely a matter of efficiency: using the vtable interface removes the need to pack arguments into variants and unpack the results.

An important feature of the dispinterface as originally conceived is that a call

```
object.method(args)
```

can be resolved at run-time (late binding), since the interface includes methods to determine whether a particular method is supported by the object, and, if it is, to map the method name onto the corresponding DispID. Thus automation objects are self-describing. However, late binding imposes overheads, and in the interests of efficiency Visual Basic and VBA can use early binding for a dispinterface if the object type is known at compile time and a type library is available to map the name to the DispID. We shall explore the early binding/late binding choice in more detail in later sections.

8.2.3 Creating automation objects

Applications that are prepared to act as servers for component objects (automation servers) provide a root-level object called the `Application` object which contains the whole of the application's object model. If the type library is available to Visual Basic at compile-time, a type-specific declaration can be used, with early binding. For example:

```
Dim xlApp As Excel.Application
Set xlApp = New Excel.Application
```

This will start an instance of Excel running, and make `xlApp` a reference to its `Application` object. An alternative method is to use the `CreateObject` function, e.g.

```
xlApp = CreateObject("Excel.Application")
```

However, the `CreateObject` function is provided mainly for use with servers that do not furnish a type library: provided that they have registered a 'Programmatic Identifier' when first installed, Visual Basic can use late binding to locate the server at run-time and create the object.

Other ways of creating instances of automation servers are discussed in Chapter 13.

8.3   The Visual Basic event model

We have seen in the previous chapter how Visual Basic facilitates event-driven programming, and the examples illustrated some simple event handlers. However, the Visual Basic event model is not restricted to external events like mouse and key operations: a control can respond to internal events, and can send events to the container, which may be dealt with by the container, or dispatched to another control. For example, an event is generated when a form is first loaded, allowing initialization of variables; events are generated when the text in a `TextBox` control changes, when a scrollbar is used or when a window is resized; a timer control can generate `Timer` events at regular intervals. These are just a few examples of what we will call *internal events*. The Visual Basic documentation lists over 200 events that can arise, but most of these are highly specific to particular ActiveX controls that are bundled with the application. The intrinsic controls respond to a relatively small number of events, which we describe in the following sections. As we shall see later in this chapter, when we define new object classes we can associate custom events with them.

8.3.1   Mouse and keyboard events

Mouse events are probably the most commonly used. Most controls allow the user to capture the following events: `Click`, `DblClick`, `MouseDown`, `MouseUp` and `Mouse-Move`. Event procedures for `Click` and `DblClick` have no arguments: procedures for the three mouse events have four arguments, e.g.

```
Private Sub Form_MouseMove(Button As Integer, _
    Shift As Integer, X As Single, Y As Single)
```

Here, X and Y are the mouse coordinates; `Button` and `Shift` are variables whose values reflect the buttons and keys pressed during the mouse move as follows. The procedure returns a value between 0 and 7 in `Button`, being the sum of three values: 1 if the left button was down, 2 if the right button was down and 4 if the middle button was down. The value returned in Shift is a similar sum: 1 if the shift key was down, 2 if the Control key was down, and 4 if the Alt key was down. Clicking a control generates MouseDown and MouseUp events in addition to the Click event. The order in which these three events occur varies from control to control. For example, for ListBox and Command-Button controls the events occur in the order MouseDown, Click, MouseUp, but for FileListBox or Label controls, the events occur in the order MouseDown, MouseUp, Click.

The keyboard events are KeyPress, KeyDown and KeyUp. The KeyPress procedure has one argument, conventionally called KeyAscii, in which it returns the ASCII code of the character corresponding to the key pressed (taking account of the Shift key). It recognizes the Space, Backspace, Return, Tab and Esc keys, together with a few combinations, e.g. Control-[for Esc, Control-M for Return, but does not recognize function keys, arrow keys etc. An interesting feature is that the argument is passed *by reference*, so that by assigning a value to KeyAscii the KeyPress procedure can spoof the control into thinking that it has received a different character. Assigning the value zero cancels the keystroke, ensuring that the control does not see a character at all. Thus if an application requires the user to enter a number in a textbox, non-digit characters can be silently discarded by defining a KeyPress event handler as follows:

```
Private Sub Text1_KeyPress(KeyAscii As Integer)
   If KeyAscii < Asc("0") Or _
      KeyAscii > Asc("9") Then _
      KeyAscii = 0
End Sub
```

The KeyDown and KeyUp events provide a much finer-grain control over the keyboard, since they report the actual state of the keyboard. The procedures have two arguments, KeyCode and Shift. The KeyCode argument returns an integer that identifies the physical key involved: these integers are defined in an in-built enumeration, so that we can refer to function keys as vbKeyF1 etc., and the arrow keys as vbKeyUp, vbKeyDown etc. We can even distinguish between zero on the main keyboard (vbKey0) and zero on the numeric keypad (vbKeyNumpad0). The second argument, Shift, behaves in exactly the same way as the Shift argument in the mouse procedures.

8.3.2 Internal events

Some common internal events generated by Visual Basic are as follows.

Change

The Change event occurs in four common contexts

1. In a TextBox control, when the user types a character, when the user edits the current contents, or when a new value is assigned to the Text property.
2. In a DriveList control, when the user clicks on an entry to change the current drive.

3. In a DirList (directory listing) control when the user double-clicks an entry to move up or down the directory hierarchy.
4. In a scrollbar or ScrollBar control when the user releases the mouse button after dragging the scroll box, clicks in the scrollbar or clicks on the scroll arrows [1].

Scroll

The Scroll event occurs as the scroll box is moved. It is this that makes it possible to provide instant update to the material being scrolled, rather than waiting until the user finishes moving the scroll box.

Timer

When enabled, a Timer control generates Timer events at an interval determined by its Interval property. (A one-shot timer is created by setting the Enabled property to false in the event procedure for the Timer event.)

Load, Initialize

The Load event occurs when a form is first loaded, allowing initialization to take place. As we shall see later, it is possible for a program to generate new instances of a form. When such an instance is created an Initialize event occurs, allowing the instance to be initialized.

UnLoad, terminate

The Unload event occurs just before a form is unloaded, which is usually the result of the user selecting Close from the menu, but can be initiated by the program. It allows the program to do tidying-up operations before the form is closed. If a program has created multiple instances of a form, these instances can later be closed by the program. A Terminate event occurs when an instance is closed by its 'parent', allowing tidying up in the same way as the UnLoad event.

Resize

This event occurs when the user resizes a form.

8.3.3 Events in automation objects

By default, external events for any automation objects are dealt with by the automation server. To make the events visible to Visual Basic, the WithEvents keyword must be added to the object variable declaration, e.g.

```
Dim WithEvents xlBook As Excel.Workbook
```

Once the component instance has been created, it is possible to write event procedures for it in Visual Basic, e.g. we could intercept a user's attempt to close a workbook with an event procedure like the following:

```
Private Sub xlBook_BeforeClose(Cancel _
    As Boolean)
  xlBook.Application.Visible = False
  MsgBox "Can't close workbook", _
    vbExclamation, "WARNING"
  xlBook.Application.Visible = True
  Cancel = True
End Sub
```

If the user clicks the Excel window's close button, the window disappears and a dialog box appears, as shown in Figure 8.2.

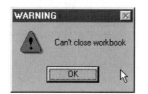

Figure 8.2   Result of capturing Excel's 'close' event

When the user clicks OK (the only option), the Excel window springs back into life.

8.4   Class modules

In Visual Basic 5 and later, a new object class can be defined in a *class module*. This is just like any other Visual Basic module, i.e. a collection of variable declarations together with procedure and function declarations: it is distinguished by being stored with the extension .cls, as opposed to .frm for a form module or .bas for a code module. Having defined a module MyNewObject.cls, you can then declare variables as instances of the class, e.g.

```
Dim Obj1 As New MyNewObject
```

The methods of the class are procedures or functions declared as Public, hence visible outside the module. Variables can be declared as Public, but it is more usual to define them as *properties* that behave like the properties of intrinsic objects. In this case the actual value of the property is stored in a Private variable, and two *property procedures*, which are Public methods, provide mediated access to the value. For a scalar property, the 'Property Let' procedure takes one argument, the value to be assigned to the property, and the 'Property Get' member of the pair behaves like a function of no arguments which returns the value of the property. (The syntax for properties that are arrays is described later.) If a 'Property Get' method is provided without a corresponding 'Property Let' method, the property becomes read-only, and, applying the same principle, a property can be made write only. If the property is itself an object, the 'Property Let' method is replaced by a 'Property Set' method.

All this will become clearer if we look at an example. Suppose we want to declare a class `Rectangle` which has properties `Width` and `Height`, and provides methods `Area()`, `Circumference()` and `Diagonal()`. For good but irrelevant reasons, attempts to set `Width` or `Height` to values greater than 5 will force the value 5 to be used. Here is the class module.

```
' Declare private variables to hold actual
' values of height and width
Private rWidth As Double
Private rHeight As Double

Public Property Let Width(w As Double)
' Allows Width to be used as a property,
' and monitors value given to actual width
  If w <= 5.0 Then
   rWidth = w
  Else
   rWidth = 5
  End If
End Property

Public Property Get Width() As Double
' Gives read access to Width
  Width = rWidth
End Property

Public Property Let Height(h As Double)
' Allows Height to be used as a property,
' and monitors value given to actual height
  If h <= 5.0 Then rHeight = h
  Else
   rHeight = 5.0
  End If
End Property

Public Property Get Height() As Double
' Gives read access to height
  Height = rHeight
End Property

Public Function Area() As Double
' Method to return Area
  Area = rHeight*rWidth
End Function

Public Function Circumference() As Double
' Method to return Circumference
```

```
      Circumference = 2.0*(rWidth + rHeight)
   End Function

   Public Function Diagonal()
   ' Method to return Diagonal
      Diagonal = _
        Sqr(rWidth*rWidth + rHeight*rHeight)
   End Function
```

If this class module is given the name `Rectangle.cls`, we can declare object variables to refer to instances of this class and set the properties, e.g.

```
   Dim R1 As New Rectangle
   R1.Width = 2.5
```

Because the `Rectangle` class defines `Width` and `Height` as a 'Property Let'/'Property Get' pair, Visual Basic knows to call the 'Property Let' procedure `Width` with the value of the right-hand side expression as its argument. Similarly, if we write

```
   W = R1.Width
```

the 'Property Get' `Width` function is called.

   A property can be an array, in which cases the index (or indices) of a particular element can be supplied as arguments to the property procedures. For example, if a property P is a two-dimensional array of double-length real numbers, the property procedures take the following form:

```
   Public Property Let P(m As Long, n As Long, _
    v As Double)
   . . .
   End Property

   Public Property Get P(m As Long, n As Long) As
   Double
   . . .
   End Property
```

Here, m, n are the array indices and v is the value to be assigned.

8.4.1 Interfaces and Polymorphism

Suppose we now define a `Circle` class, with a property `Radius` (required to be not greater than 5.0) and methods `Area()` and `Circumference()`. The class module `Circle.cls` follows the same pattern as the `Rectangle` class:

```
   Private cRadius As Double
   Private Const Pi = 3.1415926535898
   Public Property Let Radius(r As Double)
      If r <= 5.0 Then
        cRadius = r
```

```
      Else
        cRadius = 5
      End If
End Property

Public Property Get Radius() As Double
    Radius = cRadius
End Property

Public Function Area() As Double
    Area = Pi*cRadius*cRadius
End Function

Public Function Circumference() As Double
    Circumference = 2.0*Pi*cRadius
End Function
```

We can now declare instances of a circle in the same way that we declared instances of a rectangle. In conventional object-oriented programming (OOP) we could define a class `Figure`, with methods `Area()` and `Circumference()`, and then define `Rectangle` and `Circle` as sub-classes of `Figure`, which override the parent class's methods for `Area()` and `Circumference()`. If Visual Basic worked this way, we could write

```
Dim MyFigure As Figure
Dim R As NewRectangle
Dim C As NewCircle
R.Width = 2.5
R.Height = 3.5
C.Radius = 4.2
Set MyFigure = R
Debug.Print MyFigure.Area()
Set MyFigure = C
Debug.Print = MyFigure.Area()
```

The first `Debug.Print` statement would use the `Area()` method for a `Rectangle`, and the second would use the `Area()` method for a `Circle`. This is an example of *polymorphism*.

Visual Basic doesn't work the same way as traditional OOP languages, but we can still get the same effects by using the concept of *interfaces*. An interface is a class module containing property declarations and empty method declarations, thus it defines what the properties and methods are, but does not implement the methods. Once an interface has been defined, any other class can provide implementations for the members of the interface. To see how this works we shall first define an interface called `Figure`, in a file called `Figure.cls`, as follows.

```
Public Function Area() As Double
End Function

Public Function Circumference() As Double
End Function
```

We modify the definition of the `Rectangle` and `Circle` classes by specifying that they implement the `Figure` interface, and changing the method definitions. We show here the modified class module for the `Rectangle` class: the `Circle` class would be modified in a similar way.

```
Private rWidth As Double
Private rHeight As Double
Implements Figure
... 'Property procedures as before

Private Function Figure_Area() As Double
  Area = rHeight*rWidth
End Function

Private Function Figure_Circumference() _
    As Double
  Circumference = 2.0*(rWidth + rHeight)
End Function

Public Function Diagonal() As Double
  Diagonal = _
    Sqr(rWidth*rWidth + rHeight*rHeight)
End Function
```

This class implments the Figure *interface.*

Note that the `Area()` and `Circumference()` methods are now defined as `Private`, and are named to show that they are implementing methods from the `Figure` interface. The `Rectangle` class now has two interfaces: its *default interface* made up of the `Public` definitions, and `Figure`.

8.4.2 Other uses of interfaces

Interfaces have other uses besides providing polymorphism – it is quite common for a class to have multiple interfaces. One common use for multiple interfaces is handling version control. An interface once defined is set in concrete: it is a basic axiom of component-based software development that once published, interfaces cannot be changed. (You can of course change the *implementation* – that's the whole point of separating out the interface.) So if a class evolves to need changes to its default interface, this must be done by defining a new interface. Suppose we have a class `Jabberwock` whose class module (`Jabberwock.cls`) has a skeleton as follows.

```
Private Gyre As Long, Gimble As Long
Public Function Brillig(Mome As String, _
      Raths As Date) As String
  ' code for the Brillig method
End Function

Public Function Slithy(Toves As Variant)
  ' code for the Slithy method
End Function
```

Time passes, and we want to upgrade the class by adding a new method, `Beamish`, and giving `Brillig` an extra argument. To do this we must define a new interface that includes the changes and modify the code of the original class module to implement the new interface. We set up an interface (class) module called `Jabberwock2.cls` as follows:

```
Public Function Brillig( _
   Mome As String, Raths As Date, _
   Frumious As Boolean)
' Declares Brillig with an extra argument
End Function

Public Function Slithy(Toves As Variant)
' as before
   ...
End Function

Public Function Beamish(Boy As Variant) _
   As Boolean
' New method
   ...
End Function
```

and we redefine `Jabberwock.cls` as follows

```
Implements Jabberwock2
Private Gyre As Long, Gimble As Long

Public Function Brillig(Mome As String, _
   Raths As Date) As String
   ' code for the Brillig method
End Function

Public Function Slithy(Toves As Variant)
   ' code for the Slithy method
End Function

Private Function Jabberwock2_Brillig(Mome _
   As String, Raths As Date, Frumious _
   As Boolean)
   'code for new version of Brillig
End Function

Private Function Jabberwock2_Slithy(Toves _
   As Variant)
   'code for Slithy (or just call it)
End Function

Private Function Jabberwock2_Beamish(Boy _
As Variant) As Boolean
   ' code for new method
End Function
```

Now any code that uses `Jabberwock` will see the original version, since the additions are `Private` functions, but code that uses `Jabberwock2` will see the new versions.

8.4.3 Collection wrappers

A common use of class modules is to provide 'wrappers' for user-defined collections. For example, if we have a collection of objects, we might define a property whose Property Set and Property Get methods invoke the collection's `Add` method and `Item` method, respectively. In this way, access to the collection can be controlled, e.g. we can define a read-only collection by omitting the Property Set method. (The collection would be populated initially by the event handler for the `Initialize` event, described below). Taking this further, we can define a class which completely wraps a collection. The collection is declared as a `Private` variable in the class, the collection object's `count` property is exposed as a property of the class, and the methods of the collection (`Add`, `Delete` and `Item`) are mirrored as methods of the class. In this way access to the collection can be controlled, e.g. if the item to be added is an object, the wrapper can check the values of certain properties, or set default values.

An apparent drawback of this approach is that it is not possible to iterate over the items in the collection using a `For Each` loop. Recall that when given a collection object, the `For Each` loop performs an implicit `Set` statement each time round the loop, providing a reference to the next item in the collection: if the collection is hidden in a user-defined class the loop will not know that it should generate the object references on the fly. To get round this, it is necessary to provide the wrapper class with a read-only property that enumerates the items in the collection. (A collection class has such a hidden property, which is used by the `For Each` loop.) This is remarkably easy to do: if the collection is called C, we just write

```
Public Property Get NewEnum() As IUnknown
    Set NewEnum = C.[_NewEnum]
```

Having declared this property, it is also necessary to use the IDE to set its Procedure ID to −4. The whole business is best regarded as a magic incantation.

8.4.4 Events in class modules

Initialize and Terminate events

A class module can contain event handlers for the `Initialize` and `Terminate` events. If present, these handlers serve a similar purpose to the constructor and destructor functions of classical object-oriented programming, e.g. setting default values when an object is instantiated. The `Initialize` event occurs when a new instance of an object is instantiated; the `Terminate` event occurs when there are no remaining references to the object, i.e. all references have been set to `Nothing`. (The precise firing of the `Initialize` event is a little more subtle than we have stated. If we write

```
Dim myObj As myClass
Set myObj = new myClass
```

the `Initialize` event is fired by the `Set` operation. But if we write

```
Dim myObj As New myClass
```

the event will not fire until we first access a property or method of the object.)

The event handlers are `Sub` procedures with no parameters, called `Class_Initia-lize` and `Class_Terminate`. Within the body of the `Initialize` handler, `Me` can be used as a reference to the particular instance of the object that has just been created.

Custom events

The `Initialize` and `Terminate` events are internal to a class. A class module can also define *custom events* that can be raised by methods of the class to pass information to and/ or solicit responses from other parts of the program. For an example, an event could be used to report a data validation error, or to report the progress of an asynchronous task such as a file transfer. As an example of a two-way interaction, an event can be used to advise a client of an abnormal situation, and to request an OK/Cancel decision from the client. Custom events are sometimes called *outgoing interfaces*, and have an obvious relation to the callbacks found in event-driven programming systems.

A custom event is declared in the class module: the declaration provides the name of the event and a specification of the parameters that form the 'body' of the event, e.g.

```
Public Event DataChange(Msg As String)
```

Once declared, a method of the class can *raise* the event, e.g.

```
RaiseEvent DataChange("Stock Price")
```

Raising an event is one half of the communication: how does the client code register its interest in an event and listen for it? The method is simple: the client declares an object variable based on the class, using the `WithEvents` keyword, e.g. if the class is called `Deal` a client might declare

```
Private WithEvents myDeal as Deal
```

and then provide an event handler

```
Private Sub myDeal_DataChange(Msg As String)
...
End Sub
```

The name of the event handler follows the standard 'object_event' pattern: the fact that the object was declared as `WithEvents` tells Visual Basic that the event is a custom event of the object class. When any object derived from the class `Deal` raises the `DataChange` event, this handler will be called.

In this particular case, the event handler might alert the user to the data change:

```
Private Sub myDeal_DataChange(Msg As String)
  MsgBox Msg & " has changed"
End Sub
```

An event may be 'hooked' in this way by multiple clients: all the event handlers will be called when the event is raised. A potential trap here is that `RaiseEvent` is not asynchronous: once the event has been raised, execution of the method that raised it is suspended until all the event handlers activated by it have completed.

The event mechanism allows a two-way inter-process interaction: since parameters are by default passed by reference, the method raising the event can examine the value of a parameter after the event handler has completed. For example, an application might raise an event to flag an unusual transaction, requesting an OK/Cancel decision from the client as follows. In the class module for the class `Transaction` we declare an event:

```
Public Event Confirm(Msg as String, _
ByRef Cancel as Boolean)
```

(The `ByRef` is not strictly required, since it is the default. However, making it explicit reminds us that we are going to use the reply.) A method of the class module can raise this event in certain circumstances, e.g.

```
If Value > 1000 Then
RaiseEvent Confirm("Value beyond limit", _
                     Cancel)
...
End If
```

The client hooks the event by declaring

```
Private WithEvents Trans As Transaction
```

and provides an event handler which displays a dialog box soliciting a yes/no answer, setting the parameter `Cancel` accordingly:

```
Private Sub Trans_Confirm(Msg as String,_
  Cancel As Boolean)
Dim Reply As Integer
Reply = MsgBox(Msg & ": Confirm?", _
  vbQuestion & vbYesNo
If Reply = vbNo Then
 Cancel = True
Else
 Cancel = False
End If
```

To complete the interaction, we complete the server method to check the reply:

```
If Value > 1000 Then
RaiseEvent Confirm("Value beyond limit", _
                    Cancel)
If Cancel Then Exit Sub
```

8.5   Drag-and-drop

The drag-and-drop metaphor is increasingly employed in modern graphical user interfaces. Drag-and-drop was a big selling point for the Macintosh in the early days, being used as a way of moving files between folders by dragging the icon. It appeared in Windows first as a way of moving text within a document, or cells within a spreadsheet, and this later developed into the capability to move data between documents. With the advent of Object Linking and Embedding it was even possible to drag cells from an Excel spreadsheet into a Word document. When Windows 95 was introduced, drag-and-drop was extended to the desktop, in particular as a way of manipulating files in Windows Explorer.

Beneath the deceptive simplicity of the drag-and-drop interface there lies a fearsomely complex software infrastructure. An application that is prepared to engage in drag-and-drop activities has to implement a large number of COM interfaces, and has to interact with the OLE run-time API during the actual operation. In Visual Basic, all this complexity is reduced to a handful of methods, properties and events – an excellent illustration of the leverage provided by scripting languages.

Substantial run-time drag-and-drop capability is in fact built in to the Visual Basic application, though it is not enabled by default. For example, if we place two textbox controls on a form and set their `DragMode` property to automatic, then at run-time the user will be able to drag text between them. However, in this section we are concerned with 'manual drag-and-drop', where the Visual Basic programmer writes code to control the operation. Manual drag-and-drop comes in two forms. The first form, which we will call 'control drag-and-drop', allows us to develop applications in which the user initiates actions by dragging a control and dropping it on another control. The second (slightly more complex) form, OLE drag-and-drop, allows us to develop applications in which the user can move text and images from one control to another using the drag-and-drop metaphor.

8.5.1   Control drag-and-drop

We illustrate control drag-and-drop with a very simple example. The form contains three picture box controls, `Picture1`, `Picture2` and `Picture3`, and initially we are going to set up the code to allow the user to drag a picture from the left-hand box to the right-hand box, but not to the middle box. Figure 8.3 shows the initial state.

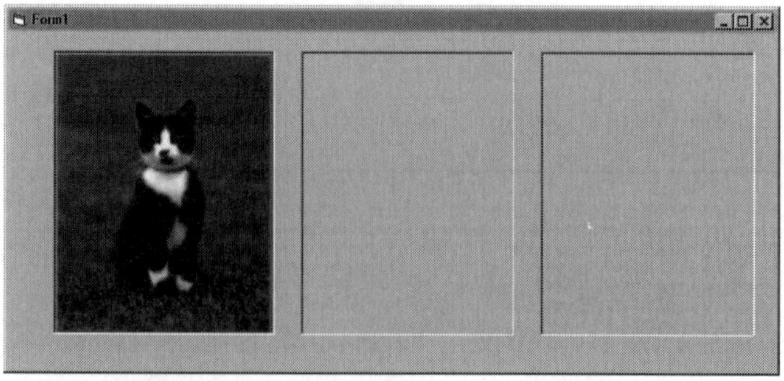

Figure 8.3   Drag-and-drop: initial state

Starting the operation

Dragging is started by calling the `Drag` method of `Picture1` in response to a mouse move with the left button pressed.

```
Private Sub Picture1_MouseMove(Button As Integer,_
    Shift As Integer, X As Single, Y As Single)
 If Button = 1 Then
   Picture1.Drag
 End If
End Sub
```

As dragging continues, Visual Basic draws a frame to show the current position (Figure 8.4)

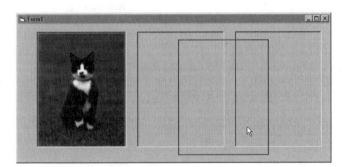

Figure 8.4 Drag-and-drop: drag in progress

Dropping on the target

When the user releases the mouse button, the control in which the mouse pointer is currently located receives a `DragDrop` event, so in our case the drop action will be controlled by the `DragDrop` event handler for `Picture3`. A `DragDrop` event handler has three arguments, a reference to the control which started the drag operation, and the mouse coordinates. It is all very simple:

```
Private Sub Picture3_DragDrop(Source _
    As Control, X As Single, Y As Single)
 Picture3.Picture = Source.Picture
 Source.Picture = LoadPicture("")
End Sub
```

We copy the `Source` picture to the target, then replace it with a null image (Figure 8.5). Drag-and-drop in five lines of code!

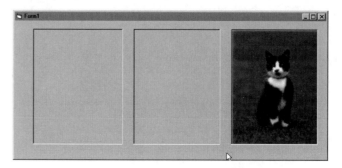

Figure 8.5   Drag-and-drop: drop completed

To implement the usual convention that if we hold the Ctrl key down while dragging, the effect is to copy rather than to move, we declare a Boolean variable `Copy` at the head of the module, and set this appropriately at the start of the drag operation.

```
Dim Copy As Boolean
Private Sub Picture1_MouseMove(Button As
Integer,_
     Shift As Integer, X As Single, Y As Single)
If Button = 1 Then
  Picture1.Drag
  If Shift = 2 Then
    Copy = True
  Else
    Copy = False
  End If
End If
End Sub

Private Sub Picture3_DragDrop(Source _
    As Control, X As Single, Y As Single)
  Picture3.Picture = Source.Picture
  If Not Copy Then Source.Picture = _
    LoadPicture("")
End Sub
```

In a real-life scenario we need to check that the control being dropped is of the same type as the drop target, otherwise there is a danger of run-time errors due to type mismatch. The `DragDrop` event handler needs to be modified to perform this check:

```
Private Sub Picture3_DragDrop(Source _
    As Control, X As Single, Y As Single)
```

```
   If TypeOf Source Is PictureBox Then
      Picture3.Picture = Source.Picture
      If Not Copy Then _
         Source.Picture = LoadPicture("")
   End If
End Sub
```

Providing user feedback

It is customary to provide feedback to the user while a drag-and-drop operation is in progress, in particular indicating whether the object being dragged can be dropped at the current position of the mouse pointer. This is done by setting the mouse pointer to the NoDrop form (like a no-entry sign) when the pointer is not over a drop target.

This is made possible using the DragOver event, which occurs when the mouse pointer enters or leaves the boundaries of a control, or moves within the boundaries. The event handler for this event has four arguments, a reference to the source control, the x and y coordinates of the mouse, and a State argument which can have values 0 (mouse entered), 1 (mouse left) or 2 (mouse moved). In our example we need to set the NoDrop pointer when the mouse leaves Picture1 or Picture3, and set it back to normal when the mouse enters Picture3.

```
   Private Sub Picture1_DragOver(Source _
       As Control, X As Single, Y As Single, _
       State As Integer)
    If State = 1 Then _
      Picture1.MousePointer = vbNoDrop
   End Sub

   Private Sub Picture3_DragOver(Source _
       As Control, X As Single, Y As Single, _
       State As Integer)
    If State = 0 Then
      Picture1.MousePointer = vbDefault
    ElseIf State = 1 Then
      Picture1.MousePointer = vbNoDrop
    End If
   End Sub
```

It is possible to provide other hints to the user, e.g. changing the background colour of a control which is an acceptable drop target.

We can very easily generalize our code to allow drag-and-drop between any pair of picture boxes by making the picture boxes a control array, with all three sharing the same event handlers. We need a global variable to remember which box started the drag operation so that we can change the mouse pointer as required, and get hold of the image when the drop takes place. A first shot at the code is as follows: the control array is called Frames(), and Src is the index of the frame which is the drag source.

```
Dim Src As Integer

Private Sub Frames_MouseDown(Index As Integer, _
        Button As Integer, Shift As Integer,_
        X As Single, Y As Single)
If Button = 1 Then
  Src = Index
  Frames(Src).Drag
End If
End Sub

Private Sub Frames_DragOver(Index As Integer, _
  Source As Control, X As Single, Y As Single, _
  State As Integer)
If State = 0 Then
  Frames(Src).MousePointer = vbDefault
ElseIf State = 1 Then
  Frames(Src).MousePointer = vbNoDrop
End If
End Sub

Private Sub Frames_DragDrop(Index As Integer, _
           Source As Control, X As Single, _
           Y As Single)
  Frames(Index).Picture = Frames(Src).Picture
  Frames(Src).Picture = LoadPicture("")
End Sub
```

This works fine except that if we drop the picture in its original frame, it gets erased. To fix this the last line of the DragDrop event procedure becomes

```
If Not Index = Src Then
  Frames(Src).Picture = LoadPicture("")
End If
```

8.5.2 OLE drag-and-drop

OLE drag-and-drop makes it possible to drag text and images from one control to another. As with control drag-and-drop, a substantial capability is built into Visual Basic: most controls support OLE drag-and-drop to some degree, and it can be enabled by setting the OLEDragMode and OLEDropMode properties of the relevant control to 'automatic'. Alternatively, the OLEDragMode property of the source can be set to automatic, leaving the drop operation under manual control. In this section we will assume that the developer wishes to provide full manual control over the drag-and-drop operations. As we shall see, the operations required to implement OLE drag-and-drop are similar to those already described for control drag-and-drop with a few significant differences.

Data objects

The key to OLE drag-and-drop is the `DataObject` object, which acts as a container for data being transferred from a component source to a component target. (In fact, a drag-and-drop operation actually passes a reference to a `DataObject` object from the source to the target.) The most important methods of the `DataObject` object are `SetData`, which places data in the object, and `GetData()`, which retrieves the data from the object. Other methods are `Clear`, which has the obvious effect, and `GetFormat()`, which allows a drop target to check what kind of data is contained before accepting the drop.

Data can be stored in a `DataObject` object in a variety of formats: the format is supplied as an argument to `SetData` and `GetData`, and can be one of the following

`vbCFText`	text (`.txt` files)
`vbCFBitmap`	bitmap (`.bmp` files)
`vbCFMetafile`	metafile (`.wmf` files)
`vbCFEMetafile`	enhanced metafile (`.emf` files)
`vbCFDIB`	device-independent bitmap (DIB)
`vbCFPalette`	colour palette
`vbCFFiles`	list of files
`vbCFRTF`	rich text format (`.rtf` files)

If `SetData` is used without specifying the format, Visual Basic will attempt to identify the format. Data can be stored in multiple formats by repeated calls of `SetData`, each specifying a different format: this allows the drop target to choose the version it requires. To avoid the inefficiency of actually storing multiple representations of the data, `SetData` can be called without specifying a data source: the drop target, having decided which format it requires, can cause the source to do a `SetData` with the data source and the desired format specified, and then use `GetData` to retrieve it.

Data is passed to the object, and returned from it, as a variant. The syntax of `SetData` and `GetData` is

```
SetData data format
GetData(format)
```

If the `DataObject` object contains a list of files selected from a drop-down file list, the object's `Files` property is set: this returns a `collection` object containing a list of the file names.

The scenario

Before going into detail it may be helpful to sketch out the overall scenario. Unlike most things in the Visual Basic application, which are internal to the application, OLE drag-and-drop involves the operating system – specifically the 'OLE run-time', since it is necessary to coordinate the source with the changing possible targets as the drag proceeds. So once a control has initiated a drag operation, the OLE run-time is in charge until the data is actually dropped on a target. However, the interaction with the OLE run-time API is mediated by the Visual Basic application, and mapped onto a handful of events, as we shall see.

When a control detects that a drag-and-drop operation is being initiated (a Mouse-Move event with the mouse button down and something selected), it calls its OLEDrag method to initialize the operation, implicitly handing control to the OLE run-time. Visual Basic raises the OLEStartDrag event for the source: the event handler for this stores the data in a DataObject object (or at least records in the object the formats supported) and by setting the value of a property, indirectly informs the OLE run-time which drop effects are permitted – move, copy or both.

As the drag proceeds, whenever the mouse pointer enters a potential target, that control's DragOver event is raised. This happens repeatedly, once when the pointer enters the control, repeatedly while it moves within the control, and finally when the pointer leaves the control. The DragOver event handler informs the OLE run-time whether the target is willing to accept a drop or not: the event handler is given the mouse coordinates as arguments, so it can base its choice on where the pointer is currently located. This information is passed to the source by raising its GiveFeedBack event, and the source can respond by changing the mouse pointer, e.g. to indicate to the user that a drop will not be accepted, or to indicate the effect of a drop (move or copy), or by modifying the selection in some way. When the user initiates a drop by releasing the mouse button, the target's OLEDragDrop event is raised, and the event handler performs whatever action is necessary to incorporate the data. Finally, the source's OLECompleteDrag event is raised so that the source can do any necessary tidying up, e.g. deleting the original data in the case of a move.

Starting the operation

We use as an example the action of dragging text from a textbox named Text1 and dropping it in another textbox. Since our purpose is only to illustrate the power of a scripting language we shall not introduce any real-life complications.

Dragging is started by calling the OLEDrag method of the source from its MouseMove event handler. When data has been selected, the mouse button is pressed and held, and the mouse is moved. This is similar to starting a control drag operation, but in this case we have to ensure that the OLEDrag method is not called when the mouse is moved to make the selection. To achieve this, we use a global Boolean variable, SelectionInProgress, which is initialized to false when the form is loaded. We set it to true if the mouse button is pressed with no text selected, and to false when the mouse button is released. The following code initiates drag-and-drop for a TextBox control called Text1.

```
Private Sub Text1_MouseDown(Button As Integer, _
      Shift As Integer, X As Single, Y As Single)
   If Text1.SelText = "" Then
     SelectionInProgress = True
   End If
End Sub

Private Sub Text1_MouseUp(Button As Integer, _
      Shift As Integer, X As Single, Y As Single)
   SelectionInProgress = False
End Sub
```

```
Private Sub Text1_MouseMove(Button As Integer, _
    Shift As Integer, X As Single, Y As Single)
Dim SelectionExists As Boolean
If SelectionInProgress Then Exit Sub
SelectionExists = Not Text1.Seltext = ""
If SelectionExists And Button = 1 Then _
    Text1.OLEDrag
End Sub
```

As explained in the scenario, OLEDrag calls the OLE run-time, which fires the OLEStartDrag event. The event handler for this has two arguments: a DataObject object, and an integer to specify the drop effects – i.e. whether the data can be copied or moved. When the event fires the handler puts the selected text into the data object and sets the desired drop effects:

```
Private Sub Text1_OLEDragStart(Data _
    As VB.DataObject, AllowedEffects As Long)
  Data.Clear
  Data.SetData Text1.SelText, vbCFText
  AllowedEvents = _
    vbDropEffectMove Or vbDropEffectCopy
End Sub
```

Dragging

When the selection is dragged over another control, the control's OLEDragOver event is fired, first as the drag cursor enters, repeatedly while it moves inside the control, and again when it leaves the control.

OLEDragOver is more complex than the simple DragOver described earlier. The event handler has seven arguments:

- Data – A reference to the DataObject object carrying the payload.
- Effect – A long integer initially set by OLEDragStart to identify the effects it supports. If the event is generated by a potential drop target, the target component checks these effects and other parameters to determine which actions are appropriate for it, and then sets this parameter to one of the allowable effects (as specified by the source) to specify which actions will be performed if the user drops the selection on the component.
- Button – An integer which acts as a bit field corresponding to the state of a mouse button when it is depressed, as in DragOver.
- Shift – An integer which acts as a bit field corresponding to the state of the Shift, Ctrl and Alt keys when they are depressed, as in DragOver.
- x,y – Numbers (type Single) that specify the current horizontal (x) and vertical (y) position of the mouse pointer within the target form or control. These values are always expressed in terms of a user-defined coordinate system. (The way this is set up is beyond the scope of a book on scripting languages.) Some objects, e.g. a textbox, do not have a coordinate system.

- State – An integer that is one of three predefined constants – vbEnter, vbOver and vbLeave – to distinguish three possibilities. The meanings are self-evident, but note that vbOver indicates that the mouse has moved within the target, *or* that the mouse button and/or modifier key has changed while the mouse is in the target.

The OLEDragOver event handler for a control which is not a drop target is simple. When the mouse pointer enters it sets the Effect value to indicate that a drop will not be accepted, while the pointer is in the control it does nothing, and when the pointer leaves the control it restores the Effect variable to its original value. Suppose we have a picture box named Pic1: this is clearly not a potential target for a text drop, so we set its event handler for the OLEDragOver event as follows:

```
Private Sub Pic1_OLEDragOver(Data as VB.DataObject, _
  Effect As Long, _
  Button As Integer, Shift As Integer, _
  X As Single, Y As Single, _
  State As Integer)
Static InitialEffect As Long
Select Case State
Case vbEnter
  InitialEffect = Effect
  Effect = vbDropEffectNone
Case vbOver
  Exit Sub
Case vbLeave
  Effect = InitialEffect
End Select
End Sub
```

In our simple example, the OLEDragOver handler for a potential target will simply set the Effect argument to indicate that a drop will be accepted. We illustrate this for a textbox control called Text2 which is prepared to accept a move operation but not a copy:

```
Private Sub Text2_OLEDragOver( _
  Data as VB.DataObject, Effect As Long, _
  Button As Integer, Shift As Integer, _
  X As Single, Y As Single, State As Integer)
Static InitialEffect As Long
Select Case State
Case vbEnter
  InitialEffect = Effect
  Effect = vbDropEffectMove
Case vbOver
  Exit Sub
Case vbLeave
  Effect = InitialEffect
End Select
End Sub
```

Giving feedback

Each time an `OLEDragOver` event handler is called, the `OLEGiveFeedback` event for the source control is raised. The event handler for this event has two arguments: a long integer containing the `Effect` value set by the `OLEDragOver` event handler, and a Boolean to specify whether the default mouse cursors are being used, or whether custom pointers are being employed. If default cursors are in use, the OLE run-time will change the mouse pointer to `vbNoDrop` (the 'no-entry' sign) whenever the `Effect` is set to `vbDropEffectNone`, so there is no need for the source control to handle this event unless it wishes to use a custom mouse pointer. We shall assume that default cursors are in use.

Dropping on target

When the user drops the source onto the target by releasing the mouse button, the target's `OLEDragDrop` event is raised. The arguments for the event handler are the same as for `OLEDragOver`, except that there is (obviously) no `State` argument. The handler for the textbox `Text2` simply retrieves the payload from the `DataObject` object, and writes it into the textbox. It also sets the `Effect` argument to indicate the type of drop (move or copy).

```
Private Sub Text2_OLEDragDrop( _
   Data as VB.DataObject, _
   Effect As Long, _
   Button As Integer, Shift As Integer, _
   X As Single, Y As Single)
Text2.Text = Data.getdata(vbCFText)
Effect = vbDropEffectMove
End Sub
```

Finally, the `OLECompleteDrag` event of the source control is raised: this has a single argument to convey how the source was dropped, as set by the `OLEDragDrop` event handler. If this was a move, the original data is deleted: the event handler will also restore the default mouse pointer if custom pointers have been used.

```
Private Sub Text1_OLECompleteDrag(Effect _
    As Long)
If Effect = vbDropEffectMove Then
 Text1.selText = ""
End If
End Sub
```

8.6   Creating ActiveX controls

We have seen that ActiveX controls can be used in Visual Basic applications as pre-built components that behave just like the intrinsic controls. Prior to Visual Basic 5, it was necessary to use C++ to write ActiveX controls, but we can now develop them entirely within Visual Basic. An ActiveX control is a lightweight automation server, i.e. it is a component that at the very least implements the automation interface (dispinterface). It is also required to be 'self-registering', that is to say, it must make its own entries in the system registry on request, e.g. when downloaded over the Internet and placed in a Web page. The minimum requirement is to supply the programmatic ID, so that instances of the control can be created using `CreateObject()`: a control may choose to register a type library as well to facilitate early binding.

An ActiveX control is implemented as a class module, which defines the properties, methods and events of the control. It may also include code modules, and if it has a visual interface it will include a form module. Telling the Visual Basic application that you are implementing an ActiveX control rather than a normal project ensures that it is packaged with the correct COM interfaces, and that a type library is generated (derived from the declarations of `Public` methods and properties).

8.6.1 In-process and out-of-process components

An ActiveX control can be created as a DLL, to run in the same process space as its host, or as a .exe file, to run in a separate process. An out-of-process control can run on the same machine as its host, or on a server located elsewhere on the network. Clearly, a control that is to run on a server cannot have a visual interface. An advantage of running out-of-process on the same machine is that when a method is invoked, execution of the function is asynchronous, giving an equivalent of multi-threading. If it is necessary to know when a method has finished its task, this is done by raising an event in the out-of-process control. The event can be hooked by the host application as described above.

8.6.2 Friend scope

So far, variables and methods in class modules have been declared `Private` – visible only in the module, or `Public` – visible in all modules in the project. There is a third scope specifier, which is useful in building ActiveX controls: `Friend`. A variable, function or property declared as `Friend` is visible in all the modules of the project, as if it had been declared `Public`, but does not form part of the control's interface as stored in the type library. Thus these elements cannot be accessed by the application hosting the control.

8.7 Interfacing to the Windows API

Visual Basic gives the user complete access to the Win32 API, making it possible to use any feature of the Windows environment. This access is provided as part of a more general facility for using 'external procedures' written in C or C++ and compiled into a dynamic link library. Using this facility requires an understanding of the API and some familiarity with C coding, so we restrict ourselves to a simple example.

Suppose we want to use the Windows API to find the colour depth of the display. From the SDK documentation we find that there is a function to do the job in `gdi32.dll`:

```
int GetDeviceCaps(HDC hdc, int nIndex);
```

The first argument is the 'device context' specifying a device, and the second argument is an integer specifying which capability is to be queried: the SDK tells us that the predefined constant BITSPIXEL specifies the colour depth, thus if hdc is the device context for the screen, the C code to find the colour depth is something like

```
col_bits = GetDeviceCaps(hdc, BITSPIXEL);
```

The first stage in using this API call in Visual Basic is to introduce it as an external function using the Declare statement:

```
Private Declare Function GetDeviceCaps _
    Lib "gdi32"_
    (ByVal hdc As Long, ByVal nIndex As Long)_
    As Long
```

Next we need to check the C header files in the Platform SDK to find the value of the constant BITSPIXEL, which is in fact 12. Finally we need to know that a form has a property, hdc, which is the device context that has to be passed to the API call. Thus with the function declared as above, the remaining code required is

```
Dim Cbits As Integer
Const BITSPIXEL = 12
...
CBits = GetDeviceCaps(Form1.hdc, BITSPIXEL)
```

In the Declare statement above, we have given the Visual Basic function the same name as the API call. This is not required: we could give it a different name, and use the Alias keyword to specify the name of the function in the DLL:

```
Private Declare Function DeviceDetails _
    Lib "gdi32" Alias GetdeviceCaps _
    (ByVal hdc As Long, ByVal nIndex As Integer) _
    As Integer
```

Alternatively, the Alias can specify the ordinal number of the DLL entry point:

```
Private Declare Function DeviceDetails _
    Lib "gdi32" Alias #00c7 _
    (ByVal hdc As Long, ByVal nIndex As Integer) _
    As Integer
```

The Lib keyword specifies the DLL containing the external procedure or function: if it is not a system DLL a full pathname is required, e.g.

```
Private Declare Sub foo _
    LIB "c:/work/mylib1.dll" (...)
```

A special feature of the Declare statement is that a parameter can be declared to be untyped, e.g.

```
Private Declare Function ChangeDisplaySettings _
   Lib "user32" _
  (lpDevMode As Any, ByVal dwFlags As Long) _
   As Long
```

This is necessary because `ChangeDisplaySettings()`, like many API calls in C, takes a parameter which is a pointer to a structure, and in some circumstances is given a null pointer. In Visual Basic the actual argument will be a UDT variable of type `DevMode`: if the `Declare` statement specified this explicitly, e.g.

```
(lpDevMode As DEVMODE, ByVal dwFlags As Long)
```

it would not be possible to pass a `NULL` when required. However, since the `As Any` declaration switches off type checking, it is potentially very dangerous and should be used only when absolutely necessary.

8.8   Accessing external databases

One of the most powerful features of Visual Basic is its provision for accessing external databases. A full discussion is beyond the scope of this book: in this section we introduce the basic ideas to demonstrate the power of scripting. We describe the facilities for database access in Visual Basic 5, which are based on the Data Access Object (DAO). Although this form of access is provided in Visual Basic 6, the emphasis in Version 6 is on ActiveX Data Objects (ADO) and 'OLEDB', which provide a more powerful paradigm for database access.

The Visual Basic programmer is provided with a uniform method of accessing a variety of databases which hides the complexity of the actual database. Databases that can be accessed in this way include:

- Microsoft Access
- Btrieve
- Dbase
- Microsoft FoxPro
- Paradox.

All of these are accessed using the Microsoft Jet database engine. This provides native support for Access databases, and loads ISAM (Index Sequential Access Method) drivers as required for the other formats. It is also possible to access Excel and Lotus 1-2-3 worksheets as if they were databases, and to access and manipulate ODBC (Open Database Connectivity) databases such as Microsoft SQL Server and Oracle.

8.8.1   Data controls and data binding

The data control

In the Visual Basic application a database is abstracted by a *data control* [2] which appears on the screen with VCR-like forward and back buttons to navigate through the database, as shown in Figure 8.6.

Figure 8.6 A data control

A data control has various properties which can be set at design time or by program. These include:

- Connect: specifies the type of database – Access, dBase, FoxPro etc. It is rarely necessary to set this property, since the type of database is usually inferred from the extension of the filename given as the value of the DatabaseName property (see below). The property is used when accessing an ODBC database by setting it to a data source name (DSN) that identifies an ODBC data source entry in the registry. The value of the Connect property can be accessed to determine the type of an open database.
- DatabaseName: the pathname of the database file, e.g.

  ```
  Data1.DatabaseName = "c:\sales\q3.mdb"
  ```

  If this property is used at run-time to open a new database, the data control's refresh method must be invoked.
- RecordSource: the name of the table to be accessed in the database.
- EOFAction: determines the behaviour at the end of file, i.e. when the user attempts to move past the last record. The default is to keep the last record as the current record. If EOFAction is set to vbEOF then when the user attempts to move past the last record, the current record becomes invalid, and the 'move next' button is greyed out. If EOFAction is set to vbAddNew, moving past the last record displays a new, blank record in which the user can enter data. Default behaviour is restored by setting EOFAction to vbMoveLast.
- BOFAction: determines the behaviour at the start of file, i.e. when the user attempts to move back over the first record. The default is to keep the first record as the current record. If BOFAction is set to vbBOF then when the user attempts to move past the first record, the current record becomes invalid, and the 'move back' button is greyed out. Default behaviour is restored by setting BOFAction to vbMoveFirst.

Once the application begins, Visual Basic uses the Data control properties to open the selected database, create a Database object and create a Recordset object. The Database object will be discussed later: the Recordset object is just that: a set of records retrieved from the specified table in the database. The data control's Database and Recordset properties refer to the newly created Database and Recordset objects, which may be manipulated independently of the Data control as we shall describe in Section 8.7.2.

Data-bound controls

The data control provides an interface for the user to move around the database table, but does not actually display any data. The display is achieved by a process called data binding, in which a visual control such as a textbox is bound to a data control. A visual control bound to a database by way of a data control is called a *data-bound control*. Most of the intrinsic controls can be data bound in this way, and Visual Basic ships with a number of useful data-bound ActiveX controls, e.g. a data-bound listbox and the DBGrid control which displays the whole database table in rows and columns with spreadsheet-like facilities for manipulating the data.

Any control that can be data-bound has `DataSource` and `DataField` properties. For example, if the `DataSource` property of a textbox control is set to the name of a data control and its `DataField` property is set to the name of a field in the database that the data control represents, then the value of that field in the current database record will be displayed in the textbox as the user navigates with the arrow buttons, and if the text in the textbox is changed, the value of the database field is automatically updated (by invoking the `Edit` and `Update` methods) when the user moves to another record, assuming that updates are allowed. A blanket ban on updating can be obtained by setting the data control's `ReadOnly` property to true. Alternatively, selective control over updating can be achieved by capturing the keystrokes when the user attempts to change the contents of a data-bound control for which updating is not allowed. For example, attaching the following event handler to a textbox control called `Text1` will render it totally unresponsive:

```
Private Sub Text1_KeyPress(KeyAscii As Integer)
   KeyAscii = 0
End Sub
```

When the contents of a data-bound control are changed by the user, the control's `DataChanged` property is set to true: this property can be tested by scripts, e.g. to do validation. More commonly, validation is performed in the event handler for the data control's `Validate` event, which is raised whenever the user moves to a different record in the database. The event handler has two arguments: an integer to give details of the move, e.g. `vbMoveNext`, and a Boolean to record whether the data in the bound control has changed.

The properties that determine the data binding may be set by the developer at design time, or by a script at run-time. For example, suppose we have an employee database with fields `Employee`, `Name`, `Department`, `Email`, `Phone`, etc. We could provide a lookup-by-name facility written in Visual Basic which displays a data control and two textboxes, one for the target name and the other for the result of the search, and a collection of option buttons to choose the field to be interrogated. If the buttons are called `optDept`, `optPhone`, `optMail` etc., and the result textbox is called `Result`, then we just have to provide a `Click` event handler for each button to set the `DataField` property of the result box, e.g.

```
Private Sub optMail_Click()
Result.DataField = "EMail"
End Sub
```

In real life we would also provide a `Load` event handler for the form to select the default option:

```
Private Sub LookUpByName_Load
optPhone.Value = True
End Sub
```

The form will then be displayed with the Phone button checked.

8.8.2 Recordsets

When a data control is connected to a table in a database, the contents of the table are made available in a Recordset object which contains a number of *records* or *rows*, each divided into *fields*. This object has a variety of properties and methods that allow direct manipulation of the data, without the intervention of the data control. Indeed, the data control can be made invisible, with navigation of the database being done 'behind the scenes' in response to user actions, e.g. button presses.

Recordset types

There are three types of recordset, defined by the RecordsetType property of the control. These are

- *Dynaset-type* (default): a dynamic set of records representing the database table. Any changes made to the records in the recordset will be reflected in the underlying database. Equally, any changes to the database made by another application will be reflected in the dynaset.
- *Snapshot-type*: a static copy of the set of records representing the database table. The recordset cannot be updated, and, being a snapshot, changes made by other applications will not be reflected in it.
- *Table-type*: an object representing the database table: only the current record is held in memory.

Navigation in recordsets

Navigation in a recordset is performed by invoking the methods of the Recordset object, which is a property of the data control. We can move to the start or end of the table:

```
Data1.Recordset.MoveFirst
Data1.Recordset.MoveLast
```

(MoveFirst sets the BOFAction property of the data control to vbMoveFirst. MoveLast sets the EOFAction property to vbMovelast.) We can move sequentially through the table in either direction:

```
Data1.Recordset.MoveNext
Data1.Recordset.MovePrevious
```

There is also a generic Move() method which takes a signed long integer as an argument and moves the Recordset pointer by that number of records. The Recordset object has properties BOF and EOF which are set true by an attempt to move to a record before the first record or after the last record, respectively.

We can also find records in a recordset that satisfy some specified criterion, e.g. if a database of information on spare parts has a column for the part number labelled PART_NO, we can search for a record that satisfies the criterion PART_NO = 1834'. (Readers who have come across the SQL database query language will recognize this as resembling the 'WHERE' specifier in an SQL query.) There are four methods, which differ only in the origin and direction of the search:

- FindFirst(): start at beginning of the recordset and search forward, i.e. find first of multiple matches
- FindLast(): start at the end of the recordset and search backwards, i.e. find last of multiple matches
- FindNext(): start at current position and search forward
- FindPrevious(): start at current position and search backwards.

Having located a desired record, it can be edited using the Edit method of the Recordset object. When editing is complete, the Update method is called to perform the actual update of the database. A more convenient way of performing operations on recordsets is to use the ActiveX DBGrid control, which displays the recordset as a table and provides spreadsheet-like capabilities for editing.

8.8.3 Using SQL

It is possible to perform SQL operations on a database using the Execute method of the Database object. This method takes an argument which is a string containing a SQL statement, and optional arguments to give finer control over the execution: the most common of these is dbFailOnError, which causes updates to be rolled back if an error occurs while executing the SQL statement. For example, assuming a database containing product information has been opened via a data control Data1, we might write

```
Dim SQLstmt As String
SQLstmt = "UPDATE Products & _
  "SET Currency = 'Euro'" & _
  "WHERE Currency = 'UKP'"
data1.Database.Execute SQLstmt dbFailOnError
```

Notes

[1] Note that in Visual Basic controls that have built-in scrollbars, the relationship between the display and the scrollbar is maintained by the control; compare Tk, where the user has to provide code to adjust the display in response to a scrollbar action and to adjust the scrollbar if the display content changes.

[2] Strictly speaking the data control abstracts the Jet database engine, which provides a uniform front-end to a variety of different databases.

## Part Three

Scripting Web clients and servers

## Chapter 9

JavaScript

JavaScript originated as a Web scripting language in the Netscape world, used for implementing interactive Web pages by client-side scripting and creating dynamic Web pages with server-side scripting. In the Microsoft world JavaScript/JScript is a general scripting language that can control scriptable applications beyond Web browsers and servers. In this chapter, we describe the core language: examples of its use in Web scripting and elsewhere and given in later chapters.

9.1 What is JavaScript?

9.1.1 LiveScript, LiveWire and JavaScript

JavaScript started life in 1995 as a proprietary Netscape product called LiveScript, incorporated in Netscape Navigator 2.0 to provide client-side scripting. The name LiveScript was changed to JavaScript in late 1995 following the launch of Java by Sun, the name 'Java' being licensed from Sun to ride on the back of the publicity (and hype) surrounding Java. Unfortunately the name leads to much confusion – as languages, the only thing JavaScript has in common with Java is the word 'Java'. The Netscape Enterprise Server 3.0. included facilities for server-side scripting for database access using the LiveWire technology using a different version of the language, called Server-Side JavaScript.

9.1.2 JScript

When it became apparent that JavaScript was becoming popular, Microsoft reverse-engineered it and produced an almost compatible version called JScript, which was incorporated in the Internet Explorer browser along with the competing VBScript, described in Chapter 10. As part of the development of the Microsoft 'Active Platform' JScript was adopted as the scripting language for Active Server Pages (a form of server-side scripting), and moved away from its Web roots, becoming a general purpose *scripting engine* that can be used to script any *scripting host* which conforms to the ActiveX Scripting Architecture. ActiveX scripting hosts include Internet Information Server, Microsoft Internet Explorer and Windows itself, using the 'Windows Script Host' (which is described in Chapter 15).

9.1.3 ECMAScript

In 1997, the European Computer Manufacturers' Association (ECMA) released Standard ECMA-262, describing a language called ECMAScript based on JavaScript 1.1 [1], and late in 1998 this was adopted as an International Standard (ISO/IEC 16262:1998). The formal position is that JavaScript and Jscript are two commercial implementations of ECMAScript, but in practice, Netscape Navigator 4.x (and later) and Internet Explorer 4.x (and later) implement different supersets of ECMAScript. In this chapter we shall follow popular custom and retain the name JavaScript – indeed, the name JScript appears only in Microsoft's technical reference documents: Internet Explorer calls the language JavaScript. Except where explicitly stated to the contrary (which is, unfortunately, quite a frequent occurrence), anything we say in this chapter applies equally to JavaScript, JScript and ECMAScript

9.2   Object models

The JavaScript core language is not computationally self-sufficient, and is not intended to be: as the ECMAScript Standard states,

> It is expected that the computational environment will provide . . . certain environment-specific host objects [which] may provide certain properties that can be accessed and certain functions that can be called from an ECMAScript program.

Thus JavaScript consists of a common core language which is extended by a collection of *host objects* (the 'object model') provided by the environment in which it is implemented. (There is an analogy here with Visual Basic for Applications, where the core language is extended by importing one or more object models. However, core VBA is computationally self-sufficient, and can be used as a general-purpose language without importing any objects.)

In the Netscape world there are two implementations of JavaScript with different object models, one in the Navigator Browser and one in the Enterprise Server. These are described as 'client-side JavaScript' and 'server-side JavaScript', respectively. As briefly stated above, in the Microsoft world the picture is different. When a JavaScript *scripting engine* is instantiated, it is bound to a *scripting host* (e.g. Internet Explorer), which supplies one or more *object models*, each described by a *type library*. In this environment 'JavaScript' (strictly JScript) can be used as a scripting language not only in a Web browser (Internet Explorer) and a Web server (Internet Information Server), but also as the scripting language for other hosts such as the Windows Script Host (WSH).

The provision of different host objects in different environments allows control over the facilities available to the user: the case of input/output and file access is a particularly apposite example. Core JavaScript does not include any facilities for access to files or devices: these are provided by objects that are reflected from the environment. Thus client-side JavaScript in Navigator and Internet Explorer has a `document` object with a `write()` method for sending text to the Web page, but scripts cannot access the local file system or other devices. However, when JavaScript is used as a server-side language or in the WSH environment, the host objects include objects representing file systems, folders and files, providing full access to the local file system.

9.3 Design philosophy

JavaScript is a one-man product: the design was the single-handed work of Brendan Eich at Netscape. In 1995 it was generally believed that HTML should be a static representation of document structure, and that dynamic effects should be achieved using the then new technology of Java applets. The idea of client-side scripting came from a recognition that users required the ability to go beyond HTML and add code to make Web pages dynamic – to make things move and respond to user input, to make new windows pop up, to open a dialog box to ask a question, with an answer necessary to proceed – things that HTML cannot express. To do this requires a programming language, but something simpler than Java or C++: languages like these are fine for professional programmers who build components, but it was recognized that there was a need to address the requirements of people who are less specialized and may be paid to do something other than programming, who want to get their code done with the minimal amount of bother.

Although there were attractions in a 'natural-language' syntax as used in Apple's HyperTalk, it was decided that the syntax should be based on Java, to assist programmers to make the transition from JavaScript to Java. (In the event, the syntax is in fact very close to that of C.) However, it was to be a simplified syntax to meet the need of non-professional programmers – describing the syntax as 'Java-lite', Eich comments that 'scripting for most people is about writing short snippets of code quickly and without fuss'.

The major simplification was to have objects without classes. This concept had been proved in the 'Self' language, development of which started at Xerox PARC (the home of Smalltalk) with the motto 'The Power of Simplicity'. The first practical implementation was at Stanford University, and in 1991 the project was transferred to Sun Microsystems Laboratories (where Java was also being developed). Another feature of Self was 'slots', which could contain either an instance value or a method: this was the origin of JavaScript's treatment of functions as another data type.

The success of the design is attested by the popularity of the language: in 1998 a Web crawler robot found over 3.5 million pages containing JavaScript, compared with around 50 000 pages containing VBScript and nearly 100 000 pages containing ActiveX controls. Since its introduction in 1995, more than 175 companies have licensed JavaScript for inclusion in their Internet software tools.

9.4 Versions of JavaScript

JavaScript has evolved very rapidly, and as a result there are a number of different versions in use. This chapter is based on JavaScript 1.3 as implemented in Navigator 4.06 and later (at the time of writing the current version is 4.7). The differences between this version and JavaScript 1.2 as implemented in Navigator 4.0–4.05 are not very great, and significant differences are flagged by marginal notes. However, many of the features described may not be present, or may be present in a different form, in the version of JavaScript used in earlier browsers.

The situation in Internet Explorer is more complex, since JScript is not incorporated directly in the browser, but is implemented as a scripting engine (JScript.dll) that can be used by any scripting host. Internet Explorer 4.x uses version 3 of the JScript engine: the language implemented is largely compatible with JavaScript 1.2, and thus this chapter applies on the whole to Explorer 4.x. In particular, references to 'JavaScript 1.2' can be taken to apply to Explorer 4.0 and later unless explicitly qualified. However, some of the features described here may not be present, or may be present in a different form, in versions of Explorer before 4.0. Explorer 5 uses version 5 of the scripting engine, and includes a number of Microsoft-specific extensions. Again, we shall try to flag significant differences between the versions. If you are developing serious JavaScript applications there is no substitute for the reference material from Microsoft and Netscape detailed in the Appendix, though it is often quicker to determine the existence or otherwise of a particular feature by writing a small script and running it in the different browsers.

9.5 The JavaScript core language

The JavaScript core language is very similar to C – it has the same operators, the same control structures, and a syntax that is largely the same. Here we concentrate on what makes JavaScript different. There are two significant lexical differences:

- The semicolon terminator is optional for one-line statements. Users who come from a C background will use semicolons out of habit, while those whose background is in BASIC can continue to work in a familiar way. This is a small but significant aspect of user-friendliness in scripting languages.
- C++ style comments (// to end of line) are recognized as well as C style comments (/*...*/).

9.5.1 Variables, types and values

JavaScript is a dynamically typed language. Although internally it recognizes numeric (IEEE double precision floating point), string, Boolean, function and object values, the programmer does not declare the type of a variable: automatic type conversion occurs as required (see below). However, the programmer can determine the type of value held in a variable using the typeof operator, which returns a string denoting the type of any value.

A variable declaration is introduced by var, e.g.

```
var first, last;
var greeting = "Hello World!";
```

As can be seen from the example, variables can be initialized at declaration time: a variable declared without initialization is given a special 'undefined' value (and the typeof operator returns the string "undefined" if used on such a variable). Use of a variable that has not been declared leads to a run-time error, unless the variable appears on the left of an assignment, in which case the assignment statement acts as an initialized declaration for the variable. It is good practice to declare all variables, since relying on implicit declaration in an assignment can lead to unintended changes to global variables. (All variables declared outside a function have global scope, being stored as properties of the *global object* – see Section 9.6.1.)

Literals (constants) are expressed in the 'usual' way, e.g.

```
1377            (decimal integer)
123.45          (floating point number)
01377           (octal integer)
1.2345E-2       ('scientific' notation)
0X9FFF          (hexadecimal integer)
```

String literals are enclosed in single or double quotes, and may contain the other type of quotes, e.g.

```
"'I say!', he exclaimed"
'"I say!", he exclaimed'
```

Backslash escapes can be used in string literals, e.g. \n for newline, \t for tab. In Navigator 4.5, Unicode characters can be introduced by \u, e.g. \u00A9 represents the copyright symbol ©. An important, apparently undocumented, feature is that a string can extend over more than one physical line if the newline character is escaped, e.g.

```
"A string that I want to split over two lines\
for my own good reasons"
```

Automatic type conversion

Automatic type conversion usually does the 'obvious' thing: for example, the Boolean values true and false are converted to the strings "true" and "false" in a string context, and to the values one and zero, respectively, in a numeric context. Conversely, in a Boolean context 0 and "" equate to false, and any other number or string equates to true. There are, however, pitfalls for the unwary.

- The operators + and – differ in the way they behave if given operands of different types. The + operator is overloaded: if either or both of its operands are of type string it will concatenate its operands as a string, if necessary converting a numeric argument to a string first. The – operator, however, always returns a numeric value, converting a string argument to a number if necessary. (If the string cannot represent a number an error is raised, except that the empty string is converted to zero.) Thus if we write

```
a = 1;
b = "10";
c = a + b;
```

  the value of c will be the string "110". If we want the + to be a numerical addition, we can write

```
c = a + (b - 0);
```

forcing numeric conversion of the value of b. In the same vein, we can convert a number to a string by concatenating it with the empty string, e.g.

```
c = a + "";
```

For more flexible conversions of strings to numbers, the functions `parseInt()` and `parseFloat()` are provided. These take a string as argument and return a numeric value: leading whitespace in the argument is ignored, as are trailing characters that cannot form part of a number. The `parseInt()` function parses integer values only: a string with an initial zero is parsed as an octal integer, and a string starting `0X` or `0x` is parsed as a hexadecimal number. (Alternatively, you can provide a second argument between 2 and 36(!) to specify the number base to be used for the conversion.) The `parseFloat()` function parses both integer and floating point values. In both cases, if the conversion fails, the function returns the special value 'not a number'. This value, printed as `NaN`, does not compare equal with any other number, including itself: it can be tested for by the function `isNaN()`.

■ The equality operators `==` and `!=` perform automatic type conversions using the following rules.

   i.   If both operands are objects, object references are compared.
   ii.   If either operand is null, the other operand is converted to an object and references are compared.
   iii. If one operand is a string and the other is an object, the object is converted to a string and the strings are compared.
   iv.   Otherwise, both operands are converted to numbers, and numeric identity is tested.

The identity operators are not implemented in versions prior to Navigator 4.06 and Explorer 5.

Strict equality can be tested with the identity operators `===` and `!==` which do not do type conversions: if the operands are of different type they are regarded as unequal. (In Navigator 4.0–4.05 the 'no conversion' behaviour can be enforced for the `==` and `!=` operators by specifying the language as 'JavaScript 1.2' in the `<SCRIPT>` tag. See Chapter 11 for details of the `<SCRIPT>` tag.)

Functions

We noted earlier that JavaScript recognizes numeric, string, Boolean, function and object values. A feature of particular note is that JavaScript functions differ in a substantive way from functions in most other languages: they are just another data type. This means that having defined a function, it can be assigned to a variable: note particularly that we are assigning *the function* as a value, not a pointer to it as in C. In addition, function literals can appear on the right of an assignment. We explore the consequences of this approach to functions in Section 9.5.4.

Objects

As we have seen, JavaScript uses host objects to interact with its environments. Objects are also at the heart of the core language: indeed, the way objects are implemented and used in JavaScript characterize the language and give it a distinctive flavour of its own. JavaScript is an *object-based* language rather than an *object-oriented* language: we maintain this distinction even though the ECMAScript Standard describes ECMAScript as an object-oriented language. The reason for this distinction is that objects in JavaScript are not derived from classes in the style of Java or C++, and do not exhibit inheritance and polymorphism. However, these behaviours can be simulated quite easily.

An innovative feature of the JavaScript object system is the duality between objects and primitive data types. In a 'pure' object-oriented language like Smalltalk, everything is an object. (This leads to the absurd situation that in the expression '2+2', one of the 2s is an object that has an 'add' method, and the other '2' is an argument to a message sent to the object – but nobody knows which '2' is the object and which is the argument.) In C++, some things are objects and others, e.g. numbers, are not. JavaScript adopts a position that everything *can* be an object, but some things don't need to be. Thus every primitive data type has an associated wrapper object, and the language allows us to move with ease between the object representation and the native representation.

The JavaScript object system is described in detail in Section 9.5.5. For the moment, all we need to know is that an object is a collection of named data items: since functions are data items in JavaScript, we can think of an object as a collection of *properties* (values) and *methods* (functions). Properties and methods are accessed using the usual 'dot' syntax, thus if obj is an object with a property p and a method m, the property value is represented by obj.p, and the method call is obj.m().

Regular expressions

The lack of any regular expression matching was a major shortcoming of early versions of JavaScript. However, JavaScript 1.2 and JScript version 3 provide a heavyweight regular expression capability, with a regular expression syntax that is to all intents and purposes identical to that of Perl, as described in Section 2.12.2. Regular expressions in JavaScript are treated as objects, and are described in detail in Section 9.6.3.

Available in Navigator 4.0 and later, and in Explorer 4.0 and later.

9.5.2 Operators

JavaScript provides 'the usual' operators: a complete list is given in Section 9.9 at the end of the chapter. The operators include a conditional operator that allows C-like conditional expressions to be written, e.g.

```
status = (age > = 18) ? "adult" : "child";
```

and a C-like comma operator evaluates its arguments in turn, returning the value of the second.

9.5.3 Control flow statements

These follow a familiar pattern, and are illustrated by a few contrived examples.

if–then–else

```
if (x > 0) {
 y = 1; alert("Positive")
}
else if (x == 0) {
 y = 0; alert("Zero");
}
else {
 y = -1; alert("Negative");
}
```

Note that there is no syntactic elseif construct, but if can follow else as shown in the example. It may be necessary to use curly brackets to avoid 'dangling else' ambiguities. If the 'then' or 'else' arm consists of a single statement the curly brackets can be omitted, but it is good practice to use curly brackets all the time.

In JavaScript 1.2, use of the assignment operator '=' in mistake for the equality operator '==' was silently corrected, so that

```
if (x = 0) {
  ...
}
```

was treated as

```
if (x == 0) {
  ...
}
```

JavaScript 1.3 only.   JavaScript 1.3 generates a run-time error in this case.

switch

```
switch (x) {
case "apples":
    price = 34;
    break;
case "oranges":
    price = 43;
    break;
default: price = "unknown";
}
```

for

```
for (var i = 0; i <= 10; i++) {
    document.write(i  + "      " + i*i;
}
```

The syntax is exactly that of C. As with the if statement, the curly brackets are not strictly necessary for a single statement.

while and do

These again are straightforward: the `while` statement is a potentially zero-trip loop; the
do statement guarantees that the body will be executed at least once.

```
var i = 0;
while (i <= j) {
    document.write(i + "\t" + i*i)
}

var i = 0;
do {
  document.write(i + "\t" + i*i)
} while (i <= j);
```

break and continue

In a `for`, `while` or `do` loop, the `break` statement causes premature exit from the loop,
and the `continue` statement causes the current iteration to be terminated, e.g.

```
while (...) {
   ...
   x = ...;
   if (x < 0) continue;
   if (x > 1000) break;
   ...
}
```

If `break` or `continue` occurs in a nested loop, it affects the innermost containing
loop. Loops can however be labelled, so that `break/continue` can control any
enclosing loop, e.g.

```
LOOPA: while (...) {
       ...
       LOOPB: while(...) {
              ...
              if (...) continue LOOPA
       }
}
```

In fact, it is possible to use `break` to achieve premature exit from other statements, e.g.
an `if` statement, provided the block has been labelled. For example:

```
TEST: if (...) {
      ...
      if (...) break TEST;
      ...
}
```

(This is similar to the 'bare block' in Perl.)

9.5.4 The JavaScript view of functions

Function declaration and call

Function declaration and call in JavaScript is, with one exception noted below, exactly the same as in C, e.g.

```
function cube(x) {
return x*x*x;
}
. . .
y = cube(z);
. . .
```

A function call is an expression whose value is determined by the `return` statement in the function body. If `return` is omitted, or has no argument, the call returns 'undefined'. Since `return` is a statement, the return value is not parenthesized.

As in C, arguments are passed by value. Local variables can be declared in the body of a function using `var`, and their scope is the entire function body, no matter where the declaration appears in the body. (Here JavaScript differs from C, where the scope extends from the point of declaration to the end of the body. However, since an assignment to an undeclared variable in JavaScript is treated as an implicit declaration anyway, the distinction is probably academic.) Function definitions can be nested, and the usual lexical (static) scoping rules apply, i.e. declaration in an inner function body hides variables of the same name declared in the enclosing function(s). We shall give a more precise account of the JavaScript scope rules after we have discussed objects.

Functions as data

As we have noted above, JavaScript functions differ in a substantive way from functions in most other languages: they are just another data type. This means that:

- Having defined a function, it can be assigned to a variable, e.g.

  ```
  myfn = cube;
  ```

  (Note that we are assigning the function as a value, not a pointer to it as in C or a reference to it as in Perl.)
- Function literals can appear on the right of an assignment, e.g. the function definition given above could be written

  ```
  var cube = function(x) {return x*x*x};
  ```

  (Readers familiar with the lambda calculus will note that the right-hand side is in fact a lambda expression, using the word 'function' as a substitute for λ.) In many ways this can be regarded as the canonical way of defining a function: the C-like syntax is essentially 'syntactic sugar', or a comfort blanket for those brought up on other languages.

  A function literal defines an anonymous function which can be passed as an argument to another function, or even invoked directly, like applying a lambda expression to an argument list, e.g.

```
    y = (function(x) {return x*x*x})(10);
```

■ A function can be converted into a string, e.g.

```
    s = cube + "";
```

(Here we force a string context by concatenating an empty string. This makes JavaScript convert the other argument of + to a string.) The resulting string contains the complete text of the function definition, possibly re-formatted. This text is legal JavaScript: the string can, for example, be given as an argument to the eval() function to be re-interpreted, provided that the function has no arguments.

Arguments

Arguments can be accessed in the function body by using the dummy variable names listed in the formal parameter list in the function declaration. They also appear as the elements of an array arguments[] which is automatically created as a local variable in the body of the function. This way of accessing arguments allows us to declare functions with a variable number of arguments (*variadic* functions, as in Perl), since JavaScript does not require a function to be called with the same number of arguments as its declaration specifies. The arguments[] array is in fact an object (as we shall see later, objects and arrays are interchangeable in JavaScript), and has a property, length, which returns the number of elements in the array. Thus, suppose we want to declare a function that has one required argument, and an optional second argument, we could use the following skeleton call.

```
function f(x) {
  //process obligatory first argument, x
  if arguments.length > 1 {
     //process optional argument (arguments[1])
   }
}
```

It would be good practice to check the number of arguments, e.g.

```
function f(x) {
  var numargs = arguments.length
  if (numargs == 0 || numargs > 2) {
    alert("Function needs 1 or 2 arguments");
    return;
  }
  ... //process obligatory first argument, x
  if (numargs == 2) {
    ... //process optional argument)
  }
}
```

alert *displays a message in the browser window.*
return *in the middle of a function body stops execution of the function and returns to the caller.*

The execution context

Unlike other languages, JavaScript is very precise as to *where* variables are stored. Every variable in a script is a property of some object. We have already seen that global variables are stored as properties of the *global object*. This object supplies an execution context for top-level JavaScript programs, providing not only global variables but also a variety of in-built functions (see Section 9.6.1). Each function has an associated *call object* in which locally declared variables appear as properties. The `arguments[]` object is also a property of the call object, which thus encapsulates all the local state.

The execution context for a function is determined by the *scope chain* which starts with the function's own call object: this is linked to the call object of the enclosing function, and the chain continues until the global object is reached. Name resolution is achieved by starting at the end of this chain with the function's call object: if the variable does not appear as a property of this object, the next call object in the chain is examined, and so on until the global object is reached.

The `with` statement adds the object given as its argument to the front of the scope chain for the duration of the following (compound) statement, and restores the scope chain to its original state at the end of the statement. This means that if a number of properties/methods of an object are being manipulated, we can save writing and make the code clearer:

```
page[i].picture[j].rectangle.width = 2.0;
page[i].picture[j].rectangle.height = 2.5;
page[i].picture[j].rectangle.colour = 'red';
```

can be written

```
with (page[i].picture[j].rectangle) {
   width = 2.0;
   height = 2.5;
   colour = 'red';
}
```

Alternatively, a common idiom is to use a temporary variable:

```
var r = page[i].picture[j].rectangle;
r.width = 2.0;
r.height = 2.5;
r.colour = 'red';
```

The argument, closure and function objects

More advanced manipulations are possible using the argument, closure and function objects. We defer discussion to Sections 9.6.4–9.6.6 below.

9.5.5 The JavaScript view of objects

As we have seen, a JavaScript object is just a collection of named pieces of data, called *properties* and *methods*. Since a JavaScript function is a data value, there is in fact no difference between properties and methods: this is the significant difference between these objects and 'classic' objects. Objects fall into three categories:

1. Predefined objects built into the language – 'native objects'.
2. Programmer-defined objects.
3. Predefined objects provided by the associated object model – 'host objects'.

Because a JavaScript object is just a collection of named data items it can be (and is) stored in an associative array: this contrasts with Java/C++ objects, which have a more complex (fixed) internal structure. The JavaScript object structure has important consequences.

- There is no difference between an object and an array.
- New properties can be added to an object at run-time. This is achieved simply by assigning a value to a non-existent property, thus

```
obj.newprop = 0;
```

creates a new property `newprop` for object `obj`, and assigns a value to it. (Internet Explorer 4.0 and later provides an option to prevent creation of new properties at run-time. Since this is completely contrary to the spirit of JavaScript, we will not discuss it further.)

- Since functions are just another data type, we can also add methods to an object: if `f` is a function defined earlier in a script, it can be made a method of an object thus:

```
obj.new_method = f;
```

Although an object is an associative array, its properties and methods are normally accessed using the customary dot syntax, as in the examples above. However, it can also be accessed with array syntax, thus `obj.prop` and `obj["prop"]` are equivalent. This is useful because it allows access to a property whose identity (as a string) is derived from some computation at run-time. (An array subscript can of course be a variable.) Compare this flexibility with Java and C++, where the instance variables and methods of an object are fixed at compile time and are accessed by identifiers only.

We can loop through the properties of an object using the `for...in` construct, e.g.

```
for (v in obj) {
  ...
}
```

Object constructors

A constructor function creates the properties of an object by assigning initial values to them. It is invoked via the `new` operator: when the statement

```
myObj = new Obj args;
```

is obeyed, the sequence of events is as follows:

1. The `new` operator creates an empty object, returning a reference to that object.
2. It then calls the function `Obj` with the arguments provided, passing the object reference to it as a hidden argument that can be accessed within the function body as `this`.

3. The function `Obj` assigns values to properties.
4. When it returns, the statement is completed by assigning the object reference to the variable `myObj`.

For example,

```
function rectangle(w, h) {
   this.width = w;
   this.height = h;
}
rect1 = new rectangle(2.0, 7.0);
rect2 = new rectangle(2.5, 7.5);
```

Methods can be created by the constructor: for example, if we want to add a method to compute the area of a rectangle we could add

```
this.area = function() {return
           this.width*this.height};
```

to the body of the constructor function. Note the use of a function literal. We could have defined a named function

```
function rectarea() {
   return this.width*this.height;
};
```

and added it as another property in the constructor with

```
this.area = rectarea;
```

but using the anonymous function literal is neater.

When a method is invoked, as in

```
x = rect1.area();
```

the function that is the value of the property `area` is called with a reference to the object passed as a hidden argument named `this`, hence the use of `this` in the body of the function `rectarea`. Although this method of creating methods via the constructor function is perfectly legitimate, it is also inefficient, since every object created has its own copy of the method function. In practice, methods are usually implemented in the object prototype, as described later.

Object initializers

Constructor functions are useful if you want to create multiple instances of objects of a particular 'class'. If you just want a single instance of an object you can use an *object initializer*, e.g.

```
myCat = {name:"Rusty", breed:"Ginger Tom",
         age:10};
```

(Note the similarity of this to the creation of an initialized hash in Perl.)

Object prototypes

In object-oriented systems like Java, a class definition defines a template from which *instances* of objects belonging to the class can be created. JavaScript takes a different approach: instances of a class are generated from a *prototypical* object. Every constructor function has an associated prototype object, and every object created by a constructor function includes an implicit reference to the prototype. When we first use the `rectangle` constructor, for example, to create a rectangle object, that object contains an implicit reference to an object called `rectangle.prototype`. Any properties subsequently defined for the prototype appear in every object of that 'class', including objects already created. So if we write

```
rectangle.prototype.colour = "red";
```

all `rectangle` objects created previously, and any created subsequently, will appear to have a property `colour` with the value `"red"`. This comes about through the mechanism used to locate property values. When a reference to a property is made, JavaScript first looks in the object to see if that property is defined. If the property is not defined, it looks in the prototype object. Thus for read access, properties of the prototype are shared by all objects in the 'class', although there is only one actual copy, the one in the prototype (c.f. class variables and methods in Java, or static data members and static member functions in C++). However, setting a value for one of the shared properties in a particular object actually creates a new property for that particular object, which hides the shared property (c.f. lexical scoping hiding an outer declaration).

Prototypes are most commonly used to define the equivalent of class methods – as we have seen, including methods in the constructor function is inefficient, but putting them in the prototype ensures that only one copy of the function body is held in memory. The prototype can also provide default values for properties, later changed by an assignment for a particular object instance. Most implementations of JavaScript attach an empty prototype to every function, in case it is used as a constructor, so we could write

```
function rectangle(w, h) {
   this.width = w;
   this.height = h;
}
rectangle.prototype.colour = "red";
```

to ensure that all rectangles created have a property `colour` with default value `red`. Since this may not always work, a commonly used technique is to start by creating an object which is immediately discarded, to guarantee that the prototype exists, e.g. preceding the last line of the code fragment above with

```
new rectangle(0, 0);
```

Similar techniques are used to set up 'class methods' in the prototype.

Since an object prototype is an object, it too can have a prototype – in the prototype created for a constructor function the implicit prototype reference is `null`, but there is nothing to stop us assigning an explicit prototype rather than using the one automatically supplied, e.g.

```
function some_obj(a,b) {
// constructor for someobj
...
}
some_obj.prototype = new some_other_obj();
// override default prototype
```

We have seen that when a property is accessed, the system first looks for the property in the named object, and if it is not present, the system follows the implicit reference to the prototype and looks for it there. If the property is still not found, the system follows the prototype's implicit reference if it is non-null. This *prototype chain* provides the basis for achieving inheritance. Thus if we want a 'class' of objects called `colouredRectangle` that inherits from `Rectangle`, we define a constructor function as

```
function colouredRectangle(hue) {
   this.colour = hue;
}
colouredRectangle.prototype =
   new Rectangle(2.0, 4.0);
```

If we now use this constructor, as in

```
red_rectangle = new colouredRectangle("Red");
```

we get a red rectangle with default values for width and height. We can use a variadic function to allow us to specify the size of the coloured rectangle in the constructor by declaring it as follows.

```
function colouredRectangle(hue) {
   numargs = arguments.length;
   if (numargs == 0) {
     alert("No arguments!");
     return;
  }
   if (numargs == 1) {//default height and width
     this.colour = hue;
     return;
  }
   if (numargs == 3) {// width and height given
    this.colour = arguments[0];
    this.width = arguments[1];
    this.height = arguments[2];
    return;
  }
   else
    alert("wrong arguments!");
}
colouredRectangle.prototype =
  new Rectangle(w, h);
```

9.5.6 Defining and using arrays

Newcomers to JavaScript are often thrown by the fact that you cannot use arrays just by assigning values, as in

```
a[0] = 127; a[1] = 255; a[2] = 64;
```

An array is an object, and so a new array must be instantiated before its elements can be referenced. A simple way to create a 'one-off' array is to use a variant of the object initializer described above, using square brackets instead of braces, e.g.

```
a = [127, 255, 64];
```

Again, note the similarity to Perl array constructors.

A more general way to create an array is to use the new operator with a constructor function to create a generic object, thus:

```
a = new Object();
```

or

```
a = new Object;
```

This creates a new object with no properties or methods, and might appear pointless. However, since objects and arrays are the same thing, what we have done is to create an empty array, which we can then populate, e.g.

```
a = new Object();
a[0] = 127; a[1] = 255; a[2] = 64;
```

If we want an associative array, we can populate it as

```
a = new Object();
a["red"] = 127; a["green"] = 255; a["blue"] = 64;
```

or even

```
a = new Object();
a.red = 127; a.green = 64; a.blue = 48;
```

We can also define a constructor function for a specialized kind of array, e.g.

```
function IndexArray(n) {
  this.size = n;
  for (i = 1; i <= n; i++)
    this[i] = i;
}
myArray = new IndexArray(128);
```

The Array( ) constructor

The Array() *constructor is not implemented in versions of Navigator prior to Navigator 4.0. It is not implemented in any version of Explorer.*

Netscape's implementation of JavaScript provides a generic array constructor, Array(). This can be used in three ways.

- Used with no arguments, as in

      myArray = new Array();

  it has the same effect as

      myArray = new Object();

  except that it gives myArray a property length, set to zero.
- Used with *n* arguments (*n* > 1), it creates an array with the first n values set to the *n* arguments, and the length property set to *n*.
- Used with one argument, as in

      myArray = new Array(n);

  it creates an empty array but sets its length property to n. (But in Navigator 4.0–4.05, if the language attribute of the <SCRIPT> tag is set to 'JavaScript 1.2' it creates an array with its first value set to the argument provided.)

An array created using the Array() constructor has the special property that it is 'elastic', since its length property is a read/write value. Setting length to a value less than its current value will change the length of the array, discarding surplus values. Setting it to a value greater than its current value will extend the array with the requisite number of undefined values.

Arrays created using the Array() constructor have a number of associated methods, including the following.

- sort(): sorts the elements of the array into alphabetical order, temporarily converting numbers to strings if required. sort(f) sorts the elements of the array into order, using f as an ordering function. Here, f should be a function that takes two arguments and returns a negative value, zero, or a positive value according as the first argument comes before, equal to or after the second argument in the desired sorting order.
- reverse(): reverses the order of the elements of the array.
- join(): converts all the elements of the array to strings, and returns a string formed by concatenating them into a single comma-separated string. join(s) converts all the elements of the array to strings, and returns a string formed by concatenating them into a single string using s as a separator.

Warning: JavaScript 1.3 behaviour differs from JavaScript 1.2.

- push() and pop(): add or remove elements at the end of an array. The push() method adds the elements given as arguments at the end of the array. In Navigator 4.0x (JavaScript 1.2) it returns the last element added, but in Navigator 4.5 (JavaScript 1.3) it returns the new length of the array. The pop() method deletes the last element of the array, adjusts the length, and returns the item deleted.
- unshift() and shift(): add or remove elements at the start of an array. The unshift() method adds one or more elements at the start of the array and returns the new length. The shift() method removes the first element of the array, adjusts the length and returns the item removed.

- `splice()`: modify an array in place. The first argument specifies the index in the array at which the modification is to take place, the second argument is a count of elements to be removed, and any further arguments are elements to be inserted. The method returns an array containing the deleted elements (an empty array if no elements were deleted). An implementation error in Navigator 4.0x affects the return value: if one element is deleted, the element is returned, not an array, and if no elements are deleted there is no return value.

Warning: JavaScript 1.3 behaviour differs from JavaScript 1.2.

Multi-dimensional arrays

In common with most scripting languages, JavaScript does not provide multi-dimensional arrays as such, but allows the use of arrays of arrays, as shown in the following example.

```
my_matrix = [[1, 0, 0], [ 0, 1, 0], [0, 0. 1]];
...
sum = 0;
for (i = 0; i <= 2; i++ {
  for (j = 0; j <= 2; j++ {
    sum += my_matrix[i][j]
  }
}
```

Alternatively, array constructors can be used:

```
row1 = new Array(1, 0, 0);
row2 = new Array(0, 1, 0);
row3 = new Array(0, 0, 1);
my_matrix = new Array(row1, row2, row3);
```

9.6 System objects

As we have remarked, objects are central to JavaScript, and many useful facilities are encapsulated in system objects. For example, every primitive data type (i.e. every type except objects and arrays) has an associated wrapper object defined for it with useful methods. Wrappers for numbers and Booleans are not of great value – we mention a few uses for them later – but wrappers for strings, regular expressions and functions provide lots of interesting and useful features. Another example is the library of mathematical functions; these are provided as methods of the `Math` object.

9.6.1 The global object

The global object encapsulates the run-time environment for scripts. Global variables are properties of the global object. Since JavaScript is always embedded in a 'scripting host', e.g. a Web browser or server, the global object is created by the host. For example, in client-side scripting the Window object acts as the global object.

Prior to JavaScript 1.3, built-in objects like `String` and built-in functions like `parseInt()` were treated as properties and methods of the global object. JavaScript 1.3 describes them as 'top level' properties and methods.

9.6.2 The string object

If we assign a string value, e.g

```
s1 = "Navigator Rules";
```

we can get the length of `s1` as `s1.length`. When we assign a string value to a variable, we create a transient 'wrapper' object: we can regard the opening and closing double quotes as the syntax for an object initializer. Alternatively, we can create permanent string objects using the `String()` constructor, e.g.

```
s2 = new String("Navigator Rules");
```

In the first example above, JavaScript converted a string value to a transient string object. This happens whenever a string value is used in a context that requires a string object; another example is

```
len = "Navigator Rules".length;
```

Similarly, JavaScript will perform automatic conversions between string objects and string values. Thus if we use the string *object* `s2` in a string context, e.g.

```
s3 = s2 + " OK!";
```

it will be converted to a string before the concatenation operator is invoked.

The string object has only one property, `length`. It has a large number of methods, which fall into two groups. Methods in the first group provide a simple string manipulation capability, e.g. extracting sub-strings, while those in the second group return a modified copy of the string.

String manipulation methods include

Warning: JavaScript 1.3 behaviour differs from JavaScript 1.2.

- `s.charAt(n)`: returns the character at position n in the string s (indexed from zero).
- `s.charCodeAt(n)`: returns the character at position n in the string s (indexed from zero). In JavaScript 1.2 it is the Latin-1 encoding: in JavaScript 1.3 it is the Unicode encoding.
- `s.indexOf(substring, n)`: index of the first occurrence of `substring` in s: search starts at character n. If n is omitted, search starts at the beginning of the string.
- `s.lastIndexOf(substring, n)`: index of the last occurrence of `substring` in s: search starts at character n. If n is omitted, search starts at the end of the string.
- `s.substring(m, n)`: returns sub-string of s starting at character m and ending just before character n.
- `s.split(delim)`: split s into sub-strings using the character/string `delim` as a boundary, and return the sub-strings in an array. (Note that this is the inverse of the `array.join` method.)

There are also four methods that perform regular expression matching on strings: these are described later, after we have introduced the `RegExp` object.

Methods which return a copy of the string modified in some way include `s.toUpperCase()` and `s.toLowerCase()` which do the obvious thing, and a whole family of methods that return a copy of the string enclosed in HTML markup tags: for example `s.bold()` returns a copy of the string enclosed between `<B>` and `</B>` tags. These methods are useful in scripts which generate HTML content 'on the fly'. A possibly useful feature is that these methods can be applied to literal strings since JavaScript will convert the string to a transient object automatically. Thus we might write

```
alert("Hello World!".fontcolor('red'));
```

to display a message in red text.

In addition to all these methods of the string object, there are some static methods which are properties of the `String()` constructor. The most useful of these is `String.fromCharCode()`. This takes one or more integer values as arguments, and returns the string generated by treating the integers as character codes. In JavaScript 1.2 the integers are treated as Latin-1 codes: in JavaScript 1.3 they are treated as Unicode codes.

Warning: JavaScript 1.3 behaviour differs from JavaScript 1.2.

9.6.3   The RegExp (regular expression) object

Like a string, a regular expression can appear in a program as a simple value or an object, and JavaScript will convert between the two forms as appropriate. Like most other languages, JavaScript uses a pair of slash (`/`) characters to denote a regular expression, e.g.

```
number_pattern = /[0-9]+/;
```

(This pattern matches any string of one or more decimal digits.) Alternatively, a regular expression object could be created:

```
number_pattern = new RegExp("[0-9]+")
```

The slash notation is by far the most common way of defining regular expressions: the special feature of the `RegExp()` constructor is that it allows regular expressions to be built up dynamically. When using the constructor, note that the argument of `RegExp()` is a string containing the characters that appear between the slashes in the simple form of regular expressions. Any qualifier appears as a second argument, e.g.

```
global_number_pattern =
    new RegExp("[0-9]+", "g")
```

has the same effect as

```
global_number_pattern = /[0-9]+/g;
```

Note also that any backslashes in the regular expression will appear as double backslash in the string given to the `RegExp()` constructor

Regular expressions are implemented in Navigator 4.0 and later, and in Explorer 4.0 and later. Readers who are not familiar with the general idea of regular expressions should read Section 2.12.1 first.

Regular expression matching

The `String` and `RegExp` objects have methods that perform pattern matching using regular expressions. The `String` object has four methods:

- The `search()` method takes a regular expression as an argument and returns the index of the start of the matching sub-string, or −1 if there is no match. Thus the expression

  ```
  "Twas brillig and the slithy
  toves".match(/brillig/)
  ```

  returns the value 5.

- The `replace()` method takes two arguments, a regular expression and a replacement string. In its simplest form it finds the first match in the target string and replaces it with the substitution string. If the regular expression has a g (global) qualifier, then *all* matching sub-strings are replaced. If the regular expression includes bracketed sub-expressions, matching sub-expressions can be denoted in the replacement string as $1, $2 etc. For example, if we have a string s which starts with a four-digit number followed by a space we can put the number at the end as follows

  ```
  new_s = s.replace(/(^\d{4}[ ])(.*$)/, "$2 $1")
  ```

- The `match()` method takes a regular expression as its argument and returns an array containing the results of the match. There are three cases to consider.

  i.   Simple (non-global) regular expression with no sub-expressions. In this case `match()` returns an array of one element, the first matching sub-string. This array has three properties, `length`, `index` and `input`. The `length` property has the value 1, `index` is the index of the start of the match, and `input` is a copy of the target string.

  ii. Non-global regular expression with bracketed sub-expressions. The first element of the array returned is the first matching sub-string, and subsequent elements contain the sub-strings matching the bracketed sub-expressions. The `length` property gives the number of elements in the array: `index` and `input` are as above.

  iii. Global regular expression. In this case `match()` returns an array containing all the matches, with the length property set to the number of matches. The skeleton code for using this is

  ```
  s = "...";
  pattern = /.../g;
  matches = s.match(pattern);
  for (i = 0; i < matches.length; i++)
      ... //process matches[i]
  ```

- The `split()` method breaks the string into an array of sub-strings, using its argument as the separator. Thus if s is a string containing words separated by arbitrary white-space possibly preceded by a comma, e.g.

```
s = "Apples, Oranges, Pears Bananas,Melons";
```

we can extract the component words with

```
words = s.split(/,\s*|\s+/);
```

(Recall that \s matches any whitespace character.)

The RegExp object has two pattern-matching methods: test() and exec(). The test() method takes a string as an argument, and returns true if the string contains a sub-string that matches the regular expression. The exec() method is similar to the match() method for strings: match() is a string method that takes a regular expression as its argument, whereas exec() is a regular expression method that takes a string argument. It behaves in the same way as match() does for a non-global pattern, i.e. it searches the string for the first match and returns an array containing the matching sub-string and the sub-strings corresponding to any bracketed sub-expressions in the regular expression. However, it also sets a lastIndex property to the index of the character in the string immediately following the end of the match, and next time the method is called, the search starts at this position, making it possible to do global matches on regular expressions with bracketed sub-expressions, retaining all the information about each match. When the match fails, lastIndex is set to zero: the programmer can set it to zero at any time to terminate a search.

In addition to lastIndex, a RegExp object has three other properties: source contains the string that forms the regular expression, global and ignoreCase are Booleans that specify the attributes attached to the regular expression.

Other features of the RegExp object

A RegExp object has a number of *class properties* (sometimes called static properties) which are set whenever pattern matching is done, providing additional information about the last match and control over the matching process. Since these are class properties, they are transient, being reset by each pattern matching operation. The properties are:

- leftContext and rightContext: the text to the left (right) of the current match
- lastMatch: the text most recently matched
- lastParen: the text matched by the last bracketed sub-expression of the last match
- $1-$9: the text matched by the first nine bracketed sub-expressions of the last match
- input: a string to be searched if exec() or test() is used without an argument
- multiline: Boolean, if true the string searched is treated as multiple lines separated by newline characters. This means that ^ and $ match the start and end of lines as well as the start and end of the string.

9.6.4 The function object

Since functions are data, they too have wrappers. There is a function() constructor that lets us define new functions at run-time:

```
var cube = new function("x", "return x*x*x;");
```

The `function()` constructor expects a number of string arguments: the last is the function body, and the preceding arguments are strings defining the formal parameters. It should be used with care, since it has to compile the function body every time the constructor is called. For an anonymous function, the function literal is usually to be preferred unless the body is built dynamically at run-time.

Warning. JavaScript 1.2 and JavaScript 1.3 differ.

We have seen that in the body of a function f, we can use `arguments.length` to find out how many arguments were passed. We can also use `f.length` (in Explorer and Navigator) or `f.arity` (in Navigator 4.0 and later) to find out how many arguments the function expected, i.e. the number of arguments in the formal parameter list in the function declaration. (In Navigator 4.0–4.05 `f.length` does not work correctly. Although `f.arity` works correctly, it is necessary to set the language attribute to 'JavaScript1.2' to ensure correct results.)

Implemented in Navigator 4.06 and later. Not implemented in Explorer.

JavaScript 1.3 provides two additional methods for the `function` object, `apply()` and `call()`. The `apply()` method allows us to invoke a function as if it were a method of another object, so that if we write

```
f.apply(obj1, args);
```

the function f is called with arguments given in the array `args`, but within the body of the function, `this` will refer to the object `obj1`. The `call()` method is similar, except that the arguments are given as an argument list rather than an array.

Static local variables

Creating new properties for a function object at run-time is a way of getting the effect of static local variables. Suppose we have a function declaration

```
function f(x, y) {
  var z;
  ...
}
```

The local variables are stored as properties of the associated call object. Additional variables can be associated with the function by assigning them as properties of the function object, e.g.

```
f.i = 3;
```

The difference between a variable like this and a local variable is that a variable stored as a property of the function retains its value between calls: local variables are initialized afresh on each function invocation. Note that when the variable is used in the function body it must be given its fully qualified name, in this case `f.i`.

9.6.5 The arguments object

The `arguments` object is not implemented in JScript. However, the `arguments[ ]` array is available in the body of a function.

The `arguments` object is created when a function is invoked, and contains the values of all the arguments that were passed to the function. It has a property length, which returns the number of arguments passed to the function, and other properties of the function described below. The automatically created local `arguments[]` array is a reference to this object. The `arguments` object should not be confused with the `arguments` property of the `function` object, use of which is deprecated.

The caller and callee properties

The `arguments` object has two further properties, `caller` and `callee`. The `callee` property is a reference to the function currently executing. This might appear pointless, but is useful if you want to define an anonymous function that calls itself recursively. Thus the classic recursive function definition,

This section applies only to Navigator 4.0 and later.

```
function factorial(x) {
    if (x > 1) return x*factorial(x-1);
    return x;
}
```

can be written

```
var factorial = function(x) { if (x > 1)
 return x*arguments.callee(x-1);
         return x;
}
```

The `caller` property refers to the `arguments` property of the function which invoked the current function. Thus the calling function can be referred to as `arguments.caller.callee`. This is likely to be of use only to the programmer who wants to play clever (or dirty) tricks.

The `caller` property of the `arguments` object should not be confused with the `caller` property of the `function` object, which is available in Internet Explorer and was provided in earlier versions of Netscape Navigator. The behaviour of this is completely different, and as it is of little utility it is not discussed further.

9.6.6   The closure object

A nested function declaration appears as a property of the enclosing function. Thus if we declare

The `Closure` object is implemented in Navigator 4.0 and later. It is not implemented in Explorer.

```
var t = 1;
function f(x) {
    var t = 0;
    function g(y) {
        ...
    }
    ...
}
```

then g can be called directly in the body of f as `g(z)`, or can be called from outside the body of f as `f.g(z)`. In either case, it is executed in the scope of f, so that an occurrence of t in the body of g is always bound to the local variable of f, not the global variable t. That is, the scope chain for g consists of its own call object, then the call object of f, then the global object, even when g is called outside the scope of f. However, caution is required if you propose to exploit this feature. The declaration

```
var t = 0;
```

in the body of f is treated as if it were written

```
var t;
t = 0;
```

Thus although a call object is created for f, with an entry for the local variable t, that variable does not receive a value until f is called. This means that a call of f.g(z) will fail if f has not been called previously.

Another way of describing what is going on is to say that a nested function is in fact stored as a *closure* ('closure' is a computer science term for the combination of a function body and its declaration environment). Explicit closures can be created: the Closure object allows us to execute a function in a different context from that in which it was declared. If we write

```
g2 = new Closure(g, h);
```

then g2 is a function identical to g except that it executes in the scope of the function h, i.e. as if its declaration had appeared in the body of h.

9.6.7 The number object

Although it is possible to create number objects, e.g.

```
n = new Number(3.14159)
```

this is unlikely to be a common (or useful) requirement. The real purpose of the Number object is to supply some useful constants as class properties. These are

Number.MAX_VALUE	Largest representable number
Number.MIN_VALUE	Smallest representable number
Number.POSITIVE_INFINITY	Value returned on overflow
Number.NEGATIVE_INFINITY	Value returned on overflow
Number.NaN	Not-a-number value

The Number object has one method, toString(), which converts a number to a string. This is an instance method, i.e. it exists for each Number object created. As with strings, if a number is used in a context where a Number object is required, a transient object will be created, so it is possible to say

```
n = 3.14159;
s = n.toString();
```

Since JavaScript usually converts numbers to strings automatically, this is not of much utility. It is in fact a survivor of earlier versions of the language, in which the `toString()` method took an argument to specify the radix to be used in conversion.

9.6.8 The Boolean object

As with numbers, it is possible, but unhelpful, to create `Boolean` objects, e.g.

```
b = new Boolean(0);
```

The utility of the `Boolean` object is its `toString()` method, which returns the string `"true"` or `"false"` depending on the value held in the object. As with numbers, transient objects are created as required, so that we can write

```
alert("Comparison returned " + (a = b).toString());
```

In JavaScript 1.2 a `Boolean` object can be used in a context where a Boolean value is required (e.g. in a condition), and its `valueOf()` method is invoked transparently to return the Boolean value. In JavaScript 1.3 `Boolean` objects should on no account be used in conditional statements, since in that context any object whose value is not `undefined` or `null` evaluates to true. So if we write

Warning. JavaScript 1.2 and JavaScript 1.3 differ.

```
var condition = new Boolean(false);
...
if (condition) {
...
}
```

the `then` arm of the `if` statement will be obeyed.

9.6.9 The math object

The `Math` object has a number of class properties and methods. The properties provide useful constants, e.g. `Math.PI`. The methods provide all the usual mathematical and trigonometrical functions, e.g. `Math.sin()`, `Math.exp()`. For mere mortals, the most useful methods are

```
Math.sqrt()      square root
Math.random()    pseudo-random number between 0 and 1
Math.round()     round to nearest integer
```

9.6.10 The date object

The `Date` object manipulates dates and times in a variety of ways. It is very rich in functionality – the description in the JavaScript 1.2 Reference Manual extends to 14 pages. (JavaScript 1.3 adds many new methods: the description of the date object now occupies 36 pages!) The simplest use of the `Date` object provides an abstraction of the system clock:

```
now = new Date();
```

or you can create an object to represent a particular day, e.g.

```
Christmas = new Date("25 December 1999");
```

Having created a `Date` object, there are methods that allow you to get and set the day, month, year, hour, minute and seconds components, e.g

```
today = now.getDay();
```

sets `today` to an integer between 0 (Sunday) and 6 (Saturday). Further methods, in particular `toLocaleString()` convert dates and times to human-readable strings. Time zones can also be queried and changed.

The method `getTime()` is useful for comparing dates: it returns the date and time in a `Date` object as the number of milliseconds since midnight GMT on 1st January 1970. The inverse operation is achieved with `setTime()`.

9.7 Advanced facilities

9.7.1 eval – on-the-fly interpretation

Like most interpreted scripting languages, JavaScript allows the interpreter to be called from within a program. The `eval()` function takes a string, which is a well-formed JavaScript script or expression, as an argument and passes it to the interpreter. The return value is the result returned by the last statement, or the result of evaluating the expression. Thus trivially,

```
y = eval("2 + 2");
```

gives `y` the value 4. In practice, `eval()` is used where it is necessary to generate JavaScript code dynamically and immediately execute it. For example, suppose we have declared a number of variables that are instances of some object class, and that the objects in this class have a property `value`. If the variable `selection` is a string containing the name of one of these variables (resulting from some previous computation or perhaps obtained from a text entry box in a Web form), we can access that variable's `value` property with

```
theValue = eval(selection + ".value");
```

9.7.2 Exception handling

This section applies to Explorer 5 only.

A weakness of the version of JavaScript that ships with Navigator 4 and Internet Explorer 4 is that it makes no provision for exception handling. This omission is remedied in Internet Explorer 5. Exception handling can get quite complex, and we do not go into great detail here.

The exception handling model is the 'try . . . catch' structure that will be familiar to C++ and Java programmers.

```
try {
  ...
}
catch(e) {
  ...
}
```

The block after `try` contains code where errors may occur: if they do the code will 'throw an exception' using the `throw` statement: this statement includes a value that identifies the nature of the exception, e.g.

```
throw "value out of range";
```

If the code does not throw any exceptions, execution continues after the catch block: if the code does throw an exception, the catch block is executed with the variable e set to the value in the `throw` statement. This makes it possible to identify which of several exceptions was thrown, and act accordingly, e.g.

```
try {
  ... // code may throw exceptions e1, e2 or e3
}
catch(e) {
  switch (e) {
    case e1:
      ...
    break;
    case e2:
      ...
    break;
    case e3:
      ...
    break;
  }
}
```

It is possible for `try...catch` structures to be nested. If the inner `catch` block does not wish to handle a particular exception it can just throw it, in which case it will be handled by the outer `catch` block, e.g.

```
try {
  try {
    ...
  if (...) throw e1;
    ...
  }
  catch(e) {
    if (e == e1) then {
    ... //deal with it
```

```
    else throw e; //pass it up one level
    }
  }
catch(e) {
  ... // exceptions other than e1 handled here
```

If a JScript run-time error occurs in a `try` block, the variable passed to the `catch` block will be a reference to an `error` object. This object has two properties, `number`, the error number, and `description`, a descriptive string. An `error` object can also be explicitly created, e.g.

```
var negTotalError = new Error(42, "Negative total");
```

or thrown using the `throw` statement. In both cases, you can add additional properties to expand the capability of the `Error` object.

9.8 JavaScript and Java

Both Netscape and Microsoft provide mechanisms for scripting Java classes: as might be expected, the mechanisms used are completely different. Here we describe the Netscape mechanism as built into Navigator: the Microsoft equivalent is part of its ActiveX technology.

The use of JavaScript to script Java classes in Navigator is one component of a proprietary Netscape technology called *LiveConnect*. The `Window` object in the browser object model (the global object) has a property `Packages` of type `JavaPackage`, which acts as the root of a hierarchy of Java classes, each of which is represented by an object of type `JavaClass`. The properties of a `JavaClass` object represent, and have the same names as, the public static fields and methods of the corresponding Java class.

The `Packages` object has three properties, `java`, `sun` and `netscape`, which are `JavaPackage` objects representing hierarchies of Java classes. Thus access to the AWT (abstract window toolkit) Java class is by `Packages.java.awt`. This can be abbreviated to `java.awt`, since the `Window` object has properties that act as short cuts to the `Packages` hierarchy. The `java.awt` object is itself a `JavaPackage` object that contains `JavaClass` objects for the classes contained in the Java AWT package.

Finally, the `JavaObject` class is a JavaScript representation of a Java object. A `JavaObject` object does not have properties and methods of its own: its properties and methods represent (and have the same names as) the public instance fields and public instance methods of the Java object it represents, in the same way that a `JavaClass` object represents the static class fields and static class methods of a Java class. The JavaScript new operator can be used with a `JavaClass` object to create a new instance of a Java class, represented by a `JavaObject` object, e.g.

```
var awt_rect = new java.awt.rectangle();
```

creates a new Java object that can be manipulated from JavaScript. LiveConnect handles all the 'plumbing', including type conversions between JavaScript's dynamic typing and Java's strict static typing.

9.9 JavaScript operators and precedence

Here are the JavaScript operators in precedence order, highest first. The second column indicates the associativity.

negation, increment		R	!	~	–	++	––	
multiply, divide		L	*	/	%	(integer remainder)		
add, subtract		L	+	–				
shift		L	<<	>>	>>>			
relational		L	<	<=	>	>=		
equality		L	==	!=				
bitwise	and	L	&					
	xor	L	^					
	or	L	|					
logical	and	L	&&	(shortcut evaluation)				
	or	L	||	(shortcut evaluation)				
conditional		R	?	:				
assignment		R	=	+=	–= etc.			
multiple evaluation		L	,					

The dot in an object property reference and the opening bracket in an array reference or function call bind tighter than any operator. The >> right shift operator propagates the sign digit: >>> is a zero-fill right shift.

Notes

[1] Microsoft documentation claims that this happened 'in response to a joint submission from Microsoft and Netscape'. However, ECMA-262 states that 'The originating technology for this ECMA Standard is JavaScript. This technology has been offered by Netscape Communications for standardization in autumn 1996'.

[2] The dot syntax for access to properties and methods of an object is suggestive of a C struct. This is not surprising – a struct has a name and has fields named by identifiers. It is perhaps of interest to note that the essential first step in creating C++ was to extend C to allow functions as components of structs.

## Chapter 10

VBScript

VBScript is an alternative to JavaScript in the Microsoft world, used for client-side scripting of Web pages, scripting Active Server Pages, and as an ActiveX scripting language. In this chapter we describe the core language: examples of its use in client-side Web scripting and with the Windows Script Host will be found in subsequent chapters.

10.1 What is VBScript?

We have already seen that after Netscape introduced JavaScript, Microsoft provided their own reverse-engineered version, JScript. They then played catch-up by producing 'Visual Basic for Applications – Scripting Edition', usually abbreviated to VBScript. This was a very cut-down version of the full Visual Basic language, incorporating just those features needed for simple client-side scripting in Internet Explorer. Subsequently, Versions 2 and 3 of the language restored some useful features such as the For Each looping construct. Version 5 (so called to bring the version numbers of Visual Basic and VBScript into synchronism – there was no Version 4), released as part of Internet Explorer 5, represents a major increment in functionality, including user-defined classes as in Visual Basic 5 and a regular expression matching capability that is not included in Visual Basic, even Version 6. (However, we shall see later that there is a back-door method of making the functionality available in Visual Basic.) In this chapter we first describe the version of VBScript as implemented in Internet Explorer 4: this is followed by a description of the new features incorporated in Version 5.

In the ActiveX scripting architecture, VBScript is a scripting language that can be used with any ActiveX scripting host, not just Explorer. At first, it seemed that VBScript was being promoted as the preferred scripting language in the ActiveX world, but there then appeared to be a growing consensus that JavaScript, a more powerful language, is the language of choice: VBScript was promoted as an easy-to-learn language, and as the language to use if you are already familiar with Visual Basic or VBA. The additional functionality included in VBScript 5 suggests that there is a move to establish it in preference to JavaScript. Time will tell.

Like JavaScript, VBScript is designed to operate in a host environment, and imports functionality from that environment in the form of collections of objects described by *type libraries*. This means that functionality of the language depends on the host environment: for example, VBScript can access the local file system when running on the Microsoft IIS Web server, but does not have that capability when hosted by Internet Explorer

10.2 The VBScript core language

In order to make this chapter self-sufficient, we give a complete account of the core language here. For readers who are already familiar with the Visual Basic core language, e.g. from reading Chapter 8, substantive differences are flagged by a marginal rule. For a complete list of the differences between VBScript and Visual Basic, refer to Microsoft's on-line documentation.

This description is based on the version of VBScript implemented in Internet Explorer 4 and later.

10.2.1 Variables, types and values

Variables

Variable names follow the usual rules: the permitted characters are letters, digits and underscore, and the first character must be a letter. There is a limit of 255 characters on the length of a variable name. Microsoft literature adopts the convention that variable names have an initial capital, and long names are made more readable by internal capitals, e.g.

```
TimeOfTheYear = "Summer"
```

However, this is pure convention, since in the long tradition of BASIC, VBScript is not case-sensitive.

Types

In VBScript all variables are of type variant, thus declarations merely specify a variable name, e.g.

```
Dim Start, End
```

If a variable is not declared, it will be implicitly declared as variant on first use. The variant type provides dynamic typing: at run-time the value has an associated tag to record the type of the value currently stored (sometimes called the *sub-type*).

Sub-types are `Byte`, `Boolean`, `Integer`, `Long`, `Single`, `Double`, `Currency`, `Date`, `String` and `Object`. Sub-types `Integer` and `Long` are 16-bit and 32-bit integers, respectively: `Single` and `Double` are 32-bit and 64-bit floating point numbers, respectively. `Currency` is a scaled integer, `xxx.yy`, with 15 digits to the left and four to the right of the point. Values of the `Date` sub-type are stored as IEEE 64-bit (8-byte) floating-point numbers that represent dates ranging from 1 January 100 to 31 December 9999 and times from 0:00:00 to 23:59:59. Note that there is no problem here with roll-over to the year 2000. Strings are variable size.

The sub-type of a variable can be interrogated by the `VarType()` and `TypeName()` functions: `VarType()` returns a numeric code to identify the sub-type while `TypeName()` returns the sub-type name as a string. There are four special values that a variant can have: `Empty`, `Null`, `Error` and `Nothing`. When a variant is first declared it is given the value `Empty`, to indicate that no value has been assigned to it. The `Null` and `Error` values can be assigned by the user to indicate that the variable contains no useful data, or that an error condition has arisen: the values `Empty` and `Null` can be tested with the functions `IsEmpty()` and `IsNull()`. The value `Nothing` is used in connection with objects (see later).

Declarations

Variables can be declared implicitly or explicitly: implicit declaration is permitted by default, but the compiler/interpreter can be told to make declarations obligatory with the statement `Option Explicit`. The first use of a new variable name constitutes an implicit declaration of the variable: it is assigned the type variant.

Variables can be declared as constants, e.g.

```
Const pi = 3.1415926536
```

(Keywords are customarily given an initial upper-case letter, but this is pure convention, since the language is not case-sensitive.)

Literal constants

Numerics and strings have the 'obvious' forms. Date literals are enclosed within number signs (#), and can be written in a variety of formats, e.g.

```
#2-Apr-98#
#April 2, 1998
#April 2, 1998 1:20 pm#
```

(A purely numerical date like `#2-4-99#` will be interpreted according to the locale set for Windows, 2 April in the UK, 4 February in the US.) Note that 2-digit dates less than 30 have 2000 added to them, while dates of 30 or greater have 1900 added to them: VBScript programs have a potential Year 2030 problem!

Enumerations ('intrinsic constants')

Enumerations provide a convenient way of mapping a collection of meaningful names on to a sequence of integers, e.g. associating the days of the week with the integers 1–7, thus making code easier to read. VBScript provides a large number of built-in enumerations to make life easier for the programmer: for example, the days of the week are mapped onto the integers 1–7 by the constants `vbSunday`, `vbMonday` etc. (The initial 'vb' indicates that this constant is defined by VBScript.) As another example, if you want to check whether a variant currently has a string value, you can remember that the sub-type for string is '8' and write

```
if VarType(myVar) = 8 Then ...
```

However, it is much less error-prone, and more readable, to use an 'intrisic constant' from a built-in enumeration and write

```
if VarType(myVar) = vbString Then ...
```

10.2.2 Operators and expressions

All the common operators are present: a full table was given in Section 7.9, together with the precedence rules. The equivalence operator compares two logical values and returns true if both are true or both are false. The implication operator is an obscure thing of interest only to mathematicians: how it got into Visual Basic is a mystery.

Type-conversion

When expressions are evaluated, any reasonable type-conversion between sub-types takes place silently and unobtrusively, e.g. if a variant of sub-type string is a valid representation of a number it will be automatically converted if used in a numeric context. The function `IsNumeric()` can be used to test whether an expression can be converted to a number, and `IsDate()` can be used to test whether an expression is a date or can be converted to a date. Explicit type-conversion functions are provided: these take an expression and coerce it (if possible) into a particular variant sub-type. The target sub-type is included (in abbreviated form) in the function name, e.g `CDbl()` converts a numeric (or valid string) value to a double. A full list of functions is

```
Cbool()   CByte()   CCur()   CDate()   CDbl()
Cint()    CLng()    CSng()   CStr()
```

There is of course no `CVar()` in VBScript, since everything is a variant anyway.

When other numeric sub-types are converted to `Date`, values to the left of the decimal point represent date information while values to the right of the decimal point represent time. Midnight is 0 and midday is 0.5. Negative whole numbers represent dates before 30 December 1899.

Built-in functions

We have already encountered some built-in functions, and we shall introduce more as we explore the language. Built-in functions that are not mentioned elsewhere include

- *Mathematical functions*: the usual collection of trigonometrical and mathematical functions – `Sin()`, `Cos()`, `Exp()` etc.
- *Rounding*: functions to round fractional numbers – `Int()` and `Fix()`. For positive arguments these are identical, and round down. For negative arguments, `Int()` rounds to the nearest integer less than the argument, so that `Int(-2.7)` rounds to –3, while `Fix()` rounds the other way, so that `Fix(-2.7)` returns –2.
- *Character conversion*: functions to convert characters to ASCII code equivalents and vice versa – `Asc()` and `Chr()`. Note that `Asc()` takes a string argument, and returns the ASCII value of the first character as an integer. On systems that support Unicode, `AscW()` and `ChrW()` can be used for Unicode conversions.
- *String manipulation*: a collection of functions for string manipulation, including

```
Len(S)          returns length of S
InStr(S1,S2)    returns position of S2 in S1 (index of first
                character)
```

```
Left(S,n)       returns leftmost n characters of S
Right(S,n)      returns rightmost n characters of S
Mid(S,n,m)      returns m characters starting an index n in S
```

Note that in VBScript the `Mid` function does not have a matching `Mid` statement.

■ *Date and time*: a collection of functions for manipulating dates and times. The functions `Day()`, `Month()` and `Year()` take an expression or variable of type `date`, and return the appropriate component as a variant of sub-type integer. `DateAdd()` adds or subtracts an interval to a date: the nature of the interval – day, month, year, hour, minute, second – being specified by one of the arguments. Thus if `d` is a date,

```
d = DateAdd("m", -1, d)
```

subtracts one month. `DateDiff()` returns the difference between two dates in units specified by an argument, e.g.

```
DaysLeft = DateDiff("d", EndOfSemester, Now)
```

■ *Formatting*: a compendious function `Format()` which converts values into strings according to a predefined or user-defined format. For example, suppose that we assign values as follows

```
Dim Today, Now
Today = #November 17, 1998#
Now = #13:09:32#
```

then

```
Format$(Now, "hh:mm:ss: AMPM")
```

returns "01:09:32 PM" and

```
Format$(Today, "dddd, mmm d yyyy"
```

returns `"Tuesday, Nov 17 1998"`. User-defined formats can give precise control over conversion of numeric values to strings, e.g. suppressing non-significant zeros, thus

```
Format$(5459.4 "##,##0.00")
```

returns `"5,459.40"`. For more information on formats, see the Visual Basic reference documentation.

10.2.3 Data structures

The only data structure provided in VBScript is the array. As in the early versions of BASIC, a fixed size array can be declared with a `Dim` statement:

```
Dim A(10), B(10, 15)
```

The lower bound for subscripts in VBScript is always zero – there is no `OPTION BASE` statement.

The function `Ubound()` takes an array name as an argument, with an optional second argument to specify the dimension to be queried (1 for first, 2 for second etc.) and returns the upper bound for that dimension. (There is also an Lbound() function to return the lower bound, but since that is always zero, use of this function is otiose.)

An array can be initialized using the Array() function:

```
Dim colours
...
colours = Array ("Red", "Green", "Blue")
```

Note that after obeying the above code, the variable Colours is a variable of type Variant whose value is of sub-type Array: the elements of the array are themselves of type Variant with sub-type String. The Array sub-type can be tested with the function IsArray().

Dynamic arrays

Dynamic arrays can be declared e.g.

```
Dim B( )
```

In this case the actual size of the array must be set before use by, e.g.

```
ReDim B(20)
```

(Note that ReDim is an executable statement, not a declaration.) The size of the array can be changed again later in the program by another ReDim. This has the effect of destroying the current contents of the array unless the Preserve keyword is used, e.g.

```
ReDim Preserve B(30)
```

However, if the Preserve keyword is used, only the *last* dimension can be changed. Thus a one-dimensional array can always be re-dimensioned preserving the contents, but if we have a two-dimensional array we can change the number of columns, but not the number of rows.

10.2.4 Statements

Statements are normally terminated by end-of-line: a statement can be continued on the next line by placing an underscore immediately before the end of the first line. Multiple statements can be placed on a single line, separated by a colon, e.g.

```
X = 1: Y = 2: Z = 3
```

(The choice of the colon as a separator is bizarre, given the otherwise almost universal use of a semicolon as a statement terminator/separator.)

10.2.5 Control structures

VBScript has all the usual control structures, though sometimes with a slightly unfamiliar syntax. A particular feature to note is that every structure has a closing 'bracket', e.g.

```
If ... End If
Do ... Loop
For ... Next
```

The explicit close means that there is no need for begin/end or curly brackets to delimit the scope of groups of repeated/conditional statements.

Conditionals

Points to note about the `If...Then...Else...ElseIf...End If` construct are

- The condition that follows the `If` can be a comparison that yields a Boolean result, or an expression that evaluates to a numeric value: zero is false and anything else is true. Unlike many other languages, there are no obligatory brackets round the expression.
- Then must be the last thing on the line (except for a comment).
- `Else`, `ElseIf` and `End If` must be the first thing on a line.
- `End If` is two words, but `ElseIf` is a single word.

Note that while Visual Basic allows a line number before `Else`, `ElseIf` and `End If` for backwards compatibility, VBScript does not.

In addition to the `If` statement there is a multi-way selection statement, the `Select Case` statement, e.g.

```
Select Case MyVar
  Case "red" document.bgColor = "red"
  Case "green" document.bgColor = "green"
  Case "blue" document.bgColor = "blue"
  Case Else MsgBox "pick another color"
End Select
```

Repetition and loops

There are two repetition statements, `Do` and `For`. (There is also a `While` statement, but this is only included for backward compatibility, and its use is deprecated.) The `Do` statement comes in two forms:

```
Do While condition
  ...
Loop
```

can be a zero-trip loop, while

```
Do
  ...
Loop While condition
```

guarantees that the body will be executed at least once. In both cases, `While` can be replaced by `Until` to negate the condition.

The simple `For` loop is straightforward, e.g.

```
For I = 1 To 100 Step 2
  A(I) = 0
Next I
```

If the increment is 1 the `Step` can be omitted. Appending the optional counter variable to the `Next` statement helps readability of nested loops.

The `For Each` statement can be used to iterate over the elements of an array (or a collection of objects, as described later). It has an obvious use in iterating over the elements of a dynamic array, e.g.

```
Dim A()
... 'computation to decide size of array
ReDim A(N)
...
ReDim Preserve A(N+10)
For Each Item in A
Print Item
Next
```

Populate the array and add some more elements. Don't need to remember size.

Loops can be terminated prematurely using the `Exit Do` and `Exit For` statements, e.g.

```
For I = 1 To N
  ...
  If A(I) < 0 Then
  Exit For
  End If
  ...
Next I
```

10.2.6   Procedures and functions

VBScript provides procedures and functions, but as a consequence of its ancestry, procedures are called 'subs' in the actual code. The term 'procedure' is used to mean 'procedure or function' when the context is unambiguous.

Procedure and function declaration and call

Examples of declarations are:

```
Sub Scream (s, n)
  ...
End Sub
Function Foo (s)
  ...
End Function
```

The body of a function must contain an assignment to the name of the function to define the return value. Execution of a procedure or function body normally terminates by 'dropping off the end', but exit from within the body is possible using the Exit Sub and Exit Function statements.

Procedure call takes the usual form, except that the arguments are not enclosed in brackets, e.g.

```
Scream "aaarrgghhh!", 42
```

Note particularly that the space after the comma is obligatory. The same syntax is used for a function call if the value returned by the function is to be discarded. However, if the value returned is to be used, the normal parenthesis notation *is* used, e.g.

```
n = Foo("aaaarrggghh!")
```

For backwards compatibility, the Call statement can be used for a procedure call, e.g.

```
Call Scream("aaarrggghh!", 42)
```

In this case too the arguments are enclosed in brackets. (Yes, this is confusing!)

Call by reference and call by value

The default is to call arguments by reference, but value calling can be specified in the declaration by adding the qualifier ByVal *before* the parameter specification, e.g.

```
Sub foo (ByVal n)
  . . .
```

10.2.7 Program structure, variable scoping and lifetime

In VBScript the scoping rules are related to scripts rather than modules, but the rules are otherwise unchanged.

1. Variables declared using Dim and constants declared using Const at the start of a script (before any procedure or function declarations) are global to the procedures and functions in the script. Their lifetime is that of the script.
2. Variables declared using Public (instead of Dim) and constants declared using Public Const at the start of a script (before any procedure or function declarations) are visible in all scripts in currently loaded documents. (The significance of this will become apparent in Chapter 11.)
3. Variables declared using Private (instead of Dim) and constants declared using Private Const at the start of a script (before any procedure or function declarations) are visible only in the script in which they are declared.
4. Variables and constants declared inside a procedure or function (explicitly or implicitly) are local to the procedure or function.

10.2.8 File I/O

VBScript does not implement the traditional BASIC I/O capabilities, thus in Internet Explorer VBScript has no access to the local file system. File I/O capabilities can be provided by the host application using an object model: in the Internet Information Server and the Windows Script Host, VBScript has access to the File System Object Model, described in Section 14.5.

10.3 Objects in VBScript

A reference to an object can be stored in a variable of sub-type `object`, which can be tested with the `IsObject()` function. Prior to version 5, VBScript did not have the ability to define its own object classes: it had the concepts of objects and properties, and the syntax for referencing them, but had no in-built object model. The enhanced object capability in Version 5 is described later in Section 10.4.6.

The usefulness of the `object` sub-type derives from the fact that VBScript can interface to any application that exposes a collection of COM objects described in a *type library*. The type library defines the properties and methods of a collection of related objects, much as a header file in C describes a collection of functions in a library: the entries in the type library are in many ways the equivalent of a set of abstract base class definitions in Java. The user specifies which type library (or libraries) is (are) to be imported at start-up, or, more commonly, accepts the default type libraries that the application designer has specified. Thus when VBScript is used in Internet Explorer, it has access to an object model describing the Web page and the document being displayed, as described in Chapters 11 and 12.

10.3.1 Working with objects

We describe here the facilities that VBScript provides for working with imported objects.

Properties

The syntax for referring to a property is

        object_id.property_name

e.g.

        ActiveCell.Value = "Annual Totals"
        v = ActiveCell.Value

Methods

In general, the syntax for referring to a method is

        object_name.method args

if the method is a strict procedure (returning no result), and

```
v = object_name(args)
```

if the method is a function returning a result.

Object variables

Many useful things can be done just by reading and setting the properties, and invoking the methods, of predefined objects. Sooner or later we want to do more complicated things, and this is where *object variables* are needed. An object variable is a variable whose value is a reference to an object. The Internet Explorer object model includes an object representing the document currently being displayed by the browser. If we write

```
Dim theDoc
Set theDoc = window.document
```

then the variable theDoc, now of sub-type object, has as its value a reference to the document object. (The keyword Set was almost certainly chosen because in the original BASIC all assignment statements had to start with the keyword Let.)

Once the reference is created, the object variable can be used in any context where the object itself could have appeared, thus theDoc appears to have all the properties and methods of the document object. Thus we can write

```
theDoc.bgColor = vbRed
```

to change the background colour of the Web page. A common idiom is to use an object variable to provide 'shortcut' access to a property. For example, if we want to reference several properties of an object that is deeply nested in the object hierarchy, e.g. frames(1).document.form1.text1, we can write

```
set tb = frames(1).document.form1.text1
tb.value = "rhubarb"
...
```

Not only does this improve readability, it is also more efficient.

The use of Set distinguishes object reference assignments from assignments of other data types: it reminds us that we are assigning a reference, not a value. To elaborate this point, suppose we declare three integer variables A, B and C. If we then write

```
A = 100
B = A
C = A
```

then B and C are each assigned a *copy* of the value of A: subsequent changes to the value of A do not affect B and C. Contrast this with the behaviour of object variables: if after setting the value of Obj1 as shown above, we write

```
Set Obj2 = Obj1
```

then both Obj1 and Obj2 refer to the *same* object, and any changes in that object will be 'seen' by both Obj1 and Obj2. Thus setting a property for Obj1, e.g.

```
Obj1.prop1 = True
```

means that `Obj2.prop1` will also have the value true. It is sometimes important to determine whether two object variables are referring to the same object: the `Is` operator tests for equivalence between two object references, i.e. returns true if two object variables are references to the same object. It can also be used to test for the value `Nothing`.

Creating automation objects

When VBScript is being used as a server-side scripting language we can use the `CreateObject()` function to actually start an automation server application and create an object representing the instance of the application, e.g.

```
Dim xlApp
Set XlApp = CreateObject("Excel.Application")
```

Note that since VBScript does not support explicit data types, creation of the object necessarily uses late binding.

When VBScript is used as a client-side scripting language, `CreateObject()` can be used to create `Dictionary` objects, but no others:

```
Dim myDict1
Set myDict1 = _
  CreateObject("Scripting.Dictionary")
```

The `Dictionary` object, which is loosely based on the Perl hash, is very useful: it is described in Chapter 14.

Collections

A *collection object* is an object that contains a set of related objects. Collections are very common in the object models that are used by VBScript: for example, the Explorer Document Object Model groups the objects representing the images on a Web page in a collection object. The only things you can do with a collection object in VBScript are to access its `count` property and to iterate through its members with a `For Each` loop, e.g.

```
Dim theImage
For Each theImage In document.images
   ...
Next
```

The Err object

The `Err` object is an intrinsic object, i.e. there is no need to explicitly create an instance of it. The properties of the `Err` object are set by the generator of an error: when a run-time error occurs, the properties of the `Err` object are filled with information that uniquely identifies the error and information that can be used to handle it. The properties of the `Err` object are:

- Number: the error number.
- Source: the name of the current project.
- Description: a string corresponding to the return of the Error function for the specified Number, if this string exists. If the string doesn't exist, Description contains the string 'Application-defined or object-defined error'.
- HelpFile: the path name of the Visual Basic Help file.
- HelpContext: the Visual Basic Help file context ID for the error corresponding to the Number property.

Since the default property of the Err object is Number, writing Err alone is equivalent to writing Err.Number. The properties of the Err object are reset to zero or zero-length strings after execution of an On Error Resume statement, and can be explicitly reset by the method Err.Clear.

A run-time error can be generated from within a program by invoking the Raise method of the Err object. This method takes the error number as an argument, so

```
Err.Raise 24
```

will cause the script to behave as if error number 24 had occurred naturally. This technique is often used to 'bounce' an error from one error handler to another.

10.4   New features in VBScript 5

10.4.1   The With statement

If several properties of an object are to be interrogated or changed, the with statement can be used:

```
With ActiveSheet.Cells(1, 1)
    .Font.Name = "Arial"
    .Font.Bold = True
    .Font.Size = 8
End With
```

10.4.2   The Execute statement and the Eval function

The Execute statement is the VBScript equivalent of the eval of Perl and Tcl. It allows the user to build a string containing one or more VBScript statements at run-time, and then immediately execute the statements. An = in the string will be treated as an assignment operation, not a test for equality. The Eval() function takes as its argument a string that is a valid VBScript expression, and evaluates the expression, returning its value. An = in the string will be treated as a test for equality.

Note that subtle scope problems can arise if the string given to Execute contains a procedure declaration: see the on-line documentation for more details.

10.4.3   Regular expressions

VBScript 5 provides powerful support for regular expressions based on an in-built object class Regexp, which has the actual regular expression as a property Pattern, thus:

```
Dim Regex
Set regex = New Regexp
regex.pattern = "(Romeo | Juliet)"
```

The regular expression syntax is identical with the JavaScript syntax, which in turn is derived from the regular expression syntax of Perl, described in Section 2.12.2. In this section we assume that the reader is familiar with regular expression matching in JavaScript or Perl.

A simple regular expression match is invoked by the Test() method, which returns true if the pattern stored in the regular expression object matches a sub-string of the target string, and false otherwise, e.g.

```
str = "Romeo, Romeo, wherefore art thou Romeo?"
If regex.Test(str) Then
   ...
End If
```

Matching is case insensitive by default: to do a case-sensitive search, set the IgnoreCase property of the regular expression object to false:

```
str = "Romeo, Romeo, wherefore art thou Romeo?"
regex.IgnoreCase = False
If regex.Test(str) Then
   ...
End If
```

The Replace() method takes two string arguments, a string to search for, and a replacement string to be substituted if the target string is found:

```
str1 = "romeo, romeo, wherefore art thou romeo"
str2 = regex.Replace(str1, "Juliet")
```

By default all occurrences of the pattern that match will be replaced. To limit the replacement to the first match, set the Global property of the regular expression object to false:

```
str1 = "romeo, romeo, wherefore art thou romeo"
regex.Global = False
str2 = regex.Replace(str1, "Juliet")
```

If the regular expression pattern includes sub-string matches, the replacement string can be constructed from the remembered values of the sub-strings. For example, suppose we set up a pattern as follows:

```
Dim regex
Set regex = new Regexp
regex.Pattern = "(\S+)(\s+)(\S+)"
```

This pattern matches a pair of words separated by whitespace. (\S+ matches one or more non-whitespace characters, \s+ matches one or more whitespace characters.) The following code swaps pairs of words in a string:

```
str1 = " ..."
regex.Global = True
regex.Replace(str1, "$3$2$1)
```

More complex pattern matching can be accomplished using the `Execute()` method of the regular expression object. This method attempts to match a regular expression in a target string, and returns a collection containing a *match object* for each successful match. Each match object provides access to the string found by the regular expression, the length of the string, and an index to where the match was found as the properties `Value`, `Length` and `FirstIndex`, respectively. The `Count` property of the collection can be tested to check the number of matches: most commonly, a `For Each` loop will be used to iterate over the matches:

```
Dim regEx, Match, Matches, str1, pat1
str1 = " ... "
pat1 = " ... "
Set regEx = New Regexp
regEx.Pattern = pat1
Set Matches = regEx.Execute(str1)
If Matches.Count = 0 Then
  MsgBox("No matches")
Else
  For Each Match In Matches
    ...
  Next
End If
```

An interesting point to note is that the regular expression object is implemented as a COM object, and is thus available to any COM-aware application. Thus, once VBScript 5 is installed, a Visual Basic programmer can write

```
Dim regExp As VBScript.RegExp
Set regExp = New VBScript.RegExp
```

and get access to the regular expression functionality.

10.4.4 Function pointers

The `GetRef()` function returns a reference to a procedure. It is provided to meet a specific requirement in Dynamic HTML, and its use is described in Chapter 12.

10.4.5 DCOM support

The `CreateObject()` function takes an optional extra argument to specify the name of the server hosting the object, e.g.

```
Set aRemoteObject = _
   CreateObject("Excel.Sheet", "\\myServer")
```

Recall that use of `CreateObject()` is, with one exception, restricted to server-side VBScript and the Windows Script Host.

10.4.6 Classes

A new object class can be declared as a `Class` block, e.g.

```
Class MyObjects
   statements
End Class
```

Within a `Class` block, members are declared as either `Private` or `Public`: using the appropriate declaration statements. Anything declared as `Private` is visible only within the `Class` block, while items declared as `Public` (the default if not specified) are also visible outside the `Class` block. `Sub` or `Function` procedures declared `Public` within the `Class` block become methods of the class. `Public` variables serve as properties of the class, as do properties explicitly declared using `Property Get`, `Property Let` and `Property Set` (see below). A default method for the class can be established by declaring a procedure as `Public Default`: a default property can be established by declaring its `Property Get` function and `Property Let` procedure as `Public Default`. Having declared a class in this way, new instances of the object can be declared:

```
Dim X
Set X = New MyObjects
```

An example

(This example will be familiar if you have read Chapter 8.) Suppose we want to declare a class `Rectangle` which has properties `Width` and `Height`, and provides methods `Area()`, `Circumference()` and `Diagonal()`. For good but irrelevant reasons, attempts to set `Width` or `Height` to values greater than 5 will force the value 5 to be used. The definition is as follows:

```
Class Rectangle
' Declare private variables to hold the
' actual height and width
   Private rWidth
   Private rHeight
Public Property Let Width(w)
' Allows Width to be used as a property:
' monitors value given to actual width
   If w <= 5.0 Then
     rWidth = w
```

```
        Else
           rWidth = 5.0
    End Property
    Public Property Get Width()
    ' Gives read access to Width
           Width = rWidth
    End Property
    Public Property Let Height(h)
    ' Allows Height to be used as a property:
    ' monitors value given to actual height
        If h <= 5.0 Then
           rHeight = h
        Else
           rHeight = 5.0
    End Property
    Public Property Get Height()
    ' Gives read access to Width
       Height = rHeight
    End Property
    Public Function Area()
    ' Method to return Area
       Area = rHeight*rWidth
    End Function
    Public Function Circumference()
    ' Method to return Circumference
    Circumference = 2.0*(rWidth + rHeight)
    End Function
    Public Function Diagonal()
    ' Method to return Diagonal
    Diagonal = _
       Sqr(rWidth*rWidth + rHeight*rHeight)
    End Function
    End Class
```

We can declare variables to refer to instances of this class and set the properties, e.g.

```
    Dim R1
    Set R1 = New Rectangle
    R1.Width = 2.5
    R1.Height = 3.5
```

Because the rectangle class defines Width and Height as a 'Property Let'/'Property Get' pair, VBScript knows to call the 'Property Let' procedure with the value of the right-hand side expression as its argument. Similarly, if we write

```
    W = R1.Width
```

VBScript knows to call the 'Property Get' function and assign the value returned to W. If a 'Property Get' function is defined without a 'Property Let' procedure, the property is read-only (and applying the same principle, a property can be made write-only). If the class had a property that was an object reference the 'Property Let' procedure would be replaced by a 'Property Set' procedure.

## Chapter 11

Scripting Web clients and servers

Netscape provides client-side and server-side scripting using JavaScript. In the Microsoft world it is possible to embed one or more scripting languages in an application: for example, JScript and VBScript are embedded in Internet Explorer and in the Internet Information Server (IIS). A script can control those aspects of the application which are exposed in its object model. In this chapter we describe client-side web scripting in Navigator and Explorer and server-side scripting of Active Server Pages in IIS: client-side scripting is explored in more detail in Chapter 12.

11.1 Client-side Web scripting

In client-side scripting as implemented in Netscape Navigator and Microsoft Internet Explorer, the browser object model reflects the HTML page and other relevant information as a collection of predefined objects that can be manipulated by scripts embedded in the page. Thus the document is represented by a *document object*, each link in a document is represented as a *link object*, every frame as a *frame object*, and so on. These objects have *properties* that describe (and possibly determine) their appearance, and methods that control browser behaviour. Some objects react to external actions, e.g. mouse clicks and moves, by raising an event. We can use scripts to define *event handlers* – scripts that will be executed whenever the associated event happens. In Navigator the objects exposed in the object model are native JavaScript objects: in Internet Explorer the scripting engine uses the type library to map the objects as native objects for the particular language.

Unfortunately, the document object model implemented in Navigator is not the same as the model implemented in Internet Explorer. The examples used in this section are based on a common sub-set: a more detailed account of the document object models is presented in Chapter 12.

11.1.1 Client-side scripting possibilities

Before launching into detail, it may help to have some idea of what client-side scripting can do. Although the Navigator object model is somewhat impoverished, it allows JavaScript to provide a variety of useful facilities for the Web author. The Microsoft object model extends the possibilities further. Client-side scripting possibilities in Navigator and Explorer include:

- *Interactive forms validation.* This is probably the most common use of scripts. Form data can be checked as it is entered, and/or when the submit button is pressed, and feedback given to the user using pop-up dialog boxes and alerts.
- *Control of overall document appearance.* Various aspects of appearance, e.g. background colour, can be selected dynamically by executing a script at the time the page is loaded. (In Explorer, document appearance can also be changed after loading.) In Navigator, styles can be defined by scripts.
- *Manipulating positioned content.* A script can change the position of items whose position is specified in absolute or relative terms, and can control their visibility.
- *Generating document content.* A script can generate HTML content that will be inserted in the page as if it had been in the original page at the point at which the script is executed.
- *Control of the browser.* A script can create new windows, change the position of windows, print their content and simulate the effect of Forward and Back buttons.
- *Customizing behaviour to the browser.* A script can determine which browser is running, down to the version number, and can thus exploit browser-specific facilities if they are present, generating different content to suit the capability of the browser.
- *Reading and writing client state.* A script can read and write cookies to simulate persistent connections.

11.1.2   JavaScript and HTML

JavaScript code can be embedded in HTML in a number of ways. The most common ways, common to both Internet Explorer and Netscape Navigator are:

- As a block of code enclosed between <SCRIPT> and </SCRIPT> tags. In this case it is usual to make the script into an HTML comment: JavaScript-aware browsers will ignore the commenting, but the script will be hidden from a non-aware browser, so avoiding confusion. It is also possible to provide explanatory comment for users of non-aware browsers by enclosing it between <NOSCRIPT> and </NOSCRIPT> tags. The <SCRIPT> tag is customarily given a LANGUAGE attribute, e.g.

```
<SCRIPT language="javascript">
...
</SCRIPT>
```

(The name is case insensitive: Internet Explorer accepts jscript as well.) In HTML 4 the preferred form is

```
<SCRIPT type=text/javascript>.
```

although the older form is retained for compatibility. If the LANGUAGE attribute is not set, and a global default has not been set by a <META> tag in the <HEAD> element, most modern browsers will default to JavaScript, but it is not safe to rely on this (except in Navigator, which does not support any other scripting language).
- From an external file by specifying an SRC attribute for the <SCRIPT> tag, e.g.

```
<SCRIPT language="javascript"
SRC="scripts/s1.js">
</SCRIPT>
```

■ As an *event handler*: here the script is the value of an attribute (e.g. onClick) within an HTML tag, e.g.

```
<FORM>
<INPUT type=button name="myBtn1" value="OK"
 onClick="...">
</FORM>
```

Here the string given as the value of onClick is a script to be executed in response to a mouse click on this button. This may consist of a number of JavaScript statements, or it may just be a function call.

There are many other ways of embedding scripts, especially in Navigator, but we do not discuss them here since they are not central to the theme of scripting languages.

11.1.3 VBScript and HTML

We have seen above how JavaScript code can be incorporated into HTML. For pages that are intended to be viewed only in Internet Explorer, VBScript code can be incorporated by setting the value of the language attribute to "VBScript" or "VBS", e.g.

```
<SCRIPT language="VBScript">
...
</SCRIPT>
```

or, in HTML 4,

```
<SCRIPT type=text/VBScript>
...
</SCRIPT>
```

Similarly, an event handler for a button click might be written

```
<FORM>
<INPUT type=button name=myBtn1
 value="Press me!"
 onClick="Alert 'You did!'"
 language="VBScript">
</INPUT>
</FORM>
```

Internet Explorer provides two alternative methods for associating event-handler code written in VBScript with an event. Suppose that a button has been defined as follows:

```
<FORM>
<INPUT type=button name=myBtn1
```

```
      value="Press me!">
</FORM>
```

A VBScript event handler for the `onClick` event can be associated with this button as follows:

```
<SCRIPT language="VBScript" for="myBtn1"
 event=onClick>
 Alert "You did!"
</SCRIPT>
```

Alternatively, we can make the event handler a procedure, and use the Visual Basic naming convention for event handlers, e.g.

```
<SCRIPT language="VBScript">
 Sub myBtn1_OnClick
   Alert "You did!"
 End Sub
</SCRIPT>
```

11.1.4   The client-side object model

The client-side object model provides some basic host objects that define the client-side implementation. The key interface is the *window object*, which reflects the current top-level browser window. This object contains:

- `navigator`: the navigator object, whose properties give information about the browser.
- `frames[]`: an array of window objects representing the frames of the top-level window.
- `location`: a representation of the URL currently being displayed.
- `history`: an object representing sites previously visited.
- `document`: an object representing the document currently being displayed. The document object has its own object model, which is very different in Navigator and Internet Explorer.

The window object

The `window` object, besides being the root of the object hierarchy, serves as the global object. It can be referred to as `window`, or `this` (outside a function definition) or `self`. In JavaScript, all variables declared (or first assigned to) outside a function body are properties of the window, thus outside a function, `v` and `window.v` are alternative ways of referring to the variable `v`. If an HTML page contains several scripts, each enclosed between `<SCRIPT>` and `</SCRIPT>` tags, it follows that global variables declared in any one script are visible in all the subsequent scripts. This is particularly useful as a way of initializing values before a page containing scripts is displayed, using a script in the `<HEAD>` of the document. Since a frame is represented by a `window` object each frame acts as its own global object, and variables in one frame can be accessed from another frame as properties of the `window` object representing the frame.

VBScript has a more simplistic approach. A 'global' variable declared as `Public` is visible in all documents currently loaded, i.e. in all frames. A variable declared as `Private` is visible only in the document (frame) in which it is declared.

The `window` object has many methods and properties: among the most useful (described with JavaScript syntax) are

- `alert(string)`: displays a message to the user in a dialog box with an OK button.
- `confirm(string)`: displays a message to the user in a dialog box with OK and Cancel buttons, returns true or false depending which one is pressed.
- `location`: an object representing the URL of the current page. The various components of the URL are made available as properties, e.g. `protocol`, `hostname`, `port` etc. The object has two methods: `reload` and `replace`. Calling `reload` is equivalent to clicking the browser's Refresh button: calling `replace` navigates to a new location without updating the history list. We shall see an example of how this is used later.
- `prompt(string1,string2)`: displays a message (`string1`) to the user in a dialog box with OK and Cancel buttons, inviting input in a text box containing `string2` (the default reply): returns the contents of the input box if OK is pressed, or an empty string if Cancel is pressed.
- `status`: a read–write property containing the text currently displayed in the status line.
- `defaultStatus`: a read–write property containing the default text to be displayed in the status line.
- `setTimeout(code, delay)`: a method which schedules the script contained in the string `code` to be executed after a number of milliseconds which is the value of `delay`.

Internet Explorer 5 adds a `print` method to the window object, so that the current page can be printed on the default printer by invoking `window.print`.

The navigator object

The `navigator` object has read-only properties that return strings containing the name of the browser, the version, a code for the language supported (e.g. EN for English, DE for German), and the hardware platform that the browser is running on. The `navigator` object gives us a way of automatically redirecting requests to browser-specific pages, e.g. to redirect requests from a Netscape browser we might include the following in the <HEAD> element of our page:

```
<SCRIPT LANGUAGE = JavaScript>
if (navigator.appName == "Netscape")
   location.replace("Netscape_page.html");
</SCRIPT>
```

The history object

The `history` object holds an array containing the URLs visited from the window, which can be accessed by three methods, `back()`, `forward()` and `go()`. The first two are equivalent to using the browser's Back and Forward buttons. The `go()` method takes a numerical argument which specifies a relative position in the list, thus `go(-2)` is equivalent to pressing the Back button twice.

For security reasons, browsers typically impose restrictions on access to the history list.

The document object

The document object represents many aspects of the current document. It has methods, including `write()`, which writes text into the page being displayed – useful for generating HTML on the fly – and properties that represent the appearance of the document, e.g. its background colour. A further set of properties represent the contents of the document, including:

- `anchors[]`: an array of `anchor` objects, one for each anchor in the document
- `forms[]`: an array of `form` objects, one for each form in the document
- `images[]`: an array of `image` objects, one for each image in the document
- `links[]`: an array of `link` objects, one for each link in the document.

These arrays can be indexed, thus `forms[1]` is an object representing the second form in the document, and `images[5]` is the sixth image. Keeping track of forms and images in this way is tedious and error prone. A better technique is to give each image and form a name, using the `name` attribute, e.g.

```
<image name="logo" src="pics/logo.jpg">
```

We can now index the `images[]` array as an associative array, e.g.

```
document.images["logo"].src =
    "pics/newlogo.jpg";
```

In fact, since both Navigator and Explorer expose the name as a property of the document object, e.g. `document.logo`, there is never any need to use the `forms[]` and `images[]` arrays explicitly, unless the index is the result of a computation. (Explorer also implements the `id` attribute, which identifies the image or form in the `document.all` collection – see Chapter 12.)

The form object

The important part of a `form` object is the `elements[]` array, which is an array of objects representing the component parts of the form – buttons, checkboxes etc. This array is rarely accessed directly: since each element has a `name` attribute, the name assigned becomes a property of the form object, thus a button named `btn1` in a form named `myform` can be referenced as `document.myform.btn1`.

11.1.5 Examples gallery

Before going on to discuss more esoteric details of client-side Web scripting we present some simple examples to give the flavour of what is involved in scripting the object model. The examples are presented using JavaScript, but could equally well be written in VBScript.

Example 1: Writing text into the status bar

This little script places some text in the browser's status bar (Figure 11.1).

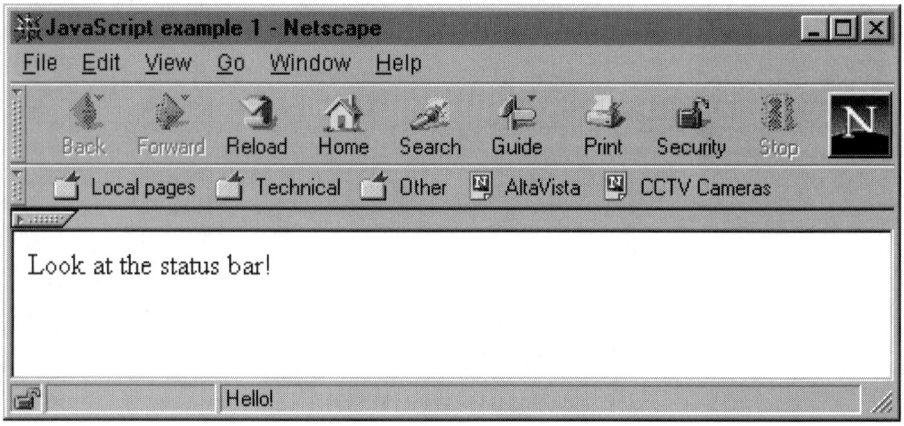

Figure 11.1   Text in the status bar

The script goes inside the
<head>, so is obeyed
before the rest of the page
is loaded. Specify
language=
"JavaScript" in case
the browser default is
something else. self is
the object representing
the current window,
defaultStatus is one
of its properties.

```
<html>
<head>
<title>JavaScript example 1</title>
<script language="JavaScript">
  self.defaultStatus = "Hello!";
</script>
</head>
<body >
...
</body>
</html>
```

Example 2: Context-sensitive help take 1

This example shows how a help message can be produced when the user points to a link. The browser window displays a line of text containing two links, and when the mouse pointer moves over the link, a message is displayed in the status bar (Figure 11.2).

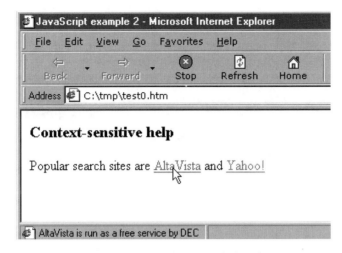

Figure 11.2 Context-sensitive help, take 1

Here is the code.

```
<html>
<head>
<title>JavaScript example 2</title>
</head>
<body>
<h3>Context-sensitive help</h3>
Popular search sites are
<a
href="http://www.altavista.digital.com"
   onMouseOver="self.status='AltaVista is \
run as a free service by DEC'; return
true">
AltaVista</a> and
<a href="http://www.yahoo.com"
   onMouseOver="self.status='Yahoo was \
founded by a couple of postgrads'; \
return true">
Yahoo!</a>
</body>
</html>
```

The value of the onMouseOver tag is a script that is the 'event handler' associated with the MouseOver event. The script must return a value true, otherwise the default status message will be displayed.

A drawback of this technique is that once displayed, the message remains in the status bar. It can be removed by adding an event handler for the *MouseOut* event which resets the status display to an empty string, thus:

```
<a href="http://www.altavista.digital.com"
   onMouseOver="self.status='AltaVista is \
run as a free service by DEC'; return true"
   onMouseOut="self.status=''; return true">
AltaVista</a>
```

Example 3: Context-sensitive help take 2

In this variation on the previous example, when the mouse pointer moves over a link the help message is displayed in a dialog box, together with an invitation to activate the link (Figure 11.3).

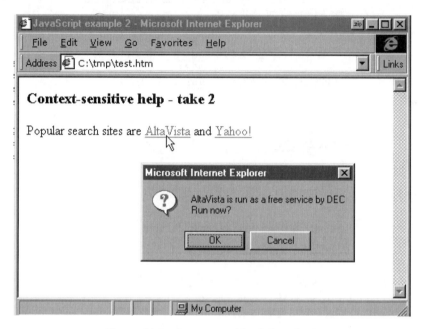

Figure 11.3   Context-sensitive help, take 2

```
<html>
<head>
<title>JavaScript example 2</title>
<script language=javascript>
function run_altavista() {
window.open('http://www.altavista.digital.com'
);
}
function run_yahoo() {
window.open('http://www.yahoo.com');
}
</script>
</head>
<body >
<h3>Context-sensitive help - take 2</h3>
Popular search sites are
<a href=""
   onMouseOver="if (confirm('AltaVista is run \
as a free service by DEC\nRun now?'))
```

```
run_altavista(); else return true;">
AltaVista</a>
and
<a href=""
  onMouseOver="if (confirm('Yahoo! was \
founded by two postgrads\nRun now?'))
    run_yahoo(); else return true;">Yahoo!</a>
</body>
</html>
```

Example 4: Buttons

This example shows how links can be replaced by buttons. Instead of links to AltaVista and Yahoo!, we provide buttons that can be pressed to start the search engine in a new window (Figure 11.4).

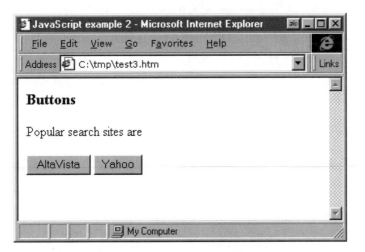

Figure 11.4   Command buttons

```
<html>
<head>
<title>JavaScript example 2</title>
</head>
<body>
<h3>Buttons</h3>
Popular search sites are<br>
<form>
<input type=button name="AltaVista_Button"
 value="AltaVista"
onClick="open('http://www.altavista.digital.com');">
<input type=button name="Yahoo_Button"
 value="Yahoo"
 onClick="open('http://www.yahoo.com');">
```

```
</form>
</body>
</html>
```

The code is straightforward. We define a `<form>` containing two button elements, which have associated event handlers for the `onClick` event. Note that `window` is the default object for open.

Example 5: A clock in the browser window

This example introduces the concept of animation, providing a constantly updated display. It displays a clock in the browser window (Figure 11.5).

Figure 11.5 Clock in the browser window

```
<html>
<head>
<title>JavaScript clock</title>
<script language="JavaScript">
function clock() {
//function will be called from a script in
//the page <body> element. Date is a built-in
//object
 var d = new Date();
 var h = d.getHours();
 var m = d.getMinutes();
 var s = d.getSeconds();
 //Add a zero in front of single digit
 //numbers.
 if (m < 10) m = "0" + m;
 if (s < 10) s = "0" + s;
 var t = " " + h + ":" + m + ":" + s;
 //string containing the time is assigned to
 //the value property of the object time,
 //contained in an object myform, which is
 //contained in the document object
 document.myform.time.value = t;
```

```
 //set a timeout to obey the script clock( )
 //after 1000 ms.
self.setTimeout("clock();", 1000);
}
</script>
</head>
<body>
<h3>The current time is:</h3>
<form name="myform">
<input type=text size=8 name="time"> <br>
</form>
<script language="JavaScript">
 //Call the function clock() to start the
 // animation
 clock();
</script>
</body>
</html>
```

Example 6: Writing to the screen

This contrived example displays a table of powers of 2 on the browser screen (Figure 11.6).

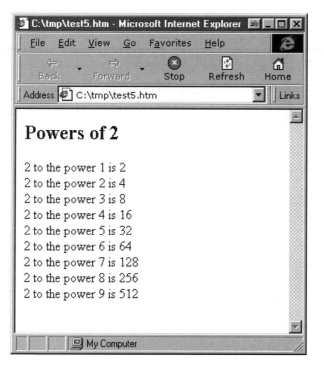

Figure 11.6   Powers of 2

```
<html>
<body>
<script language="JavaScript">
document.write("<h2>Powers of 2</h2>");
for(i=1, pwr=2; i<10; i++, pwr *= 2) {
  document.write("2 to the power " +
    i + " is " + power);
  document.write("<br>");
}
</script>
</body>
</html>
```

Example 7: Hiding code from non-aware browsers

If the previous example were run on a browser that was not JavaScript-aware, there would be problems. The <script> and </script> tags would be ignored – browsers customarily ignore tags that they do not understand – but the script in between would be regarded as text to be displayed. To avoid this, JavaScript provides a mechanism of making the script seem to be an HTML comment, and thus ignored, as shown below.

```
<html>
<body>
<script language="JavaScript">
<!--
document.write("<h2>Powers of 2</h2>");
for(i=1, power=2; i<10; i++,
    power *= 2) {
document.write("2 to the power " +
i + " is " + power)
document.write("<br>");
}
```

```
// -->
</script>
</body>
</html>
```

Another technique provides a method of alerting users of older browsers that do not support scripting, thus:

```
<script language="JavaScript">
<!-- --><h1>No scripting support!</h1>
<!--
    body of script
//    -->
</script>
</body>
</html>
```

11.1.6   Scripts and frames

If a page is divided into frames, multiple documents are being displayed, and each document can incorporate scripts. We need to consider how these scripts might interact.

JavaScript

Since a frame is represented by a window object each frame acts as its own global object, and, as noted in the preceding section, variables in one frame can be accessed from another frame as properties of the `window` object representing the frame. Thus JavaScript can execute scripts in different execution contexts, depending on the frame in which the script is being executed, but each execution context can access the other.

The names of functions declared in a frame (window) are, like variables, properties of the window, but local variables of functions are properties of the function (or, more precisely, of its call object). In general, this distinction does not matter. However, a subtle effect may occur if a function defined in one window is assigned as the value of a variable in a second window and then used in that window. This is because JavaScript will resolve variable references in the context of the current (second) window, except for local variables of the function, which will be resolved in the context of the window in which the function was declared.

Another potential problem arises if a script in a particular frame, frame 'A' say, calls a function defined in another frame, frame 'B', and that function performs a pattern-matching operation involving a `RegExp` object. Functions normally execute in the context in which they were declared: however, in this special case the class (static) properties of the `RegExp` object in the calling frame, frame 'A', will be updated. A little thought convinces us that this is the sensible thing to do.

VBScript

VBScript takes a more simplistic approach. Variables declared outside procedure or function bodies are global to the frame (window). If declared private they are visible only in that frame (window), but if declared public they are visible in all frames (windows) currently being displayed. Since VBScript does not have lexically nested scope, the potential complications relating to function definition and call described above do not arise.

11.1.7   Applets, ActiveX controls and Tclets

Things like buttons, checkboxes etc. that can appear in a form are called *intrinsic HTML controls*. An HTML page can also include external scriptable objects in the form of Java applets, ActiveX controls (Internet Explorer only) and Tcl applets (Tclets).

Scripting Java applets

A Java applet is a mini-application that is downloaded from the server when the browser encounters an `<applet>` element, and runs in the Java Virtual Machine, displaying content in an area of the page defined by attributes of the `<applet>` tag, e.g.

```
<applet code="CompanyLogo.class", name ="logo"
 width = 100 height = 50>
</applet>
```

Many applets execute independently of the rest of the page, essentially just renting some real estate on screen for their display. The display may incorporate control buttons, which are handled internally by the applet code. However, there are many benefits to be gained by making the applet scriptable. For example, suppose an applet has some animation that can be started and stopped by the user. It can display its own start and stop buttons, but if these actions are scriptable the control of the animation can be incorporated into a button bar, or indeed can be a by-product of some other user action. Another use of a scriptable applet is to perform some computationally intensive activity. The applet can be made effectively invisible by setting its window to be one pixel wide and one pixel high, and can be started by a script when required.

The document object model includes an array `applets[]`, an array of objects representing the `<applet>` elements in the document. As with the `forms[]` array, if the applets or objects have been named using the `name` attribute, those names become properties of the document object, so that the `CompanyLogo` applet of the example above can be referred to in a script as `document.logo`. (HTML 4 recommends the use of the `<object>` element for all embedded data, including applets. However, at the time of writing it is safest to use `<object>` only to introduce ActiveX controls in Internet Explorer – see below.)

Having obtained the reference to an applet, a script can invoke the public methods and read or write the public fields (properties) of the applet. Thus if the definition of the 'logo' applet includes a public method `rotate(n)` which causes the logo to rotate for n seconds, we could provide a button to spin the logo:

```
<form>
<input type=button value="Spin the logo"
  onClick="document.logo.rotate(5)">
</form>
```

(In this, as in subsequent examples, we use JavaScript: the VBScript equivalent should be obvious.) We can also associate event handlers with an applet; if our hypothetical logo applet has public methods `start()` and `stop()` to control the rotation, we might write

```
<applet code="CompanyLogo.class", name="logo"
  width=100 height=50
  onMouseOver="document.logo.start()"
  onMouseOut="document.logo.stop()">
</applet>
```

In Navigator, each entry in the `applets[]` array is a reference to a `JavaObject` object (described in Section 9.5) which represents the Java object comprising the applet, which in turn is an instance of some subclass of `java.applet.Applet`.

Scripting ActiveX controls

We have already met ActiveX controls in Visual Basic. Internet Explorer allows an ActiveX control to be placed in a Web page using the `<object>` tag, e.g.

```
<object
classid="clsid:64C28F-B22D-A30F-C169A82E891D"
width=100 height=50 id=finder>
</object>
```

On encountering this element, Explorer will use the Windows Registry to locate the control via its classid, and load it. The Explorer object model does not incorporate an `objects[]` array; the object appears as a member of the `document.all[]` collection, indexed by the value of the `id` tag. Thus having embedded a control with an id 'finder', it can be referenced as `document.all["finder"]`. Alternatively, arrays and objects being the same thing in JavaScript, we could reference the control as `document.all.-finder`. In practice, JavaScript (and VBScript) allow us to refer to the control just by its id, so that the properties and methods of the finder control can be accessed as properties and methods of `finder`, e.g. `onClick=finder.close()`.

Java–ActiveX integration

In many ways, Java and ActiveX are rival technologies – both provide the capability to download 'mobile code' from the server and execute it in the browser. Microsoft strategy appears to be to encourage the use of Java as an implementation language for ActiveX controls by providing tools which automate the generation of the necessary dispatch interfaces by which a Java class can appear as a COM object. We describe this technology very briefly, since a full account would require an in-depth knowledge of both COM and Java.

This section assumes some familiarity with Java and COM.

The Microsoft Java Virtual Machine (JVM) provides 'Automatic IDispatch' which allows a Java class to expose an `IDispatch` interface, thus making it scriptable from Visual Basic (or any other scripting host). Suppose we have a phonebook application written in Java, in a class `phonebook`. A phonebook object implements a collection of `entry` objects each of which has two instance variables, name and number. The class provides methods to set and retrieve values for these variables. The first stage is to define the interfaces in Microsoft's interface definition language (MIDL) as one would for any COM object. The interfaces will be

- `Application`: the client's first point of access.
- `Phonebook`: provides a collection of `Entry` objects, with methods to add and delete entries.
- `Entry`: has properties for name and number.

The definition of the `Entry` interface will specify the Java methods as 'property get' and 'property set' functions.

Each interface specification is then compiled into a type library by the MIDL compiler, and this is in turn processed by the 'JActiveX' tool into a source file for the compiler that will generate special codes in the class file to implement the COM interfaces. A few other bits of Java have to be written, notably to handle errors, and the various bits and pieces are added to the phonebook class to create a new class, which we will call `phonebookX`. Once this class is compiled the final step is to register it as a COM object with a fearsome looking command like

```
javareg /register /class:phonebookX
/clsid:"{4f9dfa95-32ef-11d1-b5ac-
9e4a44000000}" /progid:"PhoneBook.Application"
```

(The command would be typed in as a single line.) Here the `clsid` is the unique identifier of the COM object, and the `progid` is a human-friendly name. These will be entered in the Registry so that when a Visual Basic program refers to `PhoneBook.Application`, the system can create an instance of a `PhoneBook` object via its clsid, e.g.

```
Set myPhoneBook =
    CreateObject(PhoneBook.Application)
```

Scripting Tcl applets (Tclets)

A Tclet is a Tcl/Tk script which is included in a Web page with an `<embed>` tag, and executes when the page is loaded. To make use of Tclets, you must first ensure that the Tcl Plugin is installed in your browser. (Plug-ins are browser extensions, initially introduced in Netscape Navigator and later adopted by Microsoft for Internet Explorer, which display multimedia content inside a Web page. Each plug-in is designed to display content of a different type, and allows the browser to display pages containing elements that it does not know how to format and display itself. The Tcl plug-in is a viewer for Tcl and Tk applications: all the graphical power of Tk can be used to create exciting Web pages.)

Thus if we have created a Tcl/Tk script in a file `cool.tcl`, we can incorporate it as a Tclet in a Web page with

```
<embed src=cool.tcl width=250 height=200
str1="Use Tcl!" str2="Tk rules!">
```

Here the `height` and `width` attributes define the embedded window in which the Tclet operates. This is equivalent to the 'top-level window' in Tk, but is fixed in size, thus the Tclet must turn off geometry propagation. The remaining attributes are passed to the Tclet as name–value pairs in the array `embed_args`, so that the Tclet can access the value of attribute `str1` as `$embed_args(str1)`.

As with Java applets and ActiveX controls, there are potential security problems associated with executing scripts from unknown sources. The Tcl plug-in avoids most security risks by using a 'padded cell' approach: a Tclet is run in a safe interpreter (as described in Chapter 5) which implements the standard Safe-Tcl subset, plus a limited version of Tk, thus preventing scripts from obtaining access to the host system and isolating them from each other. In particular, the default padded cell prevents Tclets from running other programs, accessing the file system and creating top-level windows (including menus).

Version 2 of the plugin provides several different padded cells with varying degrees of padding. These are defined by a number of *safety policies* which include

- home. This policy allows the Tclet to use the socket command without an argument to make a network connection to the site from which it was downloaded, and provides access to a limited number of files in a directory that is private to the Tclet. Files in this directory persist after the Tclet exits, so providing a way of maintaining long-term state. The Tclet is also allowed access to the browser package, so it can, among other things
  - display a message in the browser status bar

    ```
    ::browser::status "Tclet calling!"
    ```

  - fetch the contents of a URL from the host from which it was loaded:

    ```
    ::browser::getURL "www.somesite.com/index.htm"
    ```

    (::browser::getURL is compatible with ::http::getURL, described in Chapter 5.)
  - display the contents of a URL from the host from which it was loaded in a frame:

    ```
    ::browser::displayURL \
      "www.somesite.com/index.htm" _blank
    ```

    or

    ```
    ::browser::displayURL \
      "www.somesite.com/index.htm" _self
    ```

    (The first of these displays the contents of the URL in a new top-level frame, the second replaces the contents of the frame containing the Tclet with the contents of the new URL.)
- inside. This policy extends the home policy by allowing socket connections to systems inside the firewall, listed in a table of hosts and ports set up by the system administrator. A similar table controls the hosts from which URLs can be downloaded.
- outside. This policy is like inside, except that network connections are only allowed to hosts outside the firewall, controlled by tables set up by the system administrator.
- javascript. This policy allows the applet to execute arbitrary JavaScript programs, to write arbitrary HTML streams into frames, and to send e-mail messages to arbitrary recipients. It does not place any limitations on file, socket and URL access: it is highly dangerous.
- trusted. This policy restores all the facilities of Tcl and Tk.

If a Tclet wants to use a non-default safety policy, it requests it by a command at the start of the code, e.g.

```
policy home
```

The plugin then consults the permission list (sometimes called the trust map) set up by the user or the site administrator. This defines one of three options for each policy:

- No Tclets can use the policy
- All Tclets can use the policy
- Only Tclets whose URL matches an entry in an allowed list can use the policy.

(Not surprisingly, the default trust map does not allow any Tclet to use the `javascript` or `trusted` policies.) It is expected that a later version of the plugin will allow certificate-based authentication of Tclets.

11.2 Active Server Pages

In the early days, a Web page was a static file of HTML, held on a server: on request, the server would send this text file to the browser, which would then render it as defined by the HTML tags. Nowadays, many Web pages are generated dynamically 'on the fly', taking information from one or more databases and building an HTML file to be sent to the browser. This technique is particularly appropriate if the pages contain information which changes frequently: changes can be made once in the database, and will automatically be reflected in all the HTML pages built from that database.

Initially, this dynamic activity was implemented using the Common Gateway Interface (CGI), but much more flexibility can be achieved by using server-side scripts to build the HTML pages. Most Web servers provide this capability in one form or another: the most advanced realization of the concept is almost certainly Microsoft's *Active Server Pages*. This technology originated in the Microsoft Internet Information Server (IIS) which is built in to Windows NT Server, but is now being ported by third parties to other Web servers: at the time of writing *OpenASP* is available for the Apache server running on Windows NT (with versions for Linux and Sun Solaris promised), and for Netscape Enterprise and FastTrack servers under Windows NT, Sun Solaris and Linux. (A functionally equivalent Open Source product has recently been announced, called PHP.)

In an Active Server Page, scripts written in JavaScript or VBScript (or any other language for which a scripting engine has been installed, e.g. PerlScript) can be run on the server: these may perform relatively simple actions, e.g. interpolating user-dependent information, or they may perform complex operations using non-visual ActiveX controls, e.g. to access a SQL database. (Netscape's 'Enterprise Server' provides similar capability in the form of server-side JavaScript and server-side applets.) When the IIS server receives a request for an active server page, recognized by the `.asp` extension, it scans the page looking for server-side scripts: any such scripts are run, and the HTML they generate is placed in the page, replacing the script. When all the scripts have been processed, the resulting HTML is sent to the browser. Note that this HTML may include client-side scripts to be run on the browser: a judicious mix of server-side and client-side scripting can be very powerful. (We note in passing that incorporating server-side and client-side scripts in the page displays a certain conceptual elegance.)

11.2.1 Incorporating server-side scripts

A server-side script is defined by setting the `RUNAT` attribute in the `<SCRIPT>` tag, e.g.

```
<SCRIPT LANGUAGE="VBScript" RUNAT="SERVER">
...
</SCRIPT>
```

More commonly, server-side scripts are enclosed in delimiters `<%` and `%>`, e.g.

```
<%
LastName = Request.Form("LastName")
%>
```

(As we shall see later, the server-side object model provides a `Request` object, one of whose properties is a `Form` collection containing the data entered in a form and sent by the POST method.) The above code has exactly the same effect as

```
<SCRIPT LANGUAGE="VBScript" RUNAT="SERVER>
   LastName = Request.Form("LastName")
</SCRIPT>
```

The default language for scripts embedded in this way is set by a directive at the start of the page, thus

```
<%@LANGUAGE="VBSript%>
```

The additional power of the 'delimiter' syntax is illustrated in the next example. Suppose an Active Server Page includes a fragment

```
<%For i = 1 To 6%>
<P>This is a pointless exercise</P>
<%Next i%>
```

The HTML page sent to the browser will contain at this point

```
<P>This is a pointless exercise</P>
<P>This is a pointless exercise</P>
<P>This is a pointless exercise</P>
<P>This is a pointless exercise</P>
<P>This is a pointless exercise</P>
<P>This is a pointless exercise</P>
```

This happens because when an Active Server Page is being processed, anything that is not part of a script is copied directly into the target HTML page. Thus the loop starts, setting the value of i to 1, the first instance of the paragraph is written, then the `Next i` script statement causes the processor to back up to the line following the `For` statement; this is repeated until i reaches the value 6, at which point the line following the `Next i` statement is examined.

A useful extension of this notation is that the value of a variable can be placed in the script by placing the variable name between the delimiters `<%=` and `%>`, thus if the variable `Now` contains the current date as a string, a document can be date-stamped thus:

```
<P>This document generated: <%=Now%></P>
```

11.2.2 Applications and sessions

Before describing the server-side object model we need to explain the concepts of applications and sessions. The HTTP protocol is stateless: having delivered a page in response to a request from a browser, the server drops the connection and loses all memory of the request. The ASP model, however, incorporates the concept of a browser *session*, in which the browser remains connected to an *application*. An ASP application is a collection of related pages and other resources, held in a single virtual directory: a shopping cart is a good example. An inactive application is started when the first user requests the front page: at that time a session is started for the user. Subsequent users each have their own session, and the application terminates when there are no active sessions. The end of a session is determined on a timeout basis, typically no user activity over a period of 20 minutes.

Application and session start and end are defined as events in the object model, and can thus be hooked by scripts. This is commonly used to establish global variables for the application, and session variables for each session.

11.2.3   The server-side object model

The object model provides objects to represent the application, the session, the HTTP request, the response (i.e. the HTML to be generated by the script), and a server object which is a catch-all to provide a number of useful methods for the developer.

The application object

The application object is used to store *application variables* – information that persists for the whole lifetime of an application (usually the whole time that the IIS server is running, but strictly until the onEnd event is raised), and which is common to all users, e.g. a page counter, or the time of the last visit to a page. If an application variable Time records the time of the last visit, this can be inserted into the page being created with

```
Last visited on <%=Application("Time")%>
```

In JavaScript this presents no problems – an object is the same thing as an associative array. But how does this work in VBScript? The answer is that in VBScript, the Application object has a hidden property which is set as the default property for the object: the value of this hidden property is a Collection object. Thus Application("Time") is seen as a reference to the hidden property, and since the default method for a collection object is Item, the reference resolves to

```
Application.HiddenProperty.Item("Time")
```

A new application variable is created by using a new name in an assignment, e.g.

```
<%Application("Time") = Now%>
```

In JavaScript this is again straightforward: it is just a case of adding a new property at run-time. Using the same syntax in VBScript, which does not have the capability to add new properties dynamically, involves a bit of chicanery: the hidden property is still the default property of the Application object, but in this particular situation, the default method for the collection item so referenced mysteriously becomes Add.

Because the `Application` object is visible to all sessions, it is possible that two users might attempt to set a particular application variable at the same time. To control this, the `Application` object has two methods, `Lock` and `Unlock`, used as follows:

```
<%Application.Lock%>
<%Application("Time") = Now%>
<%Aplication.Unlock%>
```

Note that the `Lock` method locks the entire `Application` object, not just the variable being set.

As noted earlier, the `Application` object has two events, `onStart` and `onEnd`, which can be used for initialization and clean-up. Event handlers for these events are placed in a special file called `GLOBAL.ASA`, e.g.

```
<SCRIPT LANGUAGE="VBScript" RUNAT="SERVER">
Sub Application_onStart
...
End Sub
Sub Application_onEnd
...
End Sub
</SCRIPT>
```

The Session object

The `Session` object provides session variables which behave like application variables but are local to the session, and disappear when the session terminates. When a session starts, the client is sent a cookie containing a GUID (globally unique identifier) to identify the session, and can later use this to retrieve session variables stored by the server. This identifier can be accessed as the `SessionID` property of the `Session` object.

Like the `Application` object, the `Session` object has two events, `onStart` and `onEnd`, which can be used for initialization and clean-up: handlers for these events can be placed in the `GLOBAL.ASA` file. It also has a method `Abandon`, which immediately terminates the session.

The Request object

We have seen earlier that when a form is submitted to a Web server, the data supplied by the user is packaged into a string of the form

```
name=value&name=value&name=value ...
```

Here `name` is the name of a field in the form (set as the value of a `NAME` attribute), and `value` is the value typed in by the user. In earlier chapters we saw how such a string could be parsed using regular expressions. When form data is submitted to an Active Server Page, explicit parsing is not required: instead the values are placed in a collection object, indexed by the corresponding name: this collection is the `Form` property of the `Request` object. Thus if a form has a text element called `Part_No`, the value submitted can be retrieved by

```
<%=Request.Form("Part_No")%>
```

The request object provides access to cookies in a similar way, and can be used to retrieve server environment variables: for example,

```
<%=Request.ServerVariables("HTTP_USER_AGENT")%>
```

retrieves the user agent string of the client browser.

The Response object

The `Response` object controls the content returned to the browser: in particular, it has a `Write` method which places HTML text in the page to be sent. The `<%=` notation that we have been using is in fact just a shorthand:

```
<%=stuff%>
```

is equivalent to

```
<%Response.Write stuff%>
```

When pages are being generated on the fly, undesired effects can occur if a previous version of the page is stored in the browser's memory cache. To avoid this, the `Response` object's `Expires` property can be set to zero thus

```
<%Response.Expires = 0%>
```

This ensures that the page is never cached. The `Response` object has many other properties; for example, the content type of the response can be set:

```
<%Response.ContentType = "text/html"%>
```

The Server object

The `Server` object provides a number of unrelated functions that are useful to a developer. The most important of these is `CreateObject()`, which is used to create instances of ActiveX controls, as discussed in the next section.

11.2.4 ASP components

An Active Server Page can utilize any non-visual ActiveX control: such a control is instantiated using the `CreateObject` method of the `Server` object. 'ASP components' are ActiveX controls provided by Microsoft that perform commonly required operations: we review some of these components here to convey the general flavour.

Database access component

The database access component is in fact the ActiveX Data Object (ADO) that was mentioned briefly in Chapter 9. ADO is a COM wrapper for the 'OLE DB' technology which allows you to connect to any database for which there is an ODBC driver. A detailed account is beyond the scope of this section, but a short example may illustrate the basic principles.

```
<%
dim adoConnection
dim adoRecordSet
set adoConnection = _
  Server.CreateObject("ADODB.Connection")
set adoRecordSet = _
  server.CreateObject("ADODB.Recordset")
adoConnection.Open "StudentRecords"
adoRecordSet.ActiveConnection = _
  adoConnection
...
%>
```

Here we have created a `Connection` object and a `Recordset` object. We call the `Open` method of the `Connection` object, specifying a particular database, and we then define this as the 'active connection' for the `Recordset` object. We can then access the database using the methods of the `Recordset` object.

Browser capabilities component

The browser capabilities component allows a script to access a list of features supported by the browser, e.g. does it support cookies? This list is constructed by the Web page designer, and is held in a simple text file `BrowseCap.ini`. Evidently, this is of great use when building browser-independent Web sites.

File access component

The file access component allows access to text files on the server using the `FileSystemObject` object and the `TextStream` object: see Chapter 14 for a full account of this form of file access.

Dictionary component

The dictionary component provides the same dictionary facilities as are provided in the Microsoft Scripting Runtime Library, described in Chapter 15.

## Chapter 12

Dynamic HTML and the DOM

The major use of JavaScript and VBScript is in client-side Web scripting, and the possibilities are greatly enhanced by Dynamic HTML (DHTML). This chapter explores the ways in which the scripting languages interact with Microsoft's version of DHTML, but does not attempt to give a full account of the facilities provided by DHTML. We also give a brief account of the Web Consortium's Document Object Model (DOM), and its relation to scripting languages

12.1 From HTML to Dynamic HTML

When the World Wide Web was first conceived its philosophy was one of strict separation of content and presentation. The server provided the content, marked up with HTML tags to indicate the intended purpose of each element – heading, paragraph, list element etc. Presentation was entirely the responsibility of the browser. Subject only to pre-set user preferences, the browser decided how the content would be rendered, the fonts to be used, the positioning of elements, and all other visual aspects.

This philosophy had the great advantage that the content was totally independent of the browser: any browser could be used, and could render any page that conformed to the then current version of HTML. However, as the Web developed, and moved away from its origins in the scientific community, authors of Web pages began to demand control over appearance. The initial response of Netscape, which was at the time the dominant supplier of browsers, was to bastardize HTML by introducing new tags whose purpose was to control rendering, the infamous <BLINK> tag being an extreme example. As Microsoft moved into the market, 'browser wars' developed, with incompatible extensions to HTML being introduced by both parties. The World Wide Web Consortium (W3C), the body established to set standards for the Web, played 'catch-up', releasing versions of HTML that included most of the extensions already present in the Navigator and Explorer browsers, and HTML 3.2 established a broad compatibility. When W3C introduced Cascading Style Sheets (CSS), both Microsoft and Netscape implemented the proposal in their browsers, though Netscape also introduced an incompatible version called 'JavaScript style sheets', described below.

Continuing pressure from users for more control over presentation caused a break in this consensus. Netscape broke ranks with a proposal for absolute and relative positioning of content elements based on a proprietary technology called 'layers', while Microsoft adopted the W3C's draft proposal for positioned content, CSS-P. (As a compromise, Navigator accepts CSS-P syntax for positioned content, but the underlying scriptable object remains the layer.) The split became even wider with the introduction of 'Dynamic HTML', a term used with completely different meanings by Microsoft and Netscape. W3C is attempting to bridge the gap with HTML 4 and the Document Object Model (DOM) currently under development. However, although the protagonists have committed themselves to implementing the new proposals, there is no time scale for this: for the present the battle for market share based on incompatibility continues.

12.2   Dynamic HTML

Netscape Navigator 2 was the first browser to introduce a scriptable object model, with an accompanying scripting language – LiveScript, renamed JavaScript – built into the browser. Microsoft adopted the object model and scripting language in Internet Explorer 3, also adding support for VBScript as an alternative scripting language. This object model and its use have been covered in the previous chapter. When the next generation of browsers (Navigator 4 and Internet Explorer 4) appeared on the scene, both claimed to implement a technology they called Dynamic HTML (DHTML). Although our purpose in this chapter is to explore the interaction between DHTML and scripting languages, rather than giving an account of all the facilities provided by DHTML, some background is required.

Dynamic HTML is a term that is used to describe a collection of technologies that reconcile the need for author control of appearance with the separation of content and presentation, and allow the designer to produce pages which incorporate dynamic interaction with the user. It has four main components:

- Cascading style sheets (CSS) allowing author-defined presentation preferences to be attached to elements of an HTML document
- Provision for absolute and relative positioning of document content
- Exposing HTML elements as scriptable objects whose properties can be interrogated and changed by scripts, and methods which can be invoked by scripts
- Dynamic user interaction by allowing scripts to be invoked in response to user events such as mouse clicks and movements, and browser events, e.g. page load.

From the point of view of scripting languages, we are only directly concerned with the third and fourth components listed above. However, the other components are relevant, since positioned content elements have corresponding scriptable objects in both browsers; styles are scriptable in the Microsoft document object model, and Netscape allows style sheets to be written in JavaScript as an alternative to the CSS syntax.

12.3   Document object models

The scriptable objects exposed by DHTML come under the `document` element of the object model presented in Section 11.1.4, and are described by the *document object model*. As we have already observed, Netscape and Microsoft implement very different versions of DHTML, with Microsoft's implementation being by far the more powerful: this reflects the richness of the Microsoft DOM, compared with the Netscape model.

A DOM serves two purposes:

- It provides a 'road map' of the hierarchy of scriptable objects in the currently displayed document. This hierarchy is rooted in the `document` object, which is itself a property of a `window` object representing the top-level window or a member of the `frames[]` array.
- For each scriptable object it defines the properties and methods associated with that object, and the events to which it can respond.

In the following sections we will briefly describe the DOMs used in Navigator 4 and Internet Explorer 4, and give a short account of the work of W3C towards a vendor- and language-independent document object model.

12.4   The Netscape document object model

The basic Netscape DOM was described in the previous chapter, and for convenience the main features are recapitulated here.

The `document` object has methods, including `write()`, which writes text into the page being displayed, and properties that represent the appearance of the document, e.g. its background colour. A further set of properties represent the contents of the document, including:

- `anchors[]`: an array of `anchor` objects, one for each anchor in the document
- `forms[]`: an array of `form` objects, one for each form in the document
- `images[]`: an array of `image` objects, one for each image in the document
- `links[]`: an array of `link` objects, one for each link in the document.

If images and forms are given names, using the `name` attribute, the name is exposed as a property of the document object e.g. `document.Form1`.

The important part of a `form` object is the `elements[]` array, which is an array of objects representing the component parts of the form – buttons, checkboxes etc. The name assigned to an element becomes a property of the form object, thus a button named `btn1` in a form named `myform` can be referenced as `document.myform.btn1`.

This model provides limited scope for user interaction by scripting. The background colour can be set as part of the page load operation, but once a page has been loaded there is restricted scope for changing its appearance: form elements (e.g. text on buttons or in a textbox) can be changed, and an image can be replaced by another *of the same size*.

When Navigator was extended to provide positioned content, the basic model was enhanced by the provision of objects to represent that content, as described later.

12.4.1   Styles and stylesheets

In the same way that we can centre text using the `align` attribute, e.g.

```
<P align="center">
Paragraph of centred text
</P>
```

we can attach a 'style' to a particular paragraph, e.g.

```
<P style="color:red; font-style:italic">
Paragraph of red, italicized text
</P>
```

Styles can be assigned to most elements in this way. However, it is more common to collect style definitions in a style sheet, placed in the <HEAD> element, that applies to an entire document, e.g.

```
<HEAD>
<TITLE> ... </TITLE>
<STYLE type="text/css">
H1 {color:red; }
H2 {color:blue; font-style: italic}
</STYLE>
</HEAD>
```

This specifies that first-level headings are to appear in red, while second-level headings will be in blue italic.

These settings are reflected in the tags property of the document object, thus document.tags.H1.color will have the value "red". We can assign values, e.g.

```
document.tags.H1.color = "green";
```

but this is of limited utility, since Navigator will not change the colour of headings already displayed on the page. Thus we could achieve the effect of the style sheet used above with a script in the <HEAD> element:

```
<HEAD>
<TITLE ... </TITLE>
<SCRIPT language="JavaScript">
document.tags.H1.color = "red";
document.tags.H2.color = "blue";
document.tags.H2.fontStyle = "italic";
</SCRIPT>
</HEAD>
```

Note that the CSS attribute font-style has become fontStyle in the JavaScript code, because names in JavaScript cannot include hyphens.

Navigator offers a more convenient way of doing this, the 'JavaScript Style Sheet', which takes the form

```
<STYLE type="text/JavaScript">
...
</STYLE>
```

JavaScript code enclosed between the tags is executed in the scope of the document object, i.e. with the document object in the scope chain before the window object. Thus our simple example can be written as

```
<HEAD>
<TITLE ... </TITLE>
<STYLE type="text/JavaScript">
tags.h1.color = "red";
tags.h2.color = "blue";
tags.h2.fontStyle = "italic";
</SCRIPT>
</HEAD>
```

In this simple case the CSS syntax is easier to use: JavaScript style sheets are useful only if elements of the style are to be determined by some computation.

Other components of CSS style sheets are mapped in a similar way. For example CSS allows us to define different 'classes' for elements. For example, if some first-level headings are to be capitalized, we might modify the style sheet as follows:

```
<HEAD>
<TITLE> ... </TITLE>
<STYLE type="text/css">
H1 {color:red; }
H1.ALLCAPS {text-transform: uppercase}
H2 {color:blue; font-style: italic}
</STYLE>
</HEAD>
```

We could then create a capitalized heading with

```
<H1 class="ALLCAPS"> ... </H1>
```

The object model includes a classes property that can be used to provide a JavaScript equivalent to this CSS syntax, e.g.

```
<STYLE type="text/JavaScript">
tags.h1.color = "red";
tags.h2.color = "blue";
tags.h2.fontStyle = "italic";
classes.ALLCAPS.H1.textTransform = "uppercase";
</SCRIPT>
```

A CSS class introduced with a leading dot and no preceding element name becomes a 'global' class that can be applied to any appropriate element, thus if our CSS style sheet included the rule

```
.ALLCAPS {text-transform: uppercase}
```

we could create a capitalized paragraph with

```
<P class="ALLCAPS">
...
</P>
```

In the JavaScript equivalent we use the selector `all` in place of a particular element name, e.g.

```
classes.ALLCAPS.all.textTransform =
"uppercase";
```

To complete the picture, CSS style sheets can include rules that are to apply only to an element with a specific identifier, e.g.

```
#special {text-align: center; color: red}
```

This rule will apply only to an identified element, e.g.

```
<P ID="special">
...
</P>
```

This is mirrored in JavaScript by the `ids` property of the document object: within a JavaScript style sheet we would express the rule as

```
ids.special.textAlign = "center";
ids.special.color = "red";
```

12.4.2   Positioned content

Navigator's implementation of positioned content is based on a proprietary technology using so-called *layers*, which are introduced by Navigator-specific `<LAYER>` and `<ILAYER>` elements in the HTML page. Although current versions of the browser allow the use of the CSS-P notation according to the recommendations of the World Wide Web Consortium (W3C), Navigator always implements positioning using layers, so scripting has to be done using the `layer` object, which mirrors the `<LAYER>` and `<ILAYER>` elements. An example is given later.

Layers

A layer can be thought of as a transparent sheet containing content, which can be provided between the start and end tags, or loaded from a separate file. The `<LAYER>` tag has attributes to specify the size and absolute position (as offsets from the left and top edges of the document), e.g.

```
<LAYER width=200 height=100 left=50 top=40>
...
</LAYER>
```

The `<ILAYER>` tag introduces a layer whose position is determined relative to the current flow of text in the page, rather than to the edges of the document display.

Layers can be stacked vertically to provide overlapping content: the stacking can be absolute or relative. The value of the Z-INDEX attribute in the <LAYER> tag specifies an absolute position in the vertical ordering of elements: alternatively, layers can be named using the ID attribute, and then positioned ABOVE or BELOW another named layer, e.g.

```
<LAYER ID="L1" width=200 height=100
  left=50 top=40 >
...
</LAYER>
<LAYER ID="L2" ABOVE="L1" width=100 height=50
  left=5 top=4 >
...
</LAYER>
```

Another useful attribute of a <LAYER> is VISIBILITY: if this is given the value "hidden", the layer will not be displayed when it loads, though it retains its position in the vertical stacking order. It can later be made visible by a script.

Layers in the object model

The object model is extended to include a layer object and a layers[] array – an array of references to layer objects – in the document object. Like images and frames, a layer can be referenced via the array using a numerical index, or as an associative array using the value of the ID attribute as a key. Most usually, layers are addressed by their ID, since like the name of a form or image, the ID of a layer becomes a property of the document object. Thus the layers in the HTML fragment above can be addressed in the object model as

```
document.layers[0] and document.layers[1]
```

or

```
document.layers['L1'] and document.layers['L2']
```

or

```
document.L1 and document.L2
```

It is *very important* to note that the content of a layer is represented by a document object. Thus if layer L1 contains a form Form1, it is referenced by a full hierarchic path, i.e. document.L1.document.Form1.

In technical articles, Netscape try to play down the layer nomenclature nowadays: an object that mirrors a <LAYER> element, such as document.L1 in the example above, is described as a 'Positioned HTML Element Object' (also known as a 'JavaScript Layer object'). However, you still have to use the word layers in your code if you want to access the array.

The layer object has properties that reflect the attributes of the <LAYER> tag, including top, left, z-index and hidden, so that it is possible for a script to move a layer, change its vertical stacking order, and control its visibility. For convenience, a number of methods are provided for manipulating layers as an alternative to setting values for top and left:

- `moveTo(x,y)` and `moveToAbsolute(x,y)`. Move a layer to a specified location. For a layer that is nested inside another layer, `moveTo()` uses the coordinate system of the containing layer, `moveToAbsolute()` uses page coordinates. For non-nested layers, the two methods are equivalent.
- `moveBy(dx,dy)`. Move a layer by a specified number of pixels (can be negative).
- `moveAbove(l)` and `moveBelow(l)`. Change vertical stacking order: l references another layer.

The width and height of the layer do not appear as properties, but the size can be changed by methods:

- `resizeTo(x,y)`. Set size to absolute values
- `resizeBy(dx,dy)`. Incremental change of size (can be negative).

The content of a layer can be changed by the `load()` method. (Note that layers use a method of the `layer` object, whereas for images you assign to the `src` property of the `image` object.)

As noted at the start of this section, current versions of Navigator recognize the CSS-P syntax for positioned content, e.g.

```
<SPAN style="position:absolute; left:100; top:50;
 width=100 height=75">
<IMG name="logo" src="logo.jpg">
</SPAN>
```

However, the object that mirrors an element defined in this way is a 'positioned content object', i.e. a `layer` object.

12.5 The Microsoft document object model

Unlike Navigator, Internet Explorer can re-flow a page in response to changes easily and quickly, and the Microsoft document model therefore exposes *all* the HTML elements of a page as scriptable objects. Every object representing an HTML element contains an object `all`, which is a collection of objects mirroring the elements nested within that element. Thus `document.all` is a collection of all the nested elements contained within the document. All elements have an optional `ID` attribute that can be used to assign a unique identifier to the element, and this identifier is used to index the `all` collection. Thus if we have an element

```
<someTAG ID="A26" att1="foo" att2="bar">
...
</someTAG>
```

the element will be mirrored by an object that can be referenced in the `all` collection as `document.all.A26`, and the other attributes are accessible as properties of that object, e.g.

```
document.all.A26.att1 = "foobar";
```

The object model offers an alternative to using the ID attribute to identify an element. All objects mirroring elements with a particular tag, e.g. <P>, are placed in a collection, which can be accessed using the tags() method of an all object, thus we can visit all paragraph objects with a loop of the form

```
var paras = document.all.tags("P");
var n = paras.length
for (j=0; j<n; j++) {
    ... // process paras[j]
}
```

Although the object model provides potential access to every attribute of every tag, in practice DHTML is concerned with the appearance of the page, and the main concern in scripting such pages lies in manipulating styles and positions. We explore the possibilities in the following sections.

12.5.1 Styles and stylesheets

Inline styles

Almost every HTML element can have its style specified as the value of the STYLE attribute. The object model mirrors such an 'inline style' as a style object, thus if we have a paragraph with an inline style, e.g.

```
<P ID="abstract" STYLE="color:red font-style:italic">
...
</P>
```

we can access its style object as document.all.abstract.style, and we could, for example, change the text colour in a script:

```
document.all.abstract.style.color = "yellow";
```

The style object has more than 80 properties representing the aspects of appearance that can be specified in CSS: as in Navigator, CSS properties which are hyphenated, e.g. font-style, are represented in the object model using 'interCap' names, e.g. fontStyle. Another useful property of the style object is cssText: the value of this is the string that was assigned as the value of the STYLE attribute. This property is read/write, so it is possible to set an inline style dynamically: we can give paragraph P2 the same style as P1 with

```
document.all.P2.style.cssText =
document.all.P1.style.cssText;
```

The style object represents the aspects of the style set via the STYLE attribute, not those aspects inherited from a global style sheet. However, it is possible to assign a value to a property of the style object corresponding to a feature set in the style sheet: the local assignment will take effect, in the same way that an inline style overrides a global style in the CSS model. An effective way of changing several aspects of an element's style at the same time is to define two or more classes in the style sheet, and then to use a script to change the CLASS attribute of the element from a script.

Style sheets

Style sheets are defined by a <STYLE> element in HTML, and each such element is mirrored in the document.all collection by a STYLE object (note the capitalization). However, style sheets are scripted using the styleSheet object: the object model includes a collection of these objects, styleSheets[], as a property of the document object: the collection mirrors the style sheets defined in <STYLE> elements. Having assigned an identifier e.g.

```
<STYLE ID="bodytext" TYPE="text/css">
...
</STYLE>
```

it is possible to reference the associated styleSheet object as document.style-Sheets["bodytext"].

From the point of view of dynamic behaviour, the most important features of the styleSheet object are the disabled property and the addRule() method. By setting disabled to true, e.g.

```
document.styleSheets["bodytext"].disabled = true;
```

the whole style sheet can be 'turned off'. This provides an effective way of providing multiple views of a document, by providing several style sheets and disabling all except one.

The styleSheet object includes a collection, rules[], which contains the rules comprising the style sheet. However, the only way to add new rules is by invoking the addRule() method. Thus if we want to extend our 'bodytext' style by adding a rule to say that bold text is to be rendered in blue, we would write

```
var s, ss;
ss = document.styleSheets["bodytext"];
s = ss.addRule("B", "color: blue");
```

(The addRule() method returns a value which is of no further interest to us, so it is assigned to s and forgotten.) By default, the new rule is added at the end of the style sheet. The rules of cascading make it override an existing rule for the same element in the style sheet. If this behaviour is not what is required, the position at which the rule should be inserted in the rules[] collection can be specified by a third argument to addRule(), thus

```
s = ss.addRule("B", "color: blue", 0);
```

will add the new rule at the beginning of the style sheet.

12.5.2 Positioned content

The Microsoft DOM provides a direct modelling of CSS-P syntax. Thus if we set up an element of positioned content, e.g.

```
<DIV ID="companylogo"
 style="position:absolute; left:100; top:50;
 width=100 height=75">
<IMG name="logo" src="logo.jpg">
</DIV>
```

the coordinates and size appear as properties of the `style` object that mirrors the HTML element. Thus to move the logo 50 pixels to the right from its initial position we would write

```
document.all.companylogo.style.left = "150px";
```

Note that the value assigned to `left` is a *string* containing a numerical value and a unit of measure. The same is true of the `top`, `width` and `height` properties. If it is required to perform calculations involving the position or size of an element, these properties are inappropriate. Instead we use a different set of properties:

- `pixelLeft, pixelTop, pixelHeight, pixelWidth`: numerical values in pixels
- `posLeft, posTop, posHeight, posWidth`: numerical values in the current unit of measure.

As an illustration of scripting positioned content, we present the code to centre the 'companylogo' element in the browser window.

```
var W, H; //Window width and height
var w, h; //logo width and height
var l, t; //left and top coordinates of image
var logo = document.all.companylogo;
W = document.body.clientWidth;
H = document.body.clientHeight;
w = logo.style.pixelWidth;
h = logo.style.pixelHeight;
l = Math.round(W/2-w/2);
t = Math.round(H/2-h/2);
logo.style.pixelLeft = l;
logo.style.pixelHeight = t;
```

12.5.3 Text content

In addition to making all HTML elements scriptable by providing objects to mirror them, the Microsoft DOM allows a substantial degree of control over the actual content of elements that hold text.

Inner and outer components

Suppose we have a simple paragraph:

```
<P ID="P1">
The quick brown fox jumps over the lazy dog
</P>
```

The *inner component* of this element is the character string enclosed between the `<P>` and `</P>` tags: the *outer component* comprises the whole text, i.e. the actual text and the enclosing tags.

Replacing text content

The object that mirrors this paragraph, `document.all.P1`, has four properties that reflect the text: `innerText`, `innerHTML`, `outerText` and `outerHTML`. The value of the `inner...` properties is the *inner* component of the element, and the value of the `outer...` properties is the *outer* component. The difference between the `...text` and `...HTML` properties is significant when new values are assigned. If we assign a string as the value of `innerText` it is assigned 'as-is': if we assign a string as the value of `innerHTML`, any HTML tags in the string will be recognized and the text rendered accordingly. The same is true for the `outer...` properties: `outerText` is assigned as-is, `outerHTML` recognizes HTML tags. Using these properties gives us complete control over text content, and by assigning to `outerText` or `outerHTML` we can completely change an element, e.g.

```
var para = document.all.P1;
para.outerHTML = "<H1>" + para.innerText +
"</H1>;
```

changes a paragraph into a first-level heading. (Note, however, that we cannot assign to these properties until the document is fully loaded.)

Changing text content

In addition to replacing text completely, we can add additional text using methods that are provided for every object that mirrors a text-containing element: `insertAdjacent-Text()` and `insertAdjacentHTML()`. These methods take two arguments. The first argument is a string defining the insertion point: possible values are `BeforeBegin` (before opening tag), `AfterBegin` (just after the opening tag), `BeforeEnd` (immediately before the closing tag) and `AfterEnd` (after the closing tag). The second argument is the text to be inserted.

The TextRange object

Extremely complex effects can be obtained using the `TextRange` object. This is really beyond the scope of a book on scripting languages, but we give a flavour of the possibilities with a simple example. The following fragment will search the body of a page until it finds an occurrence of the string that is held in the variable searchString: it will then scroll the page to bring the matching text into view, select the sentence in which it occurs, and cut it to the clipboard. (The code as written here assumes that the text in searchString occurs as part of a sentence in the page. Real-life code would include checks that this was indeed the case.)

```
var range = document.body.createTextRange();
range.findText(searchString);
range.expand("sentence");
range.scrollIntoView;
range.select();
range.execCommand("Cut");
```

12.6 The W3C document object model (DOM)

The W3C (World Wide Web Consortium) frequently finds itself in the position of trying to reconcile the Microsoft and Netscape approaches to HTML and the Web. When the differing versions of DHTML first appeared, W3C proposed a 'Document Object Model Level 0', which was little more than a codification of the overlapping parts of the Microsoft and Netscape models. Subsequently, a much more elaborate project was initiated to develop a comprehensive document object model. The current W3C DOM is described in the following terms:

> The Document Object Model Level 1 is a platform- and language-neutral interface that allows programs and scripts to dynamically access and update the content, structure and style of documents. The Document Object Model provides a standard set of objects for representing HTML and XML documents, a standard model of how these objects can be combined, and a standard interface for accessing and manipulating them. Vendors can support the DOM as an interface to their proprietary data structures and APIs, and content authors can write to the standard DOM interfaces rather than product-specific APIs, thus increasing interoperability on the Web . . . The goal of the DOM specification is to define a programmatic interface for XML and HTML.

The DOM is intended ultimately to be a comprehensive model incorporating not only the HTML elements but also the actual content. It is language-neutral in that the document elements are defined using an *Interface Definition Language* (IDL) – actually, the CORBA IDL – with separate sets of bindings from IDL to programming languages. Thus with a suitable set of bindings, a document conforming to the DOM could be manipulated by programs in a variety of languages. At the time of writing, bindings to Java and JavaScript have been defined.

DOM Level 1, recently issued as a W3C recommendation, is divided into two parts: Core and HTML. The Core DOM Level 1 section provides a low-level set of fundamental interfaces that can represent any structured document. The HTML Level 1 section provides additional, higher-level interfaces that are used with the fundamental interfaces defined in the Core Level 1 section to provide a more convenient view of an HTML document. The current situation is that the DOM Level 1 contains functionality for document navigation and manipulation, but style sheet functionality will not be available until Level 2. More elaborate features such as events will not be supported until even higher levels. Clearly, it will be some time before the W3C DOM impinges on client-side scripting, and we therefore concentrate on current Microsoft and Netscape technology in the remainder of this chapter.

12.7 The event model

Many of the scriptable objects that comprise the DOM can be made to respond to *events* such as user actions, e.g. mouse clicks and movements, and changes in browser status, e.g. loading or unloading of a page. The document object model specifies the events that will be recognized by each object. The page author can associate an *event handler* with any recognized event: this is a script (in JavaScript for Navigator; in any supported scripting language in Internet Explorer), which is obeyed whenever the corresponding event occurs. There is a convention for naming event handlers: the name is formed by prefixing 'on' to the event name, thus the 'Click' event has an event handler called 'onClick'.

12.7.1 Binding event handlers to elements

The event handler code has to be associated with the particular HTML element to which it applies: we describe this operation as 'binding'. The most common way of doing this is in HTML, as illustrated in Sections 11.2.2 and 11.2.3. The names of the event handlers that an object recognizes can be used as attribute names in the opening tag of the corresponding HTML element, and the event handler code is given, as a string, as the value of the attribute, e.g.

```
<INPUT type=button name="myBtn1" value="OK"
 onClick="...">
```

or

```
<INPUT type=button name="myBtn1" value="OK"
 onClick="..." language="VBScript">
```

Alternatively, Internet Explorer provides an alternative syntax for associating VBScript event handlers and elements in HTML:

```
<INPUT type=button name="myBtn1" value="OK"
<SCRIPT language="VBScript" for="myBtn1"
 event=onClick>
 ... ' VBScript code
</SCRIPT
```

and VBScript provides yet another way of making the association:

```
<SCRIPT language="VBScript">
Sub myBtn1_onclick
...
End Sub
</SCRIPT>
```

If we are using JavaScript, assigning a value to an event handler attribute in a tag, e.g. onClick="..." creates an anonymous function and assigns it as a property in the associated object with the same name (in lower case). Alternatively, the binding of the event handler to the element can be achieved dynamically, outside the HTML tags, by making the event handler a function with no arguments, then assigning this as a property of the appropriate object, e.g.

```
document.forms[0].myBtn1.onclick =
    function() {...};
```

Note particularly that the event name is in lower case: the mixed-case form used in HTML tags, e.g. onClick, is just a convention – HTML is not case-sensitive. In Internet Explorer 4 this explicit assignment can only be used in JavaScript, since it involves assigning a function. VBScript 5 provides this capability through a function GetRef(), which returns a reference to a procedure. Thus if an event handler has been defined as a procedure, e.g.

```
Sub myBtnClick
...
End Sub
```

we can associate it with the object in a similar way to the JavaScript example:

```
document.forms[0].myBtn1.onclick = _
    GetRef("MyBtnClick")
```

An attraction of this approach is that it leads to cleaner code, since event handler code is not mixed in with HTML tags. It also offers a way of changing the event handler associated with an element dynamically. In the following example, we define a button that can be pressed only twice, with different effects: subsequent presses have no effect. Note that this example, like all subsequent examples in this section, uses JavaScript.

Execute code for first press then assign a different event handler.

Execute code for second press then assign a null event handler.

```
<head>
<title>test</title>
<script language="JavaScript">
function FirstPress() {
... //code for first press
document.forms[0].B1.value = "Continue";
document.forms[0].B1.onclick = SecondPress;
}

function SecondPress() {
... // code for second press
document.forms[0].B1.value = "";
document.forms[0].B1.onclick =
function() {return true};
}
</script>
</head>
<body>
<form>
```

```
<input type=button name="B1" value="Start">
<script language="JavaScript">
document.forms[0].B1.onclick =                    Set initial event handler.
  FirstPress;
</script>
</form>
</body>
```

There is a subtle distinction between setting event handlers as object properties and setting them as values of HTML attributes. An event handler set as an object property must be a function, and will therefore execute in the scope in which it is defined. However, if the event handler is defined by assigning a string containing a script as the value of an HTML attribute, the string is executed as if it were the body of a function defined in a scope that includes all the enclosing HTML elements. Thus if we write

```
<form name="form1">
<input type="button" name="b1" value="Press"
    onClick="string">
```

the effect is the same as setting

```
document.form1.b1.onclick =
  new Closure(function() {string},
    document.form1.b1);
```

12.7.2 Event handlers

Event handlers that are commonly used include

- Mouse events: onClick, onDblClick, onMouseDown, onMouseUp, onMouseMove, onMouseOver, onMouseOut
- Keyboard events: onKeyPress, onKeyDown, onKeyUp, onFocus, onBlur
- Browser events: onLoad, onUnload, onMove, onResize, onError
- JavaScript errors: these are handled by a special mechanism described in Section 12.7.4.

(The names are self-explanatory: note that onError applies only to loading of images and objects. Consult a DHTML reference for a full list of event handlers, and for details of which objects support which event handlers.)

The functions setTimeOut() and setInterval() (which are strictly methods of the window object) define event handlers for an event which is the passage of a certain amount of time. Thus

```
setTimeOut(s, n);
```

registers the script contained in the string s as the event handler for the event which is the passage of n milliseconds:

```
setInterval(s, n);
```

does the same, but when the event occurs also re-registers the event handler for an event which is the passage of the next n milliseconds. `setTimeOut()` and `setInterval()` return a value that identifies the event, and can subsequently be used to cancel it, e.g.

```
timer1 = setInterval(script1, 1000);
...
clearInterval(timer1);
```

12.7.3 Writing event handlers

The event handler code is an arbitrary script, which can get and set properties of other objects, and can invoke methods on them. There are a few special points worth noting.

Self-reference with 'this' and 'me'

Within an event-handler script written in JavaScript, `this` refers to the object in question. In VBScript me is used for the self-reference. For example, suppose we have a number of buttons in a form and for some reason we want the text on a button to change to upper case when the mouse pointer is over the button and to revert to lower case when the mouse leaves the button. We define generic functions to change and restore the case of the button text as follows

```
<script language="JavaScript">
function UCText(button) {
  button.value = button.value.toUpperCase();
}
function LCText(button) {
  button.value = button.value.toLowerCase();
}
```

We can then set the event handlers for each button as follows:

```
<input type="button" name="button1"
value="button1"
  onMouseOver="UCText(this)"
  onMouseOut="LCText(this)">
```

Return values

A few event handlers can influence the browser in special ways by returning a true or false value. For example, if an `onClick` event handler returns `false`, the default action of the click, e.g. following a link, is cancelled. This makes it possible to intercept links, for example making them ineffective between certain hours:

```
<script language="JavaScript">
function LinkActive() {
var hour = Date.getHours();
var isOK = (hour < 9) || (hour > 12);
```

```
if (!isOK) alert("Sorry, no access until
12:00");
return isOK;
}
</script>
...
more information is available at
<a href="http://www.somesite.com"
   onClick="LinkActive()">somesite.com</a>
...
```

As another example, a form element can have an onSubmit event handler which is invoked when the user clicks on the Submit button. If this event handler returns false, the form submission is cancelled. So a common idiom is

```
<form method="post"
action="http://www.somesite.com/cgi-bin/order
  onSubmit="return IsValidOrder(this)">
...
</form>
```

where IsValidOrder() is a function which checks that all elements of the form have been completed in a consistent manner and returns true or false accordingly.

The JavaScript execution context for event handlers

We have seen that when we define a JavaScript event handler as the value of an HTML attribute, e.g.

```
<input type=Button name="btn1" value="OK"
  onClick="...">
```

the string which appears as the value of the event attribute is a script to be executed when the event occurs. It is executed rather like a function body: in particular, it has a call object containing the values of any local variables that are declared in the script. If it were treated exactly like a function body, the scope chain would consist of this call object and the global object, but as we have seen earlier, the string is executed as if it were the body of a function defined in a scope that includes all the enclosing HTML elements. Thus the scope chain for the event handler associated with a button is:

- the call object
- the button object that fired the event
- the form object containing the button
- the document object containing the form
- the window (global) object.

Thus an event handler can access properties of any of these intermediate objects, as illustrated in the fragment below, in which a button reports its name and the name of the form containing it.

```
<form name="Form1">
<input type=button name="B1" value="Press me!"
  onClick='alert("You pressed button " + name
    + " in form " + form.name);'
...
</form>
```

This behaviour applies if the event handler script is given as the value of the onClick attribute. An alternative way of associating an event handler with an event is to define the event handler as a function and then assign the function as a property of the HTML object, e.g.

```
<form name="Form1">
<input type=button name="B1" value="Press
me!">
<script language="javascript">
document.Form1.B1.onclick = function() {...};
</script>
</form>
```

In this case the event handler function for the button will execute like all functions in the context in which it was defined, so its context chain will not include the enclosing HTML elements unless we explicitly change the context by using a closure:

```
document.Form1.B1.onclick =
new Closure(function() {...},
document.Form1.B1);
```

12.7.4 JavaScript error events

When a JavaScript error occurs, the system checks to see whether a function has been assigned to the onerror property of the window object. If no function has been assigned, the system error dialog box is displayed. However, if a function has been assigned it is invoked as an event handler, and is passed parameters describing the error. If the function returns true, display of the system dialog box is not displayed, if it returns false the dialog box is displayed. Thus it is possible to handle errors in a customized fashion. (A common technique is to arrange for details of the error to be mailed to the author.)

The JavaScript error handler can only be registered by assigning to the property of the window object, e.g.

```
self.onerror = myErrorHandler;
```

The declaration of myErrorHandler is typically of the form

```
function myErrorHandler(message, URL, line) {
...
}
```

When the function is called, the first parameter, `message`, is set to a string containing a description of the error; the second parameter, URL, is set to the URL of the document containing the erroneous script, and the third argument holds the line number of the offending line.

12.7.5   The event object

Although the mechanisms described above are adequate for much of the time, they suffer from the serious limitation that the event handler does not have detailed information about the exact details of the event. For example, a mouse movement will trigger an `onMouseMove` handler if one exists for the appropriate HTML element, but the handler does not have access to the mouse coordinates. Similarly, when responding to an `onMouseDown` event, it might be important to know which button had been pressed. Navigator 4 and Internet Explorer 4 have addressed this problem by introducing the event object: unfortunately, they have done this in incompatible ways.

In Navigator 4, if the handler is assigned as an object property the event object is passed as an argument when the event handler is called, thus the skeleton definition is like

```
document.form1.mousedown = function(e) {...}
```

If the event handler is assigned as the value of an HTML tag, it is implicitly defined as a function with an argument named `event`. Internet Explorer 4 takes a different approach: the event object is available to event handlers as the value of a global variable called `event`. Fortunately, this difference in approach is not as restrictive as it might appear. If an event handler is defined as the value of an HTML attribute we can refer to the event object with the name `event` in both browsers: Navigator will take it as a reference to the formal parameter, while Explorer will treat it as a reference to the global variable. However, in an event handler that is assigned (as a function) to a property of an object, we have to use the `navigator` object (Section 11.1.4) to determine which browser is running:

```
function handleEvent(e) {
// In Navigator, e will be the event object
var browser = navigator.appName;
// Test for Explorer, if true collect event
// object
if(browser.search(/Microsoft/) != -1)
  e = window.event;
...
}
```

The event object contains useful information about the event. The information is essentially the same in Navigator and Internet Explorer: unfortunately, the names of the properties that contain the information are almost completely different, as Table 12.1 shows.

Table 12.1 Event object properties

Information	Navigator	Internet Explorer
Kind of event	`type`: string containing type name	`type`: string containing type name
Source element	`target`	`srcElement`
Mouse button	`which`: value 1, 2 or 3	`button`: value 1, 2 or 3
Keypress	`which`: value is key encoding (Unicode)	`KeyCode`: value is key encoding (Unicode)
Modifier keys	`modifiers`: bitmask	`altKey`, `ctrlKey`, `shiftKey`: Boolean values
Mouse coordinates	`pageX`, `pageY` and `screenX`, `screenY`	`clientX`, `clientY` and `pageX`, `pageY`
Mouse move context	n/a	`fromElement`, `toElement`

The names are mostly self-explanatory. The Navigator `modifiers` property is an integer that represents the keyboard modifier key(s) pressed when the event fired: 1 for the Alt key, 2 for the Ctrl key and 4 for the Shift key, with key combinations defined by the appropriate sum. Masks for these are defined as properties of the confusingly named Event object (note the capitalization: this is quite different from the event object. Thus if it is required to distinguish a Shift-click from a plain click, the `onClick` event handler would be of the form

```
function processClick(e) {
var shiftClick = e.modifiers & Event.SHIFT_MASK;
...
}
```

The `fromElement` property is a reference to the object where the cursor was located just before a `MouseOver` or `MouseOut` event: the `toElement` property is a reference to the object to which the cursor moved to trigger a `MouseOut` event.

In Internet Explorer, the event object has an additional property, `returnValue`. This can be set true or false: if it is set false then the default action of the associated element does not take place. This property is provided so that scripts written in VBScript can return values from event handlers. (An event handler in VBScript is either a sequence of statements, or a subroutine, neither of which can return a value in the sense of the JavaScript statement `return false;`. A VBScript event handler would achieve the same result with `event.returnValue = "false"`.)

12.7.6 Event propagation

In the normal course of events, a mouse click on a button, say, is handled by an event handler associated with that button. However, it is possible for the event to be handled by an object further up the hierarchy, e.g. by the enclosing form. In both Navigator and Internet Explorer it is possible for an event to be seen (and acted on) anywhere in the object hierarchy: this is due to a mechanism called *event propagation*. Unfortunately,

Netscape and Microsoft have diametrically opposite ways of arranging this. We explore the Microsoft model first, since it is a more conventional approach.

Event propagation in Internet Explorer

In software architectures that provide structured exception handling, the usual model is that an exception can be handled within the function where it occurs, or 'passed up the line' to the enclosing function. This is repeated until either some function in the hierarchy deals with the exception, or it reaches the global level at which some system-wide default action is taken. The Microsoft 'event bubbling' model is similar: an event bubbles up the object hierarchy until it is dealt with by an event handler which also specifies that the event should not be passed up to the next layer. (This means that an event can be processed by more than one event handler. This is sometimes useful, but fraught with danger.) Thus a mouse press on a button will fire the onMouseDown handler for the button if there is one. Unless the handler stops the bubbling process by setting event.cancelBubble to true, the event will be passed to the onMouseDown handler for the enclosing form. If allowed to propagate it will pass in turn to the onMouseDown handlers for the document object and finally the window object. Event bubbling is essential since the Microsoft document object model makes every HTML element potentially scriptable. To see why, suppose we have a paragraph that responds to a mouse click by changing colour:

```
<P id="para1"
onClick="document.all.para1.style.color='red';
">
This paragraph contains <em>emphasized</em>
text
</P>
```

Without event bubbling, clicking on the word 'emphasized' would have no effect, though clicking on any other word would change the colour of the whole paragraph. This is because there is no onClick event handler for the object corresponding to the <em> element. Event bubbling ensures that the event passes to the onClick handler of the <P> tag. Another example is a table, each of whose cells contains a paragraph of text. A mouse click in a paragraph will be seen first as an event for that paragraph, but a more likely situation is that the significance is that a particular cell has been singled out by the click. If we provide an onClick for the table cells but not for the paragraphs, the event bubbling will do what we want. If some paragraphs attach special significance to a mouse click, we can provide an onClick handler for them: if it does not cancel the bubble, both it and the table cell handlers will be activated.

It is important to realize that event bubbling applies only to what we might call 'primitive' events like MouseDown. Events like Click, Submit and (form) Reset do not bubble: they are regarded as 'semantic' events that are best dealt with where they occur. A mouse click is a compound event, consisting of a MouseDown event followed by a MouseUp event with the cursor on the same object. (The cursor can move out of the object between the two events – the browser still treats it as a click.) Since a click action is a combination of a MouseDown event and a MouseUp event, if there is an onMouseDown or onMouseUp handler as well as an onClick handler, that handler will be activated, and the Click event will not be recorded. Clearly, it is unlikely that anyone would provide both handlers for a single button, but if the button has an onClick handler and there is an onMouseDown or onMouseUp handler higher up in the hierarchy (at form or document level), this handler will see its event as it bubbles up, and the Click event on the button will be lost.

Event propagation in Netscape Navigator

The Navigator event model turns the event bubbling model on its head. Instead of events bubbling up through the object hierarchy from the target element to the top level (window object), events 'dribble down'. Each object in the hierarchy – window object, document object, layer object – is given the opportunity to 'capture' the event and handle it before it reaches its target element. An event handler at a higher level can choose whether to pass the event on or not: if it is passed on it can be passed either to the next level in the hierarchy, or direct to the target object (or indeed to any other object).

Event capture is controlled by methods of the window, document and layer objects: captureEvents() and releaseEvents(). Each of these takes a bitmask argument constructed from constants in the (capitalized) Event object to define the kind of events to capture or release, thus

```
document.captureEvents(Event.CLICK|Event.DBLCLICK);
```

causes all click and double click events to be processed initially by the document object. Later, the document object might choose only to intercept click events:

```
document.releaseEvents(Event.DBLCLICK);
```

Obviously, the document object must have event handlers for the captured events assigned to it:

```
document.onclick = ...;
document.ondblclick = ...;
```

Once an event has been captured, there are a number of possibilities for processing it. The event handler can examine the event object to get details of the event, and then has several choices open to it.

- Handle the event completely: the target never sees it
- Pass the event to the next level in the hierarchy, unprocessed
- Pass the event direct to its target
- Pass the event to an object other than its target
- Process the event in some way and then pass it on as above.

An event is passed down the hierarchy by the routeEvent() method of the window, document and layer objects. This method is called with one argument, the Event object. To pass the event to its target, or to another object, that object's handleEvent() method is called with the Event object as an argument. Thus for an event handler defined as a function with one argument, e, an event can be passed to its target by

```
      e.target.handleEvent(e);
```

To pass the event to an object other than its target, that object's `handleEvent()` method is called.

12.8 DHTML scriptlets

A scriptlet is a Web page that has been packaged up as an object analogous to a Visual Basic or ActiveX control, i.e. it exposes properties and methods to a container application. A scriptlet can be embedded in another Web page, using Internet Explorer, and it can also be embedded in any application that supports controls, e.g. Visual Basic. (In applications other than Explorer, the scriptlet is in fact placed in a 'scriptlet container object', which provides the ability to render the HTML.) Scriptlets thus provide an alternative to ActiveX controls for providing interactive functionality in reusable packages. An attraction of the technology is that scriptlets and controls appear identical to the scripting language: indeed, if one had a scriptlet and an ActiveX control which offered the same functionality, one could be substituted for the other without any changes to the controlling scripts.

12.8.1 Creating scriptlets

In order to convert a page into a scriptlet three distinct steps are required:

- Define the interface – the properties and methods that the scriptlet exposes.
- Specify the way in which the scriptlet responds to mouse and keyboard events.
- Specify the custom events (if any) that the scriptlet will use to communicate with its container.

The first step is covered in this section: handling of events is discussed in Section 12.8.3. The way in which the interface is defined depends on the scripting language being used, as described below.

Defining the interface in JavaScript

If we are using JavaScript, the properties and methods to be exposed are contained in the `Public_Description` object: all other variables and functions are private to the scriptlet. This is created by a script of the following form, usually placed in the `<HEAD>` element of the scriptlet page:

```
<SCRIPT LANGUAGE="JavaScript">
var Public_Description = new Interface();

Function Interface() {
  ... //definitions of properties and methods
}
</SCRIPT>
```

Note that the name of the constructor function is arbitrary: we have chosen to call it 'Interface' to remind us of its purpose. Suppose our scriptlet performs some animation effect, and we wish to expose methods to start and stop the animation. Within the body of the `Interface()` constructor we would define these methods in the usual way with

```
this.start = function () { ...};
this.stop = function () { ...};
```

(Alternatively we could put the name of a function as the value, and define the function separately.) If the background colour of the scriptlet is to be exposed as a property, we could write

```
this.bgcolor = "blue";
```

in the body of the constructor. However, a more powerful alternative is available: we can define functions to read and write the value of a property, e.g.

```
this.get_bgcolor = function() { ... };
this.put_bgcolor = function(value) { ... };
```

This technique provides controlled access to a property value: for example, by defining `this.get_bgcolor` but not `this.put_bgcolor` we can make `bgcolor` a read-only property.

Defining the interface in VBScript

VBScript before Version 5 does not allow us to create objects, so the technique of using a `Public_Description` object cannot be employed. Instead, it is necessary to use a naming convention, obviously derived from the convention used for event handlers. We define the interface by prefixing `public_` to the name of a variable or function to be exposed, at the time of declaration. (This technique can also be used in JScript, but the `Public_Description` technique is preferred.) Thus the `start()` and `stop()` methods of the example used above would be declared as

```
Sub public_Start()
  ...
End Sub

Sub public_Stop()
  ...
End Sub
```

Similarly, the `bgcolor` property could be set up by

```
Dim public_bgcolor As String
bgcolor = "blue"
```

To obtain controlled access to a property, the prefixes `public_get_` and `public_put_` are used:

```
Function public_get_bgcolor() As String
  ...
```

```
  bgcolor = ...
End Function

Sub public_put_bgcolor()

  ...
End Sub
```

12.8.2 Using scriptlets

A scriptlet is placed in a Web page using the <OBJECT> tag (as one would for an ActiveX control). The TYPE attribute is set to "text/x-scriptlet" e.g.

```
<OBJECT ID="MyScriptlet" TYPE=
    "text/x-scriptlet"
HEIGHT=100 WIDTH=200
DATA="http://somecorp.com/toys/whizzbang.html"
>
```

To use a scriptlet in another container application, it is first necessary to create a scriptlet container object. This object has two properties, Name and URL. The Name property is set to the name by which the scriptlet will be referenced, and the URL property is set to the URL of the scriptlet page.

12.8.3 The scriptlet event model

Standard events

By default, mouse and keyboard events within the scriptlet page are handled entirely within the scriptlet. However, they can be passed to the container using the bubbleEvent() method of the external object which is added to the object model to accommodate scriptlets. Thus if the <BODY> tag of the scriptlet page has the form

```
<BODY
onClick="window.external.bubbleEvent();">
```

then a click anywhere in the scriptlet will be passed to Explorer: if the <OBJECT> tag that introduced the scriptlet has a handler for the onClick event it will be fired, otherwise the event will bubble up to the enclosing element. In an alternative scenario, an event can be processed by an event handler within the scriptlet, and then passed on to the container for further processing. In either case, paranoid script writers can check that the container is ready to handle the event by checking the Boolean property window.external.frozen. If this is set to true, events will not be processed by the container application because it is not yet ready.

Custom events

Custom events provide a mechanism whereby a scriptlet can inform its container about events outwith the standard events that can be handled by bubbleEvent(). They can also be used to convey additional information about a standard event (e.g. mouse button and modifier key details), and to notify the container about changes in the scriptlet state, e.g. a change in the value of a property.

A custom event is generated by invoking the `raiseEvent()` method of the `window.external` object. This method takes two arguments: a string to identify the event and a reference to the object in the scriptlet that triggered the event (type `object` in JavaScript, `variant` in VBScript). Thus in our earlier example, the function to set the value of the `bgcolor` property might be defined as follows in the `Public_ Description` object:

```
this.put_bgcolor = function(value) {
document.bgColor = value;
window.external.raiseEvent("e_bgcolorchange", document)
};
```

This ensures that whenever the `bgcolor` property is changed, a custom event will be sent to the container.

To handle a custom event, the container application must provide an event handler for the `onscripletevent` event associated with the scriptlet. This handler has two arguments: the first is set to the string describing the event and the second is a reference to the event object generated by the event, e.g.

```
<SCRIPT LANGUAGE="JavaScript"
        FOR="MyScriptlet"
        EVENT=onscripletevent(event, eventData)
  if (event == "e_bgcolorchange") {
    ... //process colorchange
  }
  else if (event == ...)
  ...
</SCRIPT>
```

When processing the event, the properties of `eventData` include the source element that triggered the event, the mouse button and modifier key details, and other information as described earlier in this chapter.

## Part four

The Microsoft scripting model

## Chapter 13

Scripting Microsoft Office

The applications that comprise the Microsoft Office suite come with an embedded language, Visual Basic Applications Edition (VBA), as do applications from other suppliers which inter-work with the Office applications. In this chapter we show how VBA can be used as a macro language for these applications, with examples from Word and Excel, how it can be used to develop custom applications using two or more components of the Office suite, and how it can be used to manipulate OLE compound documents and ActiveX controls in Excel. We also explain how this programmability has opened the way for so-called macro viruses.

13.1   VBA

As we described in Chapter 7, the acronym VBA expands to Visual Basic for Applications, though the language is also commonly referred to as Visual Basic Application Edition. (The most recent Microsoft documentation uses the name Visual Basic Programming System – Applications Edition.) VBA is a version of the Visual Basic language embedded in the applications that comprise the Microsoft Office suite, and in applications from other suppliers which inter-work with the Office applications, e.g. Visio 2000. Using the object models exposed by these applications, it serves as a common macro (scripting) language for all these applications. In addition to scripting individual applications, it can be used to automate interactions between the applications, to provide easy access to the Windows API and the underlying file system, to add connectivity to corporate data, and to integrate with other COM-based technologies. VBA is without doubt the leading application customization technology for the Windows platform.

This chapter assumes a familiarity with Visual Basic as described in Chapters 7 and 8, since VBA is identical to the language used in the Visual Basic application. However, there is an important point of terminology to consider. Visual Basic is structured round the concept of a *project* which incorporates forms and modules. Applications such as Word and Excel that use VBA are structured round their own concepts – documents and templates in Word, worksheets and workbooks in Excel – and it is therefore necessary to establish an equivalence between these and the projects of Visual Basic. Thus in Word, the project is equivalent to a document or a template. Macros, declared as procedures with no arguments and public scope, are stored in the document/template. (Since the document/template is the project, the macros it uses must be global to the project.) In Excel the project is equivalent to a workbook. As in Visual Basic, collections of related macros can be placed in a module, with constants and procedures that are shared by several macros declared at module level.

Another difference to note is that since VBA runs within an application as an embedded language, it does not normally see external events, which are handled by the host application. In Excel, VBA code can capture a number of events, while Word has an exiguous event capability. Event handling is discussed in more detail in Section 13.7.

Within the Office suite, VBA can be used in three distinct ways:

- As a macro language for a single application, to customize the user interface and/or automate repetitive tasks.
- To allow one application to control another application or applications in the suite. This technique of *automation* can be used, for example, to build an integrated business application in Access which uses Excel to provide spreadsheet manipulation and Word to format reports.
- As a way for an Office application to access the Windows API.

We cover the first two of these uses in some detail in this chapter. Accessing the Windows API was covered in Section 8.7.

13.2 Macros and macro languages

VBA is often described in Microsoft documents as the 'macro language' for the Office applications. This is a misuse of the term macro, but one that is so firmly entrenched that it is beyond change. The term 'macro' originated as a contraction of *macro-instruction*, a feature of assembly language that allowed a group of instructions to be labelled with a name, and subsequently inserted in the source code, possibly with substitution of parameters. From this grew the macro-processor as a general string-replacement front end for a language processor.

In the early days of word processing and spreadsheets it was recognized that there were many common operations that required a number of keystrokes, and a facility for keystroke recording was incorporated in the applications. When this was switched on the system recorded subsequent keystrokes, and when recording was switched off these were stored, and associated with a keystroke combination that would cause them to be played back. This was not unreasonably called a macro, by analogy with the machine-language case. As the applications grew more sophisticated, the simple keystroke recorder was supplemented by a 'macro language', a special-purpose programming language that could be used to drive the application as an alternative to using keystrokes. Microsoft Word introduced the idea of using a customized version of an established programming language instead of a special-purpose language with WordBasic, which shipped as part of Word 6. This was a programming language that could be used to drive the Word engine. Word still provided a keystroke recorder, but this did not actually record the keystrokes: it was in effect a keystroke compiler, since it translated the keystrokes into an equivalent WordBasic program. Alternatively, WordBasic programs could be entered in text form by the user. A brief account of WordBasic is given later for the interested reader.

WordBasic was intended to be the first of a family of languages, to be followed by ExcelBasic, AccessBasic etc. However, the Excel development team decided to follow the pattern of Visual Basic, structuring their application as a collection of automation objects whose properties and methods could be scripted using a variant of the Visual Basic language, and this technology was later adopted for all the Office applications. Thus VBA has become a universal 'macro' language for all the Office applications: the same language is used, with an application-specific object model, to script all the members of the Office family. A macro in the modern sense is a public procedure written in VBA. Each of the Office applications includes an integral Visual Basic IDE (Integrated Development Environment): you define a macro by typing in the code for the VBA procedure that implements it, and it is then available for use. For more information about the mechanics of creating VBA programs, see the Visual Basic Help associated with the application (Word, Excel etc.) or consult one of the references listed in the Appendix. The procedures (macros) can be stored in a document or in a template. Macros stored in a document are only available in that document: macros stored in a template are available in any document based on that template. A common practice is to associate a macro with a toolbar button or a hot-key combination. Sometimes macros are associated with events generated by the application, e.g. whenever the user changes the value of a cell in an Excel worksheet, the `SheetChange` event is raised. If the user has provided a VBA procedure as an event handler for this event, it will be called whenever a change is made to the worksheet. This topic is explored in detail in Section 13.7.

It is important to realize that all the real work is done by the applications, through their object models. If you are working in Word or Excel, you have to use VBA as the glue language because it is embedded in the application. But you can manipulate the object models of the Office applications from outside the Office suite: all you need is a glue language which understands the automation interface. Thus we can construct a customized business application in Visual Basic which combines the functionality of two or more of the Office components; we can use the Office applications from inside a Web page or we can even access Office applications from the Windows desktop using the Windows Script Host (see Chapter 15). Programming Office applications from 'outside' is explored further in Section 13.8.

13.3 WordBasic

WordBasic was based on what was the current version of BASIC at the time of its inception. This was a reasonably modern version of BASIC incorporating structured programming facilities and data structures very similar to those in Pascal: the main differences from the current Visual Basic language are as follows.

Readers who want to get on with the main story can skip this section.

- Minor syntactic variations, e.g. `while...wend` rather than `while ... loop`.
- Data types: numbers and strings only.
- Identifiers convey type, string variables being identified by appending a $ character to the name.

This version of BASIC was enhanced by adding a large number of statements – which are actually built-in procedures – to provide access to the API of the Word engine. This provided programmed access to every operation that could be done in Word by selecting menu options. Thus in WordBasic, every menu option has a corresponding built-in procedure (statement), so there is a procedure EditSearch corresponding to the *Search* option on the *Edit* menu. Selecting this menu option displays a dialog box in which the user can enter the string to search for: the dialog box also includes a checkbox to tick if the search is to be for whole words only. The EditSearch procedure mirrors this by having two parameters: the string to be searched for and a Boolean (actually a number, zero for false and non-zero for true) to say if a whole-word match is required. This procedure might be called as follows:

```
EditSearch "Cost", 1
```

Alternatively, the procedure could be called with keyword parameters instead of the usual positional parameter syntax, e.g.

```
EditSearch .Search = "Cost" .Wholeword = 1
```

The keyword syntax allows the parameters to appear in either order, thus we could equally well write

```
EditSearch .Wholeword = 1 .Search = "Cost"
```

WordBasic also provides functions to allow the user to interrogate the environment. For example, the function CenterPara() returns 1 if all of the selected paragraphs are centred, 0 if none of the selected paragraphs is centred, and −1 if a mixture of paragraph alignments is being used. Many such functions occur as one of a pair: a procedure to achieve some effect and a function to report the current state. Thus the CenterPara() function has an associated CenterPara procedure, which applies centred alignment to the selected paragraphs. Similarly, the Font procedure, which sets a font for the selected text, has a companion function Font$() which returns the name of the font applied to the current selection. (The name is returned as a string, hence the $ in the name.)

Not all status enquiries return a single value: for example, in Word 6 the *SummaryInfo* choice on the *File* menu produced a dialog box containing 13 items. To cater for this WordBasic provides a collection of predefined UDTs called *dialog records*. The name of the type is the name of a dialog box, and the fields in the definition have identifiers that correspond to the elements of the dialog box. This is illustrated in the following example, in which we define a WordBasic program to provide a word-count facility.

```
Sub MAIN
dim dlg as DocumentStatistics
FileSummaryInfo .Update
GetCurValues dlg
docsize = dlg.words
Print docsize + "words"
End Sub
```

We declare a variable dlg as a dialog record whose type matches the *DocumentStatistics* dialog box. Thus dlg is a record structure to hold all the information about the current state of Word. Next we call a component of the Word API, FileSummaryInfo (equivalent to selecting the *SummaryInfo* option from the *File* menu) with the single parameter `.update`, to update the document statistics. (Note the use of a keyword parameter without an associated value to specify an operation. This is analogous to the C-shell notion of having an environment variable that can be set or unset but does not have an actual value associated with it.) Next we call another API procedure to get the current values (dialog box contents) and store them in the variable `dlg`. Finally we assign the field `.words`, which is the word count, to the variable `docsize` (implicitly declared as a number) and display the value in a message. (`Print` in WordBasic actually displays the output in a dialog box.) This procedure can be saved with a name chosen by the user, and then associated with a hot-key, a button on the button bar or a menu item.

13.4   The Office object models

Each of the Office applications – Access, Excel, PowerPoint and Word – has an object model described in a type library: in addition, Microsoft provides object models for a number of related products, e.g. the Data Access Object (DAO) and the ActiveX Data Object (ADO), both used for database access. The user can configure the applications to import a selection of object models into VBA at start-up, and scripts then have access to all the objects so defined. These object models provide access to the functionality of the application and to useful components of its data, with objects that represent the current state, e.g. `Document` (in Word), `Worksheet` (in Excel), `Selection` (in both). These objects have methods and properties like Visual Basic controls, but do not (normally) respond to external events. By setting the properties and invoking the methods of these objects, a VBA program can do anything that a user could do by mouse and keyboard operations, especially selecting from menus. In addition, the object models may include objects that allow operations that are not accessible via menus: for example, the Word and Excel object models provide a collection of controls which are identical to the intrinsic controls of the Visual Basic application.

These object models are immensely complex: for example, the Word object model comprises 188 objects which between them have 2300 properties and 837 methods. It also defines 192 Enums and 1969 constants. (For comparison, the Excel object model comprises 184 objects, 5956 properties, 3119 methods, 152 Enums and 1266 constants.)

To indicate the complexity of the problem, a subset of the Word object model is presented in Figure 13.1. Clearly, we can only hope to skim the surface in a single chapter.

13.4.1   Structure of an object model

Navigating the object model

An object model is a (very deep) tree whose root is the *application object*. (Strictly speaking it is not a tree but a graph, since there is not always a unique path from the root to a particular node, and there are some circular references. This significance of this will become apparent later.) Every object in the model can be referenced by a fully qualified name, e.g.

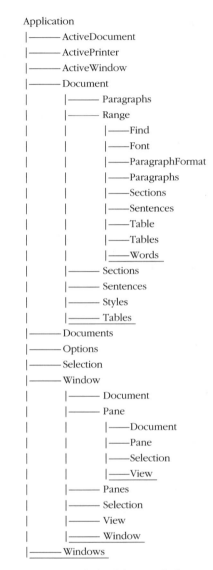

Figure 13.1 Subset of the Word object model

```
Application.ActiveDocument
Application.Workbooks(1).Worksheets(2)
```

For the convenience of the programmer, a variety of short cuts are provided. For example, many of the properties and methods of the Application object are so-called global members which can be used without qualification, thus, for example, in Word

```
Documents.Count
```

is equivalent to

```
Application.Documents.Count
```

and in Excel

```
ActiveCell.Font
```

can be used as a shorthand for

```
Application.ActiveWindow.ActiveCell.Font
```

Collection objects

Many of the objects in the object model are collection objects, e.g. in the Word model the `Application` object includes a `Documents` collection, whose members are objects representing currently open documents. In turn, each `Document` object includes collection objects `Sections` and `Paragraphs`, whose members are the objects representing all the sections and all the paragraphs in a particular document. As an example, we can use the `Paragraphs` collection to perform an operation on all the paragraphs in a document thus:

```
Dim nParas As Integer
Dim currentPara As Paragraph
...
np = Application.Documents(1).Paragraphs.Count
For i = 1 To np
 Set currentPara = _
   Application.Documents(1).Paragraphs(i)
 ... 'do something with currentPara
Next i
```

Collection objects in an object model are easily recognized by observing that their names are plural nouns, e.g. the collection of `Document` objects is called `Documents`. As noted above, most objects have a default member (property or method) which is used when a property or method is expected but not present. The default member for a collection object is `Item`, so that when accessing the `Paragraphs` collection, `Paragraphs(4)` can be used instead of `Paragraphs.Item(4)`.

Objects and reality

At run-time, the objects in the object model accessible to a VBA program mirror the current document, workbook etc. Thus if the user enters a new paragraph in Word, a `Paragraph` object will be created to represent it, and a reference to this object will be placed in the `Paragraphs` collection in the associated `Document` object. But equally, the VBA program can create a new (empty) paragraph with

```
ActiveDocument.Paragraphs.Add
```

A paragraph containing some text is set up as follows:

```
ActiveDocument.Paragraphs.Add.Range.Text = _
  "Some text"
```

(Here `ActiveDocument.Paragraphs.Add` adds a new paragraph to the `Para-graphs` collection, and also returns a reference to the `Paragraph` object created, so we can immediately access the properties of that object. You might expect a `Paragraph` object to have a `Text` property, but in practice it has a `Range` property: this returns a `Range` object which has a `Text` property. The reason for this may become apparent later.)

New objects are typically created by using the `Add` method of the appropriate collection object. A few objects can also be created within a script using the `New` keyword: these include `Application`, `Document`, `Font` and `ParagraphFormat`. Thus

```
Dim newDoc As New Document
```

creates a new document in the Documents collection, and

```
Dim anotherWord As New Application
```

starts up a new instance of Word (running invisibly).

13.5 Programming the Word object model

Although the Word object model is very large, most of the common things we want to do involve only a few objects – `Application`, `Document`, `Find`, `Range`, `Replace` and `Selection` are probably the most commonly used. In this section we just give a flavour of the possibilities available: see the references in the Appendix for sources of more detailed information, or explore Word's Visual Basic Help.

13.5.1 The Application object

As noted, the `Application` object has many properties and methods, including `Document`, `Documents`, `Options`, `Selection` and `Window`. There are also some dynamically updated properties that are particularly useful in accessing the current state of Windows. `ActiveDocument`, `ActivePrinter` and `ActiveWindow` have self-evident meanings: `Selection` is an object containing the currently selected text, or the insertion point if no text is selected. (This is in fact a gross over-simplification – as we shall see later, the `Selection` object is a complex beast.)

The following examples illustrate the use of these properties. (These examples are in fact macros used in the preparation of this book: each was associated with a keystroke combination or a toolbar button.)

Note the use of a keyword parameter.

```
Sub PageFwd()
' Advance one page
ActiveWindow.PageScroll Down:=1
End Sub
```

```
Sub PageBack()
' Back one page
ActiveWindow.PageScroll Up:=1
End Sub

Sub ProgramFont()
' Change selected text to Courier New
Selection.Font.Name = "Courier New"
Selection.Font.Size = 11
Selection.Font.Italic = wdFalse
Selection.Font.Bold = wdFalse
End Sub

Sub Hyphenate()
' Manual Hyphenation
With ActiveDocument
   .AutoHyphenation = False
   .HyphenateCaps = True
   .HyphenationZone = _
      InchesToPoints(0.25)
   .ConsecutiveHyphensLimit = 0
   .ManualHyphenation
End With
End Sub
```

Note that Autohyphenation is a Boolean property, but ManualHyphenation is a method.

Other useful members of the `Application` object are the `Quit` method, e.g.

```
Application.Quit wdSaveChanges
```

which exits Word saving any changes to the document, and the `Options` object which corresponds to the *Tools/Options* menu selection, e.g.

```
Sub SQ()
' Switch smart quotes on
Options.AutoFormatAsYouTypeReplaceQuotes = _
   True
End Sub

Sub NSQ()
' Switch smart quotes off
Options.AutoFormatAsYouTypeReplaceQuotes = _
   False
End Sub
```

13.5.2 The Document object

The `Document` object represents an open document. It appears in the object model as a child of the `Application` object, and is the root of a large and useful subset of the object model. The `Documents` collection is a collection of `Document` objects for all the open documents, and `ActiveDocument` is a reference to the `Document` object representing the currently active document, i.e. the one that has the focus. In most of the examples below we use `ActiveDocument`: this could of course be replaced by a reference to a specific document object.

Working with documents

A new document is created using the `Add` method of the `Documents` collection, e.g.

```
Documents.Add("letter.dot")
```

will create a new empty document using the 'letter' template. If the argument is omitted, `normal.dot` is used. An existing document is opened with the `Open` method, e.g.

```
Documents.Open("c:\letters\wiley3.doc")
```

This method has a large number of optional arguments, e.g.

```
Documents.Open("c:\letters\wiley3.doc", _
    ReadOnly := True)
```

opens the document as a read-only document. If the document is in fact already open,

```
Documents.Open("c:\letters\wiley3.doc", _
    Revert := True)
```

will discard unsaved changes and reload the document from the disk, while

```
Documents.Open("c:\letters\wiley3.doc", _
    AddToRecentFiles := True)
```

opens the document and adds it to the recent file list which appears at the bottom of the *File* menu. The list of recent files is mirrored by the `RecentFiles` collection, which is a property of the `Application` object. This is a collection of `RecentFile` objects, and a recently used file can be opened by invoking the `Open` method of its `RecentFile` object, e.g.

```
RecentFiles(1).Open
```

The Document object has `Save` and `Close` methods, e.g.

```
ActiveDocument.Save
ActiveDocument.Close
```

If you try to save a document that doesn't have a name, Word will display the *File Save* dialog box in the normal way. The `Close` method has an optional parameter to determine the save action, thus

```
ActiveDocument.Close(SaveChanges := _
    wdPropmtToSaveChanges)
```

will display the usual dialog enquiring whether changes are to be saved. Other possible (self-explanatory) values for the `SaveChanges` parameter are `wdSaveChanges` and wdDoNotSaveChanges. There is also a SaveAs method, which is too complex to go into here.

Document Structure

A document can be viewed as a collection of sections, or a collection of sentences, or even a collection of words. All of these views are reflected in collection objects which are properties of the Document object: Sections, Sentences, Words. (The object model even provides a Characters collection!) Note that the object model does not include objects to represent sentences or words: the Sentences and Words collections return Range objects, which are discussed in the next section. The Sentences and Words collections do not have an Add method: however, Word automatically updates the collections whenever you add or delete text from a document. The Sections collection does have an Add method, so you can add a new section with

```
ActiveDocument.Sections.Add
```

This adds a new section at the end of the document. An optional parameter specifies a range before which the section break will be inserted. A second optional parameter determines the type of section break, e.g.

```
ActiveDocument.Sections.Add(Start := _
   wdSectionNewPage)
```

adds a new section at the end of the document, starting a new page. Other possible values are wdSectionContinuous, wdSectionNewColumn, wdSectionEvenPage and wdSectionOddPage.

Spelling and Grammar

The Document object includes the following properties and methods related to grammar and spelling checks.

- ActiveDocument.CheckGrammar starts a spelling and grammar check.
- ActiveDocument.CheckSpelling starts a spelling check.
- ActiveDocument.SpellingChecked is set to true after a spelling check. Subsequent calls of CheckSpelling will have no effect unless this property is first set to false.
- ActiveDocument.SpellingErrors returns a collection which contains a range object for each word in the document identified as a spelling error: this is the ProofReadingErrors collection.

Printing

The PrintOut method prints a document, thus

```
ActiveDocument.PrintOut
```

This method has a very large number of optional arguments which correspond to all the options that can be set in the Print dialog box. We give just one example:

```
ActiveDocument.PrintOut _
    Range := wdPrintCurrentPage
```

prints the current page only.

13.5.3 Selections and Ranges

The Selection and Range objects both represent contiguous areas within a Word document. It is important, however, to realize that they represent far more than just the text in the area: they have a large number of properties, only one of which is Text.

The Selection object

The idea of a *selection* will be familiar to Windows users. You drag the mouse over some contiguous text, which is then displayed in reverse video, and this selected text can then be treated as a single entity, e.g. it can be dragged to a new location, it can be copied to the clipboard, it can be deleted, or its formatting can be changed, e.g. to italic text. The Word object model provides a Selection object to mirror this behaviour. The Selection object is a child of the Application object, and is a global property, so it is typically referred to as in the example above, e.g.

```
Selection.Font.Name = "Courier New"
```

Whenever the user makes a new selection, the Selection object is updated – there can only be one active selection at a time. However, a selection can also be created by a program, e.g.

```
ActiveDocument.Paragraphs(1).Range.Select
```

selects the first paragraph of the active document. (Note the appearance of Range again: all should be clear by the end of this section.)

The Selection object can be manipulated by the program in much the same way that a selection can be manipulated by the user. We give just a few examples.

- The selected text can be deleted using the Delete method:

    ```
    Selection.Delete
    ```

- The selected text can be cut or copied to the clipboard:

    ```
    Selection.Copy
    Selection.Cut
    ```

    (We shall see how to paste material from the clipboard when we discuss the insertion point later in this section.)
- The formatting of the selected text can be changed by setting the properties of the Font object, which is itself a property of the Selection object:

```
Selection.Font.Name = "Courier New"
Selection.Font.Size = 11
Selection.Font.Italic = wdFalse
Selection.Font.Bold = wdFalse
```

- We can manipulate the paragraphs within a selection by using its `Paragraphs` property. This returns a `Collection` object containing a `Paragraph` object for each paragraph in the selection, thus `Selection.Paragraphs(2)` returns a reference to the second paragraph in the selection. (The `Selection` object also has a `Sections` property, which can be used in the same way as the `Sections` property of the `Document` object, described earlier.)
- We can manipulate the individual words within a selection by using its `Words` property. This returns a collection object containing a `Range` object for each word in the selection, thus `Selection.Words(2)` returns a `Range` object representing the second word in the selection.
- We can insert text at the start or end of the selection, extending the selection to include the inserted text:

```
Selection.InsertBefore "START. "
SelectionInsertAfter " END."
```

- We can insert a paragraph mark at the start or end of the selection, extending the selection to include the paragraph mark:

```
Selection.InsertParagraphBefore
SelectionInsertParagraphAfter
```

- We can extend or shrink the selection.

```
Selection.Extend
```

extends the selection to the next smallest complete unit of text, thus if the current selection is a word, it is extended to the end of the sentence. The sequence of units is word, sentence, paragraph, section, document. The method can be given an argument consisting of a single character, e.g.

```
Selection.Extend Character := "*"
```

This will extend the selection forward to include the next occurrence of the character "*".

```
Selection.Shrink
```

shrinks the selection to the next smallest text unit in the sequence document, section, paragraph, word, insertion point. The `Shrink` method does not have a `Character` option.

The Range object

The `Range` object is similar to the `Selection` object, in that it describes a contiguous area of a document. The difference is that the content of the range is not highlighted on the screen, and there can be multiple Range objects coexisting at any time. The Range object appears as a property of the Document object, the Paragraph object and the Selection object. In many situations the Range and Selection objects are interchangeable (though with infuriating differences in places – to change the formatting of the selection to italic requires Selection.Font.Italic = True but if rng is a reference to a range object, the text contained in the range can be changed to italic with rng.Italic = True).

If the definition of an area of interest is to be made within the program, rather than by the user, then the choice of range or selection is largely an aesthetic one – do you want the appearance of the screen to change in response to a selection being made, or do you prefer your macro to operate silently and unobtrusively? Conversely, there are situations which dictate one or the other: if you want to process user-selected text then the Selection object is required, and if you want to have multiple areas defined, the Range object must be used. And we have noted that to access the actual text content of a paragraph we have to use the Text method of the paragraph's Range object, as in

```
str = ActiveDocument.Paragraphs(1).Range.Text
```

This reflects the fact that the Range object is a general-purpose text container: recall that the Words collection is a collection of Range objects. Finally, we note that the Range object is purely programmatic: it does not correspond directly to any part of the user interface.

The Range object appears in many places in the object model, including Document, Paragraph, Section, Selection, Words and ProofReadingErrors. A range object can be created using the Range method of the Document object, which returns a Range object defined by the given starting and ending character positions. Thus

```
Set range10c = _
   ActiveDocument.Range(Start:=0, End:=10)
```

returns a Range object that refers to the first 10 characters in the active document,

```
Set rangep1 = _
ActiveDocument.Paragraphs(1).Range
```

returns a Range object that refers to the first paragraph in the active document, and

```
Set ad = ActiveDocument
Set rangep24 = ad.Range( _
   Start:=ad.Paragraphs(2).Range.Start, _
   End:=ad.Paragraphs(4).Range.End)
```

returns a Range object that refers to the second through fourth paragraphs in the active document.

This latter example repays careful study. We see that we define the starting and ending character positions by obtaining a Paragraph object, using its Range property to get at the text, then using the Start and End properties of the Range object to identify the particular character positions required. The Range property applies to many objects, including documents, sections and paragraphs, and returns a Range object defined by the beginning and end of another object.

The Range object has many properties and methods. Here we mention just a few.

- Expand. The Expand method (which also applies to the Selection object) expands the range or selection to include whole units as specified by an argument. Thus if the range or selection is within a single sentence,

      Selection.Expand wdSentence

  or

      rng.Expand wdSentence

  will expand it to include the entire sentence. If the selection or range includes parts of two paragraphs,

      Selection.Expand wdParagraph

  or

      rng.Expand wdParagraph

  will expand it to include both paragraphs.

- FormattedText. The Text property of a range returns the enclosed text without formatting. The FormattedText property returns the text together with its formatting.

- Next and Previous. The Next and Previous methods apply to a range or a selection, and return a range. The methods take two arguments, defining a unit (word, sentence, paragraph etc.) and a count, which is the number of objects to move. Thus

      rng.Next(Unit:=wdParagraph, Count:=1)

  returns a range corresponding to the next paragraph. Note that since the method returns a range, if you want to move the selection you have to invoke the Select method on the range returned:

      Selection.Next(Unit:=wdWord, Count:=1).Select

  moves the selection to the next word. The Previous method works the same way, but moving backwards in the document. If there isn't a next or previous element, the methods return Nothing.

Setting the insertion point

The Selection and Range objects also serve another vital purpose, keeping track of the insertion point. A range or a selection containing no characters is recognized as the insertion point. Suppose we want to insert text at the beginning of a document.

      Set docstart = _
         ActiveDocument.Range(Start := 0, End := 0)

creates an empty range at character position zero, so the insertion can be done with

      docstart.Text = "Before we begin"

However, an empty range or selection is more usually created by taking an existing range or selection and collapsing it towards the start or end. Thus an alternative way of establishing the insertion point at the start of the document is

```
Set docstart = ActiveDocument.Range
docstart.Collapse wdCollapseStart
```

Here we create a range encompassing the whole document, then collapse it to its start. The attraction of this is that the symmetrical

```
Set docend = ActiveDocument.Range
docend.Collapse wdCollapesEnd
```

establishes an insertion point at the end of the document. To set the insertion point at the end of the first paragraph (strictly, at the start of the second paragraph) in the document we would use

```
Set inspoint = _
   ActiveDocument.Paragraphs(1).Range
inspoint.Collapse wdCollapseEnd
```

The same techniques can be used with the `Selection` object, e.g.

```
Selection.Collapse wdCollapseEnd
```

The insertion point can be moved around easily: after the above statement we could write

```
Selection.Move wdSentence 3
```

to move it three sentences forward.

The `Selection` and `Range` objects have a number of useful methods for inserting text. These insert the text and extend the selection/range accordingly: they are particularly useful when the range/selection has been collapsed to an insertion point. The methods are

```
InsertBefore
InsertAfter
InsertBreak
InsertDateTime
InsertParagraph
InsertSymbol
```

The names are fairly descriptive: see the Windows Visual Basic Help for full specifications. Note that `InsertBreak` has the same effect as adding a new item to the `Sections` collection and specifying the range or selection as an argument of the `Add` method as described earlier.

A detail that can catch you out is that if you use `InsertAfter` with a range or selection that refers to an entire paragraph, the text is inserted after the ending paragraph mark, thus it will appear at the beginning of the next paragraph. To insert text actually at the end of a paragraph, determine the ending point and subtract 1 from this location, since the paragraph mark is one character:

```
Set ad = ActiveDocument _
Set rng =
ad.Range(Start:=ad.Paragraphs(1).Range.End _
  - 1, End:=ad.Paragraphs(1).Range.End - 1)
rng.InsertAfter "THE END."
```

The `Selection` and `Range` objects both provide a `Paste` method. If the selection or range contains text, the text is replaced by the contents of the clipboard. If the selection or range has been collapsed, the contents of the clipboard are inserted at the insertion point so defined.

13.5.4   Find and Replace

The Find object

The `Find` object is a property of the `Range` and `Selection` objects The `Find` object's properties define the search target, and its `Execute` method actually initiates the search operation. If the search operation originates from the `Selection` object, the `Selection` is moved to the target in the event of a successful search. If the operation originates from a `Range` object, the object is redefined to encompass the target. In this section we will base all our examples on the `Selection` object.

In the notes to Chapter 7 we observed that `Find` is an object, and a search is initiated by calling the `Find` object's `Execute` method, and we observed that at first sight it would seem more appropriate to make it a method. We would then be able to do a search easily, e.g.

```
Selection.Find("Wibble!")
```

NB: This is NOT how find actually works.

However, suppose we want to search in a case-sensitive manner, recognizing whole words only: to accommodate this, our hypothetical `Find` method would need to have optional arguments. Since there are lots of possible options for searching (e.g. requiring a particular type style or typeface), the `Find` method would need a large number of optional arguments. The approach actually used in the Word object model is to provide an object whose properties match the various options available in the Find dialog box, and a method which is equivalent to the 'Find Next' button.

A simple search operation can be specified as follows:

```
With Selection.Find
  .ClearFormatting
  .Text = "Wibble!"
  .Forward = True
  .Execute
End With
```

The `ClearFormatting` method corresponds to the 'No Formatting' button in the Find dialog box, and clears any 'sticky' formatting specified in an earlier search. For simple searches, you can take advantage of the fact that all the search options that can be specified as properties of the `Find` object can also be specified as optional parameters of the `Execute` method. Thus for a simple search we can write

```
Selection.Find.Execute Text := "Wibble!"
```

As an example of a more complex search, consider

```
With Selection.Find
   .ClearFormatting
   .Text = "Wibble!"
   .Forward = True
   .MatchCase = True
   .MatchWholeWord = True
   .Font.Italic = True
   .Wrap = wdFindAsk
   .Execute
End With
```

The `Wrap` property defines the action to be taken when the target is found. here we have used `wdFindAsk`: after searching the selection, Word displays a message asking whether to search the remainder of the document. Other possible values are `wdFindContinue` (the find operation continues when the beginning or end of the search range is reached) or `WdFindStop` (the find operation ends when the beginning or end of the search range is reached).

Replacing text

A simple find-and-replace operation can be achieved by setting arguments to the `Execute` method:

```
Selection.Find Text := "Wibble!", _
   ReplaceWith := "Wobble!"
```

For more complex replacements, we define the replacement by setting the properties of the `Replacement` object, which is itself a property of the `Find` object. The properties and methods of the `Replacement` object correspond to the options in the Find and Replace dialog box. So, for example, we can replace all occurrences of '*Wibble!*' with '**Wibble!**' with the following code.

```
With Selection.Find
   .ClearFormatting
   .Font.Italic = True
   .Text = "Wibble!"
     With .Replacement
        .ClearFormatting
        .Font.Bold = True
        .Text = "Wibble!"
     End With
```

```
    .Replace = wdReplaceAll
    .Format = True
    .Execute
  End With
```

The `Format` property is set to true to indicate that formatting is to be applied to the replacement text. The `Replace` property value of `wdReplaceAll` indicates that all occurrences are to be replaced (like 'Replace All' in the Find and Replace dialog box): alternatively we could have set the value to `wdReplaceOne`.

13.6   Modifying Word's built-in dialogs

An obscure feature of Word/VBA is the ability to modify the operation of Word's dialog boxes. (The details are to be found in the on-line documentation of the `Dialogs` collection object.) For example, to force the File/Open dialog to display files with the extension `.txt` rather than `.doc`, all we need to do is to execute the following code:

```
  With Dialogs(wdDialogFileOpen)
    .Name = "*.txt"
    .Show
  End With
```

Similarly,

```
  With Dialogs(wdDialogEditFind)
    .Find = "Wibble!"
    .Show
  End With
```

will bring up the Find and Replace dialog box with "Wibble!" preset in the 'Find What' box.

13.7   Events

13.7.1   Events in Excel

The Excel object model specifies no fewer than 63 events which can be trapped by a VBA program by providing an event handler. In order to trap events, the `EnableEvents` property of the `Application` object must be set to true. This property is initially set to true by Excel: by setting it to false a program can temporarily disable event processing. The events provided fall into four categories:

- **Worksheet** events. These include
  - `Calculate`: occurs after worksheet is recalculated.
  - `Change`: occurs when cell contents are changed by the user or by an external link, e.g. a Word VBA application which has started an instance of Excel and is using the object model to populate or modify a worksheet.

- – `SelectionChange`: occurs when the selection changes.
- – `BeforeRightClick`, `BeforeDoubleClick`: these occur when the corresponding mouse operation occurs, *before* the default action is initiated.
- – `SheetActivate`, `SheetDeactivate`
- **WorkBook** events. These include
  - – `Open`: occurs when the workbook is opened.
  - – `BeforeClose`, `BeforePrint`, `BeforeSave`: these are self-explanatory.
  - – `SheetCalculate`: occurs after any worksheet is recalculated.
  - – `SheetChange`: occurs when cells in any worksheet are changed by the user or an external link.
  - – `WorkbookActivate`, `WorkbookDeactivate`
- **Chart** events. These include
  - – `BeforeDoubleClick`, `BeforeRightClick`: same as for worksheets.
  - – `Calculate`: occurs after chart plots new or changed data.
  - – `MouseDown`, `MouseUp`, `MouseMove`: occur when mouse event happens while pointer is over a chart.
  - – `DragOver`: occurs when a range of cells is dragged over a chart.
  - – `DragPlot`: occurs when a range of cells is dropped on a chart.
  - – `Activate`, `Deactivate`
- **Application** events. These replicate events in other categories for the most part, e.g.
  - – `WorkbookOpen`
  - – `SheetBeforeDoubleClick`, `SheetBeforeRightClick`
  - – `WorkbookBeforeClose`, `WorkbookBeforeSave`, `WorkbookBeforePrint`
  - – `WorkbookActivate`, `WorkbookDeactivate`

Note that a single user action may fire multiple events, e.g. if the user causes a worksheet to be recalculated, the following events fire in sequence

1. The `Calculate` event of the worksheet
2. The `SheetCalculate` event of the workbook
3. The `SheetCalculate` event of the application.

Event handlers for worksheet, workbook and chart events

Event handlers for worksheet, workbook and chart events are written in exactly the same way as Visual Basic event handlers, e.g. if you have created a worksheet object

```
Dim mySheet1 As New Worksheet
```

then the event handler for the `Calculate` event takes the form

```
Private Sub mySheet1_Calculate()
...
End Sub
```

Some event handlers are provided with arguments by Excel, e.g. the `MouseMove` event handler for a chart called `myChart1` has the skeleton

```
Private Sub myChart1_MouseMove(ByVal X _
  As Long, ByVal Y As Long)
  ...
End Sub
```

Here, X and Y are the coordinates of the mouse pointer at the moment the event fired.

Event handlers for application events

For some bizarre and unimaginable reason, Microsoft added an extra layer of complication to event handling for application events. To use application events you must proceed as follows.

- Create a new class module and declare an object of type Application, with events, in the module. For example, assume that a new class module is created and called EventClassModule. The new class module should contain the following code.

  ```
  Public WithEvents App As Application
  ```

- Select EventClassModule in the Visual Basic IDE, then choose App in the Object drop-down list box. The application events are listed in the Procedure drop-down list box, and by selecting them you can write event handlers for them. Thus if you select WorkbookBeforeClose you will get a skeleton procedure:

  ```
  Private Sub App_WorkbookBeforeClose()
  ...
  End Sub
  ```

  and you can fill in the details.
- In the code module in which you want to use application events, declare a new instance of the class module, e.g.

  ```
  Dim X As New EventClassModule
  ```

  and set the App property of X to the application object:

  ```
  Set X.App = Excel.Application
  ```

  There is an element of Catch 22 here: a natural place for this code is in the WorkbookOpen event handler, but the event will not fire until the code has been executed.

13.7.2 Events in Word

In contrast to Excel, Word is impoverished so far as events are concerned: only three events are recognized: Open, Close and New. Open and Close are self-explanatory. The New event fires when a new document is created based on the current document or template. The event handlers have skeletons

```
Private Sub Document_Open()
...
```

```
End Sub
Private Sub Document_Close()
...
End Sub
Private Sub Document_New()
...
End Sub
```

For compatibility with WordBasic, if a subroutine called `AutoOpen` exists in a document, Word will run it when the document is opened. Likewise, if a subroutine `AutoClose` exists, it will be run when the document is closed, and if `AutoNew` exists it will be run when a new document is created based on the current document. These 'Auto' macros are likely to be found in older documents: mixing 'Auto' macros and event handlers is likely to lead to confusion, and is not recommended. If you insist on mixing them, note that the 'Auto' macro always runs before the corresponding event handler.

Word also supports an `AutoExec` subroutine. If a subroutine called `AutoExec` is placed in normal.dot, or in any template that is placed in the Word Startup folder, the subroutine will run whenever Word starts up. Writers of macro viruses love this. (See Section 13.9 for an account of macro viruses.)

13.8 Automation: programming the Office suite

13.8.1 Automation servers and controllers

Automation servers and controllers were introduced in some detail in Chapter 8: for convenience we review the major features briefly in this section.

An *automation server* is an application that provides a collection of *automation objects* which are potentially useful to other applications. An automation object is a COM object that implements the COM automation interface (the *dispinterface*): any object that implements this interface can be controlled by an application which can generate calls to a dispinterface. Such an application is called an *automation controller*. Visual Basic/VBA is a prime example of the species. Applications like Word and Excel are both automation servers and automation controllers, since they make their functionality and data available as automation objects, and can control objects exposed by another application as automation objects. The Office applications expose their entire object model as automation objects described in a *type library*, which defines the properties and methods of the objects, much as a header file in C describes a collection of functions in a library. (The entries in the type library are in many ways the equivalent of a set of abstract base class definitions in C++.) The Visual Basic IDE incorporated in the application includes an object browser, so that the user can explore type libraries to find out what objects are available. This is essential, since as we have seen, the object models supported by an application such as Word or Excel are very large.

13.8.2 Accessing an automation server

To access the object model of an automation server, the controller needs an object reference to the `Application` object which is at the root of the model. All the Office applications make this an 'externally creatable object': it is, except for Excel, the only externally creatable object. (Excel includes `Chart`, `Workbook` and `Worksheet` as externally creatable objects.) The recommended way to obtain a reference to an `Application` object is to declare a variable of the appropriate object type and use the New operator:

```
Dim xlApp As New Excel.Application
```

This will start an instance of Excel running, and make `xlApp` a reference to its `Application` object. Similarly, we can start Word with

```
Dim wordApp As New Word.Application
```

Note that this technique only works in Office 97 and later. In versions of Microsoft Office prior to Office 97 it was necessary to use the `CreateObject()` function to start the server application and create the instance:

```
Dim xlApp As Excel.Application
Set XlApp = CreateObject("Excel.Application")
```

Having obtained a reference to the `Application` object, this reference can then be used as the key to the rest of the object model, e.g.

```
Dim XlApp As Excel.Application
Dim XlBook As Excel.Workbook
Dim XlSheet As Excel.Worksheet
...
Set XlApp = New Excel.Application
Set XlBook = XlApp.Workbooks.Add
Set XlSheet = XlBook.Worksheets(1)
XlApp.Visible = True
XlSheet.Visible = xlSheetVisible
XlSheet.Cells(1, 1).Value = "Hello World!"
```

Creating a reference to the `Application` object starts an instance of the appropriate automation server. What happens if we create more than one `Application` object? Some servers register themselves on installation as 'single instance servers', so that no matter how many instances of the `Application` object are instantiated, only one instance of the server is created. However, in general you should expect to create a new instance of the application for every `Application` object created. This may be what you want, but if a single instance of the server is required, the first instance should be created with New, and subsequent instances created using `GetObject()`. The code

```
Dim someAppObj As SomeApp.Application
Set someAppObj = _
GetObject(, "SomeApp.Application")
```

Note the empty first parameter.

will return a reference to the `Application` object of the application `SomeApp` if an instance of the sever is running, and will return an error (error number 429) if no instance is running [3]. Thus we can write something along the lines of

```
On Error Resume
Dim someAppObj As SomeApp.Application
Set someAppObj = GetObject(, "SomeApp.Application")
If Err.Number = 0 Then
  ...
' server was running
Else If Err.Number = 429 Then
  ...
' server was not running
Else
  ...
'something else went wrong
End If
Err.Clear
```

GetObject() can also be used in another way: for example, to create an instance of an existing Excel workbook loaded from a file we write:

```
Dim xlBook As Excel.Workbook
Set xlBook = _
    GetObject("c:\accounts\ProfitAndLoss.xls")
```

When an automation server is started, it starts running in invisible mode. This may be what you want, e.g. if you start Excel just to use its spelling checker; but if you want the user interface to be visible this must be done explicitly;

```
xlApp.Application.Visible = True
```

or more conveniently,

```
xlApp.Visible = True
```

When the automation server is no longer required, it should be closed down by invoking its Quit method, and the object variable referencing it set to Nothing:

```
xlApp.Application.Quit
Set xlApp = Nothing
```

13.8.3 An example

As an example of inter-working with Word and Excel, we present an application which takes the contents of a table in a Word document and appends it to an Excel spreadsheet. The scenario might be the transfer of sales figures from a report formatted in Word to a master spreadsheet. We assume that the application is hosted in Word, and that the first line of the table contains headings. The code is straightforward.

```
Dim wTbl As Table
Dim tblRows As Long,tblCols As Long
Dim sheetRows As Long
Dim xlApp As Excel.Application
```

```
Dim xlSheet As Excel.Worksheet
Dim range As Range

' Find the table and its size
Set wTbl = ActiveDocument.Tables(1)
tblRows = wTbl.Rows.Count
tblCols = wTbl.Columns.Count

' Start Excel, get the worksheet and find
' its boundary: the current region is a range
' bounded by any combination of blank rows and
' blank columns.
set xlApp = _
GetObject("c:\finance\sales.xls")
set xlSheet = xlApp.Worksheets(1)
range = xlSheet.Cells(1,1)
sheetRows = range.CurrentRegion.Rows.Count

' Copy table cells to worksheet, skipping
' first row (headings) and stripping off
' final paragraph mark
For i = 1 To tblRows -1
  For j = 0 To tblCols -1
    wTbl.Cell(i, j).select
    nchars = Selection.Characters.Count
xlSheet.Cells(sheetRows+i, j+1).Value = _
      Left(Selection, nchars ?1)
  Next j
Next i
' Show result
xlApp.Application.Visible = True
xlApp.Parent.Windows("sales.xls"). _
  Visible = True
```

13.8.4 OLE and compound documents

A user of Word can use Object Linking and Embedding (OLE) to create compound documents. For example, a Word document can have a portion of an Excel worksheet embedded in it by copying the required cells to the clipboard in Excel, and using the 'Paste Special' option from the *Edit* menu. The user can choose whether to embed the spreadsheet data or place a link to the Excel data in the Word document. The difference is that an embedded spreadsheet can be used from within Word using 'in-place editing', while a linked spreadsheet is edited in a separate Excel window. The spreadsheet data looks like a table in the Word document until Excel is activated by double clicking the spreadsheet. The Paste Special operation also provides the option of marking the position of the paste by an icon, rather than displaying the data.

Linked documents, but *not* embedded documents, can be created within a Word/VBA program by using the `PasteSpecial` method of the `Selection` or `Range` object. Thus if a portion of a spreadsheet has been placed on the clipboard by Excel, it can be placed into a Word document as a linked item at the start of the second paragraph by the following code:

```
Dim rng As Range
Set rng = _
   ActiveDocument.Paragraphs(1).Range
rng.Collapse wdCollapseEnd
rng.PasteSpecial DataType := wdPasteOLEObject, _
   DisplayAsIcon := True, link :=True
```

(The `PasteSpecial` method provides many other options, which we do not explore further.)

How did the Excel data get onto the Clipboard? Elsewhere in the Word/VBA program we would open the Excel spreadsheet, define a range comprising the required cells, and then use the `Copy` method of the `Range` object to place the information on the clipboard:

```
Dim xlBook As Excel.Workbook
Set xlBook = _
    GetObject("c:\accounts\ProfitAndLoss.xls")
ActiveSheet.Range("C3", "F6").Copy
```

(The arguments of the `Range` method are the cells at the top left-hand corner and bottom right-hand corner of the area to be copied.)

13.9   Using the Windows API

As an example of using the Windows API, consider the problem of finding out if an instance of an automation server is already running. As we have seen above, we can attempt to access a running instance with `GetObject`, and trap the error that results if there is no such running instance. As an alternative, we can use the API function `FindWindow`. This takes two arguments, the window class and the window name as it appears in the title bar. If this second argument is a null pointer, the window is found by class name alone. The code required is as follows:

```
Declare Function WinByClass Lib "user32" _
  Alias "FindWindowA" _
  (ByVal lpClassName As String, _
  ByVal lpWindowName As Long) _
  As Long

Function IsXL() As Boolean
Dim rv As Long
rv = WinByClass("XLMAIN", 0&)
IsXL = rv
End Function
```

Note that "XLMAIN" is the string used to define the Excel application class, and 0& is zero expressed as a long integer – the null pointer required by the API call. This call returns a non-zero value if the application is running, which is used to set the return value of the IsXL function.

13.10 Macro viruses

So called 'Macro viruses' have achieved some prominence recently. The writer of a macro virus exploits the fact that the Document_Open procedure will be obeyed when a Word document is opened. The technique is to create a document containing a Document_Open macro which does something unpleasant or undesirable, and to send it as a mail attachment, with a message 'Here is the information you asked for'. The hope (expectation) is that the user will click on the attached item, causing the document to be opened in Word: Document_Open then has its wicked way with the user's system.

The possibilities are limited only by the malefactor's imagination, since a VBA program has access to the entire system. For example, consider the following bit of trickery.

```
Private Sub Document_Open()
  Declare Function ExitWindowsEx Lib "user32 _
    (ByVal uFlags As Long _
    ByVal dwReserved As Long) As Long
  Const EWX_POWEROFF = 8
  Dim rtn As Long
  rtn = ExitWindowsEx(EWX_POWEROFF, 0&)
End Sub
```

The hapless user who opens a document containing this macro will find that Windows immediately shuts down, and if power management is enabled, the power is switched off.

One of the best known macro viruses is the 'Melissa' virus. If run on a system using Microsoft Outlook, this virus replicates itself in the form of a mail message (with attachment) to the first 50 addresses in the Outlook address book. Interestingly, all this is achieved without using the Windows API: Melissa just exploits the programmability of the Office suite. The virus starts by using the PrivateProfileString property of the System object to determine the current security settings as recorded in the Registry: if need be, it changes the PrivateProfileString and sets properties of the Options object to turn off security checking, e.g. by setting Options.VirusProtection to false. It then checks (via the PrivateProfileString) whether the system has already been infected, and if not it uses CreateObject("Outlook.Application") to start an instance of Outlook. Calling the GetNameSpace method of the object returned with an argument "MAPI" gives it access to the address book. (MAPI is the acronym for Messaging Application Programming Interface.) The virus then create an empty mail message using the CreateItem method of the Outlook object. Up to 50 entries are collected from the address book and placed in the recipient list, and the subject and body are set via the Subject and Body properties of the message object. The document itself is added as an attachment using the Add method of the Attachment property of the message object, and the Send method is invoked to send the e-mails. The virus then adds an entry to the `PrivateProfileString` to mark the system as infected, and if the day of the month expressed as a number is equal to the minute in the current time, it displays a harmless message in the current selection.

Misplaced ingenuity? Probably so, but it is an impressive example of the way in which Office applications can be made to work together.

Notes

[1] The use of VBA is not restricted just to applications that inter-work with Microsoft Office. It has recently been announced that the Corel WordPerfect Office 2000 suite is to use VBA as its common macro language.

[2] Unfortunately, the behaviour of Word and Excel with regard to visual controls is inconsistent. While these controls can be placed anywhere in an Excel worksheet, in Word they can only be placed in a *UserForm* (also known as a Custom Dialog Box), which is provided by the Word object model.

[3] The explanation given is the way things are supposed to behave, and do at the time of writing. However, in early versions of Office 97, the call `GetObject(, "Excel.Application")` always started a new instance of Excel, even if an instance was already running.

## Chapter 14

The Microsoft Scripting Runtime Library

The Scripting Runtime Library provides additional functionality to any application that can act as an automation controller. Such applications include Visual Basic, the Windows Script Host, Microsoft's IIS Web server and (subject to security restrictions) Internet Explorer. The Library provides a dictionary object which is based on the Perl hash, and a File System Object Model that provides full control of files, folders and text files. This chapter documents the objects provided, and gives examples of their use.

14.1 Scripting hosts, scripting engines and object libraries

We have by now seen several examples of languages that interact with an external environment by manipulating objects exposed by that environment. Examples include Visual Basic, Microsoft's IIS Web server and Web browsers such as Netscape Navigator and Internet Explorer. This interaction can be achieved in two ways. One approach is the Netscape Navigator model: when the browser encounters a <SCRIPT> tag in an HTML page, the subsequent lines of code up to the </SCRIPT> tag are passed for processing to the JavaScript interpreter that is built into the browser. As the interpreter processes the code it passes back instructions to the browser to manipulate the objects exposed in the Navigator object model, which mirrors the actual Web page being displayed. The interpreter and the object model are tightly bound to the browser.

An alternative approach underlies the Microsoft approach to scripting. In Chapter 8 we saw how Visual Basic decouples the language from the object model: when Visual Basic starts up it is given a list of type libraries to consult. Each type library describes an object model exposed by an application, and the Visual Basic code can 'see' all the objects in the specified object models. If we compare Visual Basic 5 with Visual Basic 6, we see that little additional functionality has been added to the core language: almost all the additional functionality is provided by new object models.

Microsoft's *ActiveX Scripting* technology builds on this idea of separation, by also allowing an application to use multiple scripting languages, with the processing of a script being detached from an application. Recall that an application that exposes a scriptable object model is called an automation server, and the object model can be scripted by any automation controller which implements the COM dispatch interface. A *scripting host* is a special kind of automation controller which can instantiate one or more *scripting engines* to process scripts. The host application does not 'understand' the script(s): instead, when it encounters a script it sends the script line by line to the appropriate scripting engine, which interprets the code and uses COM automation to manipulate the objects in the application's object models. For example, Internet Explorer uses the value of the `language` attribute in a `<SCRIPT>` tag to determine the scripting engine to be employed, and multiple scripting languages can be used in a single HTML page. Microsoft ships scripting engines for JScript and VBScript with applications like Internet Explorer and the Windows shell, but third-party scripting engines for other languages are available, e.g. PerlScript.

In this architectural framework, object libraries allow new functionality to be added to multiple applications: the Scripting Runtime Library is a good example.

14.2 The Scripting Runtime Library

The Scripting Runtime Library implements two areas of functionality.

- *Dictionary* – an object that implements associative arrays based on the Perl hash
- *File System Object Model* – a collection of objects which provide abstractions of drives, folders and files, and content of text files.

The Scripting Runtime Library can be used by any application that can control automation objects, subject to security limitations: for example, only the dictionary object is available in client-side VBScript, but server-side VBScript has access to the full File System Object Model.

14.3 The Dictionary object

The `Dictionary` object provides an efficient alternative to a collection in many situations. It is the equivalent of a Perl hash: items, which can be any form of data, are stored in an associative array with each item associated with a unique key. The key is used to retrieve an individual item and is usually a integer or a string, but can be anything except an array. It forms an alternative to the collection object in Visual Basic programs.

14.3.1 Creating a dictionary object

In Visual Basic and VBScript a dictionary object is created exactly like any other object. Thus in Visual Basic, which supports early binding, the object would be created thus:

```
Dim myDict As New Dictionary
```

In server-side VBScript we would write

```
Dim myDict
Set myDict = CreateObject("Scripting.Dictionary")
```

JavaScript (ECMAScript) does not provide a `CreateObject` function, but JScript provides an equivalent: we would write

```
Var myDict = New
   ActiveXObject("Scripting.Dictionary");
```

We can also use `Dictionary` objects in scripts embedded in HTML pages, by including the object with an `<OBJECT>` tag, e.g.

```
<HTML>
<HEAD>
<TITLE>Scripting Runtime Library Example</TITLE>
</HEAD>
<BODY>
<H2> Scripting Runtime Library Example</H2>
<OBJECT ID="myDict" WIDTH=0 HEIGHT=0
CLASSID=
   "CLSID:EE09B103-97E0-11CF-978F-00A02463E06F"
CODEBASE=
"http://msdn.microsoft.com/scripting/scrrun/x86/s
rt31en.cab#version=3,1,0,2230">
</OBJECT>
...
```

14.3.2   Using the Dictionary object

Once created, entries can be added to a dictionary using the `Add` method, e.g.

```
myDict.add "o", "Oranges"
myDict.add "a", "Apples"
myDict.add "b", "Bananas"
```

and key lookup for items in the dictionary is provided by the `Item()` property, e.g.

```
f = myDict.Item("b")
```

Since `Item` is the default method for a dictionary object, this can be abbreviated to

```
f = myDict("b")
```

The `Item()` property can also be used to assign a new value:

```
myDict.Item("a") = "Asparagus"
```

Analogously, an existing key can be changed:

```
myDict.Key("a") = "Aaaardvark"
```

The `Exists()` method can be used to check that a particular key exists:

```
If myDict.Exists("b") Then
   f = myDict("b")
```

```
Else
  MsgBox("Non-existent key b")
End If
```

An individual entry can be removed with the Remove() method, and a dictionary can be completely cleared with the RemoveAll method.

If it is required to iterate over all the entries in a dictionary, the Items method can be used to create an array containing all the items:

```
a = myDict.Items
For I = 0 To MyDict.Count - 1
   ...
Next I
```

Analogously, the Keys method returns an array containing all the keys. Apart from the syntax we might be talking about Perl hashes!

14.4 The File System Object Model

The File System Object Model abstracts all the details of the local drives and the files they contain, giving scripts full freedom to manipulate the file system as required and to read and write text files. (Random access and binary files are not supported in the current version.)

The structure of this complex object is somewhat confusing. This confusion arises because there are two different ways of viewing many operations: for example, deleting a file can be viewed as an operation on the file, or as an operation on the file system. The File System Object Model embraces both philosophies, thus many of the methods of the FileSystemObject object, which abstracts the entire file system, are duplicated in other objects, e.g. the File object, which abstracts an individual file.

14.4.1 The object hierarchy

The File System Object Model provides the following objects.

- The Drive object and the Drives collection. The Drive object represents a (local or network) drive: its methods and properties allow you to gather information about a drive attached to the system, e.g. its share name, free space etc. Note that a 'drive' is not necessarily a hard disk, but can be, for example, a CD-ROM drive. The Drives collection contains a drive object for every drive attached (physically or logically) to the system.
- The Folder object and the Folders collection. The Folder object provides methods and properties that allow you to create, delete or move folders, and to query the system for folder names, paths and various other properties. The Folders collection provides a list of all the folders within a folder.
- The File object and the Files collection. The File object represents a file: its methods and properties allow you to create, delete or move the file and to query the

system for a file name, path and various other properties. The `Files` collection contains a file object for each file in a folder.

- The `TextStream` object. The `TextStream` object allows you to read and write text files.
- The `FileSystemObject` object. The `FileSystemObject` object is the main object of the group, providing methods that allow you to create, delete, gain information about, and generally manipulate drives, folders and files. As noted above, many of the methods associated with this object duplicate those in the other objects. The important thing about this object is that it is the only object in the File System Object Model that can be externally created, thus it provides the route to all the other objects in the model.

14.4.2   Working with the File System Object Model

As noted above, the `FileSystemObject` object provides the only route to the object model, and an instance of it must therefore be created before any operations can be performed on the file system. (Note that only one instance of a `FileSystemObject` object is actually created, no matter how many instances we attempt to create.) To create a `FileSystemObject` object in Visual Basic we write

```
Dim fso As New FileSystemObject
```

In server-side VBScript we write

```
Dim fso
Set fso = _
CreateObject("Scripting.FileSystemObject")
```

and in JScript it is necessary to write

```
var fso;
fso = new
  ActiveXObject("Scripting.FileSystemObject");
```

Once created, we use the object reference to create an object representing something of interest in the file system, e.g. we open a new text file and obtain a reference to the object representing it with

```
Dim fso As New FileSystemObject
Dim myFile As File
Set myFile =_
  fso.CreateTextFile("c:\temp\test.txt", true)
```

Similarly, we can get a reference to an object representing the e: drive with

```
Dim fso As New FileSystemObject
Dim drv As Drive
Set drv = _
  fso.GetDrive("e:")
```

We can then use the properties and methods of the drive object, e.g. to check whether it is a CD-ROM we write

```
If drv.DriveType = CDROM Then
  msgBox "Can't write to CDROM", vbOKOnly
Else ...
```

(The precise way this works will become apparent later.) Alternatively, we can manipulate the file system directly using the methods of the base object.

14.5   Working with the FileSystemObject object

As we have noted above, the `FileSystemObject` object has a large collection of methods for manipulating the file system. These fall into three groups: creating and deleting files and folders, accessing existing files and folders, and miscellaneous operations.

14.5.1   Creating and deleting files and folders

- `CreateTextFile()` – creates a new file whose filespec (path name) is given as a (string) argument and returns a `TextStream` object which can be used to read and write the file. An optional second argument can be set to true if overwriting of existing files is permitted, and an optional third argument is set to true if the character coding is Unicode. Use of the `TextStream` object is described below.
- `CreateFolder()` – returns a `Folder` object representing a new folder whose filespec (path name) is given as a (string) argument. An error occurs if the named folder exists already.
- `DeleteFile, DeleteFolder` – deletes the file/folder whose filespec (path name) is given as a (string) argument. The filespec can contain wild card characters in its final component. An optional second argument is set true if deletion of files/folders with the read-only attribute set is permitted.

14.5.2   Accessing existing files and folders

- `GetFile()`, `GetFolder()` – returns a file or folder object representing the file or folder whose filespec (path name) is given as a (string) argument. Since an error occurs if the file or folder does not exist, it is prudent to check first, using the `FileExists()` or `FolderExists()` methods.
- `GetSpecialFolder()` – returns a folder object representing the special folder specified by the argument supplied. Possible arguments are `WindowsFolder`, `SystemFolder` and `TemporaryFolder`. (These are constants defined by an in-built enumeration.) Thus we can create a temporary file in the Windows TEMP directory with the following code (assuming that `fso` is a reference to a `FileSystemObject` object):

```
Set tfolder = _
fso.GetSpecialFolder(TemporaryFolder)
tname = fso.GetTempName
Set tfile = tfolder.CreateTextFile(tname)
```

(Here, GetTempName is a method of FileSystemObject which returns a unique name.)

- CopyFile, CopyFolder – copy files or folders. The first (string) argument is the filespec of the source file or folder, the second (string) argument is the filespec of the destination file or folder. If the first argument contains wild cards, multiple files or folders are copied. An optional third argument can be set to false if existing files or folders are not to be overwritten: the default is that existing files or folders will be overwritten unless the read-only attribute is set.

- MoveFile, MoveFolder – moves files or folders. The first (string) argument is the filespec of the source file or folder, the second (string) argument is the filespec of the destination file or folder. If the first argument contains wild cards, multiple files or folders are moved.

  If the source filespec contains wild cards or the destination filespec ends with a path separator (\), it is assumed that the destination specifies an existing folder in which to move the matching files. Otherwise, the destination is assumed to be the name of a destination file to create. In either case, three things can happen when an individual file is moved:
  - If the destination does not exist, the file gets moved. This is the usual case.
  - If the destination is an existing file, an error occurs.
  - If the destination is a directory, an error occurs.

- OpenTextFile() – returns a TextStream object which can be used to read and write the file whose filespec (path name) is given as a (string) argument. An optional second argument can be set to indicate the mode: possible values are the intrinsic constants ForReading, ForWriting and ForAppending. An optional third argument can be set to true to indicate that a new file is to be created if the filename specified does not exist. An optional fourth argument determines the ASCII/Unicode choice: possible values are the constants TriStateFalse (open as ASCII – the default), TriStateTrue (open as Unicode), and TriStateUseDefault (use the system default).

Miscellaneous methods

- GetDrive() – returns a Drive object for the drive name given as a (string) argument. The argument can be a drive letter e.g. "c", a drive letter with a colon appended, e.g. "c:", a drive letter with a colon and path separator appended, e.g. "c:\", or any network share specification, e.g. ("\\server\share1").
- GetExtensionName()
  GetBaseName()
  GetFileName()
  GetParentFolderName()
  GetDriveName()

Extract components of a path. Given a path as a string, GetExtensionName() returns the extension (the final part after the dot); GetBaseName() strips off the extension and returns the remainder of the path; GetFilename() returns the component of the path after the final backslash (including the extension if this has not been stripped off); GetParentFolderName() strips off the last component and returns the remainder of the path; GetDriveName() returns the drive name.

- BuildPath() – appends a name given as the second (string) argument to an existing path given as the first (string) argument, and returns the new path. If necessary a backslash will be added to the end of the original path before adding the new name.
- GetAbsolutePathName() – given a path name that is relative to the current directory as a (string) argument, returns the complete path from the root of the drive. Can also be used to resolve path names that include directory tree navigation from the current directory, e.g. "c:\...\temp.txt".
- GetTempName – return a randomly generated file or folder name
- DriveExists()
  FileExists()
  FolderExists()
  Test for existence of specified drive, file or folder. DriveExists() takes a drive letter or a complete path as argument: if the drive has removable media, it is necessary to use the IsReady property of the returned drive object to test for the presence of media in the drive. If the target of FileExists() or FolderExists() is not in the current directory, a full path must be provided, e.g. by using GetAbsolutePathName().

14.6 The Drive object

The Drive object has no methods. Its properties are
- AvailableSpace – space available to the user (bytes).
- DriveLetter – self-explanatory.
- DriveType – returns an integer denoting the drive type: the values are available as constants in an in-built enumeration: CDROM, Fixed, RAMDisk, Remote, Removable, Unknown.
- FileSystem – returns the file system type as a string: "FAT", "NTFS" or "CDFS".
- FreeSpace – free space on drive (bytes). Normally the same as the value returned by AvailableSpace, but the two may differ if quotas are enforced.
- IsReady – returns true if drive is ready, false otherwise.
- Path – returns the path of the drive. Most likely to be of use for network drives.
- RootFolder – returns a Folder object representing the root folder of the drive.
- SerialNumber – returns the serial number of the drive.
- ShareName – returns the share name of the (network) drive.
- TotalSize – returns the total size of the drive.
- VolumeName – returns the volume name of the drive. This is a read/write property, so can be used to change the volume label.

14.7 The File and Folder objects

The File and Folder objects represent files and folders, respectively. The objects have properties that give information about the file or folder (e.g. date of last update) and can be used to set certain values, e.g. attributes. The methods of these objects largely duplicate the functionality of the methods of the FileSystemObject object.

14.7.1 Properties

Properties common to File and Folder objects

- Attributes – returns the attributes of the file/folder, e.g. ReadOnly, Hidden, System, Archive as an integer. If multiple attributes are set, the value returned is the sum of the individual values. Many attributes can be set by writing to this property.
- DateCreated – returns date and time of file/folder creation.
- DateLastAccessed – returns date and time of file/folder last access.
- DateLastModified – returns date and time of file/folder last modification.
- Drive – returns drive letter of file/folder.
- Name – returns name of file/folder. The name can be changed by assigning a value to this attribute.
- ParentFolder – returns a Folder object representing the parent folder of the file/folder.
- Path – returns the path of the file/folder.
- Shortname – returns the DOS 8.3 style short name of the file/folder.
- ShortPath – returns the path using DOS 8.3 style short names.
- Size – for a File object, returns the size (in bytes) of the file. For a Folder object, returns the total size (in bytes) of the folder and all the folders/files contained in it.
- Type – returns a descriptive string, based on the extension: e.g. for a .txt file, returns Text File.

Properties specific to the Folder object

- Files – returns a collection of File objects, one for each file in the folder, including those with Hidden and/or System attributes set.
- SubFolders – returns a collection of Folder objects, one for each folder contained in the folder, including those with Hidden and/or System attributes set.
- IsRootFolder – returns true if the folder is the root folder, false otherwise.

14.7.2 Methods

Methods common to File and Folder objects

- Copy() – copies the file/folder to the destination path given as an argument.
- Delete – deletes the file or folder. (c.f. the DeleteFile() and DeleteFolder() methods of the FileSystemObject object.)

- Move() – moves the file/folder to a new location given as an argument. (Equivalent to using the MoveFile() and MoveFolder() methods of the FileSystemObject, but note that by using wild card specifications, multiple files or folders can be copied using the FileSystemObject methods.)

Method specific to the File object

- OpenAsTextStream() – opens the file and returns a TextStream object that can be used for reading and writing the file. Equivalent to the OpenTextFile() method of the FileSystemObject object. Takes optional parameters to determine the mode and the ASCII/Unicode choice, exactly as OpenTextFile(). (The TextStream object is described in Section 14.8.)

Method specific to the Folder object

- CreateTextFile() – creates a text file in the folder with the name given as an argument, and returns a TextStream object which can be used to read or write the file. Equivalent to the CreateTextFile() method of the FileSystemObject object, and takes the same optional arguments.

14.7.3   Files and folders: an example

This subroutine makes a copy of all files in a directory that have the extension .txt, the copy having the extension .bak.

```
Sub CopyToBak (targetdir As String)
' Copies *.txt to *.bak in directory
' given as argument
 Dim fso As FileSystemObject
 Dim dir As Folder
 Dim Files As Files
 Dim File As File
 Dim Path As String
 Set fso = New FileSystemObject
 Set dir = fso.GetFolder(targetdir)
 Set Files = dir.Files
 For Each File In Files
  Path = File.Path
  base = Left(Path, Len(Path) - 4)
  If StrComp(Right(Path, 4),".txt", _
    vbTextCompare) = 0 Then
    File.Copy (base & ".bak")
  End If
 Next File
End Sub
```

The code is very straightforward. We create a `FileSystemObject` object, and use its `GetFolder` method to create a folder object for the chosen directory. We then get the folder's `Files` collection, and iterate over this with a `For Each` loop. Within the loop we decompose the file path into base and extension, and if the extension is `.txt` we use the `Copy` method of the `file` object to create the copy. Using `StrComp` with the 'text comparison' option makes the comparison case-insensitive.

14.8   Text I/O with the TextStream object

The `TextStream` object provides a new and more flexible way of processing sequential character files (text files). It represents the content of a text file: its properties return information about the current position in the file (e.g. end-of-file), and its methods allow reading from the file and writing new data to the file.

A `TextStream` object comes into being as a result of creating or opening a text file: this can be done in a confusing variety of ways.

- A new text file is created using the `CreateTextFile` method of the `FileSystemObject` object or the `Folder` object:

```
Dim fso As New FileSystemObject
Dim ts As TextStream
set ts = fso.CreateTextFile("c:\temp\test.txt")
```

The operation will fail if the path provided corresponds to an existing file. This behaviour can be suppressed by specifying an optional extra argument as true:

```
set ts = _
   fso.CreateTextFile("c:\temp\test.txt", True)
```

In this case an existing file will be overwritten.
- An existing text file can be opened using the `OpenTextFile` method of the `FileSystemObject` object, e.g.

```
Dim fso As New FileSystemObject
Dim ts As TextStream
Set ts = _
   fso.OpenTextFile("c:\temp\test.txt",_
   ForReading)
```

The second parameter can alternatively be specified as `ForAppending`. The operation will fail if the file does not exist. This behaviour can be suppressed by adding an additional argument 'true':

```
Set ts = _
   fso.OpenTextFile("c:\temp\test.txt",_
   ForAppending, True)
```

In this case, a new (empty) file will be created if the file does not exist. Clearly, it is pointless to use this option in combination with `ForReading`.

- A `TextStream` object can be created using the `OpenAsTextStream` method of the `File` object:

```
Dim fso As New FileSystemObject
Dim file As File,ts As TextStream
Set file = fso.GetFile("c:\temp\test.txt")
set ts = file.OpenAsTextStream(ForReading)
```

Alternative values for the second argument are `ForWriting` and `ForAppending`.

Once the `TextStream` object is created we can use its properties to interrogate the state of the text file, and its methods to read and write data.

14.8.1   Properties of the TextStream object

- `AtEndOfLine` – returns true if at end of line.
- `AtEndOfStream` – returns true if at end of stream (i.e. EOF).
- `Column` – returns column number in current line.
- `Line` – returns line number.

14.8.2   Methods of the TextStream object

- `Read()` – reads a specified number of characters, and returns the result as a string.
- `ReadLine` – reads an entire line (up to but not including the end of line character or characters), and returns the result as a string.
- `ReadAll` – reads an entire stream and returns the result as a string.
- `Skip()` – skips a specified number of characters.
- `SkipLine` – skips an entire line: discards all characters including the end of line character(s).
- `Write()` – writes the string given as an argument to the file represented by the `TextStream`.
- `WriteLine()` – writes the string given as an argument to the file represented by the `TextStream`, followed by the end of line character(s). If no argument is provided, writes a line terminator.
- `WriteBlankLines()` – writes the specified number of line terminators to the file.
- `Close` – closes an open `TextStream` file.

14.8.3   TextStream: an example

We illustrate the use of the `TextStream` with a simple Visual Basic application, a text file browser. When the application is started, it displays the window shown in Figure 14.1. When the user clicks on 'Choose File' the standard Windows 'File Open' dialog is displayed (Figure 14.2). The user can navigate through the file system, and when the chosen file has been selected, clicking 'Open' displays its contents in a text box (Figure 14.3). The process can be repeated by clicking 'Choose File' again, and eventually the user quits using the 'Quit' button. Pressing 'Cancel' in the File Open dialog box returns the display to its initial state.

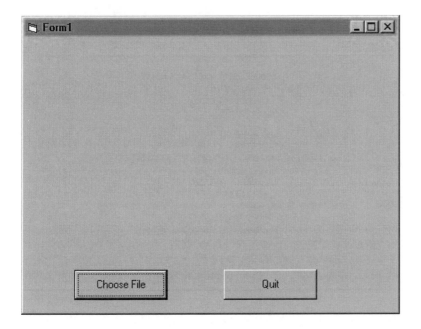

Figure 14.1   Initial screen

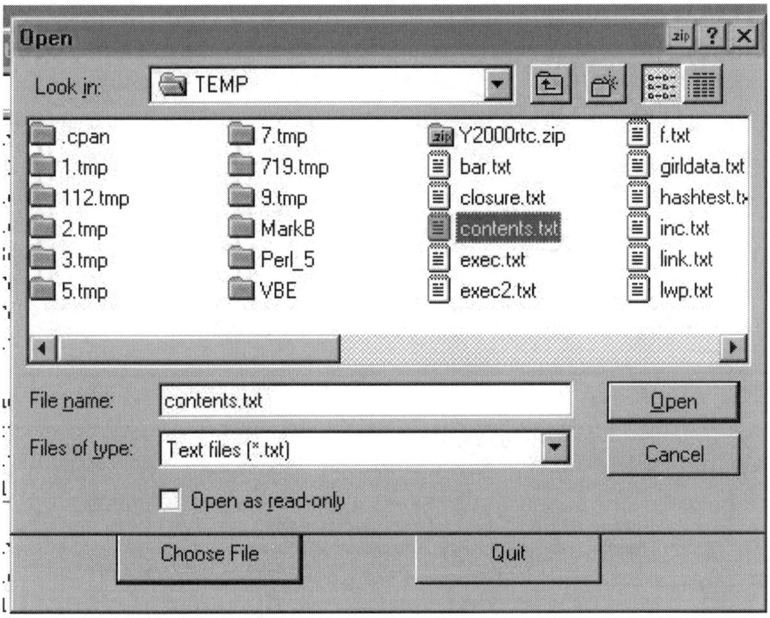

Figure 14.2   File Open dialog box displayed

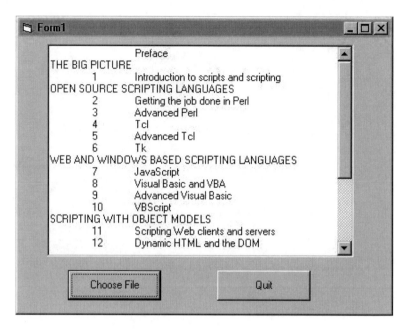

Figure 14.3 File contents display

At the design stage we created a form with a textbox control (Text1), a Common-
Dialog control (CDlg) and two command buttons, (Command1 and Command2). The
textbox control had its 'multiline' property set to true. (This property has to be set at
compile time.) The associated code is as follows.

```
Dim fso As New FileSystemObject
Dim filetext As TextStream
Dim Filename As String
Private Sub Form_Load()
Text1.Visible = False
CDlg.Filter = "Text files (*.txt)|*.txt"
CDlg.CancelError = True
End Sub
```

(Form_Load performs a few initializations. The textbox is hidden, the File Open dialog is
set to filter text files only, and the CancelError property is set to true, so that a run-time
error will be raised if the user presses the 'Cancel' button in the File Open dialog.)

```
Private Sub Command2_Click()
Unload Form1
End Sub
```

(The Quit button terminates the application.)

```
Private Sub Command1_Click()
On Error GoTo Cancel
```

```
Text1.Visible = False
CDlg.ShowOpen
Filename = CDlg.Filename
   Set filetext = fso.OpenTextFile(Filename)
   Text1.Visible = True
   Text1.Text = filetext.ReadAll
Exit Sub

Cancel:
Text1.Visible = False
Exit Sub
End Sub
```

(All the work is done in the event handler for the 'Choose File' button. The error raised by pressing Cancel is trapped: if it occurs, the textbox is hidden and the subroutine exits. CDlg.ShowOpen displays the File Open dialog: the code now blocks until the user clicks Open or Cancel. If Open is clicked, the selected file name is retrieved and the file is opened as a text stream. The ReadAll method causes the entire contents of the file to be read, and this is assigned as the value of the text property of the now visible textbox. Besides illustrating the use of a text stream, this application demonstrates the leverage that you get from the built-in controls. All the functionality of the Windows File Open dialog is yours for a couple of lines of Visual Basic code.)

## Chapter 15

The Windows Script Host and the Script Control

The Windows Script Host is a component of Windows that makes it possible to use scripting languages to automate operations in the Windows shell that would otherwise be performed manually through the Windows GUI. It forms a powerful alternative to the 'batch' capability offered in the NT command-line facility. We describe the object model used by the Windows Script Host, and give some examples of its use. The Script Control is an ActiveX control which allows any application to be a scripting host: we give a brief account of its capabilities.

15.1   What is the Windows Script Host?

The Windows Script Host [1] makes the Windows shell into a scripting host, so that scripts can be executed directly on the Windows desktop or from a command prompt window. It is an ideal host for non-interactive scripts that perform administrative tasks. Like Internet Explorer, it ships with engines for JavaScript (JScript) and VBScript, but can use any scripting engine that conforms to the ActiveX scripting architecture, e.g. PerlScript. The Script Host is available as an add-on for Windows 95 and NT4, ships with Windows 98, and will be an integral part of Windows 2000.

Scripts can be invoked from the command line using the cscript or wscript command, or directly from the desktop by double clicking files in Explorer. In both cases, the appropriate scripting engine is identified using in-built associations for the file extensions (.js for JavaScript, .vbs for VBScript). Scripts can also be invoked from the Run command.

The Windows Script Host has an object model which exposes some of the functionality of the Windows shell: it also uses the objects made available in the Scripting Runtime Library which provide comprehensive control over the file system, as described in the previous chapter. It is thus a powerful alternative to 'batch' programming. The object model provides a CreateObject method which can be used to create any OLE automation objects, not just native Windows Script Host objects. Thus, for example, a system administrator might write a script that gets data from an Excel spreadsheet to add new users in Windows NT.

15.2 The Windows Script Host object model

The root of the object model is an object called `Wscript`, which is exposed when the Script Host starts running.

15.2.1 The Wscript object

The main purpose of this object is to provide the `CreateObject` method so that connections can be established to automation servers. Thus we can create a `Dictionary` object

```
Dim myDict
Set myDict = _
  WScript.CreateObject("Scripting.Dictionary")
```

or a `FileSystemObject` object:

```
Dim fso
Set fso = _
WScript.CreateObject(_
  "Scripting.FileSystemObject")
```

(Note that we are using VBScript here and in subsequent examples.) As a more complicated example, a script can start an instance of Excel and gain access to the Excel object model:

```
Dim xlApp
Set xlApp = _
  WScript.CreateObject("Excel.Application")
```

The Script Host can optionally capture events which are exposed by the Automation object: if we add an extra parameter

```
Set xlApp = _
  WScript.CreatObject("Excel.Application",_
    "Excel_")
```

then occurrence of, e.g., the `onClose` event in Excel will cause the Script Host to call the subroutine `Excel_OnClose` in the script. Other methods of the `Wscript` object include `Echo`, which displays its (string) argument in a window or at a command prompt, and `Quit`, which quits with a specified error code.

The `WScript` object has a number of useful properties, including

- `Arguments` – a collection containing the arguments from the command line (for scripts started from a command line). The `Arguments` collection, like all collection objects, has a property `Count` (`length` in JavaScript), which returns the number of command-line parameters, and a property `Item` (the default property) which is an array of strings.
- `ScriptFullName` – the full path to the file containing the script currently running.
- `ScriptName` – file name of the script currently being run.

15.2.2   The WshShell object

This object is at the heart of shell scripting in the Windows Script Host: it gives access to the desktop and other special folders, and other aspects of the Windows shell, e.g. the environment variables. It is implemented in an ActiveX control that forms part of the Script Host, and instances are created using the CreateObject method of WScript:

```
Dim WshShell
Set WshShell = _
  WScript.CreateObject("Wscript.Shell")
```

Properties

Properties of WshShell are:

- Environment – a collection object representing the environment variables. This is in fact a collection of collections, since there are several sets of environment variables, e.g. 'System' and 'User'. Thus to access the system environment we write

```
Dim WshShell, sysEnv
Set WshShell = _
  WScript.CreateObject("Wscript.Shell")
Set sysEnv = WshShell.Environment("SYSTEM")
```

Particular environment variables are then accessed using their names, e.g.

```
nProc = sysEnv("NUMBER_OF_PROCESSORS")
```

- SpecialFolders – a collection of objects representing the Windows shell folders including the desktop folder and the start menu folder. Thus, having instantiated a WshShell object, the start menu can be accessed as

```
WshShell.SpecialFolders("START MENU")
```

Methods

The methods of WshShell include:

- CreateShortcut – creates a shortcut object. This object has properties that can be set to define the shortcut: Arguments, Description, Hotkey, IconLocation, TargetPath and WindowStyle. It also has a Save method.
- ExpandEnvironmentStrings – expands environment variables, e.g.

```
prompt = _
  WshShell.ExpandEnvironmentStrings("%PROMPT%")
```

- Popup – pops up a message box with a specified message. Also allows choice of buttons (e.g. "OK", or "OK" and "Cancel"), and returns a code indicating which button was pressed.

- RegRead, RegWrite, RegDelete – get, set or delete a key or value in the Registry.
- Run – creates a new process to execute a command with a specified window style.

15.2.3 The WshNetwork object

The WshNetwork object abstracts the 'network neighbourhood'. It is provided by the same ActiveX control as WshShell, and instances are created in a similar way:

```
Dim WshNetwork
Set WshNetwork = _
   Wscript.CreateObject("Wscript.Network")
```

The WshNetwork object gives the administrator control over many aspects of the network through its properties and methods.

Properties

The properties ComputerName, UserDomain and UserName are self-explanatory.

Methods for network drives

- EnumNetworkDrives – returns a WshCollection object containing the current network drive mappings. A WshCollection object is a collection of strings: it has a Count property (Length in JScript), and an Item property, Item(n) returning the nth item in the collection. In the object returned by EnumNetworkDrives the items are alternately local names and remote names, thus if a share \\server\data is mapped to drive Z, then in the collection, for some even value of n, Item(n) will have the value "Z:" and the following item will have the value "\\server\data".
- MapNetworkDrive – map a remote share to a local drive, e.g.

```
Dim WshNetwork
Set WshNetwork = _
Wscript.CreateObject("Wscript.Network")
WshNetwork.MapNetworkDrive "Z:", _
  "\\server\data"
```

- RemoveNetworkDrive – remove a network drive, e.g.

```
WshNetwork.RemoveNetworkDrive "Z:"
```

Methods for network printers

- EnumPrinterConnections – returns a WshCollection object containing the current remote printer connections. As with network drives, the items in the collection are in pairs, e.g. "LPT1:" followed by "\\server\printer1".

- `AddPrinterConnection` – add a remote printer, e.g.

      WshNetwork.AddPrinterConnection "LPT1:", _
        "\\server\printer1"

- `RemovePrinterConnection` – remove remote printer, e.g.

      WshNetwork.RemovePrinterConnection "LPT1:"

- `SetDefaultPrinter` – set a remote printer as the default printer, e.g.

      SetDefaultPrinter "\\server\printer1"

15.3　Examples

We illustrate the Windows Script Host with a few examples.

15.3.1　Batch copy

The subroutine `CopyToBak`, presented in the previous chapter as an example of file system manipulation, can easily be converted into a command that will run under the Windows Script Host. The objective is to be able to type a command like

      c:\> cscript copytobak.vbs d:\temp

at the command prompt to effect the copy: note that the target directory is provided as a command-line parameter. The actual command is a VBScript program stored in a file `copytoback.vbs`, with the following contents.

```
Dim fso, dir, Files, File, Path, Targetdir
Set fso = Wscript.CreateObject(_
    "Scripting.FileSystemObject")
Targetdir = Wscript.Arguments.Item(1)
Set dir = fso.GetFolder(Targetdir)
 Set Files = dir.Files
 For Each File In Files
  Path = File.Path
  base = Left(Path, Len(Path) - 4)
  If StrComp(Right(Path, 4),".txt", _
    vbTextCompare) = 0 Then
    File.Copy (base & ".bak")
 End If
Next File
```

15.3.2　Creating a desktop shortcut

Suppose that, within a script we want to create a desktop shortcut to an application, e.g. Notepad, together with a 'hot-key' assignment of Ctrl-Alt-N.

```
Set WshShell =_
  WScript.CreateObject("Wscript.WshShell")
dsk = WshShell.SpecialFolders("Desktop")
Set sc =_
  WshShell.CreateShortcut(dsk & "\npad.lnk")
sc.TargetPath =_
  WshShell.ExpandEnvironmentStrings ( _
             "%windir%\notepad.exe")
sc.WorkingDirectory = "c:\work"
sc.Hotkey = "ALT+CTRL+N"
sc.Save
```

The argument for the CreateShortcut method is the full path name of the shortcut: in our case it is a file called npad.lnk in the user's desktop folder. The TargetPath property defines the shortcut target: here we have used the ExpandEnvironmentStrings method to generate a path to notepad.exe in the Windows root directory. The Hotkey property is self-explanatory, and the Save method stores the newly created shortcut in its destination.

15.3.3   Charting data with Excel

Suppose that a system administrator needs to produce a weekly chart showing system up-time (as a percentage for each day). The script presented below enables the administrator to type a simple command with the week's data at the command prompt to produce an Excel bar chart with three-dimensional effects. A typical command would be

```
cscript uptime.vbs 99 98 100 99 100 95 99
```

The file uptime.vbs contains the following script.

```
Dim xl, xlChart, Data
Set Data = WScript.Arguments
Set xl = _
  WScript.CreateObject("Excel.Application")
xl.Workbooks.Add
For I = 0 To 6
  xl.Cells(1, I+1).Value = Data(I)
Next
xl.Range("A1:G1").Select
Set xlChart = xl.Charts.Add()
xlChart.Type = 4099
xl.Visible = True
```

This example should be straightforward for readers who have a slight familiarity with the Excel object model: for those readers who do not have this familiarity, the following explanation should suffice.

   The CreateObject function starts up Excel and returns a reference to the object representing the Excel application. This is the root of the Excel object model, and we use it to invoke the `Add` method of the `Workbooks` object to create a new workbook. We populate the first seven columns of row 1 with the data obtained from `Wscript. Arguments`, and select this range. An Excel chart always charts the current selection, so when we create a new chart with `xl.Charts.Add` it will chart the data we have entered. Finally, we select 'Bar chart with 3D effects' as the chart type, and make Excel visible. The constant '4099 used as the argument of `xlChart.Type` is the decimal representation of the hexadecimal value (FFFFEFFD) of the constant `xl3DBar`, which is defined in Excel by an enumeration: the Script Host Version 1 does not have access to the type libraries of the objects it creates, so cannot use enumerated constants.

15.4 The future of the Windows Script Host

Until recently, the future of the Windows Script Host seemed problematical. It was not heavily promoted by Microsoft, the documentation was of a low standard, and despite requests for enhancements from a small band of enthusiastic users, no new version was forthcoming. However, as this book goes to press, a beta version of Windows Script Host 2.0 has been announced, with many exciting new features, including

- Support for `StdIn`, `StdOut` and `StdErr`. For example, `WScript.stdin` returns a reference to a `TextStream` object which can be used to read standard input. Since this support is provided as part of `FileSystemObject`, it is available to any Visual Basic program once the Script Host has been installed.
- `SendKeys`, a method of `WshShell`, which sends one or more keystrokes to the active window as if typed at the keyboard (as already possible in Visual Basic).
- `AddWindowsPrinterConnection`, a method of `WshShell` which provides a programmatic equivalent to the Control Panel Printers/Add Printer dialog.
- Access to type libraries of automation objects.
- Drag and drop support.

The future of the Script Host seems assured.

15.5 The Script Control

In Chapter 14 we described the ActiveX scripting model, in which a *scripting host* is a special kind of automation controller which can instantiate one or more *scripting engines* to process scripts. The host application does not 'understand' the script(s): instead, when it encounters a script it sends the script line by line to the appropriate scripting engine, which interprets the code and uses COM automation to manipulate the objects in the application's object models. This architecture was defined by a collection of COM interfaces which were only accessible from C++. The Script Control is an ActiveX control which hosts scripting engines for JScript and VBScript, and provides a mechanism for the host application to send scripts to the engine for evaluation. Thus any application can become a scripting host: we shall limit our discussion to adding scripting capability to a Visual Basic application.

15.5.1 Using the Script Control

The following sections give a flavour of how the script control is used.

Creating a script control

A script control is created like any other ActiveX control, e.g.

```
set sc = CreateObject("ScriptControl")
```

or

```
Dim sc As New ScriptControl
```

Properties and methods of the ScriptControl object

Like any other control, the `ScriptControl` object has properties and methods. The language property selects the scripting engine to be used – possible values are `"JScript"` and `"VBScript"`. The `AllowUI` property is a Boolean which determines whether the scripting engine is allowed to display user-interface elements, e.g. message boxes. The `Error` property returns a reference to an `Error` object which contains an error number, a description of the error and the line number where the error occurred in the script.

The methods provide the mechanism whereby the application can feed scripts to the scripting engine.

- `ExecuteStatement` executes a single statement, e.g.

```
sc.ExecuteStatement "N = 0"
```

- `Eval` evaluates a single expression, e.g.

```
isZeroN = sc.Eval("N = 0")
```

- `AddCode` adds the text of a complete subroutine or function to the script control, e.g.

```
sc.AddCode Prog
```

  (Here, `Prog` is a variable with a string value which is the text of the subroutine.)
- `Run` runs a subroutine or function that has been added to the script control, e.g.

```
sc.Run "HelloWorld"
sc.Run ("SomeFunction", 10, 22)
```

Note that the Run method is given the name of a subroutine or function which has earlier been added using the `Add` method.

Some practical points

Constructing a subroutine body as a string is tedious: for example, a simple subroutine to display 'Hello World!' in a message box would be constructed in the following way:

```
Dim prog As String
prog = "Sub HelloWorld" & vbCrLf & _
      "MsgBox ""Hello World!""" & vbCrLf & _
      "End Sub"
```

An alternative for a long subroutine is to recall that the `ReadAll` method of a `TextStream` object reads the entire stream and returns it as a string, so the subroutine text can be placed in a file which is opened as a `TextStream`:

```
Dim fso As FileSystemObject
Dim ts As TextStream
Set ts = _
  fso.OpenTextFile("c:\temp\prog.txt",_
    ForReading)
sc.AddCode ts.ReadAll
```

In a similar vein, the code can be entered in a textbox:

```
sc.AddCode Form1.Text1.Text.
```

Dealing with errors

Error trapping follows the Visual Basic model described in Section 7.6.4. We illustrate it with a simple example

```
Sub RunMain(prog As String)
' Argument is a string defining a subroutine
' called "Main"
sc.AddCode prog
On Error GoTo ScriptError
sc.Run "Main"
Exit Sub ' exit here if no error

ScriptError:
msg = "Error " & sc.Error.Number & ":" & _
      vbCrLf & sc.Error.Description & _
      vbCrLf & "at line " & sc.Error.Line
MsgBox msg, vbOkOnly
End Sub
```

Notes

[1]   The Windows Script Host was originally introduced with the name 'Windows Scripting Host'. Recently the name was changed, presumably in order to emphasize the difference between a specific script host and a generic scripting host.

## Part five

And finally . . .

## Chapter 16

Loose ends

In this chapter we explore the pre-history and early history of scripting, tracing the ideas which created the climate in which scripting languages first evolved. We also look at AWK, a language that was very influential in the shaping of Perl, and at REXX, an innovative language that has regrettably never taken root outside the IBM world.

16.1 Pre-history of scripting

The origins of scripting as a form of programming can be found in the batch-processing operating systems developed for mainframes in the 1960s and 1970s. Jobs were submitted as a 'deck' of punched cards, and the purpose of the operating system was to automate the processing of a sequence or batch of jobs. (For efficiency reasons the cards were transcribed onto magnetic tape before being submitted to the mainframe: however, the user model was still one of cards.) In the earliest systems the various sections of a card deck were separated by 'control cards' with a characteristic punching to distinguish them from program and data cards (typically control cards were recognized by the presence of a dollar sign in column 1). A typical job deck might consist of:

- a job card giving the user's name and specifying resource limits (e.g. maximum runtime)
- a compile card preceding the source code
- a link card specifying library routines to be linked into the program
- a load card requesting loading of a complete executable image into memory
- an execute card to initiate execution, followed by data cards
- an end-of-job card, necessary to prevent a rogue program consuming the next job as data for itself.

It will be noted that the control information is distributed throughout the input deck, and that there is no way of omitting any steps: once started, progress through the deck is inexorable.

The IBM System/360 range, introduced in the mid-1960s, had an entirely new operating system, OS/360, which introduced the idea of a *job control language* (JCL). All the control information was collected together at the start of the job deck: the JCL statements broadly corresponded to the control cards of earlier systems, with the addition of *data definition* statements to specify where to find the source code and data for the program. A major innovation was the provision of a crude conditional facility, so that execution of a JCL

```
//C         EXEC    PGM=IEYFORT,PARM='SOURCE'
//SYSPRINT  DD      SYSOUT=A
//SYSLIN    DD      DSNAME=SYSL.UT4,DISP=OLD
//DCB=(RECFM=FBS,LRECL=80,BLKSIZE=800)
//G         EXEC    PGM=FORTLINK,COND=(4.LT.C)
//SYSPRINT  DD      SYSOUT=A
//SYSLIN    DD      DSNAME=*.C.SYSLIN,DISP=OLD
//SYSLIB    DD      DSNAME=SYSL.FORTLIB,DISP=OLD
//FT03F001  DD      DDNAME=PRINT
//FT05F001  DD      DDNAME=SYSIN
//FT06F001  DD      SYSOUT=A,DCB=(RECFM=FA,BLKSIZE=133)
//FT07F001  DD UNIT=SYSCP
//PRINT     DD      SYSOUT=A,DCB=RECFM=FA,LRECL=133)
```

Notes

1. Line 1 calls for execution of the FORTRAN compiler (IEYFORT).
2. Line 2 specifies that the listing is to go to the printer (really!).
3. Lines 3 and 4 specify where the compiled program is to be put (a tape drive) and the precise way the information is to be laid out on tape (fixed block size of 800, record length 80, corresponding to a punched card).
4. Line 5 calls for execution of the linkage editor if condition code returned by compiler is less than 4 (i.e. no compile-time errors) – note the perverse way in which the condition has to be formulated.
5. Line 6 specifies that a link-edit listing is to go to the printer.
6. Line 7 specifies that the input for the link editor is the same device that had the output from the compiler.
7. Line 8 specifies a library file to be used.
8. The remaining lines associate logical unit numbers with names used by the compiler: note the forward reference for FT05F001 which will be run-time data.

Figure 16.1   Example of OS/360 JCL

statement could depend on the exit code returned by the preceding step in the program (e.g. to abort processing if compile-time errors were reported). This was the only element of programmability in JCL, which could hardly be described as a language, and certainly not a readable one – see Figure 16.1 for an example of the JCL needed to run a FORTRAN job under OS/360. Nevertheless, JCL established the important idea of writing a 'program' to control the operating system, and it can also be seen as a very early instance of a scripting language, with the job control cards forming the script that controls the compiler, linker and loader. Figure 16.1 illustrates some of the features of JCL.

16.2   Precursors of scripting

16.2.1   Time-sharing systems

The next stage in development came with the introduction of time-sharing systems, where a number of users at remote consoles (initially hard-copy Teletype machines, later dumb terminals dubbed 'glass teletypes') were given the impression of exclusive use of a machine by time-slicing the CPU on a round-robin basis. The user interface to these systems was through a *command-line interpreter* which read command lines from the keyboard and initiated the appropriate actions. (This mode of working will be familiar to DOS and UNIX users, though Windows and Macintosh users may find it bizarre.) The idea of scripting arose from efforts to mechanize this command-line interaction.

16.2.2 Runcom, exec and the UNIX shell

CTSS runcom

The very first time-sharing system was CTSS, the 'Compatible Time Sharing System' developed on a modified IBM 7090 at MIT in the early 1960s. (The 'Compatible' in the name reflects the fact that CTSS could run background programs that were entirely compatible with the 7090 batch operating system.) CTSS provided the capability to run a short sequence of commands from a file in the background, using a program called *runcom*, which provided a simple 'keystroke playback' capability. (The name 'runcom' explains the use of 'rc' in the UNIX world to denote a file containing commands that are to be executed or definitions to be read, when some program starts up, e.g. `.newsrc` which provides initialization data for the network news reader.)

IBM CMS execs

The command language of the IBM time-sharing system VM/CMS for System/370 included a mechanism called 'EXEC Procedures' for executing statements from a file. A primitive form of programmability was provided, with variables, conditionals based on IF and GOTO, and loops. Figure 16.2 gives a taste of the horrors of EXEC programming.

The following notes may help to elucidate the example of Figure 16.2.

1. The designers of EXEC made the assumption – later demonstrated to be incorrect – that most of an EXEC procedure would consist of commands to be passed to the

```
&IF &N = 0 &GOTO -TELL
&IF &N = 1 &IF &1 = - &GOTO -TELL
&J = 1
&LOOP -X &N
  LISTFILE &&J * * (LABEL &NOHEADER
  &IF &RC = 0 &NOHEADER = NOHEADER
  -X &J = &J + 1
&IF /&NOHEADER = / &EXIT 28
&EXIT
-TELL &PRINT FORMAT IS: &FILENAME FN1 FN 2 . . .
&PRINT USES LISTFILE TO DISPLAY INFORMATION ABOUT
&PRINT ALL FILES WITH FILENAMES FN1, FN2, ETC.
&EXIT 100
```

Figure 16.2   Example of EXEC2 code – a procedure to list the files named on the command line

operating system, and they therefore adopted the convention that EXEC instructions and variables should be identified as such by an initial ampersand. They also distinguished labels (the target of GOTO statements) with an initial minus sign.

2.   The first two lines of the procedure check the arguments provided, and check for a single argument with the value ?. &N is the number of arguments, &1 is the first argument.

3.   Line 4 specifies that the loop is to be executed &N times, and comprises the subsequent lines up to and including a line starting -X.

4.   The syntax in lines 5–7 is that of the CMS 'LISTFILE' command. &RC is the return code returned by LISTFILE, and the variable &NOHEADER is set to record success.

5.   Line 8 contains a string comparison to see if &NOHEADER has a value.

6.   The last three lines display a 'help' message if the procedure is called with ? as its single argument.

The EXEC processor was built into the operating system along with the command interpreter. Incredible as it may seem to the modern reader, the text editor (XEDIT) was also 'wired in' to the operating system, and the EXEC language (and its successor EXEC2) could also be used to control the editor. In principle the language was capable of driving any utility that had a command-line interface, and as such is a clear ancestor of the modern scripting language.

16.2.3   The early UNIX shells

An important feature of UNIX was that right from Version 1 in 1976, the command-line interpreter was not part of the operating system, but was a separate program, called a *shell*, running at user level. UNIX was defined by a collection of system calls (what would nowadays be called an API), and the shell took commands typed by the user and called the relevant system functions. Another important feature was that a process (program) that normally took its input from the keyboard could have the input 'redirected' to come from a file. Since the shell was just another program, a new instance could be started up with its standard input redirected to a file, and so it was possible to execute a sequence of instructions from a file, just like a CTSS runcom or a CMS EXEC. (On start-up the shell determined whether its input was from a real terminal or a file, and in the latter case suppressed the prompt that was normally given following completion of a command.) It was at this time that the term *shell script* came into use to describe a set of UNIX commands stored in a file.

UNIX Version 1 – shell scripts with arguments

In Version 1 of UNIX, shell scripts had no programmability, though they could take arguments. A new shell was started from the command line by the sh command which had one obligatory argument, the name of the file containing the shell script, and up to ten additional arguments that were passed to the shell running the script, e.g.

```
$ sh munge foo bar foobar
```

This command starts an instance of the shell to run a set of commands from the file munge, and passes it the strings foo, bar, and foobar as arguments. More commonly, the file containing the script was given execute permission, and its name used as a command thus:

        $ munge foo bar foobar

The interactive shell recognized this construction, launching a new invocation as if the user had typed the sh command explicitly. When executing a script the shell recognized the syntax $n ($n$ = 1–9) as an instruction to substitute the nth argument from the command line.

UNIX Version 2: glimmerings of programmability

From Version 2 (1972) onward, the shell had a degree of programmability: flow control was restricted to 'goto's and labels, but a powerful if command allowed a variety of conditions to be tested: the 'man page' for the if command is reproduced in Figure 16.3. A further facility was the shift command, which discarded the first argument and re-numbered the remaining arguments, so that $2 became $1 and so on. (A similar command is an important component of Perl.) This provided a convenient way of iterating over a number of arguments, as illustrated in the following code:

NAME

    if – conditional command

SYNOPSIS

    if expr command [arg –]

DESCRIPTION

    If evaluates the expression *expr*, and if its value is true, executes the given command with the given arguments.

    The following primitives are used to construct the expr:

    -r file   true if the file exists and is readable

    -w file   true if the file exists and is writeable

    s1 = s2   true if the strings s1 and s2 are equal

    s1 != s2   true if the strings s1 and s2 are not equal

    { command }   the bracketed command is executed to obtain the exit status. Status zero is
                  considered *true*. The command must not be another *if*.

    These primaries may be combined with the following operators:

    !   unary negation operator

    -a   binary *and* operator

    -o   binary *or* operator

    (expr)   parentheses for grouping

                  (Brackets have a meaning to the shell, so must

                  be escaped as \(and \) in scripts

Figure 16.3 The if command in UNIX Version 6. Note particularly the ability to test the exit status of another command

```
:loop
if $1x = x exit
pr -3 $1
shift
goto loop
```

This script prints the files whose names are given as arguments in three-column format. The syntax $1x = x is the only way of testing for a non-existent argument, which appears as a null string.

Another elegant feature was that if the shell was invoked by giving the name of an executable file containing the script, the name of that file could be accessed within the script as $0. Thus the behaviour of the script could be made to depend on the name used to call it, facilitating implementation of a number of closely related scripts as illustrated in the following example.

```
. . .
if $0 = dee goto deecode
. . .
exit
:deecode
. . .
exit
```

Here the script is stored in an executable file called 'dum', linked (i.e. aliased to) another executable file called 'dee'. It can be called by typing dum or dee at the shell prompt, and its behaviour will depend on the name used.

Pipes and pipelines

UNIX provides a rich collection of tools for commonly used operations, and the underlying system philosophy is one of building large applications by composition of smaller units. From the earliest days, sysadmins made extensive use of the shell to build tools by linking filters in a pipeline: using the UNIX shell to create a pipeline is an early instance of employing a scripting language to glue together a set of components.

A classic example of the technique is a spell-checker realized in a two-line script. (The script is printed here as four lines for clarity. Even if typed in this form, it would appear as two lines to the shell, which treats the sequence backslash–newline as a space, thus allowing a logical line to be split over multiple physical lines.)

```
#!/usr/bin/sh
cat $1 | tr "[A-Z]" "[a-z]" |\
tr -cs "[a-z]" "[\012*]" | sort -u \
| comm -23 - dict
```

For the benefit of readers not versed in UNIX, a commentary on the script is given below.

A *filter* in UNIX is a program that reads a text file from its standard input, processes it in some way and writes it to its standard output. The default is that standard input comes from the keyboard and standard output goes to the screen: however, the shell provides syntax to indicate *diversion* of standard input or output. In particular, the vertical bar denotes a *pipe* which connects the standard output of the program on the left to the standard input of the program on the right.

If the script were stored in an executable file called 'spell', the command `spell myfile` would return a list of words that are contained in `myfile` but not in `dict`, which is a dictionary (strictly a spelling list) which contains all acceptable words, one to a line, in sorted order. The script can be dissected as follows.

`/usr/bin/sh` says that the remainder of the script is to be processed by a new instance of the shell.

`cat $1` starts the ball rolling by writing the contents of `myfile` into the pipeline. The `cat` command simply writes the contents of the file given as its argument to standard output. The notation `$1` stands for the first argument on the command line that invoked the script: this was `myfile`.

`tr "[A-Z]" "[a-z]"` is a filter which translates upper-case letters into lower-case letters.

`tr -cs "[a-z]" "[\012*]"` is a filter which translates all characters *except* lower-case letters into newline characters (octal 012) and compresses multiple newlines to a single newline. By now we have the words of the file one-to a line.

`sort -u` sorts its input alphabetically, including only a single copy of a word which appears more than once.

`comm -23 - dict` compares its standard input (denoted by the – option) with the file `dict`, returning a list of words that appear in the standard input but not in `dict`. Since this is the end of the pipeline, standard output reverts to the screen and these potential spelling errors are displayed.

16.2.4 The Bourne shell

By the early 1970s, crudely programmable control languages were available both in the IBM world (CMS EXEC) and in the UNIX world (shell). In both environments the technology was stretched far beyond its limits, creating a climate in which new developments were bound to happen. Here we describe events in the UNIX world: contemporaneous developments in the IBM world are described in Section 16.4.

In 1979 the original UNIX shell was replaced by the Bourne shell when Version 7 of the system was released. Steve Bourne had a background of research in programming languages, and he saw the essential feature of scripting, that he could write a programming language whose 'primitives' were the UNIX system calls. The programmable shell had arrived. The Bourne shell added fully programmable capabilities, including conditional branches and looping. This makes shell scripts much more powerful, since they can now test for potential error conditions: for example, we can enhance the spelling checker script to generate a sensible error message if the argument it is given is not the name of a readable file:

```
#!/usr/bin/sh
if test -r $1
then cat $1 | tr "[A-Z]" "[a-z]" |\
     tr -cs "[a-z]" "[\012*]" | sort -u \
     | comm -23 - dict
else echo "spell: cannot open $1"
fi
```

The command if test -r $1 returns true if $1 is the name of a readable file. The actual spell script appears as the 'then' arm of a conditional based on this result, with the 'else' arm producing an error message. Note the use of fi to close the if command: this is borrowed from Algol 68, a now-defunct language that Steve Bourne had encountered in his earlier work.

This example illustrates the main limitation of Bourne shell scripting: if, then, else and fi are not syntax words in the usual sense, they are built-in shell commands, and as such have to appear at the start of a line. Nevertheless, a substantial degree of programmability is provided (though this does not extend to looping structures). Another limitation of shell scripting is that UNIX provides a very limited collection of commands for text and string manipulations. A useful tool that is provided is cut, which allows us to extract fields from a line of text. For example, knowing that the full name of a user appears in the fifth field of the user's record in the UNIX password file, we can write a simple script to translate a user id into the corresponding name:

```
#!/usr/bin/sh
match=`grep "^$1" /etc/passwd`
if (test $? -eq 0)
then echo $match | cut -f5 -d:
else echo $1: not a user
fi
```

Here we use the grep command to select the line in the password file that starts with the identifier given as an argument, then use cut to select the fifth field. The complication comes from dealing with the situation when the user id given does not correspond to a valid user (i.e. there is no matching entry in the password file). Line 1 sets a variable match to the matching line, if there is one: the back-quotes enclosing the command cause it to be replaced by its output when executed. We then test the return code ($?) to see if the command was successful. If grep finds a match it will return a zero status, if it fails it will return a non-zero status. This is used to select one of two actions in the if statement starting on line 3.

This script illustrates four infelicities (there are many more) that make shell programming less straightforward than it might be.

■ An assignment like the one in line 2 must be written without spaces round the = to avoid the variable name being taken for a command name.

- The regular expression which is the first argument to `grep` has to be quoted to prevent the shell interpreting the caret, which is a meaningful character in shell syntax.
- We cannot write simple logical expressions such as `$?==0`: we have to use a `test` command to evaluate the condition, and specify the logical operator as an argument to that command with the usual shell syntax.
- Successful execution is indicated by a return status value of zero (so that different errors can be separated out by different non-zero values): this is the opposite of normal programming convention, which treats zero as false.

Apart from the true/false inversion, which is a standard UNIX convention, these restrictions arise from the way programmability is implemented in the shell. The shell is realized as a collection of C functions controlled by a very simple interpreter. The shell reads a line of input and separates it into words separated by whitespace: in the process a few transformations take place, such as file-name expansion. The first word on the line is the command: if it is an internal command it is executed by the shell, otherwise it is used to locate the appropriate C function to carry out the operation. The programmability of the Bourne shell is provided by adding internal commands. For example, as we have already noted,

```
if (...)
then ...
fi
```

looks like a programming language construct, but the `if`, `then` and `fi` are not syntactic keywords: they are internal shell commands, recognized by their appearance at the start of a line. Likewise, the round brackets surrounding the condition are not a syntactic component of the if statement: here, as elsewhere in the shell, they enclose a command to be executed in a sub-shell, and it is the return code from this statement that is collected by the `if` command to control subsequent execution. The requirement that the `==` in an assignment may not be surrounded by whitespace, and the need to evaluate the Boolean by obeying a shell command both arise because the shell does not perform any syntax analysis, but processes its input string left-to-right without any backtracking.

The other major limitation of shell scripts is that they do not provide any string manipulation capability apart from simple comparisons for equality and the simple built-in operations like `tr` and `cut`. As we have seen, system administration often involves data manipulation and reduction, and it was this requirement which led to the development of the AWK language, described next.

16.3 AWK

AWK (the name derives from its authors, Aho, Weinberger and Kernighan) was originally conceived as a tool for editing and manipulating text files which were structured as *records* (lines) divided into *fields* separated by whitespace – a commonly occurring format. The UNIX stream editor *sed* provided powerful editing features, with extensive use of regular expressions, for text files divided into lines: AWK was to be an extension of *sed* which understood fields within lines. The language was first released in 1977, and a more powerful version followed in 1985. Being an interpreted language with a simplified syntax, AWK is a useful tool for writing throw-away programs and prototyping larger applications: it also provides an acceptable substitute to C for much general-purpose programming.

The UNIX shell is reasonably good for interaction with the system, managing processes and files, but has very limited text and string processing capability: AWK is good at text and string processing, and for table manipulation. For tasks that require a mix of capabilities, a shell script which includes calls to AWK provides a solution – the shell manipulates the files, while AWK manipulates their contents. It is not an ideal solution though; as we have seen, the shell recognizes a variety of special characters, and AWK scripts within a shell script have to be quoted to prevent such characters being processed by the shell. The real problem comes when communication between shell script and AWK script is required, e.g. passing of command-line arguments to the AWK script. Shell syntax uses 'dollar' to introduce a command-line argument; AWK uses the same character to identify a field. Mixing the two – e.g. passing a field number as an argument – requires almost superhuman ability to get the quotes in the right places. Except for dedicated enthusiasts, AWK and the AWK-shell combination have been superseded by Perl.

16.3.1 Design principles

An AWK script consists of a list of *patterns* and associated *actions*. The target file is read sequentially, with each record in turn being brought into a processing buffer. As each record is loaded into the buffer, all patterns are checked against the record, and each pattern that is satisfied (true) triggers its corresponding action. The power of AWK derives from three design features:

1. A syntax is provided that allows individual fields to be identified as candidates for pattern matching.
2. The 'pattern' can be specified as matching a regular expression, or as a relationship between values in fields, i.e. a string or a numerical comparison involving expressions in which field identifiers are used a variables.
3. The action can be defined as a simple imperative operation like 'print', or an arbitrary piece of code in a C-like language, in which the fields in the record can be treated as variables. Though C-like, the syntax is greatly simplified, e.g. end of line is treated as end of statement, there are no declarations, variables are initialized on first use to numeric zero or empty string depending on context, and a string that is a valid representation of a number will be treated as such in a numerical context.

The expressiveness of AWK is enhanced by further design features:

- An action without an associated pattern is performed on all records; a pattern without an associated action causes the record to be printed (strictly sent to standard output) if the pattern is matched in that record.
- Fields contain strings, but if the string is a legitimate representation of a number the field can be used in arithmetic operations.

■ Although the default is that records are separated by end-of-line (EOL) characters, and fields are delimited by whitespace, the user can specify the record and field separators. For example, the field separator might be defined to be a comma: a more extreme case is end-of-line as the field separator and an empty line as the record separator.

These design features make AWK well suited to the manipulation of tabular data and sequential files, and for prototyping simple database applications. The designers originally envisaged it as a language for rapid prototyping and throw-away programming, though a surprising number of people used it as a general-purpose language, being attracted by the relaxed syntax and ease of use that is characteristic of interpreted languages.

16.3.2 The language

An AWK program is commonly called a *script*. It can be held in a file, or if it is short (anything less than about 5000 characters is regarded as short by AWK hackers) it can be placed in the command line. Each line is a condition/action pair, with the action enclosed in curly brackets. (This is necessary syntax so that an absent condition or action can be spotted.) Conditions can be regular expression matches or relationships between fields: special conditions BEGIN and END can be used, with obvious meaning.

Fields in a record are identified as $1, $2 etc. $0 denotes the whole record. An in-built variable NF records the number of fields in the record: another in-built variable NR holds the number of records read so far. So

```
{print $2, $1}
```

prints the first two fields of each record in reverse order: since the condition is omitted, the action applies to all records. Similarly,

```
$2 >= 5
```

prints all records for which the second field contains a numerical value that is greater than or equal to 5: as no action is specified, the action defaults to print. Note that in both cases we have processed a whole file without any explicit looping commands, and without having to open files and read lines from them.

C-style printf is available for fancy output, e.g.

```
$2*$3 > 50 {printf("?%.2f   %s\n" $2*$3, $1)}
```

selects records for which $2*$3 exceeds 50 and prints this value, with two decimal places and preceded by a pound sign, followed by spaces followed by the first field formatted as a string, the whole being terminated by a newline.

Operations that would require considerable amounts of C code can be achieved by remarkably short scripts.

■ Count the number of empty lines in a file and print the number

```
/^$/   {++x}
END    {print x}
```

This script uses a match for a regular expression anywhere in a record as the pattern, and relies on the implicit initialization of variables to 0.

- Print the records of a file in reverse order.

```
    {Line[NR] = $0}
END {i = NR
        while (i > 0) {
        print line[i]
        i--
        }
    }
```

- Given a file of student names each followed by an examination mark, separated by tab, print out the list followed by the average mark:

```
BEGIN {FS = \t}
    {print $0; total = total + $2}
END   {print total/NR}
```

The BEGIN line sets the file separator to tab. In the second line we have adopted the common style of using a leading tab to mark an absent condition.

An action can include C-like control flow, as shown in the following examples of possible actions:

```
{if ($1 > 0)
  ...
  else
  ...
}
{i = 1
  while (i <= $3) {
  ...
  i++
  }
}
{ for (i=1; i<=$3; i++)
  ...
}
```

Arrays

AWK has associative arrays but uses C-like syntax. The 'index' is a string e.g. pop["asia"]: if a numeric variable is used it is converted into a string. Arrays are one-dimensional, but the effect of a multi-dimensional array is easily obtained: since the array is stored as a table, an item like foo[2,3] goes in the table with the string 2,3 as its key. When using arrays the for loop has a useful variant: for x in y will repeat the loop body for every element actually stored in the array y, setting x equal to the 'subscript'.

16.3.3 Examples

We round off our discussion of AWK with a number of examples which illustrate the power of the language. To someone accustomed to Perl, AWK may not appear all that powerful, but when it was released in 1977 the power was breathtaking.

The examples are variations on a theme of data validation and exception report generation. The data to be validated consists of a file in which each line contains a student's name and seven marks for courses taken, the fields separated by tab characters.

Data validation

Print any record in the file which does not contain exactly eight fields, or contains mark(s) less than zero or more than 100:

```
BEGIN {FS = \t}
NF != 8
  {flag = 0
   for (i=2; i<=NF; i++) {
      if ($i < 0) flag = 1
      if ($i > 100) flag = 1
   }
   if (flag) print $0
  }
```

The first line sets the field separator to be the tab character. The second line prints any record that does not have eight fields (condition without action). The remainder of the script is a single action without a condition, and so is applied to every record in the file: it performs the check on the numeric fields and prints any records that fail. Note the explicit initialization of flag: we cannot rely on implicit initialization because we want it set to zero for each record.

Exception checking

This time we are looking for failing students, and wish to print any record which contains a mark less than 35 or for which the average mark is less than 40. In computing the average, the first mark carries double the weight of the other six.

```
BEGIN {FS = \t}
  {flag = 0
   sum = 0
   for (i=2; i<=NF; i++) {
      sum = sum + $i
      if ($i<35) flag = 1
      }
   avg = (sum + $2)/NR
   flag = flag || (avg < 40)
   if (flag) print $0, avg
  }
```

After setting the input file separator to tab, the rest of the script is a single action without a condition, processing each line in turn. The sum of the marks is accumulated so that the average can be computed, and `flag` is set if this is less than 40 or if any mark below 35 was encountered.

Flagging exceptions

This example is the same as before, except that instead of just printing details of failing students, we print out the whole table with the average mark appended to each row, flagging failing students with two asterisks.

```
BEGIN {FS="\t";OFS="\t"}
  {flag = 0
   sum = 0
   for (i=2; i<=NF; i++) {
     sum = sum + $i
     if ($i<35) flag = 1
   }
   avg = (sum + $2)/8
   if ((flag) || (avg < 40))
     print "**"$0, avg
   else print " "$0, avg
}
```

The first line sets both the input and output field separators to be tab: apart from this the code is self-explanatory. Computing column averages is left as an exercise for the reader.

16.4   REXX

16.4.1   Origins of REXX

It is interesting to note that REXX was a private development circulated over the network. Unfortunately, the net in question was IBM's internal network and as a result REXX, the great might-have-been of scripting languages, never really made it over the wall.

At the same time (1979) that Steve Bourne was developing his ground-breaking Bourne Shell for UNIX, things were also happening in IBM. Mike Cowlishaw, working at the IBM Hursley Laboratories in the UK and frustrated by the impoverished CMS EXEC language, set out to design his own language as an alternative to the EXEC processor, and called it the 'Restructured Extended Executor', REXX for short. Unusually, REXX was fully designed before any interpreter code was written. Mike Cowlishaw used the internal network linking IBM sites worldwide to obtain feedback from colleagues on his ideas, and when the interpreter was completed it was distributed over the network. Soon it was being used by large numbers of IBM staff and at this stage IBM admitted defeat and made it an official product. (But they balked at using the name: it was issued with the un-memorable name 'System Product Interpreter'.)

REXX was a fully-fledged, elegant and innovative programming language which provided a text-string interface to CMS and XEDIT, and so could be used to automate interactive sessions. Like a number of successful products, REXX was produced to meet a specific need and later found success in a quite different area: users who had acquired

REXX for its original function soon realized that they had a language well adapted to developing prototypes, and it spread from the mainframes to PCs. Today it is the recommended language for developing custom applications for OS/2.

16.4.2   Design principles

Mike Cowlishaw lists the design principles as:

- Readability
- Natural (implicit) data typing
- Nothing to declare
- No size or space limits
- Dynamic scoping
- Adaptability.

16.4.3   Features of REXX

REXX is a procedural language, with a strong resemblance to other procedural languages. However, it applies the 'no clutter' principle rigorously, and also the minimum concepts principle. For example:

- End of line is recognized as end of statement. In a neat twist on conventional approaches, instead of an explicit semicolon to end a statement REXX uses an explicit character (comma) to flag an end of line that is not the end of a statement. It also makes sensible decisions, e.g. end of line in the middle of a string or a comment is ignored.
- No declarations. All values are strings, and numerical variables can therefore be of arbitrary precision.
- No brackets for grouping statements. Grouping is achieved as part of the syntax of the DO statement (see below).

Most important is the way REXX is designed to control other applications. A valid REXX statement that is not an assignment statement must start with a REXX keyword. Any 'statement' that does not start with a valid keyword, and is not an assignment statement, is treated as a command to be passed to the external environment specified by the user, e.g. the host operating system's command-line interpreter. Since variable values are substituted before the command is passed to the environment, REXX becomes a powerful 'macro language' for any application that is driven by a command-line interface.

REXX was designed as an operating system control language (OSCL) for the VM/CMS operating system, which was also to be an expressive language. The OSCL background leads to good text handling and innovative I/O, but the CMS background leads to odd behaviour at times regarding capitalization. (CMS was an upper-case only system. REXX was designed so that programs could be written in lower case, with the system making sensible decisions about when to convert to upper case. It is those decisions, sensible in the CMS environment, that may cause odd behaviour in other environments.)

16.4.4 Language summary

Variables, values and expressions

REXX provides the usual facilities for manipulating numbers and strings. REXX values are all strings: a number is a string composed of decimal digits, optionally preceded by + or – and optionally containing a single . to denote a decimal point. When REXX uses a number it will usually be rounded to a precision defined by the NUMERIC DIGITS instruction (default nine digits). When numbers are compared, 'equality' is determined by the value of NUMERIC FUZZ – the amount by which numbers may actually differ although regarded as equal. With the default nine-digit precision, setting NUMERIC FUZZ to 1 causes equality to be checked with only eight significant digits.

Symbols are groups of characters selected from [A-Z], [a-z], [0-9], [\$@\#.!?_]. (Lower-case letters are translated to upper case before use – a hangover from the IBM mainframe inheritance). Symbols can be used as numbers, keywords, labels or variable names. Unlike other languages which provide a special 'undefined' value (e.g. undef in Perl), in REXX a variable which has not been assigned a value is given its name in upper case as its value.

Control structures

REXX provides the standard control structures – if–then–else, repetition and case (called select in REXX). The repetition statement illustrates neatly the REXX approach to combining power with minimal concepts. The basic form of the DO statement is

```
DO qualifier
    statement
    statement
    ...
END
```

If `qualifier` is absent this just acts as a grouping statement equivalent to the grouping brackets in other languages, e.g.

```
if x < 0 then do
   old_x = x
   new_x = -x
   end
```

If `qualifier` is an integer or integer variable, this indicates a repetition that number of times, e.g.

```
do 5
   y = y*y
   end
```

Other possible qualifiers are

```
FOREVER
WHILE boolean
```

```
UNTIL boolean
var = start TO finish [BY increment]
```

We see that the DO statement provides all the forms of looping that other languages provide with a number of different statements (e.g. while, for).

Two useful constructs for use in loops are LEAVE and ITERATE. LEAVE on its own causes the innermost active repetition loop to terminate as if the end condition had been satisfied. If LEAVE is followed by the name of the control variable of a currently active loop, that loop and any nested loops inside it are terminated. ITERATE on its own causes the rest of the statements in the innermost active repetition loop to be skipped, and the loop stepped. ITERATE can be followed by the name of the control variable of the currently active loop. This loop will be stepped and any nested loops are terminated as if by a LEAVE instruction.

In addition to an if–then–else construct, REXX provides a multi-way choice using the select statement, e.g.

```
select
  when x < 0 then
    x = -1
  when x > 0 then
    x = 1
  end
```

A select statement can include an otherwise then clause as the last possibility.

Data structures

REXX does not provide arrays as such, but has a feature called compound symbols which provides the effect of an array indexed by a string, like a Perl hash. (This approach to arrays is very similar to that of Tcl.) The syntax for a compound symbol is

```
stem.qualifier.qualifier. ...
```

Here stem is an identifier, and the qualifiers can be identifiers or numbers. For example:

```
thing.1 = "foo"
thing.2 = "bar"
```

The code

```
pump1 = "mild"
pump2 = "bitter"
price.pump1 = 1.85
price.pump2 = 1.95
```

sets up a table:

```
key            value
price.mild     1.85
price.bitter   1.95
```

It is possible to add a dimension dynamically:

```
brewery1 = "John Smith"
brewery2 = "Marstons"
price.pump2.brewery2 = 1.75
```

If a value is assigned to an unqualified stem, e.g.

```
pump. = 0
```

then all possible values with that stem have that value. It is as if the whole array had been initialized, though of course, the variables only come into existence when an explicit value is assigned.

The PARSE operation

REXX holds all its data as strings, and there are many situations in which we need to split a string into a number of parts, e.g.

- breaking a blank-separated list of words into its component parts, as when processing command-line arguments.
- breaking a comma-separated list of strings into its component parts, as when processing a procedure or function argument string.

These operations are achieved using the PARSE instruction. PARSE is a good example of economy of concept, since it can be used in a number of contexts. The PARSE instruction splits up a string according to a template which alternates variable names, to receive the sub-strings, and separators. The simplest template is a list of variable names separated by blanks. With such a template PARSE will treat its data as a list of blank-separated words, and assign each word in turn to the next variable in the template. The last variable in the template receives all that is left of the string, so a common use of PARSE is to strip off the first word in a string e.g.

```
PARSE VAR foo bar foo
```

Here the string to be parsed is the value of the variable foo (hence PARSE VAR): the first word is assigned to bar, and the rest of the string becomes the new value of foo. Extending this idea,

```
PARSE VAR foo first second the_rest
```

strips off the first two words as the values of first and second and puts the remainder of the string into the_rest.

Separators can be specified explicitly, e.g. a comma-separated list can be decomposed by

```
PARSE VAR foo first ',' second ',' the_rest
```

and the two forms can be mixed, e.g.

```
PARSE VAR foo first second ',' the_rest
```

will assign the string up to the first blank to `first`, the string from the first blank to the next comma to `second`, and everything to the right of the first comma to `the_rest`. The separator can also be specified by a variable name enclosed in brackets: the value of the variable is used, e.g.

```
comma = ','
...
PARSE VAR foo first second (comma) the_rest
```

has the same effect as the previous example.

Positional templates can be used, e.g.

```
PARSE VAR foo first 10 second 15 the_rest
```

will divide the string at positions 10 and 15, so that `first` gets characters up to position 10, `second` gets characters 10–14, and `the_rest` gets the rest. Signed integers can be used to specify positions relative to the place reached in the parse so far.

A useful facility in a template is the 'anonymous variable', denoted by a dot. The substring that would be assigned to a variable at this position in the template is discarded. For example,

```
PARSE VAR foo . second .
```

will extract the second word in a blank-separated string and assign it to the variable `second`.

In the examples so far, the string to be parsed has been the value of a specified variable. Alternatively the string to be parsed can be given as an expression (typically a function call) e.g.

```
    PARSE VALUE time() WITH hours ':' mins ':'
secs
```

Note the presence of the keyword `WITH` to delimit the expression.

Other uses of `PARSE` are described later in this section.

Built-in functions

A large number of built-in functions are provided, particularly for string manipulation.

Procedures and functions

In REXX the distinction between procedures and functions is one of syntactic convenience and preference. Both are instances of an underlying concept, the routine. A *routine* (strictly an *internal routine*) is a group of statements with a label attached to the first statement, finishing with a `return` instruction. (Strictly, the `return` instruction marks the dynamic end of a procedure call at run-time. REXX provides no syntax to mark the end of a routine: making `return` the last statement is just a matter of good style.) The routine can optionally return a value: this is specified by adding an expression to the `return` instruction. For example:

```
factorial:
  arg n
  if n=0 then return 1
  return factorial(n-1)*n
```

Note the recursive call in the last line. Any routine which returns a single string can be called as a function in this way: routines which return more complex results are called as subroutines using the CALL instruction with the following syntax

```
CALL name [expression] [, [expression]] ...
```

Here name is the symbol used to label the first instruction in the routine, and the square brackets indicate optional items in the usual way. Any arguments following CALL are packaged up as a string which is available to the routine for parsing by the ARG (short for PARSE ARG) instruction, which will typically be the first instruction in the routine. The arguments are passed by value. The RETURN instruction in the routine returns control to the point in the program immediately following the CALL instruction: if the RETURN instruction includes an expression, this is evaluated and assigned to the variable RESULT. If no value is returned, RESULT is uninitialized. Recursive calls are permitted.

PARSE ARG is yet another variant of the PARSE instruction. It parses the argument string according to the rules already described, with one additional feature. It regards its data as a string of strings, and a comma in the template causes it to stop parsing the current string and go on to the next member of the string of strings. Thus a function that expects two arguments might start with the instruction

```
ARG arg1 , arg2
```

to assign the arguments to arg1 and arg2. Each member of the string of strings can be subject to arbitrary parsing. For example, suppose a routine has two arguments, the first of which is a DOS-style '8+3' file name. The body might start

```
PARSE ARG name '.' extension , arg2
```

to separate the two components of the first argument.

Since a routine is defined simply by attaching a label to a statement, and since there is no syntactic delimiter for the end of a routine, it follows that variables used in a routine are global by default. Dynamic scoping can be enforced by the PROCEDURE instruction, e.g.

```
mysub:
  procedure
  ...
  return
```

The PROCEDURE instruction works in the same way as the local declaration in Perl. Following execution of the PROCEDURE instruction, all existing variables are hidden from the following instructions until a RETURN instruction is reached. At this point variables used since the PROCEDURE instruction become uninitialized, and the previous variable context is restored. A PROCEDURE instruction may optionally include the word EXPOSE followed by one or more variable names: these variables remain visible in following instructions.

As noted earlier, a routine that returns a single result can optionally be called using conventional function-call syntax. The function call must appear in a context where a value is expected, e.g. the right of an assignment, and its value is that given by the expression in the RETURN instruction.

An implementation may support calls to *external routines* written in REXX or other languages. An external routine written in REXX behaves very much like an internal routine. For a routine written in anther language, the interpreter typically delivers the argument string as a byte stream on standard input, and packages the standard output of the called routine as the result.

Input and output

Simple output is achieved with the SAY instruction, e.g.

```
SAY "Hello World"
```

The SAY instruction sends output to standard output: the LINEOUT() function allows output to other destinations in an implementation-dependent manner, typically

```
LINEOUT(STDERR, "No more data")
```

In fact, since the default destination for LINEOUT() is standard output, the statements SAY expression and LINEOUT(, expression) are equivalent. Corresponding to LINEOUT() there is a LINEIN() function whose value is the next line of input. Like LINEOUT() it allows the source of input to be specified in an implementation-dependent fashion, the default being standard input. Input data often needs to be parsed, so a common idiom is

```
PARSE VALUE LINEIN() WITH template
```

However, LINEIN() is not the normal way of getting input. A REXX program has an associated buffer called the External Data Queue, usually abbreviated to 'the queue'. (The name arises from the fact that the IBM VM/CMS operating system provides an external data queue that can be used for arbitrary inter-program communication. In PC implementations of REXX, the queue is part of the REXX system.) Input is normally done using the PARSE PULL instruction, which reads the line at the head of the queue if there is one, otherwise it reads a line from standard input. The line read is then parsed in accordance with the template, as described earlier for PARSE VAR. For example:

```
SAY 'What is your name? '
PARSE PULL name .
SAY 'Hello ' name
```

On the output side, SAY writes a line directly to standard output, PUSH writes a line to the head of the queue, and QUEUE writes a line to the tail of the queue. The queue has a variety of uses; for example, a program can generate input that will appear to have come from the user. Another use is to provide procedures with a variable number of arguments, which are passed via the queue. Also, since the queue is external to the REXX program, it can be used to allow communication between two REXX programs in an environment which permits multi-tasking.

Other unusual features

Other unusual features are INTERPRET and VALUE. The INTERPRET instruction allows the execution of instructions that have been built dynamically (like eval in other languages): its argument is a string which is interpreted as though it had been typed in. The VALUE instruction takes a variable name and returns its value. This seems of little use until you realize that it can be used more than once to provide indirect addressing (a form of pointer). For example, given

```
steak = "sirloin"
meat = steak
food = meat
```

then

```
SAY value(food)
```

prints 'steak', while

```
SAY value(value(food))
```

prints 'sirloin'.

16.4.5 An example

We round off this quick survey of REXX with an simple example of how it can be used to control a command-line application. We assume REXX is running in a DOS environment, and present a REXX program which adds an element of command-line history to the plain-vanilla DOS interface. Loosely modelled on the history mechanism of the UNIX C-Shell, it provides two facilities:

- Typing !! as a command repeats the previous command
- Typing !$ as the argument of a command causes the argument(s) of the preceding command to be used, e.g.

```
>: edit c:\foo\bar
>: print !$
```

The code is straightforward.

```
prev_command = ""
prev_args = ""
do forever
  say ">: "
  parse pull command
  parse var command cmd args
  select
    when cmd = "!!" then
      command = prev_command
    when args = "!$" then
      command = cmd prev_args
```

```
        when cmd = "exit" then
            return
        end
    prev_command = command
    prev_args = args
    command
end
```

If this REXX program is started from the DOS command line, its 'external environment' is DOS, so a statement that is not a valid REXX statement will be passed (as a string) to an instance of COMMAND.COM (using the /C option which causes a single command to be executed). After initialization the program enters an infinite loop, which issues a prompt then reads a line of input which is stored as `command` and also decomposed into `cmd` and `args`. The `select` statement deals with the special cases, constructing the appropriate command, then after saving this for future use it is sent to DOS by the penultimate line. The line `command = cmd prev_args` requires comment. The space between `cmd` and `prev_args` is in fact an operator meaning 'concatenate strings with a space between' – an example of REXX making the common operation as simple as possible. (Concatenation without a space can be done with the `||` operator.) When the user types `exit` at the prompt, the REXX program is terminated, causing a return to the normal DOS prompt.

Notes

[1] We ignore the ill-fated predecessor of CMS, called TSO (Time Shared Operation). Using TSO was once described as 'like kicking a dead whale along a beach'.
[2] The idea of the shell as a user-level program originated in the MULTICS system.
[3] In REXX, ARG is in fact shorthand for PARSE UPPER ARG, which parses in the normal way but forces the results into upper case. This was fine and dandy for CMS users, but modern day users will usually prefer to use an explicit PARSE ARG.

## Chapter 17

Epilogue

In this short essay we review the way the world of scripting languages has evolved, and speculate about the future of scripting.

The world of scripting languages is a world of shifting sands and changing landscapes – it has changed almost out of recognition even during the time that I have been preparing this book. When I first began to be interested in scripting, around ten years ago, it occupied a niche in the UNIX world: UNIX aficionados writing shell scripts, and using AWK and Perl to knock together useful tools. The first signs of the religious wars between the advocates of Perl and those of Tcl were just beginning to surface. Most important, scripting was not respectable: no manager would ship a product developed using one of these odd-ball languages (at least, not knowingly).

One of the earliest examples of scripting outside the UNIX environment was Visual Basic, but it was not recognized as a scripting language: it was seen as an end-user product, which might be used for prototyping but not application development. It was, needless to say, the Web that changed everything. As soon as the Web began to gain popularity it was recognized that CGI scripting was the key to interaction, and it didn't take long to realize that Perl was a language that might have been designed for the sole purpose of writing CGI scripts. (Unless, of course, you were an adherent of the Tcl faith.) Then in 1995 came the idea of client-side scripting. Netscape Navigator 2 shipped with LiveScript (soon to be renamed JavaScript), Microsoft played catch-up by incorporating JScript into Internet Explorer and a generation of Web page designers became programmers overnight. Another development, which was to have immense repercussions, was the decision in 1993 to use a version of Visual Basic as the macro language for Microsoft Excel, structuring Excel as an automation server that exposed a large number of automation objects.

The last few years have seen dramatic changes in the capabilities and the perception of scripting. With the release of Perl 5 in 1994, Perl threw off its image as a hacker's language, and became a serious language for large-scale software development. With an ever growing collection of plug-and-play modules, it begins to realize some of the dreams of reusable component software. Similar developments have taken place in Tcl, with Tcl 8.0 removing many of the handicaps that previously made it a poor choice for large-scale program development. With the development of the Win32 platform, Windows NT has provided a solid base for porting languages from the UNIX environment to the Windows environment. Visual Basic has moved from an end-user product to a serious professional development environment, especially for two-tier applications requiring database access.

Most important, scripting has become respectable, along with Open Source. Managers now recognize the productivity gains that come from using Perl, Tcl or Visual Basic as an alternative to C++ for application development. Employers now advertise for programmers with scripting language experience: a recent survey shows that while C++ still accounts for the largest number of job vacancies advertised, and Java accounts for the next largest number, Perl and Visual Basic vacancies come neck-and-neck in third place, with JavaScript coming up fast on the rails. (The survey didn't mention Tcl: this probably represents prejudice on the part of those who did the survey.)

A particularly significant development was the decision of Microsoft to bet their future on scripting. The integration of the Office applications, which depends on VBA, is a major selling point, and pretty well all the other Microsoft products are structured as scripting hosts, which can use a variety of scripting languages to script the objects exposed by a large collection of object models. New functionality is added to several products at once by the introduction of a new scriptable object library. The combination of server-side scripting with the database access provided by ActiveX Data Objects makes it possible for IIS to generate sophisticated dynamic Web pages using Active Server Pages. (Imitation is the sincerest form of flattery: a freeware system with similar capabilities for server-side scripting has recently been announced for other servers.)

The final feature of note is the way that the different languages are converging in functionality (though not in syntax) and in their fields of application, as they evolve into serious programming tools. Here are just three examples:

- *Regular expressions.* A major reason for Perl's popularity as a CGI scripting language was its powerful regular expression capability. Since then, a similarly powerful regular expression capability has been incorporated into Tcl and into Visual Basic and VBScript. (The regular expression capability first appeared in VBScript 5, but since it is implemented as an object model, it can be seamlessly imported into any scripting host.) Indeed, the appearance of powerful regular expressions in VBScript marks the transformation of the language from its origins as a simple language incorporating just those features needed for simple client-side scripting in Internet Explorer, to a fully-fledged development language.
- *Hashes.* Another example of convergence is the appearance of the dictionary object in the Microsoft scripting environment, giving Visual Basic and VBScript most of the functionality of the Perl hash.
- *Multi-line read.* Perl provides the ability to read an entire text file as a string using the angle bracket operator in a list context: Tcl provides the same capability with the `read` command. Now Visual Basic has the capability in the form of the `ReadAll` method of the `TextStream` object.

Another kind of convergence is seen in the fact that scripting languages are no longer confined to 'ring-fenced' application areas. At one time, CGI scripts would be written in Perl or Tcl, Web scripting was done in JavaScript or VBScript, graphical interfaces based on the X Window System were the province of Tcl/Tk, and compound documents in the Office environment were scripted in VBA. Nowadays the Web scripting can be done in any mixture of PerlScript, JavaScript and VBScript, even on the same page, and the designer can incorporate Tcl applets in the page. Tk has become a platform-independent tool for creating graphical interfaces, and can be programmed in Tcl (Tcl/Tk) or Perl

(Perl-Tk). OLE compound documents can be scripted from a Perl program. We are moving to a 'pick-and-mix' world.

What of the future? Ever since the dawn of computing, reusable software has been something of a Holy Grail: the very first book on programming [1], published in 1951, emphasizes the use of a library of subroutines, and subroutine libraries are an essential component of all modern programming systems. Reusability is one of the major benefits claimed for object-oriented programming, and the Microsoft Foundation Classes (MFC) are a prime example of software reuse. However, systems like MFC provide reusability at a price: you need to be a skilled and experienced C++ programmer to reap the benefit. Back in 1986, Brad Cox [2] developed the concept of the 'Software IC' as a unit of software reusability, drawing an analogy with the integrated circuit chips (ICs) which were transforming hardware design at the time. The analogy between integrated circuits and object classes like those in the Microsoft Foundation Classes is apt: both provide encapsulated functionality and can be used as building bricks in the construction of systems, but both require a highly skilled designer to gain the benefits.

What we want is the software equivalent of the PC expansion bus and plug-and-play expansion cards, which is provided by a combination of scriptable objects and a host architecture which specifies the interface that components present to the outside world, together with protocols for communication between components, and between a component and its host container. The Microsoft scripting architecture, with ActiveX controls which can be hosted by a variety of applications and scripted in a variety of languages, is a prime example of this. Tcl, with its ancestry as a 'glue' language is another example, and the use of Perl modules from the CPAN library is yet another. Indeed, the Perl module mechanism has achieved another of the Holy Grail objectives of the early computing world – a dynamically expandable language.

This approach to software development will continue to expand with scripting languages – programming for the rest of us – at its heart. To paraphrase an advertising slogan that will be familiar to UK readers, 'the future is bright: the future is scripting'.

Notes

[1]   M.V Wilkes, D.J Wheeler and S. Gill: *The Preparation of Programs for an Electronic Digital Computer*. Addison Wesley, 1951.
[2]   Brad J Cox: *Object Oriented Programming – An integrated approach*. Addison-Wesley, 1986.

Sources of further information

This appendix contains an annotated list of references to further material, both paper and electronic.

Note that the books referenced in this appendix are those that I have found useful in the course of writing the present volume, and the opinions expressed are strictly personal. All URLs quoted for Web resources are correct at the time of writing, but Web sites change their structure frequently, and it is likely that several of the URLs will reply '404: NOT FOUND' by the time the book appears in print.

Chapters 2 and 3: Perl

Introductory

Nigel Chapman. *Perl: The Programmer's Companion*. Wiley, 1997, 0-471-97563-X

Michael Schilli. *Perl Power! A JumpStart Guide to Programming with Perl 5*. Addison Wesley, 1999, 0-201-36068-3

Randal L. Schwartz and Tom Christiansen. *Learning Perl*. O'Reilly & Associates, Inc., 1997, 1-56592-284-0

Randal L. Schwartz, Eric Olson and Tom Christiansen. *Learning Perl on Win32 Systems*. O'Reilly & Associates, Inc., 1997, 1-56592-324-3

Nigel Chapman's book is a very accessible account, which conveys the essence of Perl effectively to the beginner, covering most of the important features. *Perl Power!* is particularly recommended if you want to use Perl in a Web context. *Learning Perl*, and its companion *Learning Perl on Win 32 Systems* are tutorial books which cover the language in considerably more detail than the books previously cited. They are aimed at the programmer who is planning to get into Perl in a serious way.

Intermediate

Larry Wall, Tom Christiansen and Randal L. Schwartz. *Programming Perl*. O'Reilly and Associates, Inc., 1996, 1-56592-149-6

Learning Perl, universally known as 'the Camel book' (or 'the blue Camel book', to distinguish it from the first edition) is the definitive source on Perl. If you are only going to own one book on Perl, this must be it. It combines a comprehensive reference account with an accessible tutorial introduction: if you are experienced in programming in another language, you can probably skip the introductory texts and go straight to the Camel book

Advanced

Sriram Srinivasan. *Advanced Perl Programming*. O'Reilly and Associates Inc., 1997, 1-56592-220-4

Tom Christiansen and Nathan Torkington. *Perl Cookbook*. O'Reilly and Associates, Inc., 1998, 1-56592-243-3

Joseph N. Hall with Randal L. Schwarz. *Effective Perl Programming*. Addison Wesley, 1998, 0-201-41975-0

Jeffrey E.F. Friedl. *Mastering Regular Expressions*. O'Reilly and Associates, Inc., 1997, 1-56592-257-3

Advanced Perl Programming covers the advanced features of Perl in more detail than the Camel book. It is a joy to read. *Perl Cookbook* contains thousands of examples, ranging from brief one-liners to complete applications, and is essential reading for the aspiring Perl guru. *Effective Perl Programming* conveys succinctly the essence of idiomatic Perl programming by addressing sixty distinct topics. Finally, *Mastering Regular Expressions* tells you more about regular expressions than you want to know.

Reference

Ellen Siever, Stephen Spainhour and Nathan Patwardhan. *PERL in a Nutshell*. O'Reilly and Associates, Inc., 1999, 1-56592-286-7

Johan Vromans. *Perl 5 Pocket Reference*. O'Reilly and Associates, Inc., 1998, 1-56592-495-9

Essential desktop companions for the serious Perl programmer.

Web resources

The primary source for all Perl information is `http://www.perl.com`, a site maintained by O'Reilly and Associates. Another useful source is the Perl FAQ – Frequently Asked Questions (and answers) – which is available at `http://www.cpan.org/doc/FAQs/`. (Note that beginning with Perl version 5.004, the Perl distribution itself includes the Perl FAQ. If everything is correctly installed on your system, the FAQ will be stored alongside the rest of Perl's documentation. Another source of information is found in the `comp.lang.perl.*` family of newsgroups. However, please look over the FAQ and related documents before posting any query to the newsgroups.

Chapters 4, 5 and 6

Tcl/Tk: general

John K. Ousterhout. *Tcl and the Tk Toolkit*. Addison Wesley, 1994, 0-201-63337-X

Mark Harrison and Michael McLennan. *Effective Tcl/Tk Programming*. Addison Wesley, 1998, 0-201-63474-0

Brent B. Welch. *Practical Programming in Tcl and Tk*. Prentice Hall PTR, 1997, 0-13-616830-2

Cliff Flynt. *Tcl/Tk for Real Programmers*. AP Professional, 1999, 0-12-261206-X

Tcl and the Tk Toolkit is the classic that launched Tcl/Tk. Unfortunately, it never went to a second edition, and as a result it is now out of date, being based on Tcl 7.3 and Tk 3.6. *Practical Programming in Tcl and Tk* is the definitive book on Tcl/Tk, covering all the new features of the latest versions, Tcl 8.0 and Tk 8.0. It is written in a tutorial style, but at the same time provides detailed reference material. *Effective Tcl/Tk Programming* is intended for developers who are building 'industrial strength' applications in Tcl: it is full of real-world advice. *Tcl/Tk for Real Programmers* is another good introduction to the language. features are introduced by examples, so you get off to a quick start. However, there is less detailed reference material than is found in Welch's book.

Tcl/Tk: reference

Paul Raines and Jeff Tranter. *Tcl/Tk in a Nutshell*. O'Reilly and Associates, Inc., 1999, 1-56592-433-9
Paul Raines. *Tcl/Tk Pocket Reference*. O'Reilly and Associates, Inc., 1998, 1-56592-498-3

Essential companions for the serious programmer.

Perl/Tk

Nancy Walsh. *Learning Perl/Tk: Graphical User Interfaces with Perl*. O'Reilly and Associates, Inc., 1999, 1-56592-314-6
Stephen Lidie. *Perl/Tk Pocket Reference*. O'Reilly and Associates Inc., 1998, 1-56592-517-3

Learning Perl/Tk is the only book on the subject: fortunately it is very good. The *Pocket Reference* lives up to its name.

Web resources

Everything you want is probably one or two clicks away in these pages:

- The 'Welcome to comp.lang.tcl' message by Andreas Kupries:
  `http://www.westend.com/~kupries/c.l.t.welcome.html`
- Larry Virden maintains a comp.lang.tcl FAQ launcher at
  `http://www.purl.org/NET/Tcl-FAQ/`
- Scriptics maintains a highly organized Tcl resource centre at
  `http://www.scriptics.com/resource/`
- Cameron Laird tracks many Tcl/Tk references of interest:
  `http://starbase.neosoft.com/~claird/comp.lang.tcl/`

Chapters 7 and 8

The bookstore shelves are full of Visual Basic books. Here I draw attention to just a few which I have found helpful.

Introductory

Peter Wright. *Beginning Visual Basic 6*. Wrox Press Ltd., 1998, 1-861001-05-3

A very clear introduction to the language and the application, which starts right at the beginning but covers some more advanced topics like database access and writing ActiveX controls.

Intermediate

Francesco Balena. *Programming Microsoft Visual Basic 6.0*. Microsoft Press, 1999, 0-73560-558-0

A very good book on more advanced VB topics. Covers sophisticated techniques and provides elegant code examples.

Advanced

Dan Appleman. *Developing COM/ActiveX Components with Visual Basic 6*. Sams, 1998, 1-56276-576-0

Provides a detailed account of how to use Visual Basic to create ActiveX controls and ActiveX document components. The book is clearly written and authoritative.

Reference

Paul Lomax. *VB & VBA in a Nutshell: The Language*. O'Reilly and Associates, Inc., 1998, 1-56592-358-8
Evan S. Dictor. *Visual Basic Controls in a Nutshell*. O'Reilly and Associates, Inc., 1999, 1-56592-294-8
Paul Litwin. *VBA for Dummies Quick Reference*. IDG Books, 1997, 0-7645-0250-6

In addition to the inevitable Nutshell Handbooks, the 'for dummies' series provides an excellent and inexpensive reference source for VBA.

Web resources

- Complete documentation of Visual Basic is available via
  `http://msdn.microsoft.com/vbasic/`
- Information on VBA can be found at
  `http://msdn.microsoft.com/vba/`

Chapter 9

David Flanagan. *JavaScript: The Definitive Guide*. O'Reilly and Associates Inc., 1998, 1-56592-392-8
Danny Goodman. *JavaScript Bible*. IDG Books, 1998, 0-7645-3188-3

JavaScript: The Definitive Guide provides excellent coverage of the language, and is particularly good at explicating the differences between the various versions of the language to be found in Web browsers. *JavaScript Bible* is a particularly comprehensive account of the language and its applications.

Web resources

- Netscape's JavaScript documentation can be found at
  `http://developer.netscape.com/docs/`
- Microsoft documentation can be found at
  `http://msdn.microsoft.com/scripting/`
- The ECMAScript standard is available at
  `http://www.ecma.ch/stand/ecma-262.htm`

Chapter 10

Paul Lomax. *Learning VBScript*. O'Reilly and Associates, Inc., 1997, 1-56592-247-6
Scott Hillier. *Inside Visual Basic Scripting Edition*. Microsoft Press, 1996, 1-57231-444-3

These books are almost entirely devoted to using VBScript for Web scripting. Lomax gives a brief introduction to the language, while Hillier merely provides an appendix listing the differences between VBScript and VBA. Since the books were published, VBScript has evolved to be very close to VB/VBA.

Web resources

Microsoft's VBScript documentation can be found at
`http://msdn.microsoft.com/scripting/`

Chapter 11

Client-side scripting

David Flanagan. *JavaScript: The Definitive Guide*. O'Reilly and Associates, Inc., 1998, 1-56592-392-8
Danny Goodman. *JavaScript Bible*. IDG Books, 1998, 0-7645-3188-3
Paul Lomax. *Learning VBScript*. O'Reilly and Associates, Inc., 1997, 1-56592-247-6
Scott Hillier. *Inside Visual Basic Scripting Edition*. Microsoft Press, 1996, 1-57231-444-3

Both Flanagan and Goodman describe the client-side scripting model, and provide extensive reference sections listing properties and methods of the objects involved. *Learning VBScript* gives a very clear account of client-side scripting, illustrated with lots of examples, but doesn't provide a reference to the objects. Hillier uses a number of extended case studies to introduce client-side scripting.

Server-side scripting

Scott Hillier. *Inside Visual Basic Scripting Edition*. Microsoft Press, 1996, 1-57231-444-3
Scott Hillier and Daniel Mezick. *Programming Active Server Pages*. Microsoft Press, 1997, 1-57231-700-0
A. Keyton Weissinger. *ASP in a Nutshell*. O'Reilly and Associates, Inc., 1999, 1-56592-490-8

In *Inside Visual Basic Scripting Edition*, Hillier uses a number of extended case studies to introduce server-side scripting. *Programming Active Server Pages* introduces the principles, then launches into a series of extended case studies to illustrate their application. The Nutshell Handbook is the perfect reference companion.

Web resources

- Lots of information about client-side scripting in JavaScript can be found at
  `http://developer.netscape.com/docs/`
- Information about client-side and server-side scripting in the Microsoft environment can be found at
  `http://msdn.microsoft.com/workshop/`

Chapter 12

Scott Isaacs. *Inside Dynamic HTML*. Microsoft Press, 1997, 1-57231-686-1
Danny Goodman. *Dynamic HTML: The Definitive Reference*. O'Reilly and Associates, Inc., 1999, 1-56592-490-8

In Chapter 12 we looked at Microsoft's DHTML. *Inside Dynamic HTML* gives a good account of this, and illustrates its capabilities with many examples. *Dynamic HTML: The Definitive Reference* is exactly what the title says it is. It provides a comprehensive reference to the objects defined by various implementations of Dynamic HTML, and cross-references them so that you can find out whether a particular object is supported in the version of DHTML that you are using.

Web resources

- Information about Microsoft DHTML can be found at
  `http://msdn.microsoft.com/workshop/`
- Information about the W3C Document Object Model (DOM) is at
  `http://www.w3.org/DOM/`

Chapter 13

Christine Solomon. *Office 97 Developer's Handbook*. Microsoft Press, 1997, 1-57231-440-0
Steve Roman. *Writing Excel Macros*. O'Reilly and Associates, Inc., 1999, 1-56592-587-4
Steve Roman. *Learn Word Programming*. O'Reilly and Associates, Inc., 1998, 1-56592-524-6

Solomon's book gives a good overview of the subject, and provides a limited introduction to the object models and how they are used. Roman's two books provide in-depth treatment of the Excel and Word object models, and are essential if you are planning to undertake any non-trivial task in VBA.

Web resources

Voluminous information is available from
`http://msdn.microsoft.com/library/`

Chapters 14 and 15

Web resources

Information can be found at
`http://msdn.microsoft.com/scripting/`

Chapter 16

Stephen R. Bourne. *The UNIX System V Environment*. Addison Wesley, 1987, 0-201-18484-2
Alfred V. Aho, Brian W. Kernighan and Peter J. Weinberger. *The AWK Programming Language*. Addison Wesley, 1988, 0-201-07981-X
M.F. Cowlishaw. *The REXX Language: A Practical Approach to Programming*. Prentice-Hall, 1985, 0-13-780735-X
Charles Daney. *Programming in REXX*. McGraw Hill Inc., 1992, 0-07-015305-1

Steve Bourne and his colleagues invented shell scripting as part of the development of UNIX Version 7. His book describes shell scripting in the commercially released UNIX System V. *The AWK Programming Language* is written by the people who designed AWK: not only is it authoritative, it is also a pleasure to read. Mike Cowlishaw's book is another definitive account by the language designer: it is a good reference, but too terse to be used to learn the language. *Programming in REXX* is an excellent tutorial introduction to the language, which also includes more advanced topics. Highly recommended.

Web resources

The REXX home site is at
`http://www2.hursley.ibm.com/rexx/`

Index

Scripting Program Index

Tcl

Tk

Visual Basic/VBA

VBScript